OXFORD STUDIES IN EUROPEAN LAW

Series Editors

PAUL CRAIG

Professor of English Law at St John's College, Oxford

GRÁINNE DE BÚRCA

Professor of Law at the European University Insitute

FLORENCE ELLINWOOD ALLEN

Professor of Law at New York University

Constitutional Disintegration and Disruption

OXFORD STUDIES IN EUROPEAN LAW

Series Editors:

Paul Craig, Professor of English Law at St John's College, Oxford,
Gráinne de Búrca, Professor of Law at the European University Insitute, and
Florence Ellinwood Allen, Professor of Law at New York University

The aim of this series is to publish important and original research on EU law. The focus is on scholarly monographs, with a particular emphasis on those which are interdisciplinary in nature. Edited collections of essays will also be included where they are appropriate. The series is wide in scope and aims to cover studies of particular areas of substantive and of institutional law, historical works, theoretical studies, and analyses of current debates, as well as questions of perennial interest such as the relationship between national and EU law and the novel forms of governance emerging in and beyond Europe. The fact that many of the works are interdisciplinary will make the series of interest to all those concerned with the governance and operation of the European Union.

OTHER TITLES IN THIS SERIES

Business Freedoms and Fundamental Rights in European Union Law
Niall O'Connor

Compliance with European Consumer Law
The Case of E-Commerce
Felix Pflücke

Legislative Authority and Interpretation in the European Union
Martijn van den Brink

Secession and European Union Law
The Deferential Attitude
Núria González Campañá

Fiscal State Aid Law and Harmful Tax Competition in the European Union
Dimitrios Kyriazis

The Abuse of Constitutional Identity in the European Union
Julian Scholtes

Judging European Democracy
The Role and Legitimacy of National Constitutional Courts in the EU
Nik de Boer

EU Values Before the Court of Justice
Foundations, Potential, Risks
Luke Dimitrios Spieker

Postnational Constitutionalism
Europe and the Time of Law
Paul Linden-Retek

The Legislative Priority Rule and the EU Internal Market for Goods
A Constitutional Approach
Eadaoin Ní Chaoimh

The Jurisprudence of Constitutional Conflict in the European Union
Ana Bobić

Reflexive Governance in EU Equality Law
Emma Lantschner

Enhanced Cooperation and European Tax Law
Caroline Heber

Legal Pluralism in European Contract Law
Vanessa Mak

Europe's Passive Virtues
Deference to National Authorities in EU Free Movement Law
Jan Zglinski

Accountability in EU Security and Defence
The Law and Practice of Peacebuilding
Carolyn Moser

Constitutional Disintegration and Disruption

Withdrawal and Opt-Outs from the European Union

OLIVER GARNER

Maurice Wohl Research Leader in European Rule of Law,
Bingham Centre for the Rule of Law, British Institute of International and Comparative Law, UK

OXFORD
UNIVERSITY PRESS

OXFORD
UNIVERSITY PRESS

Great Clarendon Street, Oxford, OX2 6DP,
United Kingdom

Oxford University Press is a department of the University of Oxford.
It furthers the University's objective of excellence in research, scholarship,
and education by publishing worldwide. Oxford is a registered trade mark of
Oxford University Press in the UK and in certain other countries

Published in the United States of America by Oxford University Press
198 Madison Avenue, New York, NY 10016, United States of America

British Library Cataloguing in Publication Data

Data available

Library of Congress Control Number: 2024948871

ISBN 9780198914105

DOI: 10.1093/9780198914136.001.0001

Printed and bound by
CPI Group (UK) Ltd., Croydon, CR0 4YY

MIX
Paper | Supporting
responsible forestry
FSC® C013604
www.fsc.org

The manufacturer's authorised representative in the EU for product safety is
Oxford University Press España S.A. of El Parque Empresarial San Fernando de Henares,
Avenida de Castilla, 2 – 28830 Madrid (www.oup.es/en or
product.safety@oup.com). OUP España S.A. also acts as importer into Spain
of products made by the manufacturer.

Series Editors' Preface

There is no doubt that Brexit sent shock waves through the European Union. The very idea that a state should wish to leave, given that the predominant modality since the inception of the European Economic Community was states wishing to join, was shocking both normatively and empirically. In normative terms, it generated complex questions concerning the desirability or not of EU membership. In empirical terms, the negotiation of exit revealed how difficult it was to disentangle a relationship that had been fifty years in the making.

Oliver Garner's book considers the mechanisms for withdrawal in Article 50 TEU (Treaty on European Union) that lead to disintegration, together with opt-outs, which are conceptualized in terms of disruption to the process of integration. The issues raised are complex and interesting in equal measure, for reasons discussed by the author. This is exemplified by the fact that disintegration through the withdrawal of a disruptive Member State may facilitate the deepening of the supranational order. It is further exemplified by the fact that opt-outs, while disruptive to some degree, may enhance integration, since reticent Member States may agree to the relevant Treaty revision, provided that they secure an opt-out, whereas they would have exercised their veto over such Treaty change if the possibility of opt-outs had not been available.

The monograph begins with the discussion of constituent power and the role of the individual. This is followed by an overview of opt-outs, with the discussion of their normative foundation and the conditions for their legitimacy. The focus then shifts to the detailed consideration of opt-outs in the principal areas where they have been used, such as Economic and Monetary Union, Schengen, and the Area of Freedom, Security and Justice. The analysis is framed by the consideration of the disruptive effects of such opt-outs. The author then turns his attention to Article 50 TEU, which is the foundation for withdrawal. There is the discussion of its telos, form, and function, followed by the detailed analysis of the different parts of Article 50 and how they were applied during Brexit. The book concludes with proposals for the reform of Article 50.

This book raises important issues concerning the EU and the way in which it functions. It will be of interest to lawyers and political scientists alike.

Paul Craig
Gráinne de Búrca

Acknowledgements

This monograph develops the PhD thesis from the European University Institute (EUI) that I defended in July 2020. All of the acknowledgments for that work remain applicable, especially to my doctoral supervisor Professor Marise Cremona; the members of my doctoral defence panel; the practitioners and academics from the EUI, the London School of Economics, my alma mater of St John's College, Oxford, the European Parliament, and beyond with whom I engaged on the project; my colleagues during the period of finishing the thesis following my return to London; and most of all the friends and family (including all the IUE Calcio *protaganisti*) who made those years from 2015 to 2019 so memorable and fulfilling.

I am grateful to the series editors of Oxford Studies in European Law, Professor Paul Craig and Professor Gráinne de Búrca, and the editorial board for accepting my proposal; Professor Jeremias Adams-Prassl for his great help at the proposal stage; the anonymous reviewers who engaged so closely with my ideas and sharpened my thinking; and all of the employees of Oxford University Press, especially Kezia Johnson, for their invaluable assistance throughout the manuscript process.

I completed this monograph during my employment for the Bingham Centre for the Rule of Law of the British Institute of International and Comparative Law, and the Central European University Democracy Institute. My line manager and now Director of the Bingham Centre, Jan van Zyl Smit, has been a crucial stabilizing presence enabling me to complete this monograph whilst also fulfilling my other engagements for the Centre. I also pass on my thanks to all the many colleagues and other members of the extended network in the London legal and policy world, including those within Parliament who have invited me to present my research to select committees, for their intellectual and practical engagement in the last five years.

In Budapest the present and former co-Directors of the Democracy Institute, Laszlo Bruszt and Renáta Uitz, have provided the opportunity for me to continue direct engagement with issues pertaining to European integration. I am particularly grateful for the lively and collegial working atmosphere created in the last four years by my past and present editorial colleagues at the Institute's *Review of Democracy* (*RevDem*): Michał Matlak, Kasia Krzyżanowska,

Robert Nemeth, Ferenc Laczó, Lucie Hunter, Teodora Miljojkovic, Alexander Lazović, Kinga Pall, Karen Culver, and all the many other editors and assistant editors. All of the academic members of the Democracy Institute and the staff based within Nádor utca have made me feel very welcome during my (sadly rare) visits to Budapest.

I developed arguments deriving from my thesis for my fellowship in the 're:constitution' programme from 2022 to 2023. I thank the co-ordinators of that programme, especially Dorit Modersitzki, and my hosts at the European Policy Centre in Brussels and the CEU Democracy Institute in Budapest for their assistance during that year of mobility periods. I am immensely grateful for the extensive exchange on our academic arguments provided by my cohort of fellows, and to Berlin for the David Bowie inspired daydreams and night walks.

The social life in London that has provided the grounding necessary to complete an academic book whilst working has inevitably revolved around sport. A particularly significant development in ensuring this vital anchoring has been the adoption, three decades too late, of the sport of cricket. Thank you to everybody at Groombridge CC, Demijohns CC, and Putney CC who have humoured me in my attempts with bat and ball in the last two years. Football remains a more long-term companion, and likewise the knowledge that each Saturday morning can be spent with King's College Old Boys Football Club—and one day a year with St John's College Old Boys Association Football Club—makes the working week worthwhile (whilst, ironically, sometimes providing far more administrative demands).

Finally, the most significant acknowledgment of all remains for those close friends, family, and companions—new and old, present and departed, continental European and British/Irish, transpacific and transatlantic—who have contributed to the flourishing of my life in the last decades. You are too numerous all to name, and all too significant to omit. I am particularly thankful to Christine for her companionship from afar (and, fleetingly, close) during the last months, which has made the distance from Ontario to London seem far shorter than five hours and 3500 miles. Family and 'clan' members Collette, Anita, Angela, and Eugene, and Rohan and Alexander have always provided support. Above all, my mother Dorothy remains the source of all the wisdom that led to this book (both hers and mine).

London, United Kingdom, 30 September 2024

Contents

Table of Cases

EUROPEAN UNION (ALPHABETICAL)

Court of Justice

General Court

EUROPEAN UNION (CHRONOLOGICAL)

Court of Justice

General Court

UNITED KINGDOM

EUROPEAN COURT OF HUMAN RIGHTS

INTERNATIONAL

Canada

Denmark

Germany

The Netherlands

United States of America

Table of Legislation

EU INSTRUMENTS

Regulations

Directives

Decisions

Other

INTERNATIONAL

NATIONAL LEGISLATION

Canada

Denmark

Germany

Ireland

United Kingdom

Abbreviations

AFSJ	Area of Freedom, Security, and Justice
CMLR	Common Market Law Reports
CSIH	Court of Session, Inner House [Scotland]
ECA 1972	European Communities Act 1972
ECB	European Central Bank
ECHR	European Convention on Human Rights
ECLI	European Case-Law Identifier
ECR	European Court Reports
ECU	European Currency Unit
EEA	European Economic Area
EEC	European Economic Community
EFTA	European Free Trade Association
EHRR	European Human Rights Reports
EMS	European Monetary System
EMU	Economic and Monetary Union
ERM	Exchange Rate Mechanism
ESCB	European System of Central Banks
EUCO	European Council
EWCA Civ	England and Wales Court of Appeal, Civil Division
EWHC	England and Wales High Court
JHA	Justice and Home Affairs
MEP	Member of European Parliament
MP	Member of Parliament
OJ	Official Journal of the EU
SCR	Supreme Court Reports [Canada]
TCA	Trade and Cooperation Agreement
TEU	Treaty on European Union
TFEU	Treaty on the Functioning of the European Union
UKHL	United Kingdom House of Lords
UKSC	United Kingdom Supreme Court
VCLT	Vienna Convention on the Law of Treaties

1
Introduction

I. The Emergence of Disintegration after Disruption

On 23 June 2016, the population of the United Kingdom was asked the referendum question 'Should the United Kingdom remain a member of the European Union or leave the European Union?'. The 52 per cent majority answer for 'Leave' sent shockwaves through Europe. An atmosphere of uncertainty prevailed at both the national level and the European level. When Article 50 of the Treaty on European Union (TEU)[1] had been established by the Lisbon Treaty the EU establishment did not envisage that it would ever be triggered. In turn, when the UK Parliament passed the European Union Referendum Act 2015, it seems that David Cameron's government also did not envisage that a result to leave would be returned. The realization of the previously unthinkable scenario of Member State withdrawal dominated the United Kingdom's legal and political arena for the next five years. The final confirmation of the United Kingdom's withdrawal on 31 January 2020 came after three extensions to the two-year period under Article 50 TEU, two changes of UK government, and two seminal UK Supreme Court cases called *Miller* that have defined the contemporary vision of the British constitution.

The impact of Brexit may have been ameliorated by the significant material crises that have emerged for Europe in the intervening four years. The date of the United Kingdom's withdrawal coincided with the emergence of the global COVID-19 pandemic. The emergency measures required, such as the re-establishment of border controls across Europe's Schengen Zone, created a state of exception that softened the alterity of post-membership for the United Kingdom. Since February 2022, Russia's invasion of Ukraine has resurrected the fear of full-scale military conflict on the European continent that the European Union has promoted itself as preventing. These shocks have provided an impetus for further European integration into the sovereign spheres of economic redistribution[2] and security and defence through military assistance

[1] Consolidated Version of the Treaty on European Union [2008] OJ C115/13 (hereafter 'TEU'), art 50.
[2] 'Recovery and Resilience Facility—European Commission' <https://economy-finance.ec.europa.eu/eueconomyexplained/recovery-and-resilience-facility_en> accessed 1 May 2024.

Constitutional Disintegration and Disruption. Oliver Garner, Oxford University Press.
 DOI: 10.1093/9780198914136.003.0001

to Ukraine.[3] Proposals for institutional reform to strengthen majoritarianism have followed. Disintegration through the withdrawal of a reticent and disruptive Member State may provide a permissive condition for such deepening of the supranational order. It remains to be seen whether a self-understanding amongst Member State nationals that they are also the constituent subjects of European supranational constitutionalism will emerge in tandem.

The consequences of the withdrawal of a Member State from the European Union reach into nearly every aspect of European law and politics. This monograph concentrates on the consequences of this phenomenon for individual citizens.[4] Rather than focusing solely on the legal rights that the nationals of a withdrawing state lose in the European Union, and that EU citizens lose in the withdrawing state territory,[5] this book takes a holistic view. The analysis also considers the implications that withdrawal has for the constitutional status from which these rights derive. This argument will not, however, focus only on the consequences of complete withdrawal. The argument is presented that disintegration has been incubated by decades of constitutional disruption. Therefore, opt-outs from the EU legal order are also examined as a manifestation of this latter phenomenon.

The 23 June 2016 referendum did not occur within a vacuum. It was the Rubicon crossed after a complicated five-decade relationship of disrupted integration within the European Union. This interplay itself had taken place within the wider drama of the seven-decade history of European integration. The scene that immediately preceded the referendum in the drama between the United Kingdom and the European Union was David Cameron's attempts in February 2016 to renegotiate the United Kingdom's membership. The result of Cameron's attempts to entrench and bolster the United Kingdom's existing opt-outs from the EU constitutional order was seven 'arrangements' including

[3] 'EU Solidarity with Ukraine—European Commission' (26 February 2022) <https://eu-solidarity-ukraine.ec.europa.eu/index_en> accessed 1 May 2024.

[4] For a recent analysis of withdrawal from the perspective of the consequences for the EU legal order see Polly Polak, 'EU Withdrawal as a Supranational Affair: The Case of Brexit' in *EU Withdrawal as a Supranational Affair* (Brill Nijhoff 2023); for an analysis centred more upon the perspective of the withdrawing Member State see Michael Dougan, *The UK's Withdrawal from the EU: A Legal Analysis* (OUP 2021); for a normative prescription of future reforms see Federico Fabbrini, *Brexit and the Future of the European Union: The Case for Constitutional Reforms* (OUP 2020).

[5] For analyses of the effect on legal rights see *inter alia* Stephanie Reynolds, 'May We Stay? Assessing the Security of Residence for EU Citizens Living in the UK' in Michael Dougan (ed), *The UK After Brexit: Legal and Policy Challenges* (Intersentia 2017); Dimitry Kochenov, 'EU Citizenship and Withdrawals from the Union: How Inevitable Is the Radical Downgrading of Rights?' in Carlos Closa (ed), *Secession from a Member State and Withdrawal from the European Union: Troubled Membership* (CUP 2017); Oliver Garner, 'After Brexit: Protecting European Citizens and Citizenship from Fragmentation' (European University Institute 2016) EUI Law Department Working Paper No 2016/22 <https://papers.ssrn.com/abstract=2871404> accessed 1 February 2017.

a Decision of the Heads of State or Governments of the Member States, a draft Decision by the European Council, and Declarations by the European Commission.

The European Council conclusions outlining these arrangements contained a declaration by the Heads of State or Government that 'this Decision will take effect on the date the Government of the United Kingdom informs the Secretary-General of the Council that the United Kingdom has decided to remain a member of the European Union'.[6] Transformational consequences for the European Union's constitutional order were inevitable regardless of the result. If 'Remain' had won, the commitments of the European Council would have led to the amendment of the Foundational Treaties further deepening disruption. In the actual event of the victory of 'Leave', the Article 50 process has led to the first example of disintegration through a Member State's complete withdrawal from the Union. This book seeks to explain and normatively critique these two phenomena through the conceptual lens of the role individuals play in constituting the European Union's supranational order.

II. Theoretical Approach: Disintegration and Disruption

This work applies a particular conception of constituent power to the European Union as a means to explicate and critique withdrawal and opt-outs. Theorists have reconstructed[7] European 'integration' as a process whereby individuals hold a 'dual-constituent' status as nationals of the Member States and as citizens of the European Union.[8] The creation of EU citizenship reconstructed nationality of a constitutional state into nationality of a Member State of the European Union. The capacity to create EU citizenship and to construct a new supranational constitutional order has been labelled the 'levelling up' of constituent power.[9] As this enables the construction of a supranational constitutional order, this may be regarded as a 'constructive power'. The conclusion of the Treaty in Rome in 1957 is regarded in this book as an initial constructive exercise of constituent power because the original six Member

[6] European Council meeting (18 and 19 February 2016)—Conclusions, Annex 1—Decision of the Heads of State or Government, meeting within the European Council, concerning a new settlement for the United Kingdom within the European Union—Brussels 19 February 2016 EUCO 1/16, 2.

[7] Markus Patberg, 'Supranational Constitutional Politics and the Method of Rational Reconstruction' (2014) 40 Philosophy & Social Criticism 501.

[8] Jürgen Habermas, *The Crisis of the European Union: A Response* (Polity Press 2013); Markus Patberg, *Constituent Power in the European Union* (OUP 2020).

[9] Markus Patberg, 'The Levelling Up of Constituent Power in the European Union' (2017) 55 Journal of Common Market Studies 203.

States utilized public international law to create a new constitutional order. The Treaty amendment capacity in Article 48 TEU has channelled this original constituent power into a constituted revisionary power. Article 49 TEU has created a mechanism to extend this 'levelling up' capacity to all qualifying constitutional states in Europe.

The retention of original constructive power by the Member States means that they also retain the power of ultimate deconstruction and complete disintegration through a unanimous decision to terminate the Treaties.[10] More partially, the constitutional mechanisms of a withdrawal clause and the unanimity requirement for Treaty amendment function as safeguards that preserve nationality as a constituent status despite levelling up. Therefore, the exercise of the withdrawal clause is conceptualized as the 'levelling down' of constituent power. As the converse of the constructive power that catalyses and maintains European integration, this process is understood as the exercise of 'deconstructive power' that results in a species of European 'disintegration'. Habermas and Patberg utilize the device of a hypothetical original constitutional convention to explicate levelling up.[11] By extension, and conversely, the very real process enacted under Article 50 TEU is conceptualized in this work as a 'deconstitutional convention'. Conceptualizing opt-outs in relation to deconstructive power is less straightforward. This phenomenon does not arise out of an explicit constitutional clause, but instead opt-outs are created through Protocols addended at the time of Treaty amendments. These Protocols are a result of resistance by Member States to the results of the reconstitution of levelling up constructive power.

The results of these processes are conceptualized as species of constitutional 'disintegration' and 'disruption'. Disintegration may be regarded as a concept that extends beyond withdrawal via Article 50 TEU to any constitutional phenomenon that challenges the existence of European integration.[12] Disruption may be regarded as extending beyond the formal mechanism of opt-outs to encompass any phenomenon that challenges the realization of the goals of European integration, but without posing an existential challenge to the European Union. The qualifier of 'illegitimate' disruption can be used to

[10] On 'entirely reversing European integration' see Markus Patberg, 'Can Disintegration Be Democratic? The European Union Between Legitimate Change and Regression' (2020) 68 Political Studies 582.

[11] Habermas (n 8); Markus Patberg, 'A Systematic Justification for the EU's Pouvoir Constituant Mixte: Principles of Constitutional Politics in Supranational Polities' (2017) 23 European Law Journal 441.

[12] See *inter alia* Douglas Webber, *European Disintegration? The Politics of Crisis in the European Union* (Red Globe Press 2018).

describe the phenomenon of 'Rule of Law backsliding' that has occurred most prominently in Poland and Hungary since 2015 and 2010, respectively.[13] There is the potential that this could degrade into illegitimate disintegration if this leads to Member States seeking to exempt themselves from the requirements of supranational integration, for example through apex courts determining that the primacy of EU law does not apply.[14] Subtler phenomena, such as Sweden's deliberate failure to fulfil the requirements to adopt the euro despite materially being able to meet these conditions,[15] may also be regarded as a species of informal disruption. A further counterfactual example of illegitimate disintegration could have arisen if calls had been followed for the United Kingdom to withdraw from the European Union purely through repeal of the European Communities Act 1972, the domestic legislation that implemented EU membership obligations, rather than through Article 50 TEU.[16]

This monograph focuses on the formal and legitimate mechanisms of Article 50 TEU and opt-outs that result in authorized disintegration and disruption. This enables explanatory and normative analysis of how these constitutional devices have been created to enable self-determination by individuals in their dual-legitimation role. Only the formal and legitimate means of disruption and disintegration concern the ultimate normative inquiry of how individuals are represented in their dual role in the supranational order, and how they can exercise input into decisions by their Member State authorities whether to level up constituent power to engage in supranational constitutionalism, disrupt levelling up in certain sectors of the supranational order, or level it down to restore nationality as the sole status of democratic self-determination.

[13] See *inter alia* Carlos Closa and Dimitry Kochenov (eds), *Reinforcing Rule of Law Oversight in the European Union* (CUP 2016); Laurent Pech and Kim Lane Scheppele, 'Illiberalism Within: Rule of Law Backsliding in the EU' (2017) 19 Cambridge Yearbook of European Legal Studies 3; Wojciech Sadurski, *Poland's Constitutional Breakdown* (OUP 2019); Petra Bárd and Viktor Zoltán Kazai, 'Enforcement of a Formal Conception of the Rule of Law as a Potential Way Forward to Address Backsliding: Hungary as a Case Study' (2022) 14 Hague Journal on the Rule of Law 165.

[14] Aleksandra Gliszczyńska-Grabias and Wojciech Sadurski, 'Is It Polexit Yet? Comment on Case K 3/21 of 7 October 2021 by the Constitutional Tribunal of Poland' (2023) 19 European Constitutional Law Review 163.

[15] Martin Höpner, 'Should Sweden Adopt the Euro?' (Swedish Institute for European Policy Studies) Issue 2017:12epa <www.sieps.se/en/publications/2017/should-sweden-adopt-the-euro/> accessed 23 April 2024.

[16] John Redwood, 'What Does Brexit Look Like? A Lot Better than Staying In' (*John Redwood's Diary*, 1 February 2016) <http://johnredwoodsdiary.com/2016/02/01/what-does-brexit-look-like-a-lot-better-than-staying-in/> accessed 6 April 2020.

2

Constituent Power, the Treaty Triptych, and the Role of Individuals

I. Introduction

Despite being a creature of international Treaty law, the role of individuals as constituent citizens differentiates the European Union's constitutional order from the paradigm of international law. Within the international legal order, the ostensible condition for norms to be binding is state consent based on external sovereignty.[1] By contrast, in the European Union's constitutional order the sovereign state parties have delegated functions to institutions representing individuals in their role as both nationals of the Member States and citizens of the European Union. These institutions can create norms through majority voting without the need for absolute unanimity of state consent. Below, the concept of constituent power will be applied and adapted to this characteristic of the supranational constitutional order.

As outlined in the previous section, the European Union is constitutional by analogy to the paradigm of national constitutional orders in which individuals should be regarded as both the authors and addressees of norms.[2] The European Union's constituent subjects are empowered as democratic subjects and juridical objects by norms that transcend national geographically limited boundaries. The ultimate authorization to participate in the construction of this order remains bound to the national level. This specific plural constellation is conceptualized as *supranational*. This is distinct from the phenomenon represented by the 'inter' prefix of international law. This signifies horizontal state relations demarcated from, rather than interconnected with, the boundaries of national legal orders. 'Supranational' is also distinct from what has been described as *transnational* law.[3] Here the prefix 'trans' indicates the interpenetration of the effects of norms throughout different national constitutional

[1] Lassa Oppenheim, *International Law: A Treatise* (Longmans, Green, and Company 1905).
[2] Jürgen Habermas, *Between Facts and Norms: Contributions to a Discourse Theory of Law and Democracy* (new edn, Polity Press 1997).
[3] Terence C Halliday, *Transnational Legal Orders* (CUP 2016).

Constitutional Disintegration and Disruption. Oliver Garner, Oxford University Press. © Oxford University Press 2025. DOI: 10.1093/9780198914136.003.0002

orders. However, the processes of norm-creation and norm-application do not have an independent constitutional basis that transcends the boundaries of national and international law.

One may consider the model of the European Union as a supranational constitutional order based upon a dual-constituent thesis as falling between two extremes on the continuum of models of European integration and the function of opt-outs and withdrawal therewithin. On one end of the scale lies the 'EU as an international treaty' model from the legal perspective[4] that coheres to a 'statist' or 'nationalist' emphasis in political theory.[5] This position would hold that EU law should be regarded merely as a 'self-contained regime' created by treaty within international law.[6] Therefore, as state consent is the predicate for the validity of international law both opt-outs and withdrawal should be regarded as being a matter purely for states, both in terms of control over the process and assessment of its consequences. The only place for consideration of the place of individuals as citizens would be at the national level. Regarding withdrawal, the national level is recognized in the Treaty through the reference to compliance with national constitutional requirements in Article 50 TEU as a condition for the decision by the state to notify intention to withdraw. For opt-outs, the relevant arena for representation of individuals is in the national ratification procedures recognized in Article 48 TEU.

The other end of the scale is the 'EU as a federal order'[7] model, which coheres with 'cosmopolitan' visions in political theory. On this reading, individuals may be regarded as the ultimate constituent subjects of the European Union with EU citizenship functioning as a 'fundamental status'[8] of last resort that encapsulates the 'right to have rights'.[9] On this reading, the only relevant consideration in determining the consequences of opt-outs and withdrawal is the impact it will have for individuals, and these citizens should also be the main subjects in control of the process. This position may provide a basis for criticism of Article 50 TEU as over-emphasizing the role of the European Council in determining the guidelines for negotiations and the Council in concluding the Withdrawal Agreement, and underplaying the role of the

[4] Bruno de Witte, 'EU Law: Is It International Law?' in Catherine Barnard and Steve Peers (eds), *European Union Law* (3rd edn, OUP 2020); Pavlos Eleftheriadis, *A Union of Peoples* (OUP 2020).

[5] David Miller, *National Responsibility and Global Justice* (OUP 2012).

[6] Bruno Simma and Dirk Pulkowski, 'Of Planets and the Universe: Self-Contained Regimes in International Law' (2006) 17 European Journal of International Law 483.

[7] Robert Schütze, *From Dual to Cooperative Federalism: The Changing Structure of European Law* (OUP 2009).

[8] Case C-184/99 *Rudy Grzelcyzk v Centre public d'aide sociale d'Ottignies-Louvain-la-Neuve* [2001] ECR I-06193, para 31.

[9] Hannah Arendt, *The Origins of Totalitarianism* (Penguin Classics 2017).

European Parliament as the direct representative of EU citizens. Similarly, opt-outs would be subject to criticism for the fact that the law that will apply to individuals can be determined by states without input from the European Parliament during Treaty amendments. This position could even lead to normative arguments that withdrawal from the European Union should not be permitted, for example on the basis that it is 'undemocratic'.[10]

The juristic model of the 'supranational constitutional order' that coheres to the political theory model of the 'dual-constituent thesis' looks to combine the elements of veracity in both of these models. Whilst recognizing the reality of state control over the legal order at times of amendment, derogation, and withdrawal, the model also emphasizes the role provided to individuals through EU citizenship in law-making and law-application that is unique from other international treaty regimes. Nevertheless, it should be recognized that Habermas' original argument was based upon the hypothetical method of a 'rational reconstruction' of reality, and so may be challenged for not cohering to the material facts of European integration. It may be posited that the statist 'EU law as international law' position is more realist than the dual-constituent position, whereas the cosmopolitan 'EU law as a federal constitutional order' position is more normatively aspirational.

Within the model of the European Union as international law, Article 50 TEU on withdrawal is simply an example of a treaty exit clause as *lex specialis* provided for by Article 54 VCLT on termination of or withdrawal from a treaty.[11] The European Union's withdrawal clause fulfils the requirement of 'withdrawal of a party . . . in conformity with the provisions of a treaty',[12] as opposed to the *lex generalis* condition of withdrawal 'at any time by consent of all the parties after consultation with the other contracting states'.[13] Upon this reading withdrawal is a process that occurs purely between states on the international plane, rather than a constitutional process involving legitimation by individuals. The references to 'constitutional requirements' in Article 50(1) TEU on this reading is merely a condition for an internationally legally valid notification, rather than being a prescriptive for a democratic process.

Opt-outs under the international law model may be regarded as a species of reservations lodged to international treaties at times of their ratification as

[10] Tore Vincents Olsen and Christian F Rostbøll, 'Why Withdrawal from the European Union Is Undemocratic' (2017) 9 International Theory 436.

[11] Vienna Convention on the Law of Treaties. Done at Vienna on 23 May 1969. Entered into force on 27 January 1980. United Nations, Treaty Series, vol 1155, p 331 (hereafter 'VCLT'), art 54.

[12] ibid art 54(a).

[13] ibid art 54(b).

regulated by Articles 19–23 VCLT on formulation, acceptance and objections, legal effects, withdrawal of reservations, and the governing procedure.[14] The description of the legal effect of reservations fits the operation of opt-outs in EU law: '[it] modifies for the reserving State in its relations with that other party the provisions of the treaty to which the reservation relates to the extent of the reservation [and vice-versa]'.[15] Article 19 outlines the conditions for reservations to come into force, including restrictions if a reservation is explicitly prohibited by the treaty, or does not fit a predefined list of permissible reservations.[16] The EU Treaties do not explicitly provide for such restrictions. Therefore, the residual condition for a legitimate reservation is triggered that it cannot be 'incompatible with the object and purpose of the treaty'.[17] This may inform arguments for parts of the EU Treaties that could be excluded from opt-outs on the basis of this international law condition, such as provisions establishing the four freedoms. For the Brexit example, this clause may have been evoked for a claim that the New Settlement provisions on the United Kingdom no longer being bound to pursue ever closer union would have been contrary to the object and purpose of the EU Treaties. The opt-outs as reservations model again would regard the legitimacy of opt-outs as being predicated purely upon compliance with these rules established in the VCLT, and would not concern itself with the democratic legitimacy of the exclusion of representation of individuals in their dual role from executive decisions to create opt-outs at times of EU Treaty amendment.

The European Union as a federal polity model would present withdrawal via Article 50 TEU as analogous to secession of a sub-state unit from a state as an internal constitutional process. Processes of secession are far more emotionally powerful in their evocation of tearing apart a pre-existing polity than the drier technical nature of treaty exits. This emotive appeal was clearly evident throughout the Brexit debate. Although the existence of the explicit Article 50 TEU may be seen to differentiate withdrawal as a legitimate legal process from many examples of secession and independence as unsanctioned and unilateral, there is precedent for legally authorized secession in the case of Quebec in Canada.[18]

A legal distinction between this example and the European Union is that secession in Canada would need to be achieved through constitutional

[14] ibid arts 19–23.
[15] ibid art 21(1)(a).
[16] ibid art 19(a) and (b).
[17] ibid art 19(c).
[18] *Reference re Secession of Quebec* [1998] 2 SCR 217 (Supreme Court of Canada) [83]–[108].

amendment, as the Constitution is silent on the issue, as opposed to the explicit presence of Article 50 TEU. However, there are parallels to notification under Article 50(1) and the negotiation of a Withdrawal Agreement insofar as the Canadian Supreme Court held that the legitimate expression of a democratic will for secession by Quebec would create a legal obligation upon the federal state to negotiate in accordance with constitutional principles.[19] These requirements were later enshrined in legislation.[20] The predicative distinction between withdrawal from the European Union and secession from the Canadian federation is unilaterality. The Canadian Supreme Court held that there could be no absolute guarantee that the outcome of negotiations would be independence;[21] by contrast, the two-year residual condition for withdrawal in Article 50 TEU operates precisely as such a legal guarantee that withdrawal can be effected regardless of the outcome of Withdrawal Agreement negotiations.[22]

By contrast to the international law model regarding exit as an exercise of state sovereignty, the federal polity model would need to regard withdrawal from the European Union as an emancipation from the overarching authority of the EU polity, and a reassertion of the sovereignty and independence of the sub-federal unit.[23] However, the retention of state sovereignty within the supranational constitutional order has seen withdrawal operate in a distinct manner to state secession with guarantee of being a sovereign and unilateral right.

Opt-outs would be regarded as a species of federal differentiation within this model. The phenomenon is distinct from the demarcation of federal and sub-unit competences and the variation between sub-units that results therefrom. By contrast, opt-outs concern areas that have been designated as 'federal'

[19] 'The clear repudiation by the people of Quebec of the existing constitutional order would confer legitimacy on demands for secession, and place an obligation on the other provinces and the federal government to acknowledge and respect that expression of democratic will by entering into negotiations and conducting them in accordance with the underlying constitutional principles already discussed': ibid [88].

[20] An Act to give effect to the requirement for clarity as set out in the opinion of the Supreme Court of Canada in the Quebec Secession Reference SC 2000, c 26 Assented to 2000-06-29. '[A]ny future referendum must have a clear majority, be based on an unambiguous question, and have the approval of the federal House of Commons': 'Clarity Act | Canadian History' (*Britannica*) <www.britannica.com/topic/Clarity-Act> accessed 23 April 2024.

[21] 'No negotiations could be effective if their ultimate outcome, secession, is cast as an absolute legal entitlement based upon an obligation to give effect to that act of secession in the Constitution. Such a foregone conclusion would actually undermine the obligation to negotiate and render it hollow.': *Reference re Secession of Quebec* (n 18) [91].

[22] See further discussion of comparisons between *Re Secession of Quebec* and *Wightman* in chapter 6 below.

[23] Some of the rhetoric around Brexit being 'independence day' may support this vision of the European Union as a federal 'super-state': Zoya Sheftalovich, 'Nigel Farage: June 23 Should Be Britain's "Independence Day" Holiday' (*POLITICO*, 24 June 2016) <www.politico.eu/article/nigel-farage-june-23-should-be-britains-independence-day-holiday-leave-eu-brexit/> accessed 23 April 2024.

competences but with exceptions for certain sub-units. The claim has been made that the only way of 'opting-out' from the United States Constitution is secession due to the supremacy claimed by the federal level.[24] The exact term 'opt-out' has been used, however, in relation to amendments to the Canadian constitution and federal–provincial shared cost programmes.[25] The former has never happened in reality, but it is a theoretical possibility under the Constitution Act 1982.[26] The crucial distinguishing factor from the European Union is that opt-outs from Canadian amendments are subject to conditions established by the federal level in the 1982 legislation, such as time limits and the possibility of re-enactment.[27] There is no such general regulation of opt-outs in the EU Treaties, and instead opt-outs are subject to the *ad hoc* conditions established in the individual Protocols.

Within the conceptual model adopted in this book, the specific phenomena of Member State withdrawal and opt-outs can only occur in a supranational constitutional order. The supranational characteristic means that, unlike state secession and independence,[28] an exercise of deconstructive power and the termination of supranational citizenship can occur without the requirement for a concurrent exercise of constituent power and the creation of a new fundamental status. The European Union is not a polity of last resort, and instead preserves national citizenship as the fundamental source of self-determination. The constitutional characteristic of the European Union illustrates, however, that the withdrawal and opt-out processes are not analogous to reservations and Treaty withdrawal in public international law.[29] This challenges the 'EU

[24] 'Is the US Constitution Voluntary? Can Any State Opt Out of It When They Wish?' (*Quora*) <www.quora.com/Is-the-US-Constitution-voluntary-Can-any-state-opt-out-of-it-when-they-wish> accessed 23 April 2024.

[25] 'Moreover, it is to be remembered that s. 33, the "notwithstanding clause", gives Parliament and the provincial legislatures authority to legislate on matters within their jurisdiction in derogation of the fundamental freedoms (s. 2), legal rights (ss. 7 to 14) and equality rights (s. 15) provisions of the Charter.': *Reference re Secession of Quebec* (n 18) [47].

[26] '[A] province may remove itself from any amendment that derogates from its existing legislative powers, proprietary rights, "or any other rights or privileges" of its legislature or government. If an amendment transfers powers relating to education or culture, the federal government must provide "reasonable compensation" to a province which opts out. Section 33 of the Constitution Act, 1982, permits a government to opt out of some sections of the Canadian Charter of Rights and Freedoms. Parliament or a provincial legislature may declare that an Act will operate "notwithstanding" sections 2 (fundamental freedoms), and 7 to 15 (legal and equality rights) of the Charter. Such a provision can last a maximum of 5 years, but may be re-enacted.': Richard Simeon, 'Opting-Out' (*The Canadian Encyclopedia*, 7 February 2006) <www.thecanadianencyclopedia.ca/en/article/opting-out> accessed 23 April 2024.

[27] Such conditions provide inspiration for the reform proposals in chapter 8.

[28] Carlos Closa (ed), *Secession from a Member State and Withdrawal from the European Union: Troubled Membership* (CUP 2017).

[29] Thomas Giegerich, 'Treaties, Multilateral, Reservations To' in *Max Planck Encyclopaedia of International Law* (Oxford Public International Law 2010) <https://opil.ouplaw.com/view/10.1093/law:epil/9780199231690/law-9780199231690-e1680> accessed 30 March 2020; Anthony Aust,

as international law' model whereby withdrawal from the European Union would not be distinct from withdrawal from any other international treaty. Instead, specific rules for democratic authorization are required due to the exercise of constituent and deconstructive power by individuals rather than just states. Finally, the characteristic of order manifests itself in the telos of Article 50. The clause mandates an 'orderly withdrawal',[30] rather than allowing an unconstrained exercise of state sovereignty. Opt-outs expose the limits of this order. The creation of opt-outs cannot be constrained by the EU legal order as they are authorized at times when this order is re-constituted under Article 48 TEU. Despite this, opt-outs are enshrined within the legal form of Protocols to the Treaties as a means to preserve the European Union's legal order once amendments are finalized.

A sufficient balance is required between the overarching yet dependent supranational order and the national orders. The perception of the scales being tipped too far towards the supranational means of norm-creation and norm-application incentivizes national actors to pursue disruptive and disintegrative policies that result in withdrawal and opt-outs.

II. The Dual-Constituent Thesis

In *The Crisis of the European Union*, Jürgen Habermas proposes the 'dual-constituent thesis' of the foundational legitimacy of the European Union.[31] Habermas proposes a hypothetical constituent moment in which nationals of constitutional states create a supranational constitutional order through the joint exercise of constituent power with the new role of citizen of the European Union. Habermas argues that 'the EU citizenry as a whole shares the constitution-building power with a limited number of "constituting states" which acquire a mandate from the peoples to collaborate in founding a supranational political community'.[32]

This position's academic origins can be excavated from the work of Jean Cohen on federations.[33] A similar conception arose during the 2002–2003

'Treaties, Termination', *Max Planck Encyclopaedia of International Law* (Oxford Public International Law 2006) <https://opil.ouplaw.com/display/10.1093/law:epil/9780199231690/law-9780199231690-e1491> accessed 30 March 2020.

[30] Case C-621/18 *Wightman v Secretary of State for Exiting the European Union*, EU:C:2018:999.
[31] Jürgen Habermas, *The Crisis of the European Union: A Response* (Polity Press 2013).
[32] ibid 11.
[33] Jean L Cohen, *Globalization and Sovereignty: Rethinking Legality, Legitimacy, and Constitutionalism* (CUP 2012).

Convention on the Future of Europe. Robert Badinter claimed that 'the sovereignty from which... [the European Union] proceeds is of double origin: First, the delegations of sovereignty granted by the Member States, through successive Treaties... Added to this sovereignty delegated by States is another source, less obvious but more direct: the citizens of the Union'.[34] The dual-constituent thesis has subsequently been developed and critiqued by numerous scholars.[35] A concurrent popular school of political theoretical thought has proposed the similar yet crucially distinct conception of 'demoicracy' and the role of constituent power therein.[36] Demoicracy was developed to recognize the reality, especially following the failure of the 2005 Constitutional Treaty, that Europe did not constitute one demos, whilst not resigning the Union to executive intergovernmentalism. Instead, the position holds that democracy is possible at the supranational level, but through cooperation between the multiple 'demoi' of the Member States.[37] Therefore, national parliaments are afforded a great deal of primacy in demoicratic arguments, especially in proposals for reform.[38]

The demoicratic position that comes closest methodologically to the dual-constituent thesis is provided by Francis Cheneval. Similar to Habermas' hypothetical original constituent assembly, Cheneval proposes a Rawlsian original position in which representatives are assigned to both the peoples of Europe

[34] Badinter, quoted in Markus Patberg, 'Supranational Constitutional Politics and the Method of Rational Reconstruction' (2014) 40 Philosophy & Social Criticism 501.

[35] See *inter alia* Markus Patberg, 'Constituent Power beyond the State: An Emerging Debate in International Political Theory' (2013) 42 Millennium 224; Patberg, 'Supranational Constitutional Politics' (n 34); Markus Patberg, 'Against Democratic Intergovernmentalism: The Case for a Theory of Constituent Power in the Global Realm' (2016) 14 International Journal of Constitutional Law 622; Markus Patberg, 'The Levelling Up of Constituent Power in the European Union' (2017) 55 Journal of Common Market Studies 203; Markus Patberg, 'Constituent Power: A Discourse-Theoretical Solution to the Conflict between Openness and Containment' (2017) 24 Constellations 51; Markus Patberg, 'A Systematic Justification for the EU's *Pouvoir Constituant Mixte*: Principles of Constitutional Politics in Supranational Polities' (2017) 23 European Law Journal 441; Peter Niesen, 'The "Mixed" Constituent Legitimacy of the European Federation' (2017) 55 Journal of Common Market Studies 183; Peter Niesen, 'Reframing Civil Disobedience: Constituent Power as a Language of Transnational Protest' (2019) 15 Journal of International Political Theory 31; Neil Walker, 'Habermas's European Constitution: Catalyst, Reconstruction, Refounding' (2019) 25 European Law Journal 508; George Duke, 'European Constitutionalism and Constituent Power' (2019) 44 European Law Review 49; Vlad Perju, 'The Asymmetries of *Pouvoir Constituant Mixte*' (2019) 25 European Law Journal 515; Markus Patberg, *Constituent Power in the European Union* (OUP 2020).

[36] See overview and discussion in Markus Patberg, *Constituent Power in the European Union* (n 35) ch 4.

[37] See Kalypso Nicolaidis, 'The Idea of European Demoicracy' in Julie Dickson and Pavlos Eleftheriadis (eds), *Philosophical Foundations of European Union Law* (OUP 2012).

[38] Sandra Kröger and Richard Bellamy, 'Beyond a Constraining Dissensus: The Role of National Parliaments in Domesticating and Normalising the Politicization of European Integration' (2016) 14 Comparative European Politics 131.

and its citizens.[39] Most relevantly to the phenomena of opt-outs and withdrawal, Cheneval argues that these dual representatives would decide upon a master principle whereby 'the accession to a specific democratic multilateral order, the exit from such an order, and the design and change of the basic rules remain in the competence of the *pouvoir constituant* of the democratic statespeople'.[40] As will be explicated further in the discussion of the European Union's 'triptych' of constituted constituent power, this position recognizes the primacy of the subject of Member State nationals in existential decisions on participation in European integration. However, the demoicratic position emphasizes this primacy to the point of exclusivity: Patberg critiques demoicratic conceptions of constituent power on the basis that they identify the national *pouvoir constituant* as being merely extended to the supranational level, rather than recognizing the unique nature of the constituent subject that makes decisions on Europe.[41] He pushes back against the demoicratic model of constituent power on the basis that it does not accurately reflect the 'politically significant relations' created *between* the citizens of Europe.[42]

Demoicracy situates constituent power exclusively in the subject of nationals of Member States, with decisions on the shape of the European Union representing an exercise of multiple cooperating constituent powers. This does not recognize the aspirations of the European Union to contain such exercises of self-determination in one status—EU citizenship—which operates in tandem with the statuses of nationality of the various Member States but has an autonomous existence as more than the mere sum of these distinct parts. Kalypso Nicolaidis argues that in a demoicracy peoples 'govern together but not as one';[43] by contrast, the dual-constituent thesis recognizes the unique feature of European integration that individuals govern together (*qua* nationals of their Member States) *and* as one (*qua* EU citizens). The demoicratic conception of constituent power may have more explanatory power for more clearly intergovernmental international organizations such as the Council of Europe, in which the Parliamentary Assembly operates on a delegation model.[44] Within the European Union,

[39] F Cheneval, *The Government of the Peoples: On the Idea and Principles of Multilateral Democracy* (Palgrave Macmillan 2011) 121.
[40] ibid 133; discussed in Patberg, *Constituent Power in the European Union* (n 36) 94.
[41] Patberg, *Constituent Power in the European Union* (n 36) 97–103.
[42] ibid 102.
[43] Nicolaidis (n 37) 254.
[44] Indeed, this would also have held for the European Union's own Parliament before direct elections were established in 1979. For a proposal to go back to this model see Jan Pieter Beetz, 'From Practice to Principle and Back: Applying a New Realist Method to the European Union's Democratic Deficit' (2018) 66 Political Studies 339.

however, the claims of autonomy of EU citizenship, and the direct representative link between individuals and the institution of the European Parliament, mean that a more holistic conception than demoicracy is necessary.

This work reconceptualizes the dual-constituent thesis, which operates hypothetically, into a *dual-legitimation* thesis, which can be applied to actual constitutional practice. The dual-legitimation thesis recognizes that the most prominent example of this duality of the role of democratic subject occurs during the ordinary legislative process in which the representative institutions of the Council and the European Parliament are co-equal.[45] Francis Cheneval's 'weak' demoicratic model recognizes this phenomenon in its advocacy of dual representation of the peoples of the Member States intergovernmentally and the citizens supranationally in ordinary law-making.[46] The explanatory power of dual legitimation should not, however, be limited to the legislative process. Echoes of this strong dual-legitimation role can also be seen in primary law-making through Treaty amendment, in which the European Parliament is represented albeit with final constructive executory power lying with the High Contracting Parties as representatives of nationals. This dual-legitimation thesis is applied in later chapters to explain and critique the disintegration and disruption caused by withdrawal and opt-outs.

Habermas asserts that the popular sovereignty founding the supranational order is split at its root into a *pouvoir constituant mixte*. He reconstructs the autonomous status of EU citizenship to evidence a desire for binding legal regulation of problems that transcend the boundaries of existing constitutional states.[47] Similarly, reconstruction of the prevalence of sovereign states reveals the intention of the original hypothetical constituent convention to preserve the states as guarantors of a particular level of freedom and justice.[48] These historical achievements could be undermined by constituting the European polity as a sovereign state entity *de novo*.[49] This functions as the argument against the position of the 'EU as federal entity' presented above. Perju has criticized Habermas' reification of the nation-state as an impediment to such a radical restructuring of European integration.[50] Although this criticism may be normatively cogent, the place for Member States assigned by Habermas has

[45] The exceptions to this co-equivalence in which the Council takes prominence may be forwarded as further evidence that nationality of a Member State remains the master constituent status.

[46] Cheneval (n 39) 144–45. Discussed in Patberg, *Constituent Power in the European Union* (n 36) 101.

[47] Patberg, 'Supranational Constitutional Politics' (n 34).

[48] Habermas, *The Crisis of the European Union* (n 31).

[49] For the legitimacy dilemma of creating polities *ex nihilo* see Hannah Arendt, *On Revolution* (Penguin Classics 2009).

[50] Perju (n 35).

explanatory validity when considering Member State withdrawal and opt-outs. A crucial factor that distinguishes the European Union from federations, and thus withdrawal and opt-outs from secession and federal differentiation, is that the claim to external sovereignty by the Member States has not been foreclosed due to the retention of nationality as the master constituent status.[51]

Habermas utilizes the dual-constituent thesis to propose prescriptive reform of the EU institutions. This could pose a methodological challenge for using the concept to analyse existing legal phenomena. As Patberg details, 'constituent power merely appears as a hypothetical assumption that highlights the discursively justifiable core of the existing construction, while the political processes in which the EU polity is shaped are not subjected to a rational reconstruction'.[52] Nevertheless, Patberg's development of Habermas' thesis primes the ground for a real-world application. Patberg argues that

> [i]n Habermas' account, the EU's constituent power only appears as a hypothetical assumption that abstracts from the fact that the EU polity 'is the work of political elites'. However, the notion of levelling up demonstrates that political communities organized in states, which have set themselves the goal of founding (or reorganizing) a supranational democracy, can actually install a dual-constituent power.[53]

Patberg argues that the normative aspirations of the dual-constituent thesis can be realized through institutional reform of revisionary constituent power.[54] The argument here is that the dual representation of individuals can be applied to analyse pre-existing phenomena without the need to take a stance on whether this dual representation should extend to primary law creation and recreation.

A particular criticism of the dual-constituent thesis is relevant for how the legal possibility of withdrawal became a reality. Niesen clarifies that the dual-constituent thesis is primarily a justificatory account of the European constitutional order: 'A rational reconstruction asks under which presuppositions a particular set-up of institutions makes *best sense* to those who participate in it'.[55] The meta-presupposition of this 'idealized participant's perspective' is

[51] By contrast see *White v Texas* 74 US 700 (1868) for the US where such claims of external sovereignty are foreclosed.

[52] Patberg, 'The Levelling Up' (n 35) 211.

[53] ibid 209–10.

[54] He proposes assigning amendment competence to the new institution of a 'Permanent Constitutional Assembly' composed of elected representatives of Member State nationals and EU citizens: see Patberg, 'A Systematic Justification' (n 35) 452–53.

[55] Niesen (n 35) 187.

that individuals will accept a constitutional order through the exercise of pure reason.[56] The presumption is that extending democratic constitutionalism beyond the nation-state, but without eschewing its freedom guaranteeing function, makes the 'best sense' for constituent individuals.

However, this seems to downplay the crucial role that *emotion* plays in the acceptance of a framework for the exercise of public power. András Sajó uses the term 'constitutional sentiments' to capture this idea.[57] This is necessary for participants to have an 'internal perspective'[58] upon the system generated, and for them to identify with and perceive themselves as belonging to the constitutional order.[59] Legitimacy is not an exogenous quantifiable substance that can be 'produced'. Heuristic devices such as 'input and output legitimacy'[60] are useful barometers for analysis but are not ultimately determinative of a system's acceptance by its subjects. Instead, emotional narratives are internalized by each member of a polity as the justification for the norms which are applied to them by those imbued with legal authority. Rejections of these narratives have been understood as exercises of 'destituent power'.[61] Legitimacy derives from a shared intersubjective narrative that explains how things are, why they ought to be this way, and why they must continue to be so. These narratives may be understood as 'foundation myths', but more accurately they are continuing serial narratives because they support the iterative development of a polity.[62]

Examples of these justificatory narratives can be found in existing constitutions.[63] The constitutional *leitmotif* of the United States of America is 'We the People', whereby a people created itself through a documentary constitution to transform a confederation of separate states into a federal state order, but with the safeguard of political powers being distributed between various branches.[64] In the United Kingdom, the narrative is 'Parliamentary Sovereignty', in which public power has gradually dissipated from one sovereign monarch to a democratically elected convention without internal revolution or external

[56] Immanuel Kant, *Critique of Pure Reason* (Bohn 1855).

[57] András Sajó, 'Emotions in Constitutional Institutions' (2016) 8 Emotion Review 44; see also András Sajó, 'Emotions in Constitutional Design' (2010) 8 International Journal of Constitutional Law 354.

[58] HLA Hart, *The Concept of Law* (3rd edn, OUP 2012).

[59] This may be considered in relation to Marco Goldoni and Michael A Wilkinson, 'The Material Constitution' (2018) 81 The Modern Law Review 567.

[60] Fritz W Scharpf, *Governing in Europe: Effective and Democratic?* (OUP 1999).

[61] Giorgio Agamben and Stephanie Wakefield, 'What Is a Destituent Power?' (2014) 32 Environment and Planning D: Society and Space 65; Kolja Möller, 'From Constituent to Destituent Power beyond the State' (2018) 9 Transnational Legal Theory 32.

[62] A parallel may be drawn to Ronald Dworkin's 'chain novel' metaphor for precedents in case law: see Ronald Dworkin, *Law's Empire* (Harvard UP 1986).

[63] See Sajó (n 57) 47–48.

[64] Arendt, *On Revolution* (n 49); Sajó (n 57) 48.

occupation, regardless of how accurately this depicts major political ruptures throughout British history.[65] In the Federal Republic of Germany, the unamendable and eternal protection of human dignity within the *Grundgesetz* (Basic Law)[66] reflects the repentant narrative of 'Never Again' following the human tragedies of the Third Reich.[67]

These distinct narratives of legitimacy inform 'constitutional identity'.[68] Michel Rosenfeld identifies seven distinct constitutional 'models',[69] and six different models of 'constitution-making'.[70] This categorization of different legitimacy narratives is analogous to Habermas' rational reconstruction of the foundations of the European Union. Rosenfeld's brief account of the 'European transnational model' resembles the dual-constituent thesis and other accounts of the European Union from the theory of federations: 'Instead, the EU model would have to promote novel vertical and horizontal apportionments of powers allowing supranational, national, and infranational governance to work in harmony without being constrained by traditional forms of federalism or confederalism'.[71] Constitutional identity concerns the predicative characteristics of the intersubjective narrative of legitimacy that individuals internalize as a justification for the constitution.[72] This must be preserved, including through adjudication,[73] to enable individuals to exercise their self-determination to participate in this shared endeavour.

Habermas' constituent thesis may be perfectly compelling as a 'rational' justification for the European Union's constitutional order. However, the dual-constituent thesis may be too convoluted for individuals to internalize as an emotional narrative of belonging to entrench 'constitutional patriotism'[74] towards

[65] Martin Loughlin, *The British Constitution: A Very Short Introduction* (OUP 2013); Martin Loughlin, 'Constituent Power Subverted: From English Constitutional Argument to British Constitutional Practice' in Martin Loughlin and Neil Walker (eds), *The Paradox of Constitutionalism: Constituent Power and Constitutional Form* (OUP 2008).

[66] Christoph Enders, 'Human Dignity in Germany' in Paolo Becchi and Klaus Mathis (eds), *Handbook of Human Dignity in Europe* (Springer 2018).

[67] Christoph Möllers, '"We Are (Afraid of) the People": Constituent Power in German Constitutionalism' in Martin Loughlin and Neil Walker (eds), *The Paradox of Constitutionalism: Constituent Power and Constitutional Form* (OUP 2008).

[68] Michel Rosenfeld, 'Constitutional Identity' in András Sajó and Michel Rosenfeld (eds), *The Oxford Handbook of Comparative Constitutional Law* (OUP 2012).

[69] Rosenfeld identifies (1) the German; (2) the French; (3) the American; (4) the British; (5) the Spanish; (6) the European; and (7) the post-colonial models: ibid 762.

[70] These are (1) the revolution-based model; (2) the invisible British model; (3) the war-based model; (4) the pacted transition model; (5) the transnational model; and (6) the internationally grounded model: ibid 766.

[71] Rosenfeld (n 68) 765.

[72] Julian Scholtes, *The Abuse of Constitutional Identity in the European Union* (OUP 2023).

[73] Christian Calliess and Gerhard van der Schyff (eds), *Constitutional Identity in a Europe of Multilevel Constitutionalism* (CUP 2019).

[74] Jürgen Habermas, 'Citizenship and National Identity: Some Reflections on the Future of Europe' (1992) 12 Praxis International 1.

the European Union. Patberg recognizes this possibility: 'one might still think that the notion of *pouvoir constituant mixte* runs the risk of scaring off citizens with excessive "Euphoria"'.[75] Patberg's rebuttal continues the appeal to reason: '"split" popular sovereignty appears as a reasonable middle ground between regional cosmopolitanism and demoicracy, the most prominent stories of political membership in the EU'.[76]

European integration has been driven by the political executives of the Member States and European institutions, with constitutional legitimacy grafted thereupon *ex post-facto*. Neil Walker refers to '"the original (and still uncorrected) sin" of a weak grounding in terms of popular legitimacy'.[77] Conceptions such as the dual-constituent thesis are necessarily reductive devices. The focus on reason rather than emotion, however, obscures the dynamics of not only the acceptance of the Union's constitutional order, but also its rejection. This argument may be reflected within one of the campaign declarations of one of the candidates for *Spitzenkandidat* of the European People's Party in the European Commission Presidency in 2019: 'Europe is a rational choice, but it needs to feel good'.[78]

One reading of the UK referendum is that the 'Remain' campaign argument for Europe as a 'rational choice' in terms of economic consequences[79] was rejected for a vague but emotionally powerful appeal to 'Take Back Control' that 'felt good'.[80] This may indicate rejection of 'split' sovereignty.[81] The division of constituent power is incompatible with the narrative of Parliamentary Sovereignty whereby the absolute power of Parliament to make and change law is legitimated by the democratic representation of individuals *qua* nationals. Such a narrative represents a zero-sum game approach to constitutional

[75] Markus Patberg, 'After the Brexit Vote: What's Left of "Split" Popular Sovereignty?' (2018) 40 Journal of European Integration 923, 933.

[76] ibid 934.

[77] Neil Walker, 'The EU's Constitutional Overabundance?' (University of Edinburgh 2016) Edinburgh School of Law Research Paper No 2016/14 <https://papers.ssrn.com/abstract=2776800> accessed 28 January 2020.

[78] Alexander Stubb, 'Stubb: "Europe Is a Rational Choice, but It Needs to Feel Good"' (*@alexstubb*, 12 October 2018) <https://twitter.com/alexstubb/status/1050707810605039618> accessed 23 January 2020.

[79] HM Government, 'Why the Government Believes That Voting to Remain in the EU Is the Best Decision for the UK—with References' (*GOV.UK*, 6 April 2016) <www.gov.uk/government/publications/why-the-government-believes-that-voting-to-remain-in-the-european-union-is-the-best-decision-for-the-uk/why-the-government-believes-that-voting-to-remain-in-the-european-union-is-the-best-decision-for-the-uk> accessed 23 January 2020.

[80] For a comprehensive overview of the reasons for the leave vote see Harold D Clarke, Matthew Goodwin and Paul Whiteley, *Brexit: Why Britain Voted to Leave the European Union* (CUP 2017) 146–74; Jack Black, 'From Mood to Movement: English Nationalism, the European Union and Taking Back Control' (2019) 32 Innovation: The European Journal of Social Science Research 191.

[81] Patberg, 'After the Brexit Vote' (n 75).

identity.[82] This emotional drive to simplicity in the legitimation narratives of a polity may militate more closely towards the model of the European Union as international law, with clear separation from the national level on the basis of state sovereignty.

The critique from emotion may also inform reform of the dual constitution of the European Union. Niesen envisages such a possibility: '[D]ependence on already existing political forms should not be thought to take away either *pouvoir*'s freedom to re-invent themselves (in a process of co-evolution with their other *persona*)'.[83] Patberg claims that

> [a]s the method of rational reconstruction examines practices from within, the argument for the *pouvoir constituant mixte* applies not only to processes of polity formation but also to forms of constitutional politics that would take the EU and its Member States in the direction of new forms of political organization—and certainly it does not foreclose such a development.[84]

Member State withdrawal reveals the fault-line within the dual-constituent foundations of the European Union whereby it is no longer sustainable for certain individuals to retain the perspective of both national of a Member State and citizen of the Union. It remains to be seen whether Brexit's rejection of EU citizenship in favour of an absolute nationality will lead to a counter-rejection of nationality in favour of an autonomous EU citizenship.[85] Reconstitution of Europe and the Member States may occur through separation of the dual subject rather than 'co-evolution' between the two personae.[86]

Despite challenges to the dual-constituent thesis as the justificatory narrative for the foundational legitimacy of European integration, the equality of the dual role in the creation and application of norms has explanatory validity for the ordinary functioning of the supranational constitutional order. However, the creation and successive amendments of the constitutional order are more difficult to attribute to a dual-constituent power. The constituted institutions of the European Parliament and the Council have an informative role through participation in the Convention established under Article 48 TEU. Yet the final

[82] Thomas Bryant, 'How the British Conception of Sovereignty Makes EU Membership Untenable' (*BrexitCentral*, 27 September 2019) <https://web.archive.org/web/20241005040621/https://brexitcentral.com/how-the-british-conception-of-sovereignty-makes-eu-membership-untenable/> accessed 2 April 2020.

[83] Niesen (n 35) 190.

[84] Patberg, 'A Systematic Justification' (n 35) 453.

[85] Oliver Garner, 'The Existential Crisis of Citizenship of the European Union: The Argument for an Autonomous Status' (2018) 20 Cambridge Yearbook of European Legal Studies 116.

[86] See the Conclusion for a brief redux of this idea.

executory power to construct and reconstruct the order lies with the plenipotentiaries of the High Contracting Parties acting through the conference of representatives.[87]

Original constituent power was exercised by states in international law to create the European Union's constitutional order. Subsequently, these High Contracting Parties have constituted revisionary constituent power to reconstruct the order. This may seem to cohere with the 'demoi-cratic' conception of constituent power. However, this power has been utilized to create an autonomous and coexistent legitimation status of citizenship of the European Union, comprising the dimensions of both democratic subject and juridical object. The Member States' control over constructive and revisionary constituent power enables reservation by certain Member States and the creation of opt-outs. Furthermore, exercises of power to deconstruct the order through withdrawal lie solely with the nationals of each Member States. EU law has been created by the exercise of a form of 'constituent power' by *states* in international law, which in terms of democratic legitimation is authorized solely by individuals in their role as nationals of constitutional states. Withdrawal from the European Union, and thus extinction of EU citizenship as a democratic and juridical status, is both legally permitted and normatively permissible precisely because the current state of the EU Treaties has *not* created the preconditions for the supranational status to be a co-equivalent constituent status alongside nationality of a Member State.

III. The Principles of Levelling Up Constituent Power

Levelling up and levelling down of constituent power may require the concurrent amendment of the national constitutional order. The principle of citizen participation in revisions manifested itself through specific constitutional mechanisms in the United Kingdom, Ireland, and Denmark. In the latter two states provisions of a formal constitution mandate amendment.[88] Specific provisions also enable the levelling up of power to the supranational level.[89] In the former case of the United Kingdom revisions and authorization

[87] For a classic state-centric 'intergovernmental' explanatory account, see Andrew Moravcsik, *The Choice for Europe: Social Purpose and State Power from Messina to Maastricht* (Cornell UP 1998).

[88] The Constitutional Act of Denmark of 5 June 1953, s 88; Constitution of Ireland enacted by the People on 1st July 1937 in operation as from 29th December 1937, art 46.

[89] The Constitutional Act of Denmark (n 88) s 20; Constitution of Ireland (n 88) art 29.

of levelling up were achieved through ordinary law-making in statutes passed by Parliament.[90] These mechanisms played their role in realizing disruption and disintegration at the national level. In reality, these principles were assumed to be fulfilled by the original six Member States, before the progressive iteration of accession conditions culminating in the Copenhagen Criteria for accession.[91] These principles apply when the Council acts during exercises of 'constituted constituent power' through the triptych of Article 48 TEU, Article 49 TEU, and Article 50 TEU.

Markus Patberg disaggregates Habermas' hypothetical convention into three stages—the intra-demos, the inter-demoi, and the across-demoi stages. He extrapolates concrete principles for each stage that build upon the basic principle of equality between citizens.[92] At the first domestic stage, Patberg adds the principle of basic rights to participate in processes of supra-state constitutional politics.[93] The principles at the levels beyond the nation-state that pertain to nationals of the Member State are the political autonomy of the members of the state demoi; the equality of the state demoi; the pluralistic representation of the state demoi; and the discursive interaction of representatives.[94] The principles pertaining to representation of citizens of the European Union are the political autonomy of the members of the cross-border demos and the equality of the members of the cross-border demos.[95] Patberg's principles can be condensed into a normative statement that, in the ordinary functioning of the supranational constitutional order, and the decisions concerning its construction, individuals *qua* Member State nationals and *qua* citizens of the Union should be able to express their will autonomously and co-equivalently through representative institutions. The desiderata of equality should also be utilized to assess whether the application and reliance of EU law norms for individuals *qua* juridical objects vindicates their self-determination.

These principles may be appropriated to analyse the converse phenomena of levelling down of constituent power through withdrawal leading to disintegration, and the processes of opt-out formation leading to disrupted integration. The principles can be used to explain and critique the direct representation of EU citizens in levelling up, reconstruction, and levelling down of constituent

[90] See European Communities Act 1972; European Union Act 2011.
[91] 'Accession Criteria' (*European Neighbourhood Policy And Enlargement Negotiations—European Commission*, 6 December 2016) <https://ec.europa.eu/neighbourhood-enlargement/policy/glossary/terms/accession-criteria_en> accessed 17 December 2018.
[92] Patberg, 'A Systematic Justification' (n 35).
[93] ibid 449.
[94] ibid 450.
[95] ibid 452.

power. Formal equality may be guaranteed through the democratically constituted European Parliament serving as the means to represent individuals *qua* EU citizens under Article 50 TEU. However, the limited role of the European Parliament in Treaty amendment means that individuals *qua* EU citizens cannot regulate the reservation of constituent power by Member States. A tentative claim is that opt-outs violate the principles as they do not reflect an expression of democratic self-determination by individuals *qua* EU citizens.[96] The principles are drawn upon at various points throughout this monograph to consider whether decision-making is fully inclusive of individuals in their dual role.

IV. The Triptych of Constituted Constituent Power (and the *Ad Hoc* Anomalies)

The conclusion of the Treaty of Rome by the states of Germany, France, Italy, Belgium, the Netherlands, and Luxembourg was an exercise of original constituent power through the source of international treaty law. Complete disintegration is similarly possible if all of the constituent powers of the Member States so agree.[97] This would be legitimated in public international law by the Vienna Convention rules on termination of treaties.[98] To prevent disintegration being the only means for legitimate change, the constituent powers have established a triptych of Treaty articles in 'Title VI—Final Provisions' of the Treaty on European Union. This triptych constitutionalizes the procedures for the exercise of constituent power following the initial levelling up of constituent power during construction.

Article 48 TEU functions as a means of constituted revisionary power. This mandates the reconstruction of the supranational constitutional order. The process of levelling up constituent power is reactivated through the representation of individuals by national and supranational institutions. The ordinary revision procedure empowers the government of any Member State, the European Parliament, or the Commission to propose to the Council amendment of the Treaties.[99] The simplified revision procedure is limited to Part Three TFEU on internal policies and actions.[100] In the ordinary procedure, the

[96] See further elaboration of these claims in chapter 7.

[97] Markus Patberg, 'Can Disintegration Be Democratic? The European Union Between Legitimate Change and Regression' (2020) 68 Political Studies 582.

[98] VCLT, art 54.

[99] TEU, art 48(2).

[100] TEU, art 48(6).

Council submits the proposals to the European Council, notifying national parliaments. The European Council, after consultation with the European Parliament and the Commission, may then adopt a simple majority decision to establish a Convention to examine the amendments.[101] In the simplified procedure, the European Council may adopt the decision for amendment by unanimity without the need for a Convention after consultation with the European Parliament and Commission, and the European Central Bank (ECB) if relevant.[102] There are substantive and formal safeguards to compensate for the lack of Convention: the decision may not increase Union competences,[103] and any national parliament may veto the decision within six months.[104] To adopt the decision, the European Council acts by unanimity with the consent of the European Parliament.[105]

In the ordinary procedure the Convention is composed of national parliament representatives, the Heads of State or Government of the Member States, the European Parliament, the Commission, and the ECB if relevant.[106] However, consensus in the Convention does not lead to amendment, but only a recommendation to a conference of representatives of the governments of the Member States. This conference determines by common accord the amendments to be made.[107] The unanimity of the Member States recognizes the necessity of consent of all of the original constituent powers. The amendments may then only enter into force if ratified by all Member States in accordance with their respective constitutional requirements.[108] This provides a final filter whereby all individuals *qua* nationals of the constitutional states must approve exercises of revisionary power. Unanimity requirements in amendment of the EU Treaties are crucial as a manifestation of the retention of nationality as the ultimate status with control over the deepening of European integration, no matter how fully the functioning of the supranational order may touch upon issues that are traditionally regulated through national sovereignty. Unanimity is the predicative factor behind the emergency of legitimate disruption through opt-outs due to the potential for any Member State to reserve its consent to level up constituent power into new areas.

[101] TEU, art 48(3).
[102] TEU, art 48(6).
[103] TEU, art 48(6).
[104] TEU, art 48(7).
[105] TEU, art 48(7).
[106] TEU, art 48(3).
[107] TEU, art 48(4).
[108] ibid.

Article 49 TEU functions as a means to replicate the original levelling up of constituent power for any European State which respects and is committed to promoting the Union's Article 2 values.[109] This reconstructs the constituent nationals of the candidate state into holders of the quadripartite role, as explicated further below. The accession application is addressed to the Council, which acts unanimously after consulting the Commission and receiving the consent of the European Parliament. The European Council establishes conditions of eligibility to be taken into account. This stage allows the input of the pre-existing individuals *qua* Member State nationals and *qua* EU citizens.

The conditions of admission and the necessary adjustment to the Treaties are the subject of an agreement between the Member States and the applicant state. This legal structure, rather than an agreement between the European Union and the applicant state, recognizes that the conferral of the status of EU citizenship upon a new class of nationals requires the agreement of all of the constituent powers. Further consent is required at the national level through the requirement of ratification by all contracting states in accordance with their constitutional requirements. After two decades of abeyance following the challenges of the 'Big Bang' enlargement in 2004, the functioning of Article 49 TEU and accession has become a live issue in Europe again following Ukraine's application for membership at the beginning of the Ukraine invasion in February 2022, with the decision to open negotiations in December 2023,[110] and the further applications from Georgia, Moldova, and Kosovo. The challenges of 'accession through war'[111] have seen proposals for radical overhaul of the Article 49 process, including arguments for immediate accession,[112] and for a form of differentiated accession.[113] Such modifications could challenge the primacy of Member State nationals over decisions to confer the constituent status of EU citizenship to new European democratic subjects.

Article 50 TEU provides a deconstructive power for each Member State. The chapters below fully explicate the telos and operation of this clause. Finally, the a-constitutional anomalies of Protocols to the Treaties legally enshrine the

[109] TEU, art 49.

[110] 'Ukraine' (*European Council*) <www.consilium.europa.eu/en/policies/ukraine/#candidate> accessed 24 April 2024.

[111] Roman Petrov, 'Applying for EU Membership in Time of War: "Accession through War" of Ukraine' (*IAI Istituto Affari Internazionali*, 3 May 2023) <www.iai.it/en/pubblicazioni/applying-eu-membership-time-war-accession-through-war-ukraine> accessed 24 April 2024.

[112] Dimitry Kochenov, 'Immediate EU Membership for Ukraine? In Conversation with Dimitry Kochenov' (*Review of Democracy*, 20 April 2022) <https://revdem.ceu.edu/2022/04/20/immediate-eu-membership-for-ukraine-in-conversation-with-dimitry-kochenov/> accessed 24 April 2024.

[113] Irakli Sirbiladze and Elena Ventura, 'The EU's Eastern Enlargement and Differentiated Democracy Support' (*Carnegie Europe*, 11 September 2023) <https://carnegieeurope.eu/2023/09/11/eu-s-eastern-enlargement-and-differentiated-democracy-support-pub-90488> accessed 24 April 2024.

reservation of constituent power by certain Member States.[114] The requirement of unanimity in Article 48 TEU enables this resistance, and the unravelling of the supranational constitutional order allows for amendment despite such reservations. These Protocols, the object of study in the chapters below, are afforded their legal status through Article 51 TEU: 'The Protocols and Annexes to the Treaties shall form an integral part thereof'.[115]

V. The Role of Individuals

Within all democratic constitutional systems individuals should function both as *democratic subjects* in the creation of norms by the constituted legislative institutions, and as *juridical objects* in their reliance upon norms, and the application by the constituted juridical institutions. The supranational constitutional order that is dependent upon the dual role of individuals as nationals and EU citizens for its legitimacy is no exception. The resulting *quadripartite* role of individuals in the order can be used as a means to analyse constitutional phenomena such as disruption and disintegration. There are four distinct roles for individuals in the European Union: (1) EU citizen *qua* democratic subject; (2) EU citizen *qua* juridical object; (3) national of a Member State *qua* democratic subject; (4) national of a Member State *qua* juridical object. This may be regarded as the 'quadripartite conception' of the individual within the European Union. Sensitivity to all four roles is crucial to understand the consequences of disintegration and disruption comprehensively.

The terminology of 'subjects and objects' of EU law has been utilized by *inter alia* Samo Bardutzky and Elaine Fahey,[116] and Joseph Weiler.[117] Päivi Johanna Neuvonen[118] and Susanna Lindroos- Hovinheimo[119] have advanced

[114] TEU and TFEU, Protocol (No 15) on certain provisions relating to the United Kingdom of Great Britain and Northern Ireland; TEU and TFEU, Protocol (No 16) on certain provisions relating to Denmark; TEU and TFEU, Protocol (No 17) on Denmark; TEU and TFEU, Protocol (No 19) on the Schengen *acquis* integrated into the framework of the European Union; TEU and TFEU, Protocol (No 20) on the application of certain aspects of Article 26 of the Treaty on the Functioning of the European Union to the United Kingdom and to Ireland; TEU and TFEU, Protocol (No 21) on the position of the United Kingdom and Ireland in respect of the area of freedom, security and justice; TEU and TFEU, Protocol (No 22) on the position of Denmark; TEU and TFEU, Protocol (No 36) on transitional provisions.

[115] TEU, art 51.

[116] Samo Bardutzky and Elaine Fahey (eds), *Framing the Subjects and Objects of Contemporary EU Law* (Edward Elgar Publishing 2017).

[117] JHH Weiler, 'Van Gend En Loos: The Individual as Subject and Object and the Dilemma of European Legitimacy' (2014) 12 International Journal of Constitutional Law 94.

[118] Päivi Johanna Neuvonen, 'Retrieving the "Subject" of European Integration' (2019) 25 European Law Journal 6.

[119] Susanna Lindroos-Hovinheimo, 'There Is No Europe—On Subjectivity and Community in the EU' (2017) 18 German Law Journal 1229.

recent interpretations of the subject of European integration. Weiler's starting point is the Court of Justice's dicta that individuals are 'subjects' of the EU legal order: '[T]he Community constitutes a new legal order of international law for the benefit of which the states have limited their sovereign rights, albeit within limited fields, and the subjects of which comprise not only Member States but also their nationals'.[120] Weiler uses the term 'objects' to criticize the potential de-politicization resulting from the juridical empowerment of individuals: 'In the European Union with its defective democratic machinery where the individual has far less control over norm creation, direct effect has the paradoxical effect of objectifying him or her—an object of laws over which one has no effective democratic control'.[121]

The nature of Bardutzky and Fahey's endeavour to 'reframe' the objects and subjects of EU law means that they investigate numerous iterations of these concepts, including the 'object' being the law itself. One specific instance coheres with Weiler's understanding: 'individuals are, or should be, both subjects (the source of the law) and objects (objects of the law). In other words, they are all *both* subject *and* object *at one and the same time*'.[122] Bardutzky and Fahey's contribution confirms that the same physical individuals are the root of these processes, just as Habermas confirms that the dual-constituent subject does not refer to ontologically separate individuals. The processes themselves, however, are qualitatively distinct. Weiler uses the term 'object' in a critical sense to describe law application with deficient democratic input. By contrast, in this monograph it is used in a normatively neutral sense to capture the qualitative distinction for individuals between adjudicative and legislative processes.

Weiler recognizes that the juridical architecture of the EU legal order empowers individuals as juridical objects through *inter alia* the preliminary reference procedure, direct standing rules, the doctrines of direct effect, primacy, *effet utile*, and Francovich damages. These are the elements of European integration that enable democratic self-actualization and accordingly are threatened by disruption and disintegration. He argues that

> as a socio-legal phenomenon, direct effect harnesses the *private* economic, political, and social interests of the individual in vindicating those rights

[120] Case 26/62 *Van Gend En Loos v Nederlandse Administratie Der Belastingen* [1963] ECR 1, para 3.

[121] Weiler (n 117) 102.

[122] Elaine Fahey and Samo Bardutzky, 'Introductory chapter: *The Subjects and Objects of EU Law: Exploring a Research Platform* (Cheltenham: Edward Elgar Publishing, Forthcoming [at time of publication])' (*City, University of London Institutional Repository*, 18 July 2016), 9 <https://openaccess.city.ac.uk/id/eprint/15217/1/Framing%20the%20subjects%20and%20objects-%20%20Introductory%20Chapter.pdf> accessed 18 February 2025.

> to the public interest of ensuring the rule of law at the transnational level. With each individual effectively becoming in that way a 'legal vigilante' of the public rule of law, an effective civil society monitoring system is put in place.[123]

Individuals can vindicate their own private interests against the manifestations of domestic and European constituted power. This decentralized role as 'Private Attorney Generals'[124] empowers individuals to rely upon norms to enact their plans for self-fulfilment within the territory of the European Union.

Mattias Kumm develops this further and argues that such juridical empowerment promotes *democratic* self-determination.[125] This may be a step too far if we wish to preserve a separation in the normative functioning between legislative and judicial institutions, and the role of individuals as democratic subjects and juridical objects. Kumm captures the interdependence when he claims that 'judicial review of rights is not in tension with democratic legitimacy but a necessary complement to it'.[126] However, he conflates the different forms of legitimacy that legislation and adjudication represent. The value of adjudication and democracy should be complementary rather than identical. Kumm's claim may instead be interpreted as a holistic statement on the role of adjudication in social and personal self-actualization.[127] This claim functions as a foundational principle of the levelling up of constituent power explicated by Patberg.[128] Democratic legitimation and juridical empowerment are the two dimensions of constitutional self-determination, but remain qualitatively distinct.

Weiler claims that the present structure of the Union's constitutional order is misbalanced towards output legitimacy and does not make sufficient provision for democratic self-determination. This perceived democratic deficit is one of the prime motivations for Habermas' use of the dual-constituent thesis to propose prescriptive reforms. To delineate the multifaceted role of individuals here it suffices to establish the role of democratic subjecthood, regardless of its imperfect realization.

123 Weiler (n 117) 96.

124 ibid.

125 Mattias Kumm, 'Institutionalising Socratic Contestation: The Rationalist Human Rights Paradigm, Legitimate Authority and the Point of Judicial Review' (2007) 1 European Journal of Legal Studies 153.

126 ibid 156.

127 See Mark Dawson and Floris De Witte, 'Self-Determination in the Constitutional Future of the EU' (2015) 21 European Law Journal 371.

128 Patberg, 'A Systematic Justification' (n 35).

i. Democratic subjects

Democratic subjecthood empowers the EU legislative institutions to create binding legal norms following the election of representatives. European Parliament elections held under Article 223 TFEU, and national elections that lead to the appointment of Ministers are the 'norm-creator' processes. Following their appointment, the supranational 'norm-creation' process is mandated by Article 289 TFEU. Individuals *qua* Member State national and *qua* EU citizen are recognized as equal democratic subjects through the co-equivalence of the Council and the European Parliament in the ordinary legislative procedure. Article 289(2) TFEU also recognizes 'special' legislative procedures in which the European Parliament does not have the power to amend proposals, and which are determined on an *ad hoc* basis within the Treaty. This shows that the predominance of the Member States in the creation, amendment, and termination of the Treaties can spill over into the ordinary functioning of the constitutional order.

The (conditional) equality of the statuses also explains some unusual features of the supranational legislative processes: Qualified Majority Voting (QMV) within the Council and the degressive proportionality of the European Parliament. According to Peter Niesen, 'what appears as anomaly at first sight may in fact provide the key to deciphering the normative logic'.[129] Habermas argues that 'when there are extreme differences in size between the participating states, the principle of state equality must not be invalidated by the legitimation requirement of democratic equality'.[130] This is rooted in the retention of nationality as a constituent status. Habermas states that 'the prejudice in favour of the member states anchored in the structure of the [hypothetical] constituent convention itself now impacts upon the design of all the institutions'.[131] These features may also result from the balance sought between the institutions following their input under Article 48 TEU.

The representation of individuals balances the principle of equality of Member State nationals and the principle of equality of EU citizens. Markus Patberg presents a thought experiment to explain the creation of these roles and the normative guidelines that would guide this process.[132] Patberg recognizes

[129] Niesen (n 35) 187.
[130] Jürgen Habermas, 'Citizen and State Equality in a Supranational Political Community: Degressive Proportionality and the *Pouvoir Constituant Mixte*' (2017) 55 Journal of Common Market Studies 171, 177.
[131] ibid 178 (emphasis removed).
[132] Patberg, 'A Systematic Justification' (n 35).

the potential schism between the roles: 'In emphasizing the role of the (future) members of the supranational polity, the last step of the thought experiment seems to contradict the results of the previous step, which put the citizens of the states involved in the driver's seat'.[133] The principles underpinning the roles may come into conflict with one another. The role of democratic subject is one of formal co-equivalence, but this equality is founded on the shifting sands of uncertain foundations as to which role takes primacy within the constitutional order. The interplay between the two roles can combust into contradiction and conflict and arguments that mutual accommodation is not possible.[134] In these disruptive and disintegrative scenarios, the retention of constituent power by the Member States and the prospect of withdrawal suggests that that the original status of Member State nationality ultimately takes precedence.

ii. Juridical objects

Individuals are juridical objects of EU law because they are the addressees of the norm-application processes by EU and national judiciaries. Habermas focuses his attention on the hypothetical creation of the legislative institutions. He places less emphasis on why it would make 'best sense' for the hypothetical constituent subject to form the Court of Justice of the European Union. Habermas does, however, include the 'primacy of supranational law over the national law of the monopolists on the means for the legitimate use of force'[135] as the first innovation enabling supranational democracy. He ties this explicitly to the rational reconstruction of the dual-constituent subject: 'the subordination under European Law can be understood as a result of the fact that, from the very beginning, two different subjects were involved who cooperated in bringing about a supranational political community'.[136]

The historical equivalent of Habermas' hypothetical is the Court of Justice's iterative empowerment of individuals *qua* EU citizens.[137] This story of the subordination of national norms has been told extensively in the dicta of the Court,[138] and secondary commentary

[133] ibid 452.

[134] Margaret Thatcher, 'House of Commons Statement: Rome European Council, Hansard HC 178/869-92 ("No No No")' (*Margaret Thatcher Foundation*, 30 October 1990) <www.margaretthatcher.org/document/108234> accessed 2 April 2024.

[135] Habermas, *The Crisis of the European Union* (n 31) 20.

[136] ibid.

[137] Garner (n 85).

[138] Opinion 2/13 of the Court on the accession of the EU to the ECHR, EU:C:2014:2454 (Grand Chamber, 18 December 2014).

thereupon.[139] These narratives justify the legal doctrines and principles that enable the uniform application of EU law throughout the Member States.[140] These principles aspire to formal equality between all individuals who hold EU citizenship regardless of their nationality. The distinct roles performed through EU citizenship and Member State nationality *qua* juridical object are harder to establish than the democratic roles.

One interpretation is that the supremacy claim of EU law means that the individual *qua* citizen of the Union and *qua* national of a Member State are not co-equivalent; instead, the former takes precedence over the latter. This raises the question of the legitimacy of the role of EU citizen being dominant over the role of national of a Member State when it comes to legal norms. On the one hand, this position may be justified by emphasizing the greater 'quantity' of input into EU law norms by each individual through two channels, and in turn by individuals of all the Member States rather than just one. On the other hand, it may be argued that the primacy of the EU citizens *qua* juridical object is democratically deficient due to the more proximate representative link and greater quality of domestic norm-creation through national legislatures.

A more salient distinction focuses not on status but on the source of law. Individuals may be conceived as the juridical objects of EU law, and the juridical objects of national law. The former role will (conditionally) take precedence over the latter in cases of conflict.[141] The crucial caveat is provided by the roles of national courts: 'in their interpretation of the European Treaties, [they] can conceive of themselves as legitimate guardians of the democratic legal substance of the constitutions of their respective member countries'.[142] As outlined above, the primacy of EU law may be justified because it has been legitimated by other individuals beyond the scope of any one constitutional order. To ensure these individuals can rely upon this law effectively throughout the territory of the European Union, the norms must have a uniform scope of application. However, the national constitutional orders may empower their courts to protect the 'democratic legal substance'—the greater quality and

[139] See *inter alia* Karen J Alter, 'Who Are the "Masters of the Treaty"? European Governments and the European Court of Justice' (1998) 52 International Organization 121; Miguel Poiares Maduro, *We the Court: The European Court of Justice and the European Economic Constitution: A Critical Reading of Article 30 of the EC Treaty* (Hart Publishing 1998); Thomas Horsley, *The Court of Justice of the European Union as an Institutional Actor: Judicial Lawmaking and Its Limits* (CUP 2018); Justin Lindeboom, 'Why EU Law Claims Supremacy' (2018) 38 Oxford Journal of Legal Studies 328.

[140] TEU, art 19.

[141] On conditional primacy of EU law see Oliver Garner, 'The Borders of European Integration on Trial in the Member States: Dansk Industri, Miller, and Taricco' (2017) 9 European Journal of Legal Studies 1.

[142] Habermas, *The Crisis of the European Union* (n 31) 27.

proximity of the legislative process—when specific characteristics are threatened by EU law.

The national and supranational judiciaries do not operate in hermetically sealed vacuums. Instead, a 'symbiotic relationship' exists.[143] The Treaties determine that all Member State courts are also EU courts.[144] The innovation of the preliminary reference procedure[145] enables a pathway for individuals with standing as juridical objects of domestic law to vindicate claims as juridical objects of EU law.[146] The continuing application of the preliminary reference procedure during the Article 50 process ensures that nationals of the withdrawing state can continue to rely upon their juridical objecthood to ensure that the treaties cease to apply in a legally valid manner. This is complemented by the fast-track of direct standing before the Court of Justice when the role as object of EU law is activated by acts 'of direct and individual concern'.[147] Weiler argues that '[t]he member states' courts "are not alone" when confronted with the higher norm of the international Treaty. The symbiotic relationship works also in the opposite direction. The European Court "needs" the national courts not only to "activate" and initiate the European norm. But also for the compliance pull issue.'[148]

The juridical architecture of the supranational constitutional order is available to all individuals *qua* juridical objects, regardless of whether they hold the constituent status of EU citizenship or not. The residual juridical objects of the order who do not exercise democratic subjecthood, Third-Country Nationals, are also able to vindicate legal claims if they fulfil the objective standing criteria. By contrast to Third-Country Nationals, the core of the unique value of EU citizenship as a juridical status is the right to free movement and associated rights to enable integration into any of the Member States of the Union.[149] Article 21 TFEU declares that '[e]very citizen of the Union shall have the right to move and reside freely within the territory of the Member States, subject to the limitations and conditions laid down in the Treaties and by the measures adopted to give them effect'.[150] EU citizens are also granted the right to vote

[143] Weiler (n 117) 97.

[144] TEU, art 19.

[145] TFEU, art 267.

[146] The preliminary reference procedure enabled UK nationals *qua* objects of EU law to ensure the legal validity of the Article 50 withdrawal process in the *Wightman* litigation.

[147] TFEU, art 263.

[148] Weiler (n 117) 97.

[149] Floris De Witte, 'Freedom of Movement Needs to Be Defended as the Core of EU Citizenship' in Rainer Bauböck (ed), *Debating European Citizenship* (Springer 2019).

[150] TFEU, arts 20(2)(a) and 21. For the 'limitations and conditions laid down . . . by the measures adopted to give them effect' see Directive 2004/38/EC of the European Parliament and of the Council of 29 April 2004 on the right of citizens of the Union and their family members to move and reside freely within the territory of the Member States [2004] OJ L 158/77.

in local and European Parliament elections in their adopted Member State.[151] This juridical core of free movement rights has been a key arena for the Court of Justice's development of the supranational constitutional order. The development of free movement has also exposed cleavages between individuals who identify more with their nationality or their EU citizenship in the pursuit of self-fulfilment.[152] The rights that underpin EU citizenship as a status of democratic subjecthood and juridical objecthood are mutually reinforcing. The physical integration of individuals in the territory of other nations requires that they have a form of local and supranational representation, and the outcome of these democratic processes informs the development of the juridical free movement and residence rights.

The physical placement of the norm-creation processes in Brussels and Strasbourg has no territorial significance in constitutional terms.[153] By contrast, norm-application is traditionally predicated more upon territory than the identification of the individuals as objects to whom it applies. Territorial legal orders within the Union within which norms cannot be relied upon undermines the central telos of individuals as juridical objects in the foundational case law. This raises a further point of normative significance regarding the relationship between the roles of democratic subject and juridical object. As Habermas outlines: 'Democratic self-government means that the addressees of mandatory laws are at the same time their authors. In a democracy, citizens are subject only to the law which they have given themselves in accordance with a democratic procedure'.[154] Constitutional disruption and disintegration threaten to undermine this normative goal. Member State opt-outs disrupt the equality of all individuals *qua* juridical objects by demarcating national legal orders in which individuals cannot rely upon certain EU law despite their input into its creation.[155] Withdrawal represents a full disintegration of the role of individual *qua* juridical subject of EU law through the disapplication of this legal source in the territory of a former Member State.[156]

[151] TFEU, art 21.
[152] Garner (n 85).
[153] There is, however, geopolitical significance in vindicating French state interests through sharing the European Parliament between Strasbourg and Brussels.
[154] Habermas, *The Crisis of the European Union* (n 31) 14.
[155] See chapter 7 for the full argument on the normative deficiencies of opt-outs.
[156] See chapter 7 for the full argument on the normative deficiencies of withdrawal.

3

Opt-Out Protocols

Telos, Form, and Function

I. Overview and Normative Foundations

These next two chapters of the book analyse the phenomenon of disrupted integration contained within the legal Protocols enabling Member State opt-outs. The constitutional sectors in which at least two of the Member States opted out are the Economic and Monetary Union (EMU), the Schengen *acquis*, and the Area of Freedom, Security and Justice (AFSJ). This chapter compares the different methods of operation of Protocols (No 15), (No 16), (No 17), (No 19), (No 20), (No 21), (No 22), and (No 36). The historical case of the United Kingdom's Social Policy opt-out demonstrates that opt-outs can be reversed. The 'quasi' opt-out from the Charter of Fundamental Rights illustrates the threshold for a Protocol to disapply EU law rather than merely clarify its operation.

The origins and development of these opt-outs show that the driving logic is not the necessity to preserve equality between the democratic subjects of the supranational order on the basis of the precept to 'treat different cases differently'. Instead, the opt-outs have been driven by executive attempts to secure state interests and preferences at Treaty amendments. The overview will also consider whether Member State actors have been unwilling or unable to level up constituent power because of the constraints of the national constitutional order. A major normative issue arising from executive preferences to opt out from policy areas is the negative externalities caused for those Member States that do participate fully in European integration, and the spillovers and path dependencies that can be created from decisions to opt out leading to deepening disruption.

Opt-outs are not created through a single constitutional clause. Instead, they arise from the reservation of constituent power at Treaty amendments under Article 48 TEU. Nevertheless, the consequences of opt-outs are comparable to withdrawal as individuals of the opt-out Member State will not participate in the creation of norms *qua* nationals, and these norms will not apply to EU citizens *qua* juridical objects in this territory. Rather than disintegration,

Constitutional Disintegration and Disruption. Oliver Garner, Oxford University Press. © Oxford University Press 2025. DOI: 10.1093/9780198914136.003.0003

opt-outs are an example of *disrupted* integration. This disruption is legitimate and authorized because Protocols to the Treaties enable this non-uniform application of EU law. This contrasts opt-outs from examples of *illegitimate* disruption, such as failures to apply EU law[1] or deliberate resistance to EU values.[2] A typology could be briefly introduced whereby breaches of EU law may be regarded as 'unsanctioned norm-specific derogation', and deliberate resistance may be regarded as 'unsanctioned intentional sector-specific derogation'. A number of factors may be forwarded as distinguishing opt-outs from failures to implement EU law: perhaps most prominently, the EU legal order's enforcement architecture included within *inter alia* Article 263 and Article 267 TFEU has been designed to ensure a coherent legal response to the former phenomenon. By contrast, the opportunity for disrupted integration through opt-outs derives from the extensive authority retained by the High Contracting Parties. The states unravel and rework the constitutional fabric of the European Union during amendment. Therefore, rather than legal forms of enforcement, the political process is required to deal with this resistance through the creation of Protocols to accommodate disruption and positivize norms not being applied in particular Member State territory.

Another important distinction may be drawn between such opt-outs as 'sanctioned sector-specific derogation' and the discrete exceptions to EU law[3] contained within the text of primary and secondary law that may be regarded as 'sanctioned norm-specific derogation'. The key difference in the origins, form, and function of these two species is that exceptions are fully under the control of the constitutional legislator of the High Contracting Parties or the Council and European Parliament for primary and secondary law respectively. By contrast, opt-outs are dependent upon the will of individual Member States in their retentions of constituent power. This legal form also distinguishes opt-outs and disrupted integration from the differentiated integration that occurs through enhanced cooperation.[4] Within the typology, the derogation that

[1] Ben Smulders and Luca Prete, 'The Coming of Age of Infringement Proceedings' (2010) 47 Common Market Law Review 9.

[2] Kim Lane Scheppele, Dimitry Vladimirovich Kochenov and Barbara Grabowska-Moroz, 'EU Values Are Law, After All: Enforcing EU Values through Systemic Infringement Actions by the European Commission and the Member States of the European Union' (2020) 39 Yearbook of European Law 3.

[3] Ton van den Brink and Virginia Passalacqua (eds), *Balancing Unity and Diversity in EU Legislation* (Edward Elgar Publishing 2024).

[4] See *inter alia* Daniel Thym, '"United in Diversity"—The Integration of Enhanced Cooperation into the European Constitutional Order' in Philip Dann and Michał Rynkowski (eds), *The Unity of the European Constitution* (Springer 2006); Sebastian Zeitzmann, 'A Rather Strange Animal, This "Enhanced Cooperation"—May It Serve as King of the European Zoonion? Or: Is Enhanced Cooperation Anywhere Near a Constitutional Principle?' in Thomas Giegerich, Desirée C Schmitt and Sebastian Zeitzmann (eds), *Flexibility in the EU and Beyond: How Much Differentiation Can European Integration Bear?* (Nomos/Hart 2017).

arises may be regarded as 'unchosen sector-specific derogation' by the Member State(s) who do not participate in the enhanced cooperation because they are excluded from the application of norms not through any exercise of sovereign choice to not level up constituent power in certain areas at times of Treaty amendment, but rather through the choice of other Member States. Article 20 TEU and Articles 329 to 334 TFEU ensure that enhanced cooperation is subject to conditions established by the supranational constitutional order, with specific roles for the representative institutions. This creates a general and reproducible framework and conditions for when enhanced cooperation can occur, by contrast to opt-outs being created in an *ad hoc* manner due to the context of Treaty amendment. Furthermore, the Court of Justice remains the final arbiter of the constitutionality of such differentiated measures.[5] By contrast, opt-outs are subject to no such constitutional safeguards for individuals *qua* democratic subjects and *qua* juridical objects.[6]

If individuals are from a Member State which has an opt-out then they are not represented by their national Ministers in the norm-creation process in this legal sector, although they are represented *qua* EU citizen by Members of the European Parliament. This undermines the co-determination of norms by individuals relying equally upon the statuses of nationality and EU citizenship. The consequences for individuals *qua* juridical objects are that, if they are a national of an opt-out Member State, they are unable to rely upon or be subject to norms created in this area within the territory of the opt-out state. This is particularly egregious for individuals from Member States that do not opt out, as they have legitimated these norms in both their role as Member State national and EU citizen.

Divergences in the democratic self-determination and juridical self-fulfilment of individuals arise on the basis of their nationality. Inequality is not based upon the perception and construction of 'objective' differences between Member States that are then enshrined through legal exceptions. Instead, inequality derives from the executive discretion of the representatives of individuals *qua* nationals. These consequences may be regarded as illegitimate because individuals in their dual roles have not consented to an explicit Treaty mechanism to regulate Member States reserving the levelling up of constituent power.[7] From the supranational perspective, the normative desideratum is that Member States should only pursue opt-outs if the self-actualization of

[5] For example see Case C-274/11 *Spain and Italy v Council*, EU:C:2013:240.

[6] The extent to which the enhanced cooperation mechanisms can provide inspiration for greater regulation of opt-outs through an explicit Treaty clause is considered in chapter 8.

[7] See chapter 8 for a reform proposal to create such a Treaty mechanism.

individuals *qua* Member State nationals is compromised by the levelling up of constituent power in certain areas of norm-creation. This normative critique provides a bridge towards the reform proposals for how the reservation of constituent power could be brought within the triptych of constituent power, and how the existence of such opt-outs could be subjected to conditions established within the supranational constitutional order.

As opposed to the focus on explaining differentiation within political science literature,[8] legal literature has been more explicitly normative. The focus has been on whether the creation of opt-out mechanisms is constitutionally acceptable as well as legally feasible.[9] The disquiet over opt-outs concerns the essential characteristics of EU law as established by the Court of Justice of the European Union. This indicates a focus upon distortions in the capability of all individuals *qua* EU citizens to rely upon EU law norms in the pursuit of their life-plans without variation. The capacity for Member States to determine which norms will apply in their legal orders challenges the ideal of an autonomous juridical constitution with the 'uniform' application of EU law.

The critical strain in the literature immediately followed the creation of the opt-out Protocols at the Maastricht Treaty. Deirdre Curtin warned of the implications of it 'being possible for an individual Member State to plead and obtain a "ring-fence" of unlimited duration around, inter alia, specific national constitutional provisions'.[10] This critical strain continued in reaction to the development of the opt-out Protocols at the subsequent Treaty amendments.[11] Daniel Thym bridges the explanatory political science perspective and the normative perspective from legal scholarship. He explicates the dominant

[8] See *inter alia* Alexander Stubb, 'A Categorization of Differentiated Integration' (1996) 34 Journal of Common Market Studies 283; Alkuin Kölliker, *Flexibility and European Unification: The Logic of Differentiated Integration* (Rowman & Littlefield 2006); Dirk Leuffen, Berthold Rittberger and Frank Schimmelfennig, *Differentiated Integration: Explaining Variation in the European Union* (Palgrave 2012); Frank Schimmelfennig and Thomas Winzen, *Ever Looser Union? Differentiated European Integration* (OUP 2020).

[9] Bruno De Witte, 'The Law as Tool and Constraint of Differentiated Integration' (European University Institute 2019) Robert Schuman Centre for Advanced Studies Research Paper No RSCAS 2019/47 <http://cadmus.eui.eu//handle/1814/63604> accessed 26 April 2020.

[10] Deirdre Curtin, 'The Constitutional Structure of the Union: A Europe of Bits and Pieces' (1993) 30 Common Market Law Review 17, 49.

[11] Patrick Twomey and David O'Keefe, *Legal Issues of the Amsterdam Treaty* (Bloomsbury 1999); Gráinne De Búrca and Joanne Scott (eds), *Constitutional Change in the EU: From Uniformity to Flexibility?* (Hart Publishing 2000); Bruno De Witte, Dominik Hanf and Ellen Vos, *The Many Faces of Differentiation in EU Law* (Intersentia 2001); Bruno De Witte, Andrea Ott and Ellen Vos, *Between Flexibility and Disintegration: The Trajectory of Differentiation in EU Law* (Edward Elgar Publishing 2017).

conceptual ideal types of differentiation: 'multi-speed Europe', 'Federal core Europe', and 'flexibility *à la carte*'.[12]

Constituent power being split between nationality and the derivative yet autonomous subject of EU citizen informs which conception of differentiated integration is compatible with the dual-legitimation thesis and the quadripartite conception of the individual within the supranational constitutional order. The '*à la carte*' model of European integration and differentiation, whereby Member State executives should be free to choose their participation in the *acquis communautaire* on the basis of their conception of the national interest, undermines the constituent role of EU citizenship. Similarly, a 'multi-level' or 'core' Europe conception of permanently differentiated membership and participation on a 'club' basis undermines the underpinning equality of individuals *qua* EU citizens. This conception precludes future generations of EU citizens from participation in further European integration due to a decision made by the government of the day in one moment of time about whether to join the core Europe or not. The United Kingdom's proposed opt-out from 'ever closer union' during the February 2016 renegotiation falls within the auspices of this normative concern.

From the perspective of dual-constituent power Patberg argues that:

> As long as we are dealing with temporary opt-outs from constitutional arrangements that are in principle meant to include all member states, there is no need for conceptual adjustments. However, should a situation arise in which differentiated integration is pursued on a permanent basis, the need would arise for a plurality of (differently composed) higher-level constituent powers.[13]

The only legitimate model of differentiation within the dual-legitimation thesis is 'multi-speed' Europe. Differentiation may only be legitimate as a means to establish a vanguard of constituent subject nationals who are willing and able to level up more constituent power to the European level. The choice should remain open to the other constituent subjects to follow suit at a time when they themselves are willing and able to transfer this power. This conception does not preclude the capacity of all individuals to participate in further integration as EU citizens, but instead limits it to conditions which are set

[12] Daniel Thym, 'Competing Models for Understanding Differentiated Integration' in Bruno De Witte, Andrea Ott and Ellen Vos (eds), *Between Flexibility and Disintegration: The Trajectory of Differentiation in EU Law* (Edward Elgar Publishing 2017).

[13] Markus Patberg, *Constituent Power in the European Union* (OUP 2020) 157.

clearly by the supranational constitutional order. The conditions to determine the willingness and capacity for levelling up constituent power become crucial within this conception.

Permanently differentiated membership in a core Europe would permanently undermine equality amongst individuals *qua* EU citizens. By contrast, unconditional discretion for Member State executives to choose participation on the basis of national interests would iteratively undermine EU citizenship as a constituent status. Therefore, the dual-legitimation thesis leans towards 'multi-speed Europe' as the only legitimate model for differentiation that vindicates the interests of both sides of the coin of the European constituent subject. When applied to opt-outs as a reservation of constituent power, the argument is that disrupted integration is only legitimate as a temporary deferral of levelling up constituent power rather than a permanent reservation. Opt-outs should only be created on the basis of strict conditions to vindicate the self-determination of individuals *qua* nationals. The purpose of restoring convergence if feasible is necessary to prevent a permanent cleavage in the supranational constituent status.

Thym states that '[d]ifferentiated integration may stabilise the rule of law by accommodating internal tensions and heterogeneities, while it may, at the same time, undermine the infrastructure of the European project'.[14] The accommodation of internal tensions and heterogeneity vindicates the inherent differences between the holders of the constituent role of nationality of a Member State. Such accommodation may create cleavages in the co-equal constituent status of citizenship of the Union. A balance must be found for the legitimate provision of differentiation that vindicates both constituent roles. This balance informs the normative conditions legitimating the creation of opt-outs.

Bruno de Witte provides an overview of the legal parameters within which opt-outs must operate.[15] Law plays the double role of providing the tools to translate political will into a binding form, but also sets the constraints on that political action.[16] The specific characteristics of the EU's juridical system also, however, provide the constraints upon how far the law may be used as a tool to achieve these political goals. De Witte argues that three concepts of the EU legal order achieve this constraining function: (1) hierarchy through primary law prevailing over secondary law, which remains most relevant to enhanced

[14] Thym (n 12) 28–29.

[15] Bruno De Witte, 'The Legal Feasibility and Constitutional Acceptability of Differentiated Integration' (Kick-off Meeting H2020 Project InDivEU Integrating Difference in the European Union, European University Institute, 24 January 2019); De Witte, 'The Law as Tool and Constraint' (n 9).

[16] De Witte, 'The Legal Feasibility' (n 15).

cooperation; (2) primacy of EU law over national law; and (3) autonomy whereby the EU legal order may not be eroded by external agreements. The Protocols addended to the Treaties enshrine the political will of Member States to reserve constituent power. This context means that the principles of EU law function only to constrain the operation of the Protocols rather than their creation. These constraints are evident in the cases preventing divergent understandings of the scope of the United Kingdom's AFSJ opt-out.[17]

De Witte expresses further constraints upon opt-outs as 'things that may be formally possible but would affect the integrity of the EU constitutional system'.[18] Differentiated and disrupted integration could regress the European Union to a more primitive state. This would have deleterious effects for the standards of democracy and accountability, and the representation of individuals by the supranational institutions.[19] The acceptance of opt-outs suggests that it is more conducive to the integrity of the EU legal order for a Member State to be exempt from the application of EU law norms than the situation in which EU law is formally adopted but not enforced in practice. Legitimate derogation prevents illegitimate breaches and primacy challenges. Historically, the United Kingdom pursued formal opt-outs and Treaty declarations amidst concern over breaching EU law by not applying measures relating to the elimination of border controls.

The question arises as to whether legal constraints require particular sectors to be insulated from the possibility of opt-outs. The key characteristics of what Tuori calls the 'framing' juridical and political constitutions may be regarded as fault lines.[20] De Witte corroborates this precept with the argument that there should be no differentiation on values contained in Article 2 TEU, fundamental rights, nor on the rule of law.[21] This explains why formal opt-outs from the Charter of Fundamental Rights, as opposed to declarative clarifications, would not have been constitutionally acceptable.[22] A sacrosanct constitutional space is demarcated within which fundamental structural principles and values cannot be the subject of Member State opt-outs. This is justified because these values and principles enable individuals to function as the democratic subjects and juridical objects of the supranational constitutional order. The United Kingdom's attempts to renegotiate its commitment to ever closer

[17] See further discussion in chapter 4 below.
[18] De Witte, 'The Legal Feasibility' (n 15).
[19] ibid.
[20] Kaarlo Tuori, *European Constitutionalism* (CUP 2015).
[21] De Witte, 'The Legal Feasibility' (n 15).
[22] See discussion at the start of chapter 4.

union among the peoples of Europe challenged this demarcation. The New Settlement declared that '[t]he United Kingdom ... is not committed to further political integration into the European Union'.[23] This may have jeopardized the Member State's commitment to vindicate democratic subjecthood in the supranational constitutional order.

Any similar fault lines within the EU's substantive policies would establish further constraints on opt-outs. The implication is that differentiation is less acceptable within the EU's 'core' policies.[24] No *de jure* distinction has been drawn between core and peripheral policies. A *de facto* distinction may be inferred from constitutional practice. Procedurally, 'core' policies may be indicated by Treaty bases with an amplified role for the supranational institutions through Qualified Majority Voting. The policies in which Member State unanimity is required may indicate more peripheral supranational policies. The United Kingdom's renegotiation of membership pushed the limits of substantive core policies. The original proposal to seek concessions on free movement of people was rejected on the basis that they would not be acceptable to the European Council. This accords with de Búrca's conceptualization of the Single Market as the 'core' of the EU legal order,[25] and Floris de Witte's argument that free movement is the 'core' of EU citizenship as a juridical status.[26]

The *de facto* core and periphery thesis on the basis of norm-creation rules is supported by the Schengen and AFSJ opt-outs. These sectors were formerly Third Pillar policies in which Member States retained more autonomy.[27] A pathway dependence led to the creation of opt-outs as these policies were supranationalized. This analysis is challenged by the EMU opt-outs. This is the most highly centralized core policy with extensive executive roles for the European Central Bank and the Commission. The validity of the core–periphery analysis may therefore be limited to the incorporation origin of opt-outs. Pathway dependence is not applicable to the creation of constitutional sectors *de novo*. Instead, one should look to the extent to which these Member States felt that core aspects of national sovereignty and thus self-determination for individuals *qua* nationals were challenged by these new

[23] European Council meeting (18 and 19 February 2016)—Conclusions, Annex 1—Decision of the Heads of State or Government, meeting within the European Council, concerning a new settlement for the United Kingdom within the European Union—Brussels 19 February 2016 EUCO 1/16, 16.

[24] Gráinne De Búrca, 'Differentiation within the Core: The Case of the Internal Market' in Gráinne De Búrca and Joanne Scott (eds), *Constitutional Change in the EU: From Uniformity to Flexibility?* (Hart Publishing 2000).

[25] ibid.

[26] Floris De Witte, 'Freedom of Movement Needs to Be Defended as the Core of EU Citizenship' in Rainer Bauböck (ed), *Debating European Citizenship* (Springer 2019).

[27] See detailed explanation in chapter 4 on the Maastricht Treaty.

areas. Substantively, the core–periphery argument on the basis of the norm-creation rules is challenged by the intimate connection between the Schengen *acquis* and free movement as a benefit for individuals *qua* juridical objects regarding norm-application. This also holds for the AFSJ insofar as these norms concern significant issues such as access to justice and the migration rights of Third-Country Nationals.

The core–periphery dynamic may be a more appropriate explanation and justification from the perspective of national constitutional orders. The perspective and reasoning of national executive actors rather than supranational actors drive the creation of opt-outs. One may consider whether the national sectoral policies that are levelled up to the supranational level and excluded from exclusive national competence are sufficiently sensitive to justify a demand for opt-outs. Leuffen, Rittberger, and Schimmelfennig argue that differentiation has increased as European integration has moved into more politically and socially sensitive areas.[28] Jachtenfuchs and Genschel claim that differentiation increases when integration moves into areas regarded as 'core state powers'. These powers concern the twin monopolies over force and taxation and have high visibility and high symbolic value.[29]

Within the dual-legitimation thesis, core state powers are the constitutional sectors that are most relevant for the exercise of self-determination by individuals *qua* Member State nationals. As Jachtenfuchs and Genschel indicate, these areas are crucial because they are constitutive of the state.[30] Within Habermas' explication of the dual-constituent thesis, the state's operation as the guarantor of the hitherto achieved levels of freedom and security is the *raison d'être* for the retention of nationality as a constituent status. Supranational attempts to level up these areas are most likely to generate resistance. The normative task is to scrutinize the validity of these self-determinative claims.

i. Normative justifications for opt-outs

A synthesis of pre-existing normative justifications can be used to establish a model of legitimate opt-outs. Bellamy and Kröger identify normative justifications within the schemata of institutional, constitutional, and legislative

[28] Leuffen, Rittberger and Schimmelfennig (n 8).
[29] Philipp Genschel and Markus Jachtenfuchs (eds), *Beyond the Regulatory Polity? The European Integration of Core State Powers* (OUP 2013).
[30] ibid.

differentiation.[31] The third category is inapplicable to opt-outs as primary law. Schimmelfennig and Winzen provide a similar distinction between instrumental and constitutional differentiation.[32] Institutional differentiated integration for Bellamy and Kröger involves 'opt-outs or exclusions from participating in policies designed to produce collective goods at the EU level'.[33] Constitutional differentiated integration involves 'an opt-out from a given policy or measure because it conflicts with a domestic constitutional norm or cultural practice'.[34] Schimmelfennig and Winzen contend that instrumental differentiation is 'motivated by efficiency and distributional concerns'[35] whereas constitutional differentiation is 'motivated by concerns about national sovereignty and identity'.[36] These authors also identity different origins for the two forms of differentiation. Whereas instrumental differentiation arises at times of enlargement, constitutional differentiation emerges at times of Treaty revision.

Opt-outs have arisen exclusively at Treaty amendments. They may equally be motivated by the desire not to participate in certain collective policies on the basis of efficiency concerns and by concerns for sovereignty and national identity. The reasons for their creation encompass both institutional and constitutional logics. From the perspective of the dual-legitimation thesis and normative justification, constitutional differentiation provides the most compelling fit. Issues of 'national sovereignty', 'identity', and 'domestic constitutional norms' identified by Bellamy and Kröger, and Schimmelfennig and Winzen respectively are directly related to the exercise of self-determination by individuals in their role as nationals of a Member State. The consideration of normative justifications and limitations upon the creation of opt-outs will be considered through this lens.

Bellamy and Kröger identify the democratic grounds of fairness, impartiality, and equity as benchmarks for assessing legitimacy in a homogenous polity. These principles may be regarded as the desiderata for the legitimate functioning of a constituent status. In a heterogeneous, composite, and dual-legitimated polity such as the European Union these grounds are augmented. This is because of the proportionality, partiality, and difference problems:

[31] Richard Bellamy and Sandra Kröger, 'A Demoicratic Justification of Differentiated Integration in a Heterogeneous EU' (2017) 39 Journal of European Integration 625.
[32] Frank Schimmelfennig and Thomas Winzen, 'Instrumental and Constitutional Differentiation in the European Union' (2014) 52 Journal of Common Market Studies 354.
[33] Bellamy and Kröger, 'A Demoicratic Justification' (n 31) 627.
[34] ibid.
[35] Schimmelfennig and Winzen (n 32) 355.
[36] ibid.

> [T]he proportionality problem ... can justify excluding, temporarily or permanently, some member states from participation in certain club goods ... the partiality problem ... allows for those who conceive of themselves as a distinct public with divergent public norms to make their own decisions as to what collective goods they should support ... the difference problem suggests that when groups with different interests and values belong to a club, then collective rules need to accommodate these differences to some degree.[37]

Bellamy and Kröger outline how these problems can justify the pursuit of opt-outs by Member States. They define the effects of opt-outs as 'an asymmetric retention of power by certain Member States in matters that most countries agree can be EU competences'.[38]

Through the dual-legitimation lens, the partiality and the difference problems are the most relevant issues. The persistence of diverse publics with divergent public norms and different conceptions of the telos of constitutionalism arises through the retention of the constituent status and orders generated through nationality of the Member States. The Member State executives and legislatures retain an obligation to preserve these divergent partialities in the representation of their nationals. The differences in interests and values justify collective rules allowing differentiation as a means to ensure that the constituent status of nationality is not subsumed by the constituent status of EU citizenship. This is recognized by Bellamy and Kröger: 'So far as the Treaty-making and accession processes are concerned, the EU remains a union of Member States and their peoples rather than straightforwardly of European citizens'.[39] This is factually correct and highlights how the conditions for the creation of unilateral opt-outs arise. Normatively, this observation raises the question of whether the treaty-making and accession processes are deficient in ensuring the representation of individuals in their dual roles.

The proportionality problem arises through objective differences in 'population size, varieties of capitalism, economic specialisation and wealth ... leading to different stakes'.[40] These characteristics indicate a condition for assessing the legitimacy of opt-outs: 'objective' differences in the material constitution of each state leading to distinct relationships between the demoi of the Member States and the telos of European integration. Regarding instrumental differentiation, these differences are not utilized as a justification for why a

[37] Bellamy and Kröger, 'A Demoicratic Justification' (n 31) 633.
[38] ibid.
[39] ibid.
[40] ibid 634.

Member State may be constrained from participation. Instead, the differences are utilized to forward divergent bargaining preferences through the logic of economic utility. Hence the claim is that 'it becomes rational to employ instrumental forms of DI that reduce the club involved in producing a given collective good to a smaller group than the whole so as to overcome the proportionality problem'.[41] Bellamy and Kröger point towards a normative limit to instrumental forms of derogation: 'an injustice might be thought to be committed where the stake an excluded country has in a collective arrangement is greater than those that are included'.[42] This raises the possibility of a role for either national or supranational institutions to make an objective assessment of the stake of each Member State in a particular policy.

The intergovernmental analysis of European integration tends to neglect individuals as subjects of the supranational constitutional order. Such justifications for the pursuit of opt-outs may only be justified if coupled with 'constructivist' arguments. These arguments hold not only that it may be rational for the welfare of the nationals of that Member State to pursue such a policy, but also that a retention of national competence is crucial for the exercise of self-determination of the collective as nationals.[43] The United Kingdom's opt-out from EMU is such an example: economic rationality arguments and constructivist identity and sovereignty arguments coalesced.[44] It is problematic to argue for a multi-speed Europe of those who are willing because this creates divergences between individuals *qua* EU citizens on the basis of instrumental concerns.

The issues surrounding the interests of individuals *qua* Member State nationals emerge more clearly in the partiality problem. Bellamy and Kröger recognize that, since Maastricht, the Treaties have recognized constitutional differentiation to address the partiality problem. The rationale forwarded by Bellamy and Kröger provides a compelling fit with the dual-legitimation thesis:

> [T]he different demoi of the member states have already developed their own constitutional and juridical orders that reflect the distinctive and diverse public cultures of their citizens. As a result, impartiality in the application of constitutional norms may not be possible at the EU level. Even if all the member states endorse broadly the same set of rights and democratic principles, they may have legitimately different views about their scope and

[41] ibid.
[42] ibid.
[43] Leuffen, Rittberger and Schimmelfennig (n 8).
[44] See discussion in chapter 4 below on the run-up to the Maastricht Treaty.

> relative weighting with regard to both each other and other important values and interests that reflect valid cultural differences.[45]

This goes to the heart of the hypothetical process of 'levelling up' of constituent power explicated by Markus Patberg. The partialities arise from the diverse manners in which the constitutional orders of the Member States manifest the principles for constitutional politics. These divergences continue to inform the interaction between the polities of these Member States even beyond the mutual recognition of the necessary preconditions to construct EU citizenship for themselves.[46] The crucial question is whether it is legitimate for these divergences to continue after the construction of the supranational order. Should Member States be able to evoke distinct constitutional identities to justify opt-outs from the *acquis communautaire*?

One view is that the 'levelling down' of constituent power provided by Article 50 TEU should displace any other forms of contestation once levelling up has occurred. A more nuanced view holds that, in order to avoid this nuclear option, a graduated response to such claims can be envisaged. The conception of Treaty amendments as part of a triptych of constituted constituent power legitimates these challenges: Article 48 TEU provides for a reconstruction of the supranational constitutional order in which the principles of levelling up are reactivated. This provides procedural legitimacy for Member State executives to revive the partiality problem. These national interests should lay dormant during the ordinary constitutional functioning of the Union as Member State executives act as supranational legislators.[47] The national divergences could legitimate opt-outs on the basis that the levelling up of constituent power would undermine the self-determination of nationals, but not to the extent that continuing participation in supranational constitutional politics is untenable. Justifications for opt-outs may be constructed between the two extremes of homogeneity and disintegration. Bellamy and Kröger echo legal commentators in establishing juristic limitations on this process: 'basic rights if not EU law can limit how much constitutional differentiation is justifiable'.[48]

Bellamy and Kröger discuss the difference principle in relation to legislative differentiation: '[t]he formulation of specific EU secondary law has allowed for flexibility that acknowledges the need on grounds of equity to recognise

[45] Bellamy and Kröger, 'A Demoicratic Justification' (n 31) 636.
[46] See detailed discussion in chapter 2.
[47] This is why the United Kingdom's and Ireland's opt-outs from the AFSJ are normatively egregious. See conclusions in chapter 7.
[48] Bellamy and Kröger, 'A Demoicratic Justification' (n 31) 636.

relevant differences.'[49] These differences are also relevant to the demand for opt-outs at Treaty revisions. The differences that inform legislative differentiation involve both economic and social factors that inform the proportionality problem and constitutional differences concerning the partiality problem. The authors utilize Aristotle's equitable maxim that one should treat like cases alike, and unalike cases differently: 'a difficulty arises in deciding when a difference is relevant or not with regard to the policy at hand'.[50] Bellamy and Kröger label this difficulty the difference problem. The initial question is whether the Member States should have to advance relevant differences to justify opt-outs. If so, the next question is how to establish the barometer of relevance. The final question is what institutions should be given the competence to make such a decision.[51] The authors conclude their own normative survey with a principled argument for differentiation. A constitutional order that 'addresses the problems by sharing the costs and benefits of differential treatment reciprocally . . . will only operate in a fair and impartial manner that respects difference to the extent the proportionality and partiality problems are taken into account'.[52]

Bellamy and Kröger's more recent statement on the normative justifications for differentiated integration intersects more closely with the dual-legitimation thesis.[53] The objectives of excavating the philosophical foundations of differentiated integration are to develop an account of input (procedural) and output (substantive) legitimacy of participation in a fair scheme of cooperation. These dimensions cohere specifically to the dual role played by individuals as democratic subjects and juridical objects respectively. The objective is to establish the conditions in which the three models of differentiation—multi-speed Europe, variable geometry, and Europe *à la carte*—could be justified.[54] The authors claim that the justifications for differentiation, and thus opt-outs, vary depending on the model of EU integration theory.

The authors identify two possible constituent subjects and corresponding models: (1) states (statism); (2) citizens (cosmopolitanism). The statist model holds that, in terms of procedural or input legitimacy, if the creation of opt-outs involves the elected representatives of the states it is acceptable. With

[49] ibid.
[50] ibid 632.
[51] See chapter 9 for engagement with these questions.
[52] Bellamy and Kröger, 'A Demoicratic Justification' (n 31) 632.
[53] Richard Bellamy and Sandra Kröger, 'Differentiated Integration as a Fair Scheme of Cooperation' (European University Institute 2019) Robert Schuman Centre for Advanced Studies Research Paper No RSCAS 2019/27 <https://cadmus.eui.eu/bitstream/handle/1814/62246/RSCAS%202019_27.rev.pdf?sequence=4&isAllowed=y> accessed 30 January 2025.
[54] See also Thym (n 12) in which 'core Europe' is used instead of 'variable geometry'.

regard to substantive or output legitimacy, opt-outs are legitimate so long as they are 'Pareto optimal', address morally obligatory global goods, and respect human rights. The cosmopolitan model emphasizes that opt-outs will be procedurally fair so long as their creation involves the elected representatives of individuals *qua* EU citizens. Substantively, they are legitimate so long as they promote equality among all individuals.[55]

The conceptions of legitimacy depend on the theoretical approach adopted, a key component of which is identifying different actors as the constituent power. This poses a challenge for the augmented approach of the dual-legitimation thesis. This recognizes that the legitimacy of the EU's legislative process is shared between individuals as nationals of their state and citizens of the EU. However, the explanatory validity of mixed constituent power is challenged by the primacy of states' representatives in the Treaty amendment process. This requires a more nuanced approach to ensuring the vindication of individuals *qua* Member State nationals and *qua* EU citizens that recognizes these different roles in the creation of primary and secondary law. A synthesis of the statist and cosmopolitan justifications is necessary to establish the conditions for legitimacy of opt-outs in a dual-constituted supranational constitutional order.

ii. The conditions for legitimacy of opt-outs

The minimum baseline for an opt-out to be created is for the elected representatives of the Member States to be involved. This requires the involvement of representatives of all Member States, rather than solely the resistant Member State. Substantively, the bare minimum requirement is the need to respect the basic rights and values established in the Treaties and the Charter of Fundamental Rights. Although the creation of opt-outs may be acceptable within the conditions for Treaty amendment, they create normatively problematic effects for the ordinary functioning of the supranational constitutional order. Procedurally, this arises from the insufficient representation of individuals *qua* EU citizens in the creation process. This may be legally justifiable whilst constitutionally unacceptable.

The application of the principles of levelling up constituent power further conditions legitimacy.[56] Opt-outs undoubtedly function as 'expressions of the

[55] Bellamy and Kröger, 'Differentiated Integration' (n 53) 8–11.
[56] See chapter 2 for the explication of the principles.

political self-determination' of the nationals of the Member State in question. The formal equality of the demoi in this process is doubtful due to the unilateral proposal of opt-outs. There is no means to approve or reject opt-outs that is independent from approval of the entire Treaty amendment. A counter-argument is that so long as any Member State is empowered to pursue such opt-outs the principle of equality is fulfilled. However, statements from the European Commission and European Parliament regarding ending the era of opt-outs suggest that this route will be precluded for the future.[57]

A further condition is that the creation of the opt-out is predicated upon a pluralistic representation of the state demoi. This would require discursive interaction at the national level between multiple stakeholders beyond the government at times of the creation and appraisal of opt-outs. In the United Kingdom, the executive dominated the process with little opportunity afforded to actors from across the political spectrum.[58] The Danish experience more closely coheres with this vision of pluralistic representation due to the national compromise following the rejection of the Maastricht Treaty. This has been bolstered by reaffirmation in referendums on the EMU and AFSJ opt-out Protocols.[59]

There are serious doubts as to whether opt-outs respect the condition of the discursive interaction of state representatives. Nothing has prevented the text of opt-out Protocols being presented at the final hour of negotiations. This limits the opportunity for 'representatives at the supra-state level to determine the content of the constitutional order on the basis of an exchange of reasons'.[60] This failure to pursue opt-out and opt-in policies on the basis of an exchange of reasons informed the United Kingdom's approach to the maintenance of opt-outs. The approach of Treaty negotiations has spilled over into the ordinary legislative procedures through the discretion to opt in to AFSJ measures without the need to provide reasons.

These problems are even more acute when regarded from the 'across demoi' perspective.[61] The exclusion of the European Parliament from decisions to create opt-outs undermines the political autonomy of individuals

[57] Jean-Claude Juncker, 'State of the Union Address 2017' (*European Commission*, 13 September 2017) <https://ec.europa.eu/commission/presscorner/detail/en/SPEECH_17_3165> accessed 27 April 2020; European Parliament resolution of 16 February 2017 on possible evolutions of and adjustments to the current institutional set-up of the European Union [2018] OJ C 252/201.

[58] See discussion of the narrative of disruption in chapter 4.

[59] See discussion of the Danish experience in chapter 4.

[60] Markus Patberg, 'A Systematic Justification for the EU's Pouvoir Constituant Mixte: Principles of Constitutional Politics in Supranational Polities' (2017) 23 European Law Journal 441, 450.

[61] See chapter 2.

qua EU citizens whereby 'constitutional decisions are expressions of the political self-determination of the citizens of the (future) supranational polity'.[62] The equality of individuals *qua* EU citizens in the processes of constitutional opinion and will formation is undermined by whether their Member State of nationality pursues opt-outs are not. This leads to inequality between individuals *qua* EU citizens regarding the territory within which they can rely on EU law norms.

Substantively, the barometers established in Bellamy and Kröger's conceptions of European integration can be utilized to consider the legitimacy of opt-outs for individuals *qua* juridical objects. Opt-outs may be scrutinized on the basis that they promote or inhibit equality among individuals. The dual-legitimation conception is distinct from the cosmopolitan conception because equality only pertains as an obligation and ideal to be achieved between individuals who hold the same status. The objective should be the promotion of democratic and juridical equality for all those who hold the status of EU citizenship. The conception that those holding the status do form a polity, albeit a supplementary one, is distinct from Bellamy's republican view that Member State institutions are subject only to an obligation of non-discrimination between individuals.[63]

The dual-legitimation perspective argues for an equal stake for all EU citizens in the creation of norms, and equality in the application of these norms. The legitimacy of differentiated participation and application must be evaluated against whether such inequality is justified by an overriding objective reason arising from the needs of individuals *qua* nationals of a Member State. The condition is that these objective reasons make certain nationals so 'unalike' from other EU citizens that their case must be treated differently.

II. The Legal Form and Operation of the Opt-Outs

The legal form and operation of the opt-out Protocols reflect their distinct origins in different EU Treaty amendment procedures by different Member States. The shared feature of the Protocols is that they exempt certain Member States from the application of EU law norms in defined sectors of the *acquis*. However, the extent to which these Member States have the flexible ability to

[62] Patberg, 'A Systematic Justification' (n 60) 451.
[63] Richard Bellamy, *A Republican Europe of States* (CUP 2019).

'opt in' to norms, and the legal formulae by which the exemption takes place, differ across the Protocols.

i. Economic and Monetary Union (EMU)

A. Protocol (No 15): The United Kingdom's tailored opt-out from EMU
Protocol (No 15) of the Treaties on certain provisions relating to the United Kingdom contains the norms which enabled derogation from EMU. The Preamble recognizes that the constitutional requirements for the United Kingdom to adopt the euro were 'a separate decision to do so by its government and parliament'.[64] The Preamble records the historical notification by the United Kingdom to the Council in 1996 and 1997 of its intention not to participate in the Third Stage of EMU.

Paragraph 1 reads that '[u]nless the United Kingdom notifies the Council that it intends to adopt the euro, it shall be under *no obligation* to do so'.[65] This represents a reservation and deferral of the choice to level up constituent power that usually occurs at Treaty amendments. Paragraph 3 confirms that the United Kingdom retained its powers in the field of monetary policy according to national law. This affirms that the individual *qua* national of the United Kingdom remained the only democratic subject and juridical object for the creation and application of norms establishing and regulating monetary policy. The individual *qua* EU citizen was not afforded a role in this sector.

Paragraph 4 provides a detailed overview of the Treaty articles from the Economic and Monetary Policy chapter which did not apply to or within the United Kingdom.[66] The object of the opt-out was the substance of the norms rather than the mechanisms by which they were promulgated and enforced. The continuing functioning of the juridical constitution ensured that the United Kingdom was able to bring claims regarding the scope of the opt-out before the Court of Justice.[67] The paragraph ensured institutional separation by clarifying that 'references to the Union or the Member States shall not

[64] TEU and TFEU, Protocol (No 15) on certain provisions relating to the United Kingdom of Great Britain and Northern Ireland, preamble.
[65] ibid para 1 (emphasis added).
[66] 'Articles 119, second paragraph, 126(1), (9) and (11), 127(1) to (5), 128, 130, 131, 132, 133, 138, 140(3), 219, 282(2), with the exception of the first and last sentences thereof, 282(5), and 283 of the Treaty on the Functioning of the European Union shall not apply to the United Kingdom. The same applies to Article 121(2) of this Treaty as regards the adoption of the parts of the broad economic policy guidelines which concern the euro area generally': ibid para 4.
[67] See T-496/11 *United Kingdom v ECB*, EU:T:2015:133.

include the United Kingdom and references to national central banks shall not include the Bank of England'.[68]

Paragraph 5 created a soft obligation for the United Kingdom to 'endeavour to avoid an excessive government deficit'.[69] This contrasts to the quantitatively precise hard obligation for Members States within the Eurozone to 'avoid excessive government deficits'.[70] Accordingly, the application of oversight mechanisms regarding deficits and balances of payment is limited to those which apply to the Member States with a derogation that have not fulfilled the economic criteria.[71]

Paragraph 6 declares that 'the voting rights of the United Kingdom shall be suspended in respect of acts of the Council referred to'.[72] This confirms that UK citizens did not exercise democratic subjecthood *qua* Member State nationals in the creation of norms within the constitutional sector of EMU. The principles of political autonomy, equality of state demoi, pluralistic representation, and discursive interaction did not apply to the United Kingdom in relation to EMU. UK nationals did not participate in the formation of norms that apply to all individuals *qua* EU citizens within the Eurozone. UK nationals were, however, represented *qua* EU citizens by the Members of the European Parliament that they had elected. They exercised one form of input into the norms that apply to them when they are within the territory of the Eurozone. This ring-fencing in derogation from EU law may be advanced as evidence for the distinct constituent roles played by nationals and EU citizens in the constitutional order.

Paragraph 7 contains the norms by which the United Kingdom derogated from participation in the institution of the European Central Bank (ECB). This ensured further isolation from the supranational constitutional order due to the unique character of the ECB as a highly centralized executive supranational institution.[73] The Articles of the Protocol on the Statute of the European System of Central Banks (ESCB) and of the European Central Bank that did not apply to the United Kingdom are listed.[74] Paragraph 8 clarifies that

[68] TEU and TFEU, Protocol (No 15) on certain provisions relating to the United Kingdom of Great Britain and Northern Ireland, para 4.

[69] ibid para 5.

[70] TFEU, art 126(1).

[71] 'Articles 143 and 144 of the Treaty on the Functioning of the European Union shall continue to apply to the United Kingdom. Articles 134(4) and 142 shall apply to the United Kingdom as if it had a derogation': TEU and TFEU, Protocol (No 15) on certain provisions relating to the United Kingdom of Great Britain and Northern Ireland, para 5.

[72] ibid para 6.

[73] TFEU, art 127.

[74] 'Articles 3, 4, 6, 7, 9.2, 10.1, 10.3, 11.2, 12.1, 14, 16, 18 to 20, 22, 23, 26, 27, 30 to 34 and 49 of the Protocol on the Statute of the European System of Central Banks and of the European Central Bank ("the Statute")': TEU and TFEU, Protocol (No 15) on certain provisions relating to the United Kingdom of Great Britain and Northern Ireland, para 7.

Article 141(3) TFEU and Articles 43–47 of the Statute would still take effect in relation to tasks that needed to be performed in the third stage owing to the UK decision not to adopt the euro, and to provide a basis for ECB advice for the preparation of a Council decision on the United Kingdom's reversal of the opt-out if this had occurred.

Paragraph 9 contains the means by which the opt-out may have been extinguished: 'The United Kingdom *may* notify the Council at any time of its intention to adopt the euro . . . provided only that it satisfies the necessary condition . . . The Council . . . shall decide whether it fulfils the necessary conditions'.[75] The use of the permissive language indicates that it was a conditional sovereign right of the United Kingdom executive to participate in the EMU *acquis*. The imposition of Council conditions that must be determined by all individuals *qua* Member State nationals means that the United Kingdom's decision to revoke its reservation of constituent power would not have been entirely unshackled. It would have been submitted to the control of the supranational constitutional order and its democratic subjects.

Paragraphs 9(a) and (c) clarify that the default constitutional clause of Article 140 TFEU for assessing whether a Member State has made sufficient progress to adopt the euro applied.[76] Article 140(2) TFEU ensures that individuals *qua* EU citizens will have input into this process through the consultation of the European Parliament.[77] The procedure includes reports provided to the Council by the ECB and the Commission on the compatibility between the national legislation and the statutes of its national central bank with the Statute of the ESCB and the ECB, and examination of whether the Member State has achieved a high degree of sustainable convergence with reference to the criteria of price stability, the sustainability of the government financial position, the observance of normal fluctuation margins in the Exchange Rate Mechanism, and the durability of convergence achieved by the Member State.

This raises the legal question of whether the United Kingdom would have been obliged to join the Exchange Rate Mechanism before it could have proceeded to the third stage of EMU, particularly as Article 140(1) TFEU makes reference to these fluctuation margins being maintained for at least 'two years'. This would have provided an additional time-constraint amongst the conditions for adoption. The Council is obliged to consult the European Parliament

[75] ibid para 9 (emphasis added).
[76] ibid paras 9(a) and (c).
[77] TFEU, art 140(2).

and discuss with the European Council before deciding on a proposal from the Commission on whether to abrogate the derogation. The Council makes a decision within six months on the basis of a qualified majority of those among its members representing Member States whose currency is the euro.[78] If this is fulfilled, unanimity is required amongst the Member States whose currency is the euro for the Council to irrevocably fix the rate at which the euro shall be substituted for the currency of the Member State concerned.[79]

Supranational conditionality contrasts sharply to the United Kingdom's opt-out Protocol from the AFSJ, which imposed no conditions upon participation beyond temporal limits. This unshackled permission for the United Kingdom to level up constituent power was selective as it allowed participation on a piecemeal legislation-by-legislation basis. By contrast, paragraph 9 of Protocol (No 15) preserved the integrity of the constitutional sector of the EMU. The extinction of the opt-out would have been ensured through the final sentence of paragraph 9: 'If the United Kingdom adopts the euro pursuant to the provisions of this Protocol, paragraphs 3 to 8 shall cease to have effect'.[80]

B. Protocol (No 16) and (No 17): Denmark's EMU opt-out by reference to the derogation states

Protocol (No 16) of the Treaties on certain provisions relating to Denmark is the legal basis for this Member State's opt-out from EMU. The Preamble notes the historical activation of these provisions 'given that, on 3 November 1993, the Danish Government notified the Council of its intention not to participate in the third stage of economic and monetary union'.[81] The Preamble also makes note of the constitutional requirements at the national level for reversing the opt-out: 'the Danish Constitution contains provisions which may imply a referendum in Denmark prior to Denmark renouncing its exemption'.[82]

Paragraph 1 of the Protocol outlines that, in view of the notice given to the Council by the Danish government notifying its intention not to participate in the third stage of EMU, 'Denmark shall have an exemption. The effect of the exemption shall be that all Articles and provisions of the Treaties and the Statute of the ESCB referring to a derogation shall be applicable to Denmark'.[83] In contrast to the United Kingdom's tailored declarations, the nature of Denmark's

[78] TFEU, art 140(2).
[79] TFEU, art 140(3).
[80] TEU and TFEU, Protocol (No 15) on certain provisions relating to the United Kingdom of Great Britain and Northern Ireland, para 9.
[81] TEU and TFEU, Protocol (No 16) on certain provisions relating to Denmark, preamble.
[82] ibid. See discussion on the Danish case study in chapter 4 on reversing the EMU opt-out.
[83] ibid para 1.

opt-out places it in the same position as a 'derogating Member State' which has not yet fulfilled the conditions for participation.

Paragraph 2 outlines that 'the procedure referred to in Article 140 shall only be initiated at the request of Denmark'.[84] The Danish government retains executive discretion to reverse its reservation of constituent power. The legal structure of the Protocol is more conducive to the integrity of the supranational constitutional order than the United Kingdom's tailored opt-out. Denmark is placed within a regulatory structure of derogation that is generally applicable on the basis of conditions established by the supranational constitutional order. However, the legal fiction of Denmark as a 'Member State with a derogation' despite fulfilling convergence criteria undermines the equal application of these conditions to all individuals *qua* juridical objects. Paragraph 3 of the Protocol makes provision for its own invalidation following such a decision to abrogate the exemption status. Protocol (No 17) clarifies the competence of the National Bank of Denmark to carry out existing tasks with regard to the territory of Denmark that is not part of the Union, namely Greenland, following its 'withdrawal' from the Union in 1985.[85] The differences in the form of the UK and Danish opt-outs reflect the different degrees of resistance of these Member States during the Maastricht negotiations, as will be discussed in the narrative of disruption in the next chapter.

ii. The Schengen *acquis*

A. Protocol (No 19): The United Kingdom and Ireland's flexible opt-out from Schengen

Protocol (No 19) made provision for the United Kingdom's derogation from the Schengen *acquis* during its membership and continues to make provision for Ireland's derogation. This derogation is given effect by exclusion from the list of Member States in Article 1 who are 'authorised to establish closer cooperation among themselves in areas covered by provisions defined by the Council which constitute the Schengen *acquis*'.[86] This paragraph refers to the incorporation of the provisions of an international agreement within the institutional and legal framework of the European Union.[87] The legal text reflects

[84] ibid para 2.

[85] See discussion of origins of withdrawal in chapter 5.

[86] TEU and TFEU, Protocol (No 19) on the Schengen *acquis* integrated into the framework of the European Union, art 1.

[87] See discussion on the early development of opt-outs in chapter 4 for detailed explanation.

the origins of Schengen as a use of international law by a vanguard of Member States to pursue integration by excluding the other constituent powers of the Union.

Article 4 of the Protocol makes provision for opt-ins to Schengen measures on an iterative basis:

> Ireland and the United Kingdom ... may at any time request to take part in some or all of the provisions of the Schengen *acquis*. The Council shall decide on the request with the unanimity of the members referred to in Article 1 and the representative of the Government of the State concerned.[88]

This provided for the United Kingdom, and provides for Ireland, a mechanism to reverse the reservation of constituent power selectively. Protocol (No 19) ensures that selective applications of constituent power must be approved by all individuals *qua* Member State nationals as represented in the Council. This echoes the unanimity requirements for the original reconstructions of constituent power at Treaty amendments that legitimated the creation of norms in the Schengen *acquis*.

Article 5(2) contains further provisions that enabled the United Kingdom, and enables Ireland, to notify the Council in writing, within three months, that they do not wish to take part in such a proposal or initiative. The Protocol provides a great degree of flexibility in whether to participate or not in the sector. The Council, and residually the European Council, regulate the procedures of participation and non-participation.[89] Four declarations are attached to the Treaty in relation to the operation of the Protocol. Schutte provides a pithy cricket analogy to summarize this complex procedure.[90]

B. Protocol (No 20): The United Kingdom's and Ireland's national powers

Protocol (No 20) further defined the scope of the United Kingdom's, and continues to define the scope of Ireland's, Schengen opt-out by reference to the

[88] TEU and TFEU, Protocol (No 19) on the Schengen *acquis* integrated into the framework of the European Union, art 4.

[89] ibid arts 5(3) and 5(4).

[90] 'First the UK is out, but it can request to be in, and when authorized, it is in. For proposals building on where it is in, it is deemed to be in, but it may notify its wish to be out, in which case it is out unless it withdraws its notification, in which case it is in. If it notifies its wish to be out, it is out of the whole game if that is so decided by the other players. But the other players should discuss the matter seriously and try to keep it in, so that it can remain in while it is out. If they do not know what to do, another team of players may be brought in. If that team cannot decide whether it is in, it shall be out, unless it withdraws its wish to be out in which case it is in again. But when it is definitely out it shall pay a round of beer to all the other players': Julian Schutte, 'UK v EU: A Continuous Test Match' (2011) 34 Fordham International Law Journal 1346, 1363.

national measures which the opt-out Member States are entitled to maintain.[91] This Protocol covers derogation from norms created through a Treaty base contained within Chapter 2 of Title V of Part Three TFEU. This evidences the overlap and interdependence between the Schengen and AFSJ opt-outs. The AFSJ now covers the substance of the original Schengen Convention with regard to border controls. Protocol (No 20) could be considered as part of a general opt-out from the *political* area of Justice and Home Affairs.

The Schengen opt-out is not only defined negatively by reference to the supranational norms that these Member States are not obliged to apply; it is also positively defined through identifying norms that may be applied at the national level. Article 1 entitled the United Kingdom, notwithstanding Articles 26 and 77 TFEU, to exercise controls on persons seeking to enter the United Kingdom at its frontiers with other Member States. The conditions were that the government considered these controls necessary for the purpose of verifying the right of citizens of Member States and their dependents to enter the United Kingdom, and for determining whether or not to grant Third-Country Nationals permission to enter the country.[92]

Article 2 extends the scope of the Protocol to Ireland. This is conditional upon the maintenance of the Common Travel Area regime of reduced border controls with the United Kingdom: 'as long as they maintain such arrangements, the provisions of Article 1 of this Protocol shall apply to Ireland under the same terms and conditions as for the United Kingdom'.[93] The requirement is that these arrangements respect the rights of EU citizens referred to in Article 1 of the Protocol. The Common Travel Area displaces the operation of Articles 26 and 77 TFEU in relation to Ireland and the United Kingdom. Article 2 is a juridical manifestation of the claim that Ireland's reservation of constituent power was compelled by the United Kingdom's position.[94] Article 3 raises a legal question as to how Ireland's permission to implement border controls is enshrined after the United Kingdom's withdrawal. The text of the Protocol remains unamended at the time of writing. The constituent powers may decide that Ireland's maintenance of the Common Travel Area with the former Member State is a sufficient condition, despite Protocol (No 20) no longer being the legal basis for the United Kingdom's border controls over EU citizens and Third-Country Nationals.

[91] TEU and TFEU, Protocol (No 20) on the application of certain aspects of Article 26 of the Treaty on the Functioning of the European Union to the United Kingdom and to Ireland.

[92] TEU and TFEU, Protocol (No 20) on the application of certain aspects of Article 26 of the Treaty on the Functioning of the European Union to the United Kingdom and to Ireland, art 1.

[93] ibid art 2.

[94] See discussion of the origins of Ireland's opt-outs in chapter 4.

Article 3 provides a permission to the other Member States to reciprocate in the exercise of border controls over anyone entering their territory from the United Kingdom or Ireland. This distinguishes the Schengen opt-out Protocol from the EMU and AFSJ opt-out Protocols. In these areas, the opt-out state nationals will still be subject to EU law norms when in the territory of Member States without an opt-out. Article 3, by contrast, empowers these Member States not to apply EU law in relation to individuals of the opt-out Member States *qua* juridical objects.

The Protocol deactivates the juridical component of EU citizenship that enables movement through the frontiers of the constituent Member States without administrative formalities. The capacity for the opt-out Member States to determine whether or not to grant Third-Country Nationals permission to enter their territory undermines the equality of this residual juridical status as determined by the Treaties. The corollary is that the opt-out Member State nationals *qua* democratic subjects have the capacity to determine the conditions for the entry of Third-Country Nationals into their territory. This determination is not shared with all other individuals from other Member States *qua* nationals and EU citizens. However, opt-out Member State nationals do still legitimate Schengen norms through their representation in the European Parliament.

C. Protocol (No 22): Denmark's national and international law implementation of Schengen

Article 3 of Protocol (No 19) determines the international law basis for Denmark's implementation of the Schengen *acquis* by reference to Protocol (No 22): 'The participation of Denmark in the adoption of measures constituting a development of the Schengen acquis, as well as the implementation of these measures and their application to Denmark, shall be governed by the relevant provisions of the Protocol on the position of Denmark'.[95] Denmark opts out from the *method* of supranational constitutionalism, rather than the substance of the Schengen norms. The Protocol does not provide for Denmark's participation in the supranational constitutional order, but for the replication of its effects through national and international law, mimicking the original legal basis of the Schengen Agreement.

Article 4 of Protocol (No 22) provides for Denmark's participation in Schengen *acquis* measures within six months after a decision is made. The

[95] TEU and TFEU, Protocol (No 19) on the Schengen *acquis* integrated into the framework of the European Union, art 3.

government ostensibly has discretion whether to implement this measure in national law, thus creating an obligation under international law between Denmark and the other Member States. Ostensibly, the individual *qua* national of Denmark maintains democratic control over border policy without the participation of nationals of other Member States. However, this discretion is restricted by the statement in Article 4(2) that 'if Denmark decides not to implement a measure of the Council as referred to in paragraph 1, the Member States bound by that measure and Denmark will consider appropriate measures to be taken'.[96]

Article 4(1) of Protocol No (22) states that if Denmark decides to participate 'this measure will create an obligation under international law between Denmark and the other Member States bound by the measure'.[97] Bruno de Witte argues that this statement is 'either legally redundant . . . as all Member States are bound by all parts of EU law on the basis of international law, or it assumes that the Schengen Agreement . . . will continue to exist as an international agreement . . . governing the relations between Denmark and the other [Member States]'.[98] De Witte's first scenario seems to ignore the supranational means of norm-formulation and norm-application which are an additional layer upon the skeleton of obligations binding in international law. Denmark's Protocol may be regarded as a threat to this process of supranational constitutionalism. Rather than accepting the legitimacy of norm-creation and norm-application by the supranational legislature and judiciary, Denmark instead re-establishes the traditional international and national law model of implementation.

iii. The Area of Freedom, Security and Justice (AFSJ)

The legal mechanisms which allowed the United Kingdom, and allow Ireland and Denmark, to opt out from measures promulgated under Title V of Part Three TFEU are Protocol (No 21) on the position of the United Kingdom and Ireland in respect of the Area of Freedom, Security and Justice, Protocol (No 22) on the position of Denmark, and Protocol (No 36) on transitional provisions. The specific structure of Protocol (No 21) allowed the United Kingdom and allows Ireland to decide whether to participate in specific new measures

[96] TEU and TFEU, Protocol (No 22) on the position of Denmark, art 4(2).
[97] ibid art 4(1).
[98] Bruno De Witte, 'Old-Fashioned Flexibility: International Agreements between Member States of the European Union' in Gráinne de Búrca and Joanne Scott (eds), *Constitutional Change in the EU: From Uniformity to Flexibility?* (Hart Publishing 2000) 33.

without the caveat from Protocol (No 19) concerning Schengen norms that the Council must unanimously agree. These 'tailored' opt-in mechanisms are qualitatively distinct from the United Kingdom's opt-out from EMU during membership, and Denmark's opt-out from the AFSJ in Protocol (No 22), on the basis that they enable selective participation in the creation and application of norms.

These mechanisms are also qualitatively distinct from the opt-out and opt-in mechanisms enabled by Article 10 of Protocol (No 36). This mechanism enabled the United Kingdom to notify the Council that it did not accept the powers of the supranational institutions over police and judicial cooperation after the Treaty of Lisbon amendments. The consequence of this decision was the 'wholesale' disapplication of the measures regarding police and judicial cooperation in force before Lisbon. The United Kingdom was subsequently allowed to opt in to police and judicial cooperation measures that ceased to apply to it, but subject to the conditions of practical operability and coherence.[99] No such substantive conditions are imposed on decisions to opt in under Protocol (No 21). This crossed the Rubicon to full executive discretion for Member States to decide whether to participate in the ordinary legislative procedure on an iterative basis.

A. Protocol (No 21): The United Kingdom and Ireland's flexible opt-in mechanism

The overlap in the subject matter regulated by Protocol (No 21) and the Protocols enabling opt-outs from the Schengen *acquis* is evidenced by the Preamble: 'having regard to the Protocol on the application of certain aspects of Article 26 of the Treaty on the Functioning of the European Union to the United Kingdom and to Ireland'.[100] Article 1 establishes the default opt-out position of the United Kingdom during its membership, and of Ireland to the present. Democratic subjects *qua* Member State nationals are excluded from the norm-creation process: 'the United Kingdom and Ireland shall not take part in the adoption by the Council of proposed measures'.[101] The Protocol does not deauthorize the exercise of legislative authority by representatives of the opt-out Member States *qua* EU citizens in the European Parliament.[102]

[99] TEU and TFEU, Protocol (No 36) on transitional provisions, art 10(5).

[100] TEU and TFEU, Protocol (No 21) on the position of the United Kingdom and Ireland in respect of the area of freedom, security and justice, preamble.

[101] ibid art 1.

[102] See arguments regarding this feature in Deirdre Curtin and Cristina Fasone, 'Differentiated Representation: Is a Flexible European Parliament Desirable?' in Bruno De Witte, Andrea Ott and Ellen Vos (eds), *Between Flexibility and Disintegration: The Trajectory of Differentiation in EU Law* (Edward Elgar Publishing 2017).

The scope of application of the Protocol concerns measures adopted pursuant to Title V of Part Three TFEU. The final two sentences of Article 1 ensure the continuing functioning of the decision-making rules. Unanimity in the AFSJ is determined 'with the exception of the representatives of the governments of the United Kingdom and Ireland'.[103] A qualified majority is still defined in accordance with Article 238(3) TFEU. The fact that the United Kingdom's population was, and Ireland's population will still be, accorded weight when determining a qualified majority evidences Habermas' claim that the Qualified Majority Voting rule functions as a means of residual representation of individuals *qua* EU citizens in the decisions of the Council.[104] The first clause of the Article—'Subject to Article 3'—points towards the exception to this deauthorization. Article 3 provides for the selective and discretionary reauthorization of legislative power by representatives of the opt-out Member State.

Article 2 establishes the effects of the opt-out mechanism for individuals *qua* juridical objects. The relevant EU law 'shall [not] be binding upon or applicable in the United Kingdom or Ireland'.[105] The conjunction denotes the dual-character of EU law that will be disapplied: EU law as international treaty law with binding effects upon the relevant states, and EU law as domestic public law within the constitutional orders of the relevant states. The latter means that it is not necessary for the opt-out Member State to make explicit provision in domestic constitutional law for the non-application of EU law deriving from Title V. As the United Kingdom's 'conduit pipe' of the European Communities Act 1972 specified that 'any' provisions of the Treaties were directly applicable as an independent and overriding source of law, this included the particular sentence of Article 2 of the Protocol. By contrast, and despite the lack of legal necessity, Article 29 of the Irish Constitution implements domestically the legal basis for the 'options or discretions' under the opt-out Protocols.[106] Both Houses of the Irish Parliament must approve of executive decisions under the Protocol, providing a further layer of representation for Irish nationals *qua* democratic subjects.

The non-application of the EU law listed in Article 2 is stated to occur 'in consequence of Article 1 and subject to Articles 3, 4 and 6'.[107] This confirms

[103] TEU and TFEU, Protocol (No 21) on the position of the United Kingdom and Ireland in respect of the area of freedom, security and justice, art 1.

[104] Jürgen Habermas, 'Citizen and State Equality in a Supranational Political Community: Degressive Proportionality and the Pouvoir Constituant Mixte' (2017) 55 Journal of Common Market Studies 171.

[105] TEU and TFEU, Protocol (No 21) on the position of the United Kingdom and Ireland in respect of the area of freedom, security and justice, art 2.

[106] Constitution of Ireland enacted by the People on 1st July 1937 in operation as from 29th December 1937, art 29(7).

[107] TEU and TFEU, Protocol (No 21) on the position of the United Kingdom and Ireland in respect of the area of freedom, security and justice, art 2.

that the legitimate application of EU law norms in the territory of a Member State is predicated upon democratic legitimation by individuals in their dual role. The fact that UK nationals were not, and Irish nationals are not, represented in the Council in norm-creation means that the application of these norms would be illegitimate. Article 2 lists the sources of law that are not applicable to an opt-out Member State by virtue of the Protocol: (1) none of the provisions of Title V of Part Three TFEU; (2) no measure adopted pursuant to that Title; (3) no provision of any international agreement concluded by the Union pursuant to that Title; and (4) no decision of the Court of Justice interpreting any such provision or measure.

The categorization broadly coheres to the supranational constitutional hierarchy of primary law, the EU's international agreements, secondary law, delegating acts, and judge-made common law. This aims to ensure a coherent conception of the relationship between norms in the AFSJ. Nevertheless, the exact scope and meaning of the term 'adopted pursuant to Title V' was a rich vein of litigation between the United Kingdom and the Union institutions.[108] A further practical issue is the extensive regime of executive delegating acts in Title V. Although this source of law is not explicitly covered in the categorization, it may be inferred that these acts are covered by the concept of 'measures'. This term denotes a broader scope than the corpus of Directives, Regulations, and Decisions which form the main body of secondary law.

The final sentence of the Article delineates the autonomy that the opt-out Member States have secured through the Protocol: 'no such provision, measure or decision shall in any way affect the competences, rights and obligations of those States'.[109] There is a question over whether this refers narrowly to the competences, rights, and obligations of the United Kingdom and Ireland as *Member* States of the Union, or more holistically to their role as states in public international law and national constitutional law. The fact that the 'Member' qualifier is not used points towards the latter interpretation.

The respect for the autonomy of the opt-out Member States is supplemented by the statement that 'no such provision, measure or decision shall in any way affect the Community or Union *acquis* nor form part of Union law as they apply to the United Kingdom or Ireland'.[110] This ensures respect for the legal order that is generated for individuals *qua* EU citizens. It is ambiguous how measures taken pursuant to the AFSJ or decisions thereupon could affect the

[108] See discussion of the functioning of the United Kingdom's opt-outs at the end of chapter 4 below.
[109] TEU and TFEU, Protocol (No 21) on the position of the United Kingdom and Ireland in respect of the area of freedom, security and justice, art 2.
[110] ibid.

EU legal order. One interpretation is that this provision seeks to preserve the integrity and autonomy of the EU legal order in the face of the authorization for certain Member States not to participate in the creation nor application of this law. As with EMU, this confirms that the effect of the opt-out Protocol does not alter the legal character of these norms. A further argument could be that this qualification insulates the scope of the opt-out from interference by measures promulgated on another legal basis. This was a practical issue that informed the United Kingdom's attempts to renegotiate the operation of the Protocol in February 2016.[111]

Article 3 is the predicate of Protocol (No 21) as an innovative prospective opt-in mechanism. Paragraph 1 provides for the abrogation of the opt-out and *à la carte* participation in Title V measures. This opt-in mechanism operates *after* a measure has been proposed but *before* it has been formally adopted and promulgated as EU law. The executive discretion for the opt-out Member State government is confirmed in the wording that they 'may notify' their intention to participate. The legal formality is notification to the President of the Council in writing. The procedural condition is that this notification is provided 'within three months after a proposal or initiative has been presented to the Council'.[112] The Member State expresses its intention to participate in the 'adoption and application of any such proposed measures'.[113] These two terms cover the norm-creation process and the norm-application process. The condition for such an intention to take effect is automatic, as indicated by the final clause: 'whereupon [the notification is made in writing of the intention to participate] that State shall be entitled to do so'.[114]

The next paragraph clarifies the decision-making rules in light of the potential for opt-ins: 'The unanimity of the members of the Council, with the exception of the member which has not made such a notification, shall be necessary for decisions of the Council which must be adopted unanimously'.[115] This is supplemented by the confirmation again that qualified majority is defined in accordance with Article 238(3) TFEU. The next sentence confirms the legal effect that any measures adopted 'under this paragraph' shall be binding upon all Member States which took part in its adoption. This confirms the abrogation

[111] See discussion of the Treaty of Lisbon to the New Settlement in chapter 4 below.
[112] TEU and TFEU, Protocol (No 21) on the position of the United Kingdom and Ireland in respect of the area of freedom, security and justice, art 3(1).
[113] ibid.
[114] ibid.
[115] ibid.

of Article 1 and Article 2, and that EU law will have binding effect for individuals *qua* juridical objects in the territory of that state if there is a decision to opt in.

The third paragraph of Article 3(1) is the only provision that indicates that the opt-ins could be subjected to further substantive conditions. For measures promulgated on the basis of Article 70 TFEU, there is an obligation for the Commission and the Council to 'lay down the conditions for the participation of the . . . [opt-out Member State] in the evaluations concerning the areas covered by Title V of Part Three'.[116] Article 70 TFEU outlines these conditions as 'objective and impartial evaluation[s] of the implementation of the Union policies referred to in this Title by Member States' authorities, in particular to facilitate full application of the principle of mutual recognition'.[117]

The European Parliamentary Research Service has conceptualized this clause as a 'peer review mechanism'.[118] The obligation for the legislative institutions to set the conditions for participation by the opt-out Member State in these evaluations recognizes their status as only partial adherents to the constitutional purpose of the AFSJ. It would be inappropriate for the opt-out Member State to have executive discretion to participate in these peer review mechanisms and to evaluate the practice of other Member States from the perspective of mutual trust. The exercise of this obligation manifested itself in the Commission proposal for a Regulation on the establishment of an evaluation mechanism to verify application of the Schengen *acquis*.[119] The Regulation stated that, because the United Kingdom and Ireland did not participate in the policy to maintain an area without internal border controls, they 'will not participate in adoption of this Regulation and will not be bound by it or subject to application thereof'.[120] This suggests that an opt-out Member State will only be entitled to engage in peer review evaluation of the areas in which they participate. This may prevent holistic evaluation of measures adopted pursuant to the AFSJ.

[116] ibid.

[117] TFEU, art 70.

[118] Daniela Vincenti, 'MEPs Launch Counterattack Against Schengen Deal' (*Euractiv*, 13 June 2012) <www.euractiv.com/section/justice-home-affairs/news/meps-launch-counterattack-against-schengen-deal/> accessed 15 October 2024. For criticism that this mechanism excludes the European Parliament, and thus the representation of individuals qua EU citizens, see 'Schengen: MEPs Angry at Council Attack on Democratic Powers' (*European Parliament News*, 12 June 2012) <https://web.archive.org/web/20220901050749/https://www.europarl.europa.eu/news/en/headlines/security/20120612STO46654/schengen-meps-angry-at-council-attack-on-democratic-powers> accessed 23 January 2020.

[119] Proposal for a Regulation of the European Parliament and of the Council on the establishment of an evaluation mechanism to verify application of the Schengen *acquis*, Brussels, 16.11.2010, COM(2010) 624 final.

[120] ibid.

Article 3(2) of the Protocol is a safeguard clause in the event that the opt-in power is activated but the adoption process has been obstructed. The clause states that '[i]f after a *reasonable period* of time a measure referred to in paragraph 1 cannot be adopted with the United Kingdom or Ireland taking part, the Council may adopt such measure in accordance with Article 1 without the participation of the United Kingdom or Ireland'.[121] This clause enables the Council to ensure the coherent functioning of the norm-creation process whilst accommodating differentiated participation. In contrast to the defined period of three months to notify participation, the timeframe to trigger the clause remains under-determined as a 'reasonable period'. This affords considerable flexibility to the Council to determine what is reasonable, and to consider the background context and purpose of the provision in question.

The opt-in mechanism provided by Article 4 of the Protocol is the sister provision to Article 3. The clause enables opt-ins *after* the adoption of a measure pursuant to Title V of Part Three TFEU. In contrast to the three-month window under Article 3, the opt-out Member State is given complete discretion as to when it may decide to adopt a provision.[122] In the case that this notification is given 'the procedure provided for in Article 331(1) of the Treaty on the Functioning of the European Union shall apply *mutatis mutandis*'.[123] This is a legal transplant of the procedure provided for under Article 20 TEU for the participation of Member States in an enhanced cooperation that is already in progress. This provides evidence of a generalized link in the realization of differentiated integration. This procedure affords primacy to the EU institutions, in particular the Commission and residually the Council, to determine whether the conditions for the participation of a Member State in EU law have been fulfilled. The provision establishes a timeframe of four months from the date of receipt of the notification to confirm this participation, and a discretion to set a deadline for the re-examination of the request in the event of a negative decision.

One issue with this *mutatis mutandis* transplant is that the Commission is authorized under Article 331 TFEU to assess whether the conditions of participation for enhanced cooperation have been fulfilled. By contrast to Article 20 TEU,[124] Article 3 of Protocol (No 21) sets no substantive conditions for

[121] TEU and TFEU, Protocol (No 21) on the position of the United Kingdom and Ireland in respect of the area of freedom, security and justice, art 3(2) (emphasis added).

[122] ibid art 4.

[123] ibid.

[124] TEU, art 20. See Federico Fabbrini, 'Enhanced Cooperation under Scrutiny: Revisiting the Law and Practice of Multi-Speed Integration in Light of the First Involvement of the EU Judiciary' (2013) 40 Legal Issues of Economic Integration 197.

participation in AFSJ measures before their promulgation. After their promulgation, the decision is not entirely unilateral. Such conditionality is necessary to ensure the coherence of the EU legal order and its uniform application when opt-out Member States have not participated in the creation of these norms. There is no coherent reason for why the Commission is the dominant institution to determine AFSJ opt-ins whereas the Council is the dominant institution to determine Schengen opt-ins. This was demonstrated most starkly in the United Kingdom's Protocol (No 36) opt-ins requiring separate decisions by the institutions.

Article 4a was an addition to the Protocol made at the Treaty of Lisbon.[125] Paragraph 1 extends the scope of opt-out mechanisms 'also to measures . . . *amending* an existing measure by which they are bound'.[126] This represents an inroad into the situation whereby Article 3 and Article 4 re-establish the status quo of membership for such measures. This contrasts to Protocol (No 19). Instead, the opt-out Member State retains the capacity to reactivate its dissident constituent power when norms undergo amendment.

Paragraph 2 provides a caveat to the discretion to opt out from amendments. The Council can determine if an opt-out 'makes the application of that measure *inoperable* for other Member States or the Union'.[127] If this condition is fulfilled, the Council is empowered to 'urge [the opt-out Member State] to make a notification under Article 3 or 4 [to opt in]'.[128] This triggers a two-month extension to the three-month period from the date of this determination. The concept of 'operability' was also used to regulate the United Kingdom's decision to opt in to police and judicial cooperation measures under Protocol (No 36). Operability functions as a structural principle to ensure that opt-outs and opt-ins do not undermine the constitutional integrity of the AFSJ. Article 4a(2) goes on to clarify the consequences of the expiry of this two-month period: 'the existing measure shall no longer be binding . . . or applicable . . . unless the Member State concerned has made a notification under Article 4 before the entry into force of the amending measure'.[129] The final sentence of the paragraph clarifies that the de-application of the measure will take effect from the date of entry into force of the amending measure, or the expiry of two months.

[125] Jean-Claude Piris, *The Lisbon Treaty: A Legal and Political Analysis* (CUP 2010) 199.
[126] TEU and TFEU, Protocol (No 21) on the position of the United Kingdom and Ireland in respect of the area of freedom, security and justice, art 4a (emphasis added).
[127] TEU and TFEU, Protocol (No 21) on the position of the United Kingdom and Ireland in respect of the area of freedom, security and justice, art 4a(2) (emphasis added).
[128] ibid.
[129] ibid.

The fact that the Council has no power to compel a Member State to adopt a measure even when it determines that this will make the measure inoperable underlines the ultimate sovereignty that is reserved for the opt-out Member States. This situation would create deleterious effects for individuals *qua* juridical objects if it were identified that an AFSJ measure is inoperable.

B. Protocol (No 22): Denmark's simple AFSJ opt-out

Protocol (No 22) on the position of Denmark provides for a simple opt-out from both AFSJ and Common Security and Defence Policy measures. The Preamble premises the creation of the Protocol as a resolution to the situation created by the Edinburgh Agreement that enabled Denmark to ratify the Maastricht Treaty:[130]

> [T]he continuation . . . of the legal regime originating in the Edinburgh decision will significantly limit Denmark's participation in important areas of cooperation of the Union, and . . . it would be in the best interests of the Union to ensure the integrity of the *acquis* in the area of freedom, security and justice.[131]

The Preamble also clarifies that the preference is to establish a legal framework that will provide an option for Denmark to participate in AFSJ measures.

Article 1 clarifies simply that 'Denmark shall not take part in the adoption by the Council of proposed measures pursuant to Title V of Part Three'.[132] Article 2 replicates the list of Article 2 in Protocol (No 21) to identify the EU law measures that do not apply to Denmark. However, there is no analogue to Article 3 of that Protocol whereby Denmark may iteratively opt in to AFSJ measures. Article 5 of the Protocol establishes Denmark's derogation from measures adopted pursuant to Article 26(1), Article 42 and Articles 43–46 TEU. Denmark does not participate in the elaboration and implementation of decisions and actions of the Union which have defence implications. Article 7 makes provision for Denmark's reversal of the opt-out 'in accordance with its constitutional requirements'.[133] The national constitution is recognized as the area for the decision to reverse the reservation of constituent power. This familial resemblance with the 'constitutional requirements' conditions in Article 48, Article 49, and Article 50 TEU is further evidence that the Protocols are interconnected with this triptych of constituted constituent power.

[130] See discussion on the background context in chapter 4 below.
[131] TEU and TFEU, Protocol (No 22) on the position of Denmark, preamble.
[132] TEU and TFEU, Protocol (No 22) on the position of Denmark, art 1.
[133] ibid art 7.

Article 7 states that Denmark may inform the other Member States that it no longer wishes to avail itself of all or part of the Protocol. The consequence is that Denmark will apply in full all relevant measures in force.[134] This constitutes a complete reversal. Denmark also has the option to transfer to a flexible opt-in mechanism. The final annex to the Protocol contains 9 Articles which mirror the flexible opt-out held by the United Kingdom during its membership, and by Ireland to the present. Article 8(1) of the Protocol establishes that Denmark may decide in accordance with its constitutional requirements to notify the other Member States that Part I of the existing opt-out will be replaced by the provisions in the annex. Article 8(2) also stipulates that in this event all Schengen measures that are binding upon Denmark in international law would become binding upon Denmark in EU law. This would extinguish the Schengen 'opt-out' and fully integrate Denmark into the supranational constitutional order in this sector. In December 2015, the Danish government attempted to fulfil these constitutional requirements through a national referendum. However, the population rejected the replacement of Part I with the annex and thus the Member State retains its rigid opt-out.[135]

C. Protocol (No 36): The United Kingdom's retrospective opt-out

A final provision of relevance to the AFSJ is Article 10 of Title VII of Protocol (No 36) on transitional measures after the Treaty of Lisbon came into force. Paragraph 1 established a transitional regime whereby the enforcement powers of the Commission under Article 258 TFEU would not apply to police and judicial cooperation measures adopted before the entry into force of Lisbon for five years.[136] The Court of Justice's jurisdiction would remain the same as the old intergovernmental regime.[137]

Paragraph 4 determined the right specifically for the United Kingdom to notify the Council that it did not accept the powers of the supranational institutions in the field of police cooperation and judicial cooperation in criminal matters.[138] The consequence of this notification was that all police and judicial cooperation acts referred to in paragraph 1 of the Article ceased to apply to the Member State from the date of expiry of the transitional period of five years. This functions as a *de facto* capacity for a Member State to disapply the binding force of EU law norms that it has already exercised its constituent power to

[134] ibid.
[135] See conclusions to the Danish narrative in chapter 4 below.
[136] TEU and TFEU, Protocol (No 36) on transitional provisions, art 10(1).
[137] See discussion of the Lisbon Treaty amendments below in chapter 4.
[138] TEU and TFEU, Protocol (No 36) on transitional provisions, art 10(4).

create and apply. *De jure* the integrity of the supranational constitutional order is preserved by the disapplication being a mandated reaction to the rejection of the supranational institutions by the United Kingdom.[139] The Protocol is comparable to Denmark's opt-out from Schengen under Protocol (No 22) as reservation of constituent power in relation to the method of supranational constitutionalism.

Paragraph 5 then created a flexible opt-in mechanism for the United Kingdom. The Member State 'may, at any time afterwards, notify the Council of its wish to participate in acts which have ceased to apply to it pursuant to paragraph 4'.[140] This provided an ostensibly unlimited time discretion akin to Article 4 of Protocol (No 21). The decision to opt in activated the relevant opt-in provisions of Protocol (No 19) or Protocol (No 21) depending on whether the measure was part of the Schengen *acquis* or the AFSJ beyond Schengen. By contrast to these provisions, decisions to opt back in were subject to substantive conditions of operability and coherence:

> [T]he Union institutions and the United Kingdom shall seek to re-establish the widest possible measure of participation of the United Kingdom in the acquis of the Union in the area of freedom, security and justice without seriously affecting the practical operability of the various parts thereof, while respecting their coherence.[141]

On 24 July 2013, the UK government formally notified the European Council under Article 10(4). The Council adopted a Decision on the consequential and transitional arrangements of this action on 27 November 2014.[142] The Decision identified fifty-nine police and judicial cooperation measures which ceased to apply to the United Kingdom. The United Kingdom also activated the opt-in provisions of Article 10(5). The application of these opt-ins of Protocol (No 19) for Schengen measures and Protocol (No 21) for non-Schengen measures required separate decisions of the Council[143] and the

[139] See chapter 4 for discussion of the extent to which this represents deconstructive power.

[140] TEU and TFEU, Protocol (No 36) on transitional provisions, art 10(5).

[141] ibid.

[142] Council Decision 2014/836/EU of 27 November 2014 determining certain consequential and transitional arrangements concerning the cessation of the participation of the United Kingdom of Great Britain and Northern Ireland in certain acts of the Union in the field of police cooperation and judicial cooperation in criminal matters adopted before the entry into force of the Treaty of Lisbon [2014] OJ L 343/11.

[143] Council Decision 2014/857/EU of 1 December 2014 concerning the notification of the United Kingdom of Great Britain and Northern Ireland of its wish to take part in some of the provisions of the Schengen *acquis* which are contained in acts of the Union in the field of police cooperation and judicial

Commission.[144] The United Kingdom opted back into twenty-nine police and judicial cooperation measures on this date.

iv. The functioning of the United Kingdom's opt-in mechanisms

The UK government published an annual report to the UK Parliament from 2010 for its decisions to opt in to Schengen and AFSJ measures under Protocol (No 19) and Protocol (No 21). From 2011 onwards these annual reports included an explanation for why the Minister decided to opt in or not. Protocol (No 19) and (No 21) do not impose supranational duties to give reasons for or justify opt-out decisions to the Council nor to the European Parliament. This legitimacy lacuna in Protocol (No 21) was mitigated by the practice of accountability at the domestic level at least for the democratic subject *qua* national.

The decision whether to participate in measures that are dual-legitimated within the supranational constitutional order is only justified to individuals *qua* nationals of the opt-out state. The opt-out Member State is not obliged to consider the interests of all the nationals of the Member States through engaging in argumentation in the Council. This undermines the principle of discursive interaction between the representatives of individuals.[145] Even without formally notifying participation, the United Kingdom was known to engage in discussions in an attempt to influence the development of measures before making a decision to opt in or not. One consequence of the justifications practice is that it enables assessment of the reasons given by an opt-out Member State, in contrast to the traditional opt-outs in which these reasons for derogation at times of Treaty amendment can only be reconstructed *ex post facto*.

The practice of justifications allows a number of claims to be tested by reference to the UK government documents: (1) exclusive executive accountability at the national level means that the intergovernmental bargaining logic prevalent in Treaty negotiations will prevail in decisions whether or not to opt in or opt out; (2) language that reflects the 'preferences' and 'interests' of the state in question will predominate and the arguments will not engage with whether

cooperation in criminal matters and amending Decisions 2000/365/EC and 2004/926/EC [2014] L 345/1.

[144] Commission Decision 2014/858/EU of 1 December 2014 on the notification by the United Kingdom of Great Britain and Northern Ireland of its wish to participate in acts of the Union in the field of police cooperation and judicial cooperation in criminal matters adopted before the entry into force of the Treaty of Lisbon and which are not part of the Schengen *acquis* [2014] OJ L 345/6.

[145] See the discussion of the principles of constitutional politics in chapter 2.

participation would be in the best interests of constituents in their role *qua* EU citizens; (3) the Member States will opt in to measures which they perceive will provide them with more rights or power in their representation of nationals; they will opt out from measures that are perceived to impose more obligations or constraints in the interests of all individuals *qua* EU citizens, and Third-Country Nationals.

The initial normative claim is that this behaviour undermines the Council as a representative forum for deliberation. The lack of supranational oversight means that government representatives are not required to take into account the interests of any Member State nationals other than their own. The discretion to choose measures also skews the integrity and coherence of the policy area. Compensatory measures counterbalance the control that Member States surrender over internal security and border control. The opt-out Member State may opt in to these compensatory measures without applying the initial obligations. The consequences for the juridical order were exacerbated by the United Kingdom's attempt to enforce a broad interpretation of the scope of its opt-out.

The analysis of the justifications advanced by the government focuses on the second annual report of decisions taken between 1 December 2010 and 30 November 2011. This covers a period after the Treaty of Lisbon when the new Protocol fully came into force, but before the announcement by David Cameron in 2013 that a referendum on membership would take place. The assumption is that this represents a period in which ministerial decisions were focused on the endogenous merits of the particular legislative procedure, rather than exogenous concerns over the wider political palatability of European integration.

The report from 2010 to 2011 identifies key opt-in decisions.[146] In relation to the opt-in to the EU Passenger Name Records Directive, the government argued that such records 'help our law enforcement agencies to prevent, detect, investigate and prosecute terrorists and other serious criminals',[147] emphasizing the increased powers. It concludes by arguing that 'the draft directive as it stands is not perfect, but it is right that we work with our European partners to get a directive that best serves Britain's interests'.[148] This is a paradigmatic

[146] Ministry of Justice and Home Office, 'Report to Parliament on the Application of Protocols 19 and 21 to the Treaty on European Union (TEU) and the Treaty on the Functioning of the European Union (TFEU) ("the Treaties") in Relation to EU Justice and Home Affairs Matters (1 December 2010–30 November 2011)' (2012) 5–6.

[147] ibid 11.

[148] ibid.

intergovernmental bargaining approach to the supranational constitutional process of legislation. This approach is reiterated by the statement that 'the Home Secretary pressed the argument for it at the ... Justice and Home Affairs Council meeting, where 15 member states supported the UK's position to include intra-EU data'.[149] The United Kingdom was relieved from the obligation to deliberate on the basis of the exchange of reasons and compromises within the Council because if its preferences were not fulfilled it could simply opt out from the legislation in question.

The second and third identified key opt-in decisions pertain to the Directive on establishing minimum standards on the rights, support, and protection of victims of crime, and a Regulation on civil protection measures respectively. In relation to the former, the government is explicit that 'the proposed Directive will benefit UK citizens who are victims in other EU member states'[150] without any mention of reciprocity for EU citizens in the United Kingdom. The effects on the legislative process are evidenced by the statement that 'by opting into this directive the UK will have the opportunity to strongly influence the text and ensure that the minimum standards victims can expect throughout the EU are clear, appropriate and affordable'.[151] In relation to the latter Regulation on civil protection measures, the government advanced the reasoning that 'it will benefit vulnerable people in Britain who may now feel more confident to travel within the EU due to greater protection'.[152] Again, the reciprocal situation for all other individuals *qua* EU citizens is omitted. However, this justification does recognize one of the key purposes of the juridical status of EU citizenship, namely the exercise of free movement rights, and accordingly seeks to vindicate these rights for UK nationals.

The fourth key decision concerned the decision to opt out from the Directive on the right of access to a lawyer in criminal proceedings. The government based this on the reasoning that 'a number of provisions ... go beyond the requirements of the European Convention on Human Rights ... and would have an adverse impact on our ability to investigate and prosecute offences effectively and fairly'.[153] This comes despite the recognized 'benefit [for] UK nationals subject to the criminal justice systems of other Member States'.[154] The government prioritized the powers of the executive within the national legal

[149] ibid.
[150] ibid 14.
[151] ibid.
[152] ibid.
[153] ibid 16.
[154] ibid.

order over the extension of protection for UK nationals when they exercised their rights *qua* EU citizens.

Attempts to influence the legislation from a position of non-participation are evident again: '[w]e are working very closely with our European partners to develop an improved text ... If our concerns are dealt with, we will consider whether to apply to opt in once it has been adopted'.[155] This exposes a particularly egregious asymmetry for the quadripartite role. Individuals *qua* nationals of the United Kingdom were still represented through *de facto* influence on the creation of norms even though officially these representatives had excluded themselves from exercising this role. This influence was exercised even though it was uncertain whether these norms would eventually be applied to these individuals *qua* juridical objects due to the retention of the decision whether to opt in during the first three months after adoption.

The final key decisions from the report are the UK government's decisions not to opt in to the Directive on the minimum standards on procedures in Member States for granting and withdrawing international protection, and to the Directive laying down minimum standards for the reception of asylum seekers. The justifications regarding both Directives display some generalized concern rather than pure self-interest: '[t]he Government was concerned that the Directive would subject Member States' asylum systems to unjustified regulation and focus excessively on enhancing the rights of all asylum seekers where their claims are valid or not'.[156] This prioritizes the national legal systems of all the Member States over the rights of residual juridical objects who do not fulfil the role of democratic subject either as national or EU citizen. This is further evidenced by the concerns expressed in relation to the former Directive that the 'proposals ... would allow asylum seekers to work after six months if a decision at first instance had not been reached and would place stringent restrictions on Member States' ability to detain asylum seekers when necessary'.[157] In relation to the latter Directive, the government expressed its concern about 'the proposed restrictions on accelerated procedures, and on the making of asylum appeals non-suspensive (where a right of appeal can be exercised out of country only)'.[158]

In both instances, the United Kingdom insisted that national administrative procedures obviated the requirement for supranational oversight. In the former case, the government considered the 'restrictions on detention to be unnecessary

[155] ibid.
[156] ibid 15.
[157] ibid.
[158] ibid.

in a system such as the UK's where detainees have the right to apply to the Courts for release on bail, or to bring a legal challenge against their detention'.[159] In the latter case, the government expressed concern for the endangerment of 'a number of systems that the UK operates to manage straightforward asylum claims effectively—in particular the UK Border Agency's Detained Fast Track which provides speedy but fair decisions for any asylum seekers whose claims are capable of being decided quickly'.[160] The United Kingdom's opt-out decisions in relation to the protection of Third-Country Nationals are predicated upon the perception that the domestic constitutional order provides superior mechanisms to ensure the protection of these individuals *qua* residual juridical objects.

A theme that emerged from the UK government's justifications was the belief that it could unilaterally pursue an opt-out if it believed a legislative measure concerned Justice and Home Affairs. This policy is detailed in the second annual report as a means of 'protecting the application of the opt-in Protocol':

> It is vital for UK interests that the opt-in Protocol is applied in a consistent manner. The Government has, during the past 12 months, noted the publication of measures in non-JHA policy areas which include provisions imposing JHA obligations, but which do not cite a Title V legal base (the normal TFEU legal base for a JHA proposal). It is the Government's position that the UK is not bound by such measures, unless it has opted into them pursuant to the Protocol.[161]

This policy was predicated upon a 'political' understanding of the sectors into which the EU legal order is divided. The 'JHA' has ceased to be a formal sector of the Treaties and instead is a configuration for the Council. The constitutional propriety and legality of this practice was scrutinized by the House of Lords European Union Committee.[162] Legal certainty over the norms an opt-out Protocol covers is crucial to ensure that the reservation of constituent power does not undermine the uniform application of EU law.

A related interpretative disagreement arose concerning the meaning of the wording 'pursuant to' in Article 1 and Article 2 of Protocol (No 21) in relation

[159] ibid.
[160] ibid.
[161] Ministry of Justice and Home Office, 'Fifth Annual Report to Parliament on the Application of Protocols 19 and 21 to the Treaty on European Union (TEU) and the Treaty on the Functioning of the European Union (TFEU) ("the Treaties") in Relation to EU Justice and Home Affairs (JHA) Matters (1 December 2013–30 November 2014)' (2015) 5.
[162] House of Lords European Union Committee, 'The UK's Opt-in Protocol: Implications of the Government's Approach' (House of Lords European Union Committee 2015) Ninth Report of Session 2014–2015 (HL Paper 136).

to provisions in international agreements between the European Union and Third Countries.[163] The UK government argued that 'pursuant to' Title V is 'a broader test which . . . extends to any provision in an international agreement that contains content where the EU competence for negotiating, signature and conclusion of that agreement flows from Title V . . . [this is] JHA content'.[164] By contrast, the European Commission advanced the interpretation that the phrase 'pursuant to' means 'that the measure in question must have a provision in Title V of Part Three of the Treaty as its legal basis'.[165] The Commission argued that there is 'a logical connection between not taking part in the adoption of a measure and not being bound by it. Yet the Government's position implies that the United Kingdom, after having taken part in the adoption of a measure, may subsequently consider itself not to be bound by some of its provisions'.[166] This threatened the functional purpose of the opt-out Protocol to ensure legal certainty for individuals *qua* juridical objects.

The Commission recognized this argument: 'It [the UK government's interpretation] would create considerable uncertainty as to when and whether Protocol No 21 applies'.[167] The House of Lords European Union Committee concluded that 'the potential of the Government's policy to create real legal uncertainty is very considerable indeed. The unilateralism of the Government's approach also raises serious questions about the UK's acceptance of the uniform application of EU law, the defining trait of the rule of law in the European Union'.[168] The Committee report also raised the issue of whether the unilateral interpretation of 'pursuant to' undermined the duty of sincere cooperation under Article 4(3) TFEU. Expert witness Damian Chalmers argued that 'the Court has held that unilateral action dissociating a State from a common agreed strategy which grants a mandate to the EU institutions to negotiate violates that duty'.[169] The inroads into the ordinary legislative practice represented by Protocol (No 21) and Protocol (No 19) encouraged the United Kingdom to assert its sovereign right to decide unilaterally despite the efforts to provide legally bounded parameters to the opt-in procedure. This exacerbated the spillover of the unbound exercise of constituent power at Treaty amendment into the ordinary functioning of the constitutional order.

[163] See chapter 4 for the origins of these cases.
[164] House of Lords European Union Committee (n 162) 19.
[165] ibid 20.
[166] ibid.
[167] ibid 31.
[168] ibid 32.
[169] ibid 34.

The pursuit of an exceptionalist strategy that sought only to vindicate the interests of individuals *qua* nationals was evident in a Ministerial response to the Committee. When questioned on whether the government's interpretation of 'pursuant to' could have implications for the interpretation of the term in the other ninety-eight instances in the Treaties, the Justice Secretary replied that this would not be an issue because '[m]y issue, as Secretary of State for this Government, is looking after the interests of the United Kingdom'.[170] This mindset suggests that accommodating recalcitrant Member States poses a threat to the uniform interpretation of EU law. The disputes show that the supranational institutions should have the final authority to determine the scope of opt-out mechanisms to preserve the integrity of the constitutional order for all individuals *qua* EU citizens. Allowing a unilateral determination by the opt-out Member State in the interests of its own constituent nationals undermines supranational uniformity. The following chapter will excavate how this situation as it stood before 23 June 2016 was allowed to manifest itself. The chapter will reconstruct the narrative whereby the constituent powers of the European Union at times of Treaty amendment allowed a situation in which their desire to progress European integration forward also created the incentives to enable disruption through opt-outs for the United Kingdom, Denmark, and Ireland.

[170] ibid 20.

4

Pre-Brexit

A Narrative of Disruption

I. Origins of Opt-Outs

The narrative of opt-outs is interwoven with the story of successive amendments of the foundational Treaties between the Single European Act signed on 17 February 1986 and coming into force on 1 July 1987, and the Treaty of Lisbon[1] signed on 13 December 2007 and coming into force on 1 December 2009. These constitutional amendments are bookended by two international agreements which are the prologue and the epilogue of the story: the Schengen Agreement[2] signed on 14 June 1985 and coming into force on 26 March 1995, and the Decision of the Heads of State or Government, Meeting Within the European Council, Concerning A New Settlement for the United Kingdom Within the European Union,[3] agreed on 19 February 2016, and coming into force upon the unrealized event of the United Kingdom notifying its intention to remain a Member State.

The United Kingdom, Ireland, and the Kingdom of Denmark have reserved constituent power to create Protocols addended to the Treaties that disapply the validity of EU law norms. As the Member State that opted out from all three of these sectors during its membership, and the only Member State that has also pursued disintegration, the narrative will focus predominantly upon the United Kingdom. Analysis of Ireland's opt-outs from Schengen and AFSJ, and Denmark's opt-outs from Schengen and EMU, will be utilized to complement this narrative.

[1] Treaty of Lisbon amending the Treaty on European Union and the Treaty establishing the European Community, signed at Lisbon, 13 December 2007 [2007] OJ C 306/1; Single European Act [1987] OJ No L 169/1.

[2] The Schengen *acquis*—Agreement between the Governments of the States of the Benelux Economic Union, the Federal Republic of Germany and the French Republic on the gradual abolition of checks at their common borders [2000] OJ L 239/13.

[3] European Council meeting (18 and 19 February 2016)—Conclusions, Annex 1—Decision of the Heads of State or Government, meeting within the European Council, concerning a new settlement for the United Kingdom within the European Union—Brussels 19 February 2016 EUCO 1/16.

Constitutional Disintegration and Disruption. Oliver Garner, Oxford University Press. © Oxford University Press 2025. DOI: 10.1093/9780198914136.003.0004

Amendments have prompted the creation of opt-outs for two reasons: the creation of new constitutional sectors, and the incorporation of prior international agreements. The 'deepening' of European integration into new policy areas prompts reluctance from certain Member States to acquiesce to the extension of supranationalism. The paradigm of this origin is the Third Stage of EMU, agreed upon and created in the Treaty of Maastricht.[4] The United Kingdom and Denmark opted out through Protocols addended to the final Treaty.[5]

The paradigm for the incorporation of previously concluded international agreements into the supranational constitutional framework is the Schengen *acquis*. Agreed upon in 1985, and finally coming into force in 1995, the international agreement was constitutionalized by the Treaty of Amsterdam.[6] The two Member States that had not consented to the international agreement, Ireland and the United Kingdom, secured opt-outs from the newly minted sector.[7] Denmark retained its national and international law basis for Schengen cooperation.[8]

The origins of the other opt-outs may be situated between the poles of the creation of new sectors and the incorporation of existing agreements. The AFSJ[9] never had an autonomous existence as a separate international agreement. However, its previous existence as the Third Pillar in the Maastricht Treaty distinguished it from the fully supranational First Pillar of the then European Community.[10] Before homogenization into the current two-Treaty structure, this sector existed between intergovernmental cooperation through international law agreements, and full supranational constitutionalism. The opt-outs arose through the contestation of the transfer of policies from the

[4] Treaty on European Union signed at Maastricht on 7 February 1992 [1992] OJ C 191/1.

[5] TEU and TFEU, Protocol (No 15) on certain provisions relating to the United Kingdom of Great Britain and Northern Ireland; TEU and TFEU, Protocol (No 16) on certain provisions relating to Denmark; TEU and TFEU, Protocol (No 17) on Denmark 17; TEU and TFEU, Protocol (No 19) on the Schengen *acquis* integrated into the framework of the European Union; TEU and TFEU, Protocol (No 20) on the application of certain aspects of Article 26 of the Treaty on the Functioning of the European Union to the United Kingdom and to Ireland; TEU and TFEU, Protocol (No 21) on the position of the United Kingdom and Ireland in respect of the area of freedom, security and justice; TEU and TFEU, Protocol (No 22) on the position of Denmark; TEU and TFEU, Protocol (No 36) on transitional provisions.

[6] Treaty of Amsterdam amending the Treaty on European Union, the Treaties establishing the European Communities and certain related acts [1997] OJ C 340/1.

[7] TEU and TFEU, Protocol (No 19) on the Schengen *acquis* integrated into the framework of the European Union.

[8] TEU and TFEU, Protocol (No 17) on Denmark.

[9] TFEU, Part III, Title V.

[10] For more on the pillar structure see David O'Keeffe and Patrick M Twomey (eds), *Legal Issues of the Maastricht Treaty* (John Wiley & Sons 1994).

Third Pillar to the First Pillar, and then subsequent constitutionalization at Lisbon.[11]

The United Kingdom's former Social Policy opt-out presents further ambiguity. The sector was created as an 'Agreement'[12] between all of the Member States except the United Kingdom during the Maastricht Treaty negotiations. Whether this Agreement was a creature of the European Union's constitutional order or the international legal order remained ambiguous until the Court of Justice adjudicated upon the agreement.[13] In direct opposition to the Schengen example, when Social Policy was fully constitutionalized in the Treaty of Amsterdam[14] the UK government 'reversed' its opt-out and fully committed to the new constitutional sector.[15]

The final and most ambiguous example is the 'quasi opt-out' from the Charter of Fundamental Rights of the European Union.[16] Debate emerged over whether this Protocol fulfilled the conditions to be a sector-specific opt-out. First, the Charter is a constitutional guarantee for individuals rather than a substantive sector. Second, rather than disapplication, the wording arguably only declares and clarifies the operation of the norms. Protocol (No 30) again falls between the origins of creation and incorporation of norms. The issue was not the form of these norms as either international or supranational, but the question of whether they were legally binding upon the Member States or merely declaratory.

The Charter was first proclaimed at the Nice European Council on 7 December 2000. The legal 'force' of the Declaration would be 'considered later'.[17] This occasion arose with the Intergovernmental Conference for the Treaty of Lisbon, resulting in the new Article 6 TEU's confirmation that the Charter 'shall have the same legal value as the Treaties'.[18] The corollary to this confirmation of legally binding status as primary law was the decision by the

[11] TEU and TFEU, Protocol (No 21) on the position of the United Kingdom and Ireland in respect of the area of freedom, security and justice; TEU and TFEU, Protocol (No 22) on the position of Denmark 22.

[12] Protocol on Social Policy of the Treaty on European Union signed at Maastricht on 7 February 1992 [1992] OJ C 191/1.

[13] Case T-135/96 *UEAPME v Council* [1998] ECR II-2335.

[14] Now contained within TFEU Part 3, Title X.

[15] Julia Lourie, 'The Social Chapter' (House of Commons Library 1997) Research Paper 97/102 <http://researchbriefings.files.parliament.uk/documents/RP97-102/RP97-102.pdf> accessed 27 January 2020.

[16] See Catherine Barnard, 'The "Opt-Out" for the UK and Poland from the Charter of Fundamental Rights: Triumph of Rhetoric over Reality?' in Stefan Griller and Jacques Ziller (eds), *The Lisbon Treaty: EU Constitutionalism without a Constitutional Treaty?* (Springer 2008).

[17] European Council, 'European Council – Nice, 7–10 December 2000: Conclusions of the Presidency' <www.europarl.europa.eu/summits/nice1_en.htm> accessed 27 January 2020.

[18] TEU, art 6(1).

UK and Polish governments to pursue the attachment of a Protocol[19] to the Treaty seeking to restrict the operation of the Charter.

Protocol (No 30) states that the Charter does not extend the ability of the Court of Justice or of nationals courts to find that legal actions of the United Kingdom were, or Poland are, inconsistent with fundamental rights, freedoms, and principles.[20] The Charter did not create justiciable rights except if Poland and the United Kingdom provided for such rights in national law.[21] At the time of the Lisbon amendment, debate emerged over whether the Protocol constituted an opt-out or not.[22] Catherine Barnard conditionally endorsed the views of Alan Dashwood and the House of Lords EU Select Committee that the Protocol functions as an unequivocal statement of the legal situation rather than an opt-out.[23] Although the origin of the Protocol may be regarded as a species of disrupted integration, its operation did not lead to disapplication of supranational norms. This illustrates the distinction between political declarations contained within and pertaining to the Treaties and legally binding opt-outs.

The New Settlement for the United Kingdom within the European Union would have represented a paradigm shift for the origins of opt-outs. Formally, the simplified international agreement would have bound the Member States to the deepening of opt-out Protocols in advance of a Treaty amendment. This contrasts to the Edinburgh Agreement, which established opt-outs for Denmark *after* the Treaty of Maastricht.[24] In terms of substance, opt-outs were sought from established provisions of EU law rather than norms that were being incorporated or created *a novo* in the supranational constitutional order. Most dramatically, the United Kingdom sought to 'opt out' from the EU's telos statement of ever closer union amongst the peoples of Europe. The Decision states that 'the United Kingdom is . . . not committed to further political integration into the European Union'.[25] The implication is that even if the United Kingdom had not triggered Article 50 TEU it may still have ceased the levelling up of constituent power to the supranational level in practice thus ossifying disrupted integration.

[19] TEU and TFEU, Protocol (No 30) on the application of the Charter of Fundamental Rights of the European Union to Poland and to the United Kingdom.
[20] ibid art 1(1).
[21] ibid arts 1(2) and 2.
[22] Barnard (n 16).
[23] ibid.
[24] See chapter 4 for the origins of the Danish opt-outs.
[25] European Council meeting (18 and 19 February 2016)—Conclusions, Annex 1—Decision of the Heads of State or Government, meeting within the European Council, concerning a new settlement for the United Kingdom within the European Union—Brussels 19 February 2016 EUCO 1/16, 16.

II. The 1972 Member States and Disrupted Integration

The United Kingdom was not the only 'awkward partner' in the process of European integration. The description of Denmark's history of interaction with the European Union as 'limited engagement, fragmentation, and pragmatism'[26] may be applied to all three Member States that acceded in 1972. This is not to say, of course, that these three were the only 'awkward' Member States. From different perspectives and regarding different aspects, all Member States may well be described as awkward at different times. Each Member State of the European Union has its own experience of European integration, and the interaction of the national constitutional order and the European constitutional order will vary based on the differing 'constitutional identities' of the states.[27]

Nevertheless, there are certain shared aspects of the 1972 Member States' experiences in the European Union. All three states have strong cultures of parliamentary primacy in the constitutional order.[28] All three states have also experienced judicial and democratic clashes with the EU constitutional order. The boundaries between the national legal order and the EU legal order have been questioned in national courts in, *inter alia*, the *Factortame*[29] cases in the United Kingdom, the *Grogan*[30] case in Ireland, and the *Dansk Industri*[31] case in Denmark. A major contrast between the 1972 Member States is that the procedures for levelling up constituent power are contained within a constitutional higher-law in Denmark and Ireland. These mechanisms are found in Article 29 of the Irish Constitution, and Section 20 of the Constitutional Act of Denmark.[32] Within the United Kingdom's uncodified constitution the only constitutional norm pertaining to the further levelling up of constituent power was the constraint of the 'referendum lock' in the now repealed constitutional statute of the European Union Act 2011.[33]

[26] Mikael Rask Madsen, Henrik Palmer Olsen and Urška Šadl, 'Competing Supremacies and Clashing Institutional Rationalities: The Danish Supreme Court's Decision in the *Ajos* Case and the National Limits of Judicial Cooperation' (2017) 23 European Law Journal 140, 145.

[27] Michel Rosenfeld, 'Constitutional Identity' in András Sajó and Michel Rosenfeld (eds), *The Oxford Handbook of Comparative Constitutional Law* (OUP 2012).

[28] *R (Miller) v Secretary of State for Exiting the European Union* [2017] UKSC 5; Madsen, Olsen and Šadl (n 26).

[29] *R (Factortame Ltd) v Secretary of State for Transport* [1990] UKHL 13.

[30] Case C-159/90 *The Society for the Protection of Unborn Children Ireland Ltd v Stephen Grogan* [1991] ECR I-04685.

[31] Danish Supreme Court case 15/2014 *Dansk Industri, acting on behalf of Ajos A/S v Estate of A.*

[32] Constitution of Ireland enacted by the People on 1st July 1937 in operation as from 29th December 1937, art 29; The Constitutional Act of Denmark of 5 June 1953, s 20.

[33] European Union Act 2011, s 6.

Regarding the role of individuals as democratic subjects, all three states have returned negative votes towards Europe in national referendums. The Irish population returned 'No' votes to the Nice and Lisbon Treaties in 2001 and 2008 respectively, both of which were reversed in later referendums.[34] The Danish electorate initially returned a 'No' vote to the Maastricht Treaty in 1992,[35] and another 'No' vote on the relaxation of the opt-out from the AFSJ in 2015.[36] Most infamously, the UK population returned their 'No' vote to membership in 2016. As most clearly demonstrated in the Danish case, reluctant popular legitimation has been a direct causal influence on the creation of the opt-out Protocols. Although the United Kingdom, Denmark, and Ireland share these similarities, they were not the only Member States that have contested supranational constitutionalism through the judiciary, the political elites, and/or the demos.

The judiciary of arguably the most pro-European Member State, the Federal Republic of Germany, has most prominently and frequently contested supranational constitutional boundaries.[37] The constitutional courts in other Member States, such as Czechia[38] and Italy,[39] have also protected the boundaries of national constitutional identity. The Hungarian population were asked the question of whether to comply with EU policy on refugee admissions in 2015. Although the vote went against the European order, the national threshold for validity was not reached.[40] More dramatically, the Treaty establishing a Constitution for Europe was halted abruptly by 'No' votes from the Dutch and French electorates in 2005.[41]

[34] 'Ireland Rejects Nice Treaty' *The Guardian* (London, 8 June 2001) <www.theguardian.com/world/2001/jun/08/eu.politics> accessed 18 April 2020; Henry McDonald and Allegra Stratton, 'Irish Voters Reject EU Treaty' *The Guardian* (London, 13 June 2008) <www.theguardian.com/world/2008/jun/13/ireland> accessed 18 April 2020.

[35] Torben Worre, 'First No, Then Yes: The Danish Referendums on the Maastricht Treaty 1992 and 1993' (1995) 33 Journal of Common Market Studies 235.

[36] Henriette Jacobsen, 'Denmark Rejects Further EU Integration in Referendum' (*Euractiv*, 4 December 2015) <www.euractiv.com/section/justice-home-affairs/news/denmark-rejects-further-eu-integration-in-referendum/> accessed 23 January 2020.

[37] Dieter Grimm, Mattias Wendel and Tobias Reinbacher, 'European Constitutionalism and the German Basic Law' in Anneli Albi and Samo Bardutzky (eds), *National Constitutions in European and Global Governance: Democracy, Rights, the Rule of Law: National Reports* (TMC Asser Press 2019).

[38] David Kosař and Ladislav Vyhnánek, 'Constitutional Identity in the Czech Republic' in Christian Calliess and Gerhard van der Schyff (eds), *Constitutional Identity in a Europe of Multilevel Constitutionalism* (CUP 2019).

[39] Federico Fabbrini and Oreste Pollicino, 'Constitutional Identity in Italy' in Christian Calliess and Gerhard van der Schyff (eds), *Constitutional Identity in a Europe of Multilevel Constitutionalism* (CUP 2019).

[40] Andrew MacDowall, 'Voters Back Viktor Orbán's Rejection of EU Migrant Quotas' (*POLITICO*, 2 October 2016) <www.politico.eu/article/hungary-referendum-eu-migration-viktor-orban/> accessed 23 January 2020.

[41] 'French Say Firm "No" to EU Treaty' (*BBC News*, 30 May 2005) <http://news.bbc.co.uk/1/hi/world/europe/4592243.stm> accessed 23 January 2020; 'Dutch Say "No" to EU Constitution' (*BBC News*, 2 June 2005) <http://news.bbc.co.uk/1/hi/4601439.stm> accessed 23 January 2020.

Both France and the Netherlands were members of the 'Original Six' signatories to the Treaty of Rome in 1957. Nearly two decades on from these votes, both the Netherlands and France have seen surges in electoral popularity of nationalist parties advocating withdrawal from the European Union.[42] Following national electoral defeats and Brexit, these withdrawal strategies were revised into anti-supranational strategies to reform the European Union into an intergovernmental alliance of independent nation-states.[43] It remains to be seen whether Geert Wilders' unexpected victory in the 2023 Dutch general election could alter the country's position on EU membership.[44] Despite these examples of resistance to European integration, no Member States other than the United Kingdom, Denmark, and Ireland constitutionalized such disruption in the form of Protocols exempting them from the creation and application of EU law.

III. The Single European Act to the Treaty of Maastricht

i. Schengen

The original Schengen Agreement was concluded between the States of the Benelux Economic Union (the Kingdom of Belgium, the Kingdom of the Netherlands, and the Grand Duchy of Luxembourg), the Federal Republic of Germany, and the French Republic on 14 June 1985.[45] This agreement was

[42] Eline Schaart, Pieter Haeck and Jakob Hanke Vela, 'Far-right Leader Geert Wilders Wins Dutch election' (*POLITICO*, 22 November 2023) <www.politico.eu/article/far-right-leader-geert-wilders-wins-dutch-election-exit-poll/> accessed 1 December 2023; Michael Stothard, 'Could France's Marine Le Pen Deliver Frexit?' *Financial Times* (Paris, 15 March 2017) 3; James Fontanella-Khan, 'Geert Wilders Outlines Case for a Dutch 'Nexit' from the EU' *Financial Times* (The Hague, 7 February 2014) 3. See for deeper analysis of the Le Pen strategy Théo Fournier, 'From Rhetoric to Action, a Constitutional Analysis of Populism' (2019) 20 German Law Journal 362.

[43] Rym Momtaz, 'French Far Right Wants to Scrap European Commission' (*POLITICO*, 15 April 2019) <www.politico.eu/article/marine-le-pen-national-rally-french-far-right-wants-to-scrap-european-commission/> accessed 23 January 2020; Stijn van Kessel, 'Geert Wilders Is No Longer so Keen on Pushing for a "Nexit"—and It's Because Dutch People Don't Want It' (*EUROPP*, 2 March 2017) <https://blogs.lse.ac.uk/europpblog/2017/03/02/nexit-evolving-euroscepticism-geert-wilders/> accessed 23 January 2020.

[44] Steve Anglesey, 'Does Geert Wilders's Election Mean Nexit Is on the Horizon?' (*The New European*, 25 November 2023) <www.theneweuropean.co.uk/does-geert-wilderss-election-mean-nexit-is-on-the-horizon/> accessed 1 December 2023.

[45] The Schengen *acquis*—Agreement between the Governments of the States of the Benelux Economic Union, the Federal Republic of Germany and the French Republic on the gradual abolition

eventually implemented via a Convention which came into force in 1990.[46] The Agreement was promulgated with a prospective focus. The obligations and rights pertaining to the gradual abolition of checks at common borders are split into two Titles: Title I details 'Measures Applicable in the Short Term', whereas Title II details 'Measures Applicable in the Long Term'. Steve Peers claims that 'the Commission supported such measures as an interim solution, hoping that the time would one day come when Member States could agree to address these issues using Community law'.[47] The resort to international law as a means to predetermine the exercise of supranational constituent power provided the conditions whereby certain Member States would eventually decide to reserve the levelling up of constituent power. The telos of Schengen is embodied within the declarations of the preamble to the Agreement. The State Parties declare that 'the ever closer union . . . should find its expression in the freedom to cross internal borders for all nationals of the Member States' and therefore that they will 'achieve the abolition of checks at their common borders on the movement of nationals of the Member States'.[48]

It is noteworthy that the benefits are prescribed as being for individuals as nationals of the Member States, as the original Agreement predated the creation of EU citizenship. Nevertheless, despite the references to movement of goods, it is clear that the Parties intend to serve the interests of individuals rather than merely instrumentalize their movement for the realization of the Internal Market. The purpose of the Parties was to provide legal rights for nationals of the Member States to pursue life plans without the obligations of internal border checks. This focuses on the 'output legitimacy' for individuals *qua* juridical objects. The 'input legitimacy' for individuals *qua* democratic subject is limited to representation by their heads of state or government through the state consent necessary to create obligations in international law. The agreement to enable individuals to move between common borders represents a supranational inroad into the traditionally intimate relationship between a

of checks at their common borders [2000] OJ L 239/13 13; for detailed analysis of the origins in French-German cooperation and the terms of the Agreement, see Julian Schutte, 'Schengen: Its Meaning for the Free Movement of Persons in Europe' (1991) 28 Common Market Law Review 549.

[46] The Schengen *acquis*—Convention implementing the Schengen Agreement of 14 June 1985 between the Governments of the States of the Benelux Economic Union, the Federal Republic of Germany and the French Republic on the gradual abolition of checks at their common borders [2000] OJ L 239/19.

[47] Steve Peers, *EU Justice and Home Affairs Law: EU Justice and Home Affairs Law: Volume I: EU Immigration and Asylum Law* (4th edn, OUP 2016) 71.

[48] The Schengen Agreement (n 45), preamble.

state's internal and external sovereignty and its territory.[49] Traditional legal theory presents state-based legal orders as geographically differentiated on the basis of territory. Within this territory, the state's authority is theoretically absolute.[50] Loïc Azoulai claims that Schengen, free movement, and EU citizenship have transformed the concept of 'Member State territory' into the concept of 'Union territory'.[51]

It is appropriate to discuss the original Schengen Agreement within the framework of the supranational constitutional order despite its origins as a creature of public international law. The preamble makes reference to the EU's *raison d'être* of ever closer union amongst the peoples of Europe.[52] This declaration is evidence that the 'centre of gravity' around which the 'Satellite Treaty' orbited was the Union legal order.[53] Ever closer union provided the pathway for the incorporation of the Schengen *acquis* into the EU's constitutional order. The purpose of the Agreement was to function as an *avant-garde*[54] for a unified supranational regime to abolish the operation of internal borders between Member States in relation to EU citizens.

This prompts the question of why such goals were not pursued within the auspices of the supranational constitutional order from the outset. An *inter se* international agreement to pursue European integration is a paradigmatic case of 'old-fashioned flexibility'.[55] Recourse to international law was necessary due to the failure to secure unanimous consensus for supranational amendment. Schutte outlines the 'fundamental difference of view between the Member States as to . . . [the] implications for the existing regime of checks on persons when crossing borders between Member States'.[56] The legitimacy of extra-constitutional forms of integration is debated. Peers uses the evocative term

[49] As evidenced by criterion (b), 'a defined territory' for statehood outlined in the Montevideo Convention on the Rights and Duties of States, Signed at Montevideo, 26 December 1933, art 1.

[50] Hans Kelsen, *General Theory of Law and State* (The Lawbook Exchange 1945); Hans Lindahl, *Authority and the Globalisation of Inclusion and Exclusion* (CUP 2018).

[51] Loïc Azoulai, 'Transfiguring European Citizenship: From Member State Territory to Union Territory' in Dimitry Kochenov (ed), *EU Citizenship and Federalism* (CUP 2017).

[52] TEU, art 1.

[53] See Bruno De Witte, 'Old-Fashioned Flexibility: International Agreements between Member States of the European Union' in Gráinne de Búrca and Joanne Scott (eds), *Constitutional Change in the EU: From Uniformity to Flexibility?* (Hart Publishing 2000).

[54] See Daniel Thym, 'Competing Models for Understanding Differentiated Integration' in Bruno De Witte, Andrea Ott and Ellen Vos (eds), *Between Flexibility and Disintegration: The Trajectory of Differentiation in EU Law* (Edward Elgar Publishing 2017).

[55] De Witte, 'Old-Fashioned Flexibility' (n 53); Bruno De Witte, 'Variable Geometry and Differentiation as Structural Features of the EU Legal Order' in Bruno De Witte, Andrea Ott and Ellen Vos (eds), *Between Flexibility and Disintegration: The Trajectory of Differentiation in the EU* (Edward Elgar Publishing 2017).

[56] Julian Schutte, 'UK v EU: A Continuous Test Match' (2011) 34 Fordham International Law Journal 1346, 1348.

'black-market' European integration to describe the Schengen Agreement.[57] By contrast, Bruno de Witte has emphasized that international agreements are an acceptable tool to resolve coordination problems when unanimity is not possible.[58]

The Member States that would eventually create opt-outs were described as 'dissidents' in the Schengen process since its inception.[59] Peers claims that 'four Member States (the United Kingdom, Ireland, Denmark, and Greece) did not believe in the abolition of internal border controls'[60] and 'two Member States—the UK and Ireland—maintained for some time that the abolition of internal border controls was not part of the European integration process at all'.[61] These claims suggest that the predilection against Schengen may not have been rooted purely in national self-interest. There is a constitutional perspective in the argument that such legal norms are detrimental rather than beneficial for constituent citizens. This has been framed as a 'battleground' between 'States' desire to retain discretion over control of their borders as a key aspect of their sovereignty [and] the need to ensure effective protection of rights and liberties'.[62] This indicates the inherent tension between guaranteeing the fulfilment of individuals *qua* immobile nationals of a Member State and individuals *qua* mobile EU citizens. Control over the entry of individuals into the territory of the polity pursues the former goal, whereas reducing the burdens to enable individuals to travel between Member States pursues the latter objective. The constitutional disquiet over this new frontier of European integration developed into the decisions of these Member State to opt out when the *acquis* was constitutionalized within the Treaties.

Before the Treaty of Amsterdam, the international law Schengen *acquis* and the number of State parties increased in tandem with attempts to consolidate within the supranational constitutional order.[63] The 'original sin' for the incorporation of the Schengen *acquis* was the dispute over the interpretation of ex Article 8a EEC, now Article 26 TFEU.[64] The 1987 Single European

[57] Peers (n 47) 68.

[58] De Witte, 'Old-Fashioned Flexibility' (n 53); De Witte, 'Variable Geometry and Differentiation as Structural Features of the EU Legal Order' (n 55).

[59] Rebecca Adler-Nissen, *Opting Out of the European Union: Diplomacy, Sovereignty and European Integration* (CUP 2014) 116.

[60] Klaus-Peter Nanz, 'The Schengen Agreement: Preparing the Free Movement of Persons in the European Union' in Roland Bieber and Jörg Monar (eds), *Justice and Home Affairs in the European Union* (European Interuniversity Press 1995) 45–46; see also Alkuin Kölliker, *Flexibility and European Unification: The Logic of Differentiated Integration* (Rowman & Littlefield 2006) 212.

[61] Peers (n 47) 68.

[62] ibid.

[63] For a brief yet detailed overview of this process see ibid 69–75.

[64] TFEU, art 26.

Act sought to create a 'great leap forward' in European economic integration. Article 8a obliged the supranational institutions to adopt measures to establish the internal market as an area without internal frontiers before the end of 1992. Some Member States regarded this prerogative as requiring the abolition of border checks, thereby replicating and eventually absorbing the Schengen norms. Others disputed this interpretation. Nanz claims that 'only the five Schengen countries could clearly accept the Commission's interpretation of [ex] Article 8a EEC'[65] as a legal competence for the Schengen *acquis*. Schutte details the view of the resistant Member States that 'this Article does not require the full abolition of checks on persons at internal borders and therefore does not guarantee a right of free circulation for everyone legitimately present within EC territory'.[66] The United Kingdom argued further that the abolition of border checks only needed to be extended to nationals of Member States, excluding Third-Country Nationals.[67]

The centrifugal forces leading to the Schengen opt-outs were set in motion by the five original Schengen states. The decision of these Member States to fulfil their interpretation of the EU's mission statement without the necessary consent of all representatives set the course for the reservation of constituent power. The continuing disagreement over free movement of persons set in motion by this decision would not only lead to opt-outs, but would ultimately manifest itself in the United Kingdom's attempts to renegotiate its membership in February 2016.

ii. Economic and Monetary Union (EMU)

Superficially, the opt-outs from EMU seem to arise from resistance to new sectors of the *acquis communautaire* created in the Treaty of Maastricht. A more nuanced analysis identifies the reservation of constituent power as the culmination of fragmented participation in the two prior stages of EMU. Before Maastricht, 'the EMS [European Monetary System] already recognised that non-participation need not always be based on motives pertaining to the Member States' socio-economic performance'.[68] This incremental method may have created a pathway dependence whereby participation in what Kaarlo Tuori calls the 'macroeconomic constitution' was regarded as an executive

[65] Nanz (n 60) 45.
[66] Schutte, 'Schengen: Its Meaning' (n 45) 564.
[67] Peers (n 47) 70.
[68] Filip Tuytschaever, *Differentiation in European Union Law* (Hart Publishing 1999) 176.

elective.[69] This contrasts to the 'microeconomic' elements of the supranational constitutional order which have been enshrined in binding primary law since the Treaty of Rome.[70] This observation illustrates a qualitative difference to the Schengen opt-out origins. This was rooted in a dispute over the *ex post facto* interpretation of a legal provision.[71] In EMU, by contrast, there was *prospective* resistance to the creation of such a source of legal norms. This explanation may have power for the United Kingdom. It has less explanatory validity for Denmark, which participated in the EMS from 1979. This discrepancy may be confronted by distinguishing between the contestation of macroeconomic supranationalism as an executive preference, and constraints upon levelling up imposed by national constitutional structures. Whereas the UK government actively pursued a policy of resistance to EMU, Danish governments have been prevented from following an integration-friendly policy by a lack of popular will.

The telos of EMU may be reconstructed from the declarations contained within the 'Werner Report'[72] of 1970 and the 'Delors Report' of 1989.[73] The former presents the ordoliberal justification for EMU as a necessary element to complete the single market: 'general economic disequilibrium in the member countries . . . is likely to compromise seriously the integration realized in the liberation of the movement of goods, services and capital'.[74] Integration is not merely presented as an objective *per se*. Reference is made to the 'realization of the objectives of growth and stability'.[75] This terminology would persist in the evolution of EMU.[76] These concepts are the macroeconomic conditions necessary to ensure that undue disruption is not caused for individuals in their pursuit of self-fulfilment. This supports the EU's telos to ensure that Europe will not fall back into armed conflict. The devastating impact of the global financial crash in the 1930s and hyperinflation in the Weimar Republic is regarded as a condition that allowed the Nazi regime to come to power, eventually leading to

[69] Kaarlo Tuori, *European Constitutionalism* (CUP 2015) 174–226.

[70] ibid 127–73; but for a nuanced account see Gráinne de Búrca, 'Differentiation within the Core: The Case of the Internal Market' in Gráinne de Búrca and Joanne Scott (eds), *Constitutional Change in the EU: From Uniformity to Flexibility?* (Hart Publishing 2000).

[71] TFEU, art 26.

[72] Pierre Werner, 'Report to the Council and the Commission on the Realisation by Stages of Economic and Monetary Union in the Community ("Werner Report")' (1970) Supplement to Bulletin II-1970 of the European Communities.

[73] Jacques Delors, 'Report on Economic and Monetary Union in the European Community by Committee for the Study of Economic and Monetary Union Presented 17 April 1989' (1989) EU Commission—Working Document.

[74] Werner (n 72) 8.

[75] ibid.

[76] Treaty on Stability, Coordination and Governance of 2 March 2012 T/SCG.

the Second World War.[77] The objectives of growth and stability feed into the overriding imperative to preserve the necessary preconditions for individuals to exercise self-determination in order to pursue self-fulfilment.

These objectives are defined in the report as effecting 'a lasting improvement in welfare in the Community'[78] and achieving 'simultaneously satisfactory growth, a high level of employment, and stability'.[79] The statements on the adoption of a single currency are most pertinent for the United Kingdom's and Denmark's opt-outs:

> From the technical point of view the choice between these two solutions [maintenance of national monetary symbols or the establishment of a sole currency] may seem immaterial, but considerations of a psychological and political nature militate in favour of the adoption of a sole currency which would confirm the irreversibility of the venture.[80]

Political and psychological factors transcend economic rationales. The single currency became a symbol for the mutation of European integration into political union and the consequent threat to state sovereignty. These political and psychological factors expose a cleavage between whether nationality or EU citizenship is the appropriate status to legitimate monetary policy. This explains why EMU became the locus for the compromise that was necessary to ensure that the Maastricht Treaty was ratified.

In March 1971, the Member States declared 'their political will to establish an economic and monetary union'.[81] Various mechanisms in the 1970s and the 1980s prepared the ground. The 'Snake' was established in 1972,[82] the European Monetary Cooperation Fund in 1973,[83] and Council Directives on stability, growth, and full employment were adopted in 1974.[84]

[77] Lewis E Hill, Charles E Butler and Stephen A Lorenzen, 'Inflation and the Destruction of Democracy: The Case of the Weimar Republic' (1977) 11 Journal of Economic Issues 299.

[78] Werner (n 72) 9.

[79] ibid.

[80] ibid 10.

[81] Member States of the European Community, 'Resolution on the Achievement by Stages of Economic and Monetary Union in the Community' (European Parliament—Committee on Institutional Affairs 1982).

[82] 'The Snake—Historical Events in the European Integration Process (1945–2009)' (*CVCE.eu by Uni.lu*) <www.cvce.eu/en/education/unit-content/-/unit/02bb76df-d066-4c08-a58a-d4686a3e68ff/1b3433df-a25b-455a-b872-dec04270f820> accessed 27 January 2020.

[83] European Central Bank, 'European Monetary Cooperation Fund (1973-93)' (*European Central Bank*) <www.ecb.europa.eu/ecb/access_to_documents/archives/emcf/html/index.en.html> accessed 27 January 2020.

[84] Council Directive 74/121/EEC of 18 February 1974 on stability, growth and full employment in the Community [1974] OJ L 63/19.

The momentum for macroeconomic integration continued in 1979 with the creation of the Exchange Rate Mechanism (ERM) within the EMS and the European Currency Unit (ECU).[85] These integration mechanisms challenge the origin paradigm for the creation of the opt-outs. The iterative development of economic and monetary policy through forms of intergovernmental cooperation outside amendment of the Treaties preceded the creation of the sector at Maastricht. The participation of the United Kingdom and Denmark in these predecessor mechanisms indicates the executives' attitudes towards macroeconomic cooperation. After departing from the 'Snake' as early as 1972,[86] the United Kingdom only joined the ERM as late as 1990 after eleven years of abstention.[87] It was forced to withdraw from the mechanism ignominiously in 1992 in the wake of 'Black Wednesday' when the pound dropped below the agreed lower limit.[88] At this point, the UK government had already decided to opt out from the third stage of EMU. The negative effects of this experience and its inextricable association with European integration hardened political attitudes against future participation in EMU. Stephen Wall asserts that 'our withdrawal from the ERM helps explain the persistent hostility in Britain to the single currency. We linked our currency to those of our partners and were forced into what looked like a humiliating defeat'.[89]

The arguments against participation in the ERM were broadly coherent with the arguments against EMU in general. The latter was the final crystallization of the price stability goals of the former. The statements of senior UK politicians in this period indicate that economic arguments were combined with constitutional arguments against the policy. Wall claims that 'EMU and the European superstate were to become increasingly associated in people's minds'.[90] The economic arguments were generally applicable to all the Member States and may be interpreted as concerned with all individuals *qua* EU citizens. The constitutional arguments were peculiar to the situation of the United

[85] 'The European Monetary System—Historical Events in the European Integration Process (1945–2009)' (*CVCE.eu by Uni.lu*) <www.cvce.eu/en/education/unit-content/-/unit/02bb76df-d066-4c08-a58a-d4686a3e68ff/1040d119-5eba-4c7b-a850-ed254556c43c> accessed 27 January 2020.

[86] 'The Difficulties of the Monetary Snake and the EMCF—Research Corpora' (*CVCE.eu by Uni.lu*) <www.cvce.eu/en/collections/unit-content/-/unit/56d70f17-5054-49fc-bb9b-5d90735167d0/2d84f078-672e-4ae9-92d5-b4969911442a> accessed 27 January 2020.

[87] 'The ERM and the Single Currency' (*UK Parliament*) <www.parliament.uk/about/living-heritage/evolutionofparliament/legislativescrutiny/parliament-and-europe/overview/britain-joins-erm-to-introduction-of-single-currency/> accessed 27 January 2020.

[88] Larry Elliott, Will Hutton and Julie Wolf, 'September 17 1992: Pound Drops out of ERM' *The Guardian* (London, 17 September 1992) <www.theguardian.com/business/1992/sep/17/emu.theeuro> accessed 27 January 2020.

[89] Stephen Wall, *A Stranger in Europe: Britain and the EU from Thatcher to Blair* (OUP 2008) 142.

[90] ibid 81.

Kingdom, and therefore sought only to protect individuals *qua* nationals of that Member State. The UK government's reasons for joining the ERM were ultimately economic. The Chancellor, Nigel Lawson, argued that 'it would reduce exchange rate fluctuations and we would be able to use it to assist us in our anti-inflationary policy'.[91] The Prime Minister, Margaret Thatcher, also expressed economic arguments against participation in the EMU. Wall claims Thatcher believed that 'if one could find an objective standard to act as a spine, there was no need for an ECB or a single currency. It was only necessary that all ERM members should adopt sound economic and monetary policies'.[92]

The contestation which set the course for the United Kingdom's non-engagement was rooted in an ideological position beyond economic arguments. The move to a single currency rather than a common currency was not economically necessary; it was pursued for political and psychological reasons to symbolize the irreversibility of integration.[93] This was mirrored in Margaret Thatcher's opposition to EMU being interweaved with concern for the sovereignty of the United Kingdom beyond economic arguments:

> A number of fundamental issues . . . will be transferred from national parliament to a rather amorphous group of people whose duties and rights are not specifically defined but who are not publicly accountable . . . It would be the biggest transfer of national sovereignty that we have ever had and I do not think it would be acceptable at all to the British Parliament that we should transfer certain fundamental rights over the Budget, over the Budget Deficit, over economic structure and over monetary policy to another group.[94]

There are no legal limitations on the substance of what can be levelled up to the supranational level in the United Kingdom's uncodified constitution. Thatcher's speech, however, indicates that there are political conceptions of such limits, which included economic and monetary policy.

Wall delineates these political limits: 'a national currency and national decision-making on economic and monetary policy were among the most substantial attributes of sovereignty in the modern world'.[95] This may be contrasted

[91] ibid.
[92] ibid 93.
[93] Delors (n 73) 15.
[94] Margaret Thatcher, 'Press Conference after Madrid European Council' (*Margaret Thatcher Foundation*, 27 June 1989) <www.margaretthatcher.org/document/107711> accessed 27 January 2020.
[95] Wall (n 89) 103.

with the counter-limits on supranationalism proposed by other Member State constitutional actors, such as the German Constitutional Court, in which monetary policy is not afforded such primacy.[96] The United Kingdom's initial resistance was not parochial to the Member State's own nationals. The government expressed its concern generally for the nationals of all of the Member States from the United Kingdom's particular perspective on sovereignty: 'EMU was [regarded as] a vehicle by which the sovereignty which defined the independence of nation-states would be undermined'.[97]

Denmark had participated in the ERM since its inception in 1979. Following a change of government economic policy in 1983, it was an enthusiastic proponent of EMU.[98] The Danish political class and economic system converged towards the predicative requirements of EMU: price stability, liberalization of capital, and the independence of central banks.[99] Marcussen outlines that this 'sound policy strategy' 'became consensually shared and achieved a taken-for-granted quality among the elites within the Danish macroeconomic organizational field'.[100]

Rebecca Adler-Nissen corroborates the susceptibility of the Danish political class towards EMU: 'most of the parties in the Danish Parliament, the various Danish governments and the politico-administrative-economic elite are, at least in principle, favourable to joining the euro . . . Denmark is not the same kind of euro-outsider as the UK'.[101] The reforms to the economic system in the 1980s meant that the Danish executive did not contest the validity of EMU on the basis of economic arguments. Instead, concerns relating to political sovereignty played the key role within Denmark. Two factors distinguish the Danish sovereignty concerns from the United Kingdom. Rather than a particular *formal* conception of absolute Parliamentary Sovereignty, in Denmark the national 'fault line' is a *substantive* conception of the welfare state.[102] Unlike the United Kingdom's absolutist doctrine, 'semi-sovereignty is completely taken-for-granted and accepted praxis in the Danish polity'.[103] However, the Danish welfare state is 'sacred' and was placed in direct contestation with the

[96] *Lisbon*, Judgment of the Second Senate of 30 June 2009, BVerfG, 2 BvE 2/08.
[97] Wall (n 89) 104.
[98] Martin Marcussen, 'EMU: A Danish Delight and Dilemma' in Kenneth Dyson (ed), *European States and the Euro: Europeanization, Variation, and Convergence* (OUP 2002).
[99] ibid.
[100] ibid 123–24.
[101] Adler-Nissen (n 59) 80.
[102] For more on the distinction between UK and Danish conceptions of sovereignty see chapter 2 and Oliver Garner, 'The Borders of European Integration on Trial in the Member States: Dansk Industri, Miller, and Taricco' (2017) 9 European Journal of Legal Studies 1.
[103] Marcussen (n 98) 123.

economic logic of the 'sound policy' paradigm.[104] Marcussen argues that '[t]he sacredness of welfare was . . . a critical point which had somehow to be decoupled from EMU if the euro was to have any chance of being "sold" convincingly to the Danish electorate'.[105] Attempts to either decouple or synthesize the supranational constitutional telos of EMU and the national constitutional significance of the welfare state were attempted in the run-up to the 2000 referendum on adopting the euro.[106]

The second difference between the United Kingdom and Denmark is that the sovereignty concerns were not an executive preference of the Danish government. Resistance manifested itself within the national electorate.[107] Section 20(2) of the Danish Constitution[108] makes the levelling up of constituent power dependent upon a successful referendum if there is no five-sixths parliamentary super-majority.[109] The determination of whether there has been a delegation of powers to international authorities is made by the Danish executive. Although ultimately a popular decision is necessary to transfer sovereignty, the executive retains the discretion to determine that such a constitutional event is in play.[110] At the time of Maastricht, the UK executive had a similar but unfettered discretion whether to submit levelling up to referendum.[111] By virtue of the first-past-the-post voting system, a simple majority of loyal Members of Parliament meant that the executive could secure its preferences. Rebellion may challenge this majority, as was the case for John Major in implementing the domestic legislation on the Treaty of Maastricht.[112]

In Denmark, by contrast, in the absence of a super-majority the decision automatically becomes one for the people: 'The Danish constitution . . . prevented it from making an advance commitment to a single currency'.[113] Maya Sion-Tzidkiyahu makes the dramatic claim that in Denmark the electorate

[104] ibid 136.
[105] ibid 138.
[106] See discussion later in this chapter.
[107] Jens Henrik Haahr, '"Our Danish Democracy": Community, People and Democracy in the Danish Debate on the Common Currency' (2003) 38 Cooperation and Conflict 27.
[108] The Constitutional Act of Denmark of 5 June 1953, s 20.
[109] See further Helle Krunke, 'From Maastricht to Edinburgh: The Danish Solution' (2005) 1 European Constitutional Law Review 339.
[110] ibid. Krunke outlines that in 1986 a decision was made that the Single European Act did not involve a transfer of sovereignty, whereas in 1992 the decision was made that it did.
[111] The Constitutional Reform and Governance Act 2010 and the European Union Act 2011 have subsequently made the transfer of powers to the EU and other bodies subject to 'referendum locks' similar to the Danish constitutional situation.
[112] HC Deb 23 July 1993, vol 229, cols 625–724.
[113] Adler-Nissen (n 59) 80.

functions as a 'veto player' in European integration.[114] This may correspond to an ideal model of levelling up of constituent power as a decision made by individuals *qua* democratic subject without interference from constituted powers.[115] National constitutions which subject Treaty amendments to popular referendums may vindicate 'actual' constituent power more than the Member States in which solely the constituted powers of the state decide on conclusion and ratification. This constitutional fault line would be exposed by the referendum rejecting the ratification of the Treaty of Maastricht. The management of this rejection by the government would inform Denmark's pursuit of an opt-out from EMU.

iii. Area of Freedom, Security and Justice (AFSJ)

The Treaty of Rome to the Treaty of Maastricht has been described as an '"informal" intergovernmental period'[116] for cooperation in the areas that would become the AFSJ. The creation of norms exclusively involved representatives in international law of individuals *qua* nationals, with no norm-creation role for the supranational institutions representing individuals *qua* EU citizens.[117] The source of norms was limited to Conventions binding in international law. For individuals *qua* juridical objects, there was no recourse to the Court of Justice of the European Union: '[a]s for the EU's Court of Justice, there was no interest in giving it jurisdiction to interpret intergovernmental measures, except for those dealing with civil cooperation.'[118] In the absence of democratic subjecthood for individuals *qua* EU citizens, juridical objecthood *qua* EU citizen was also omitted. Norm application occurred exclusively through national courts. Individuals were represented again in 'dualist' systems in the creation of implementing legislation. Before Maastricht, the constitutional consensus was that areas pertinent to Justice and Home Affairs were the exclusive sphere of the constituent states as guarantors of self-determination for nationals. No wholesale levelling up to the supranational level was attempted. The Member State governments exercised their constituent power

[114] Maya Sion-Tzidkiyahu, 'Comparing Opt-Outs: How Different Is Differentiated Integration' in Thomas Giegerich, Desirée C Schmitt and Sebastian Zeitzmann (eds), *Flexibility in the EU and Beyond: How Much Differentiation Can European Integration Bear?* (Hart Publishing; Nomos Verlag 2017).

[115] See the discussion of these principles of levelling up in chapter 2.

[116] For the framework prior to the Maastricht Treaty see Peers (n 47) 7–8.

[117] ibid 7.

[118] ibid.

purely through the traditional means of public international law and national constitutional law. The Treaty of Maastricht substantially reformed this intergovernmentalism.

IV. The Treaty of Maastricht to the Treaty of Amsterdam

i. Schengen

Between the Single European Act and the Treaty of Amsterdam attempts were made to accommodate the international and supranational sources of norms. This has been referred to as 'two divergent processes of integration first outside, and then inside, the EU legal framework'.[119] The Maastricht Treaty created the 'Third Pillar'. This included measures overlapping with the international law Schengen *acquis* such as external border and visa policy. The Third Pillar did not confirm Union competence over internal borders: 'the issue of whether the [European Union] had competence over internal border issues was still open'.[120] The European Parliament brought a legal action against the Commission for failure to act in 1992.[121] This was dropped when the Commission proposed three Directives on border controls. The continuing opposition of the United Kingdom and Ireland to such measures meant that the unanimity requirements for the legislation under ex Article 100 EC were not fulfilled.[122]

Concurrent with the supranational failure, the international Schengen *acquis* deepened and widened after coming into force in 1995.[123] Following the accession of eight new Member States, the autonomous Executive Committee proceeded to adopt 'a wide range of decisions in most of the areas covered by the convention'.[124] The supranational constitutional order was transcended in order to pursue integration goals that were hamstrung by the supranational

[119] ibid 68.
[120] ibid 73.
[121] Order of the Court of 11 July 1996 in Case C-445/93 *European Parliament v Commission* [1996] OJ No C 336/15.
[122] Peers (n 47) 73.
[123] The Schengen *acquis*—Convention implementing the Schengen Agreement of 14 June 1985 between the Governments of the States of the Benelux Economic Union, the Federal Republic of Germany and the French Republic on the gradual abolition of checks at their common borders [2000] OJ L 239/19; Schutte, 'UK v EU' (n 56) 1352.
[124] Wall (n 89) 114.

requirements of unanimity. The two sources of norms would finally be reconciled through the Amsterdam incorporation. The price of constitutional unity would be the reservation of constituent power by the Member States that never accepted the legitimacy of the policy area.

ii. Economic and Monetary Union (EMU)

The final decision by the United Kingdom to retain constituent power in EMU was influenced by the economic concerns of Thatcher's successor as Prime Minister. 'John Major's main preoccupation . . . was with the economic viability. He was particularly concerned about the lack of economic convergence'.[125] The author concludes that 'his reservations were not so much about sovereignty or defence of the pound as about the credibility of trying to move to a single currency without adequate economic convergence'.[126] The 'wait and see' policy of the Major government would establish an equivocal institutional design for the opt-out Protocols. Member States could decide at a later stage to reserve their opt-out and level up constituent power. This policy was influenced by concerns that an *inter se* treaty could be used to exclude the United Kingdom.[127] Yet the UK government did accept this method being used to bring the Social Policy Protocol into force.[128] This discrepancy indicates the perception of the significance of EMU. This interplay in the preferences of the constituent powers explains how the present paradigm of tailored opt-out Protocols came to exist, as opposed to alternative more general exemption procedures akin to enhanced cooperation.

Before the Maastricht negotiation Major set out his arguments against EMU:

> [T]o move to a single currency without the convergence of national economies would be an economic catastrophe. That is why we are negotiating a Treaty which would . . . allow the British Government and the British Parliament to take the decision on whether to join such a single currency when the option is a realistic one.[129]

[125] ibid.
[126] ibid.
[127] ibid 113.
[128] See discussion earlier in this chapter on reversal of opt-outs.
[129] John Major, 'Mr Major's Speech to the Lord Mayor's Banquet – 11 November 1991' (*Sir John Major KG CH*, 11 November 1991) <www.johnmajorarchive.org.uk/1991/mr-majors-speech-to-the-lord-mayors-banquet-11-november-1991/> accessed 20 April 2020.

This presents a vision of the EMU opt-out not as an outright restriction on levelling up of constituent power, but as a deferral of this decision to a time after the Treaty amendment. The need for the opt-out to be enshrined in a legally binding form may be explained by internal constitutional dynamics: 'Parliament would not accept a treaty that provided for automatic moves to EMU provided certain economic conditions were met'.[130] This suggests that guarantees to insulate nationals from the operation of EU legal norms must be provided in the supranational constitutional order rather than just national law. The experience with Schengen, where the United Kingdom could have been subject to infringement proceedings for non-implementation of Article 8a of the Single European Act, may have been instructive.[131] The preferences of the UK executive for clarity in the EMU case also served to promote legal certainty for individuals *qua* judicial objects in the supranational constitutional order.

Major's address to the House of Commons on 20 November 1991 illustrated the balancing between the two constituent roles of individuals:

> A single currency would be the means of safeguarding anti-inflationary policies for the whole of the European community. That would be a great prize . . . the price is that it would take from national governments the control of monetary policy . . . We cannot take that step now, but nor should we exclude it.[132]

This form of temporal disruption prevented the perception of an irreversible fault-line in the supranational constitutional order.[133]

Major warned against the creation of a 'core Europe': 'I think that would be fatal for Europe if we were to go ahead in that fashion . . . because it would be extremely difficult for those countries that did not go ahead in that inner core to subsequently become part of that inner core'.[134] These remarks also addressed the Eastern and Central European candidate states which would become 'Member States with a derogation' regarding EMU. This demonstrates a more general concern beyond the parochial self-interest of the United Kingdom that extends to those with the *potential* to become constituent citizens of the Union.

[130] Wall (n 89) 131.
[131] See discussion of the origins of the Schengen opt-out earlier in the chapter.
[132] HC Deb 20 November 1991, vol 199, col 274.
[133] For the concept of 'temporal differentiation' see Tuytschaever (n 68).
[134] Wall (n 89) 117.

The UK government's resistance to a core Europe at Maastricht arguably preserved the default principle of equality in the application of norms for future citizens of the Union.[135] Non-application to certain Member State nationals was limited to the exceptional scenario of specific opt-out Protocols.

Stephen Wall suggests that the legal form of the opt-out was pre-determined by pre-Intergovernmental Conference negotiations: 'Major argued against an opt-out clause from EMU that was UK-specific. But Mitterrand [President of France] was resistant. He did not want to see Britain isolated but nor did he want to offer a temptation to others to open up the issue in a few years' time.'[136] The United Kingdom's initial proposals were for an opt-out clause that would be generally available to all Member States. This would have avoided a distinction in the application of norms on the basis of nationality being enshrined in the constitutional text. This general form of derogation was rejected on the basis of the centrifugal effects it could have. This would have undermined the telos of the Third Stage of EMU to move beyond voluntary intergovernmental mechanisms such as the ERM towards a macroeconomic policy that was fully constitutionalized within the Union legal order. Ironically, however, this concern for integration set in motion the path of Member State specific disruption rather than the alternative of a general mechanism of derogation.

The EMU opt-out broke from the United Kingdom's policy against a two-speed Europe. Dyson and Featherstone outline that 'the shift was, in significant part, owing to what was seen as the intransigence and isolation of the British position'.[137] A disconnect was growing between the UK government's perspective of the interest of its nationals, and the EU institutional representation of individuals *qua* EU citizens. The terminology of a 'firebreak' on EMU that would be generally available to all Member States before the transition from the Second to the Third stage was replaced by the terminology of a specific opt-out. This was the Rubicon crossed towards safeguarding the capacity for self-determination and self-fulfilment of only UK nationals. The perceived necessity of an opt-out from the national level was consolidated by the position taken at the supranational level:

> Jean-Claude Trichet argued in a French paper to the IGC in April 1991 that the transition to stage 3 should be based on the twin principles of 'no coercion and no veto': no member state could be forced to enter into it, nor could

[135] For arguments regarding the implications of core Europe for EU citizenship see Thym (n 54).

[136] Wall (n 89) 133.

[137] Kenneth Dyson and Kevin Featherstone, *The Road to Maastricht: Negotiating Economic and Monetary Union* (OUP 1999) 652.

any government stop the rest from going ahead. Such principles seemed to underscore the notion of an opt-out.[138]

The UK negotiators presented legal arguments for why a political declaration would be insufficient:

> First, a declaration outside the Treaty would not confer the necessary legal certainty. Secondly, the right of a member state to take a separate decision must be contained within the Treaty. Finally, there was no rule of EC law that Community obligations should necessarily be binding on all states if there were good reasons for not making them so.[139]

These features distinguish disrupted integration from outright breaches of EU law. The argument for legal certainty and clarity ensures that individuals *qua* juridical objects are fully aware of which norms apply to them within the territory of different Member States.

The structure of an intergovernmental conference to enact constitutional change informed the legal nature of the opt-out Protocol. The political brinkmanship of negotiations between heads of state with compromises at the 'thirteenth hour' would condition the legal text that was adopted. 'On the opt-out, the Major government played its cards close to its chest. It [the government] wanted to avoid Britain's [EU] partners dissecting in detail a draft protocol in advance of Maastricht, for fear that it might be undermined'.[140] Wall continues that '[w]hat Britain's partners had not expected was the detailed legal text written up . . . and only tabled when Major judged that it was too late for others to try to rewrite it'.[141] Dyson and Featherstone note that '[t]he implication was that such negotiation was an unexpected intrusion into British affairs. Yet the protocol would be part of a Treaty binding on all: twelve EC states . . . would have to ratify the British protocol'.[142] The nature of intergovernmental negotiations meant that the text of provisions that would have consequences for all individuals *qua* citizens of the Union was not opened up to scrutiny before adoption.

Deirdre Curtin criticizes this paradigm from a constitutional perspective:

[138] ibid 654.
[139] ibid 657.
[140] ibid 655.
[141] Wall (n 89) 136.
[142] Dyson and Featherstone (n 137) 660.

> It is truly extraordinary that the revision of a 'constitutional charter based on the rule of law' takes place behind closed doors in a *diplomatic* conference. Part and parcel of such diplomatic negotiations is the natural desire of *governments* to retain the maximum in the inter-governmental sphere and to avoid parliamentary and judicial control of their activity.[143]

This 'extraordinary' phenomenon is evidence of the tension between the ultimate grounding of the Union in international treaties, and the supranational constitutionalism that these treaties generate.[144] This demonstrates the distance between the reality of European integration and the hypothetical scenario of Habermas' dual-constituent thesis.

The opacity and late date of introduction of the opt-out Protocol undermined throughput legitimacy. The creation of the Protocol did not comply with the principle that such reconstructions of the supranational constitutional order should be based on a discursive exchange of reasons between representatives.[145] None of the executives representing all the other nationals of the Member States were able to influence the legal form of this provision. This undermined the juridical objecthood of these individuals because they would not be able to rely upon norms their representatives had agreed upon within the territory of a constituent Member State.

The constitutional tension between the objectives of EMU and the preservation of the welfare state informed the Danish government's approach to the Maastricht intergovernmental conference. The UK government criticized the Danish approach:

> There was some frustration amongst the British over how the Danish delegation was pursuing the opt-out goal. It was seen as deserting the cause . . . the British felt the Danes were being too lax in the drafting of an opt-out. The Danes were more ready to accept an individual solution.[146]

Adler-Nissen corroborates this account: 'Because the UK essentially fought the battle over the EMU in the early 1990s, Denmark hid behind the UK during the negotiations, and its reluctance passed almost unnoticed'.[147]

[143] Deirdre Curtin, 'The Constitutional Structure of the Union: A Europe of Bits and Pieces' (1993) 30 Common Market Law Review 17, 66.
[144] See further discussion of this tension in the conclusion to this monograph.
[145] See the discussion of the principles of supranational constitutional politics in chapter 2.
[146] Dyson and Featherstone (n 137) 658.
[147] Adler-Nissen (n 59) 80.

This may be explicable on the basis that the Danish executive did not have integral concerns regarding the economic or constitutional feasibility of the Third Stage of EMU. The government did not pursue a strategy of contesting its existence and legitimacy in the same manner as the United Kingdom. Instead, they were cautious about the perception of feasibility and legitimacy amongst the nationals whom they represented. These concerns came to fruition in the negative referendum result in 1992 against the Treaty. The attempts to assuage the electorate through the creation of an opt-out Protocol failed. Following the rejection, the Danish executive and legislature were compelled to frame the opt-outs in a manner that would persuade the electorate to accept the Treaty.

The Danish convergence with the economic telos of EMU means that the crucial question is not why the Member State contested the policy. Instead, the issue is why the immediate triggering of the opt-out Protocol was proposed as a means to appease the electorate. The Danish executive found itself in a similar position to the UK electorate after the Brexit referendum in 2016.[148] The constituted powers' position on European integration clashed with an expression of popular sovereign will. Whereas in the United Kingdom's case a renegotiation was pursued before the referendum, in the Danish case the renegotiation was pursued afterwards. This reflects a qualitative difference between a referendum on the ratification of a Treaty, which may lead to withdrawal if the conflict is not resolved, and a referendum on membership *per se*.

The phenomenological connection between opt-outs and withdrawal was evident after the Danish rejection of Maastricht. The failure to ratify the Treaty could have led to *de facto* withdrawal. Stephen Wall notes the sentiment amongst the other Member State executives that 'this was a good opportunity for the rest of the EC to "let the Danes go"'.[149] The Danish executive contemplated this eventuality: '[t]he Danes themselves seemed all too ready to contemplate just such an outcome, not because it was what their government wanted, but because they felt the breath of some of the larger member states aggressively hot on their necks'.[150]

Deirdre Curtin indicates the potential legal form of such a *de facto* withdrawal in the pre-Article 50 era: 'a frightening crescendo of voices was to be heard stressing the applicability of general principles of international law to the Communities and the ability of the . . . "group of 11" to withdraw from the European Communities en masse, leaving their erstwhile Danish partner'.[151]

[148] See discussion in chapter 6 of the Brexit narrative of disintegration.
[149] Wall (n 89) 139.
[150] ibid.
[151] Curtin (n 143) 67–68.

The Danish political establishment managed to avoid this withdrawal scenario through the conclusion of the 'Edinburgh Agreement'.[152] This followed the domestic process of establishing a 'people's compromise', which mandated the holding of a second referendum on Maastricht.

Krunke outlines that, following the referendum defeat, the Danish government and Parliament had to 'interpret' the outcome of the referendum.[153] They chose to interpret it as a general expression of concerns regarding the transfer of sovereign authority to the European Union: '[t]he Danish "no" to European Union on 2 June 1992 reflected the fact that the majority of Danes do not want a United States of Europe. It was not . . . a "no" to . . . membership'.[154] Krunke corroborates this through national polling: '[m]any voters were concerned about ceding sovereignty and creating "The United States of Europe" and about specific political areas, about European Citizenship, the common defence policy, a European currency and the social dimension'.[155] The national compromise and Edinburgh Declaration were the Danish government's attempts to re-address this balance. This provides the clearest example of opt-outs resulting from the direct reconstruction of the conditions for the levelling up of constituent power by nationals of a Member State.

The Edinburgh Agreement triggered the EMU opt-out by Denmark, in addition to the creation of further Protocols containing norm-specific declarations on EU citizenship and second homes. The national compromise went beyond the eventual 'exceptions' and included general declarations on democracy, openness, and transparency.[156] These arguments were relevant to all individuals *qua* EU citizens rather than simply Danish nationals. They may have been attempts to shape the general reconstruction of the supranational constitutional order. However, the outcome remained specific to the situation of Denmark. With regard to EMU, the relevant declaration was that 'Denmark . . . will not participate in the third stage of Economic and Monetary Union'.[157]

Despite some debate over whether the Edinburgh Agreement functioned as a ratification reservation, Annex 1 refers to a 'decision of the Heads of State and Government, meeting within the European Council'.[158] The Agreement was registered by the United Nations, and the Danish government's own position was that the Decision was binding under international law.[159] The exceptions

[152] Denmark and the Treaty on European Union [1992] OJ C 348/1.
[153] Krunke (n 109) 341.
[154] ibid.
[155] ibid 341–42.
[156] ibid 343.
[157] Denmark and the Treaty on European Union [1992] OJ C 348/1, 2.
[158] ibid.
[159] Krunke (n 109) 350.

relating to the AFSJ and Common Security and Defence Policy were eventually incorporated into the Protocols to the Amsterdam Treaty, extinguishing the Agreement as a live legal instrument.[160] The use of international law to 'pre-bind' the EU's constitutional legislators indicated how the Member States can utilize their external sovereignty to direct the supranational constituent process. The Edinburgh Agreement set a precedent in form and substance for the United Kingdom's attempts to renegotiate its own membership in 2016.

Denmark triggered the EMU opt-out Protocol once the Maastricht Treaty was ratified following a successful second referendum. Krunke argues that 'a new referendum was not necessary (and might legally even be not possible)'[161] because the five-sixths parliamentary majority had now been achieved. The reservation of constituent power has had a transformative effect upon the national constitutional order. The conditions for the creation and revocation of opt-outs are autonomous from the general conditions for transfers of sovereignty. The constitutional mutation manifested itself in a referendum lock as a condition to revoke any of the four exceptions. This applied in Denmark's 2015 referendum on Protocol (No 22) on the AFSJ.[162] The lock also applied to the exceptions that did not entail a transfer of sovereignty under Section 20 of the Constitution.

Henning Koch argues that such mutations are constitutionally justified on the basis of a 'constitutional convention taking form, according to which referendums on transferring sovereignty to the European Union can take place even though five-sixths of parliament support it'.[163] An analogy may be drawn to Vernon Bogdanor's argument that there is an informal constitutional convention in the United Kingdom to hold referendums on major constitutional issues.[164] Bogdanor argued that a referendum should have been necessary at the time of Maastricht due to the transfer of powers from Westminster: 'MPs are entrusted by the electorate with legislative power, but they are given no authority to transfer that power. That authority requires a specific mandate from the people'.[165] In Denmark, the constitutional convention displaced the

[160] See discussion of this moment later in the chapter.

[161] Krunke (n 109) 345.

[162] See discussion of the referendum later in this chapter.

[163] Henning Koch, 'Grundlovsstridige EU-Folkeafstemninger (Unconstitutional EU Referenda)' in Henning Koch (ed), *Politik og jura. Festskrift til Ole Espersen* (Forlaget Thomson 2004) 520; Krunke (n 109) 351.

[164] Vernon Bogdanor, 'After the Referendum, the People, Not Parliament, Are Sovereign' *Financial Times* (London, FT Weekend 10 December 2016) 14.

[165] Vernon Bogdanor, 'Why the People Should Have a Vote on Maastricht: The House of Lords Must Uphold Democracy and Insist on a Referendum, Says Vernon Bogdanor' (*The Independent*, 8 June 1993) <www.independent.co.uk/voices/why-the-people-should-have-a-vote-on-maastricht-the-house-of-lords-must-uphold-democracy-and-insist-1490346.html> accessed 21 April 2020.

permissions for the constituted powers under Section 20. The Danish parliament agreed not to enact a Bill with a majority of five-sixths to ratify the Maastricht Treaty. Constitutional transformation has also been evident in the increased parliamentary scrutiny of European integration, further empowering the constituent subject of national of Denmark.[166]

iii. Area of Freedom, Security and Justice (AFSJ)

The Maastricht amendment established nine items pertinent to Justice and Home Affairs in the 'Third Pillar' of the Treaty on European Union.[167] Curtin describes this as 'a grafting technique [that] was preferred over a technique of absorption or expansion'.[168] Peers argues that the convoluted structure was a 'compromise agreement whereby certain aspects of visa policy were included within the EC Treaty, but all other measures remained subject to the intergovernmental system established by the Maastricht Treaty'.[169] The rationale for the 'Pillars' metaphor derives from the different rules for the adoption and application of legal norms. These rules were distinguished as the 'community method' and the 'intergovernmental method'. The former is supranational constitutionalism with its commitment to equality between nationals of the Member States and citizens of the Union. The latter emphasizes unanimity between the High Contracting Parties as sovereign equals. The compromise set in motion the eventual reservation of constituent power as Justice and Home Affairs norms were converted from intergovernmentalism at Maastricht to full supranational constitutionalism at Lisbon.

Peers identifies the distinctions between the First and Third Pillars.[170] The supranational institutions were diminished in the Third Pillar: '[it] largely use[d] the Council as an instrument of intergovernmental cooperation and pass[ed] over in silence the role of the Commission (as initiator) and the European Parliament'.[171] A specialized 'Coordinating Committee' was established exclusively for the Third Pillar. The use of a Union legislative institution as an 'instrument' is evocative of the manner in which *inter se* international law

[166] Krunke (n 109) 353.
[167] Hans Ulrich Jessurun d'Oliveira, 'Expanding External and Shrinking Internal Borders: Europe's Defence Mechanisms in the Area of Free Movement, Immigration and Asylum' in David O'Keeffe and Patrick M Twomey (eds), *Legal Issues of the Maastricht Treaty* (John Wiley & Sons 1994) 261–62.
[168] Curtin (n 143) 23.
[169] Peers (n 47) 7.
[170] ibid 5.
[171] Curtin (n 143) 28.

agreements have similarly appropriated the institutions.[172] The Member States as constituent powers in international law utilized supranational institutions without vindicating the dual representation of individuals. Curtin illustrates the normative problems of intergovernmentalism for democratic subjecthood and juridical objecthood: 'the result [is] that parliamentary and judicial control is extremely minimal'.[173]

Peers' second distinction concerns the Court of Justice: 'the third pillar provided for special rules which significantly restricted the Court's jurisdiction'.[174] Curtin clarified at the time that 'the only possibility is that conventions . . . may stipulate *express jurisdiction* for the Court of Justice to interpret their provisions and to rule on any disputes'.[175] The Third Pillar restricted the Court of Justice to the role of an international arbiter with *ad hoc* jurisdiction mandated by the State parties. This predicated the Court's vindication of individuals' juridical objecthood *qua* EU citizens upon the will of the Member States. Establishment of the Court of Justice's supranational jurisdiction in the AFSJ after the Treaty of Lisbon became the driver and legal condition for the creation and activation of the United Kingdom's opt-out under Protocol (No 36).[176]

The final two distinctions also relate to norm application. The First Pillar used the orthodox Directives, Regulations, and Decisions whereby EU secondary law takes effect today. In contrast, 'third pillar law used different instruments, although those instruments changed with the adoption of the Treaty of Amsterdam'.[177] Before the Treaty of Lisbon, primacy, direct effect, the interpretative obligation for Directives, and remedies applied only to norms created under the First Pillar. Third Pillar norms were not imbued with the specific characteristics that determine the EU's juridical constitutional identity.[178] One may argue that these norms were not incorporated fully within the supranational constitutional order but instead were peripheral cases of EU law. The amendments between Maastricht and Lisbon would seek to eliminate these divergences progressively.

The Three Pillar structure meant that, before the Treaty of Lisbon, it may be argued that the European Union did not represent a complete levelling up of constituent power. Hans Ulrich Jessurun d'Oliveira captures this in his

[172] See De Witte, 'Old-Fashioned Flexibility' (n 53); De Witte, 'Variable Geometry and Differentiation' (n 55).
[173] Curtin (n 143) 25.
[174] Peers (n 47) 6.
[175] Curtin (n 143) 29 (emphasis in the original).
[176] See discussion of the post-Lisbon period later in this chapter.
[177] Peers (n 47) 6.
[178] See Tuori, 'Crossing the Limits but Stuck behind the Fault Lines?' (2016) 7 Transnational Legal Theory 133, and the discussion in chapter 2 on constitutional identity.

description of the Third Pillar as 'co-operation among the Member States . . . inside the Union, but outside the European Community'.[179] This cooperation is a partial form of levelling up beyond international law but beneath the threshold of full incorporation of legislative and judicial power into the supranational constitutional structure. Resistance from the representatives of the United Kingdom, Denmark, and Ireland to complete levelling up of constituent power in this area was the key driver for opt-outs at Amsterdam. This is a specific form of the 'incorporation' origin of opt-outs. Rather than resistance to the incorporation of international law norms into Union law, Member States resist the levelling up of constituent power from a partial intergovernmental form into a complete supranational form.

The shift to constitutionalize Justice and Home Affairs measures into the First Pillar was envisaged at the time of Maastricht: 'Article K.9 . . . explicitly contemplates, albeit under very strict conditions, the transfer of certain matters relating to justice and home affairs from the third pillar to Article 100c of the Treaty establishing a European Community'.[180] The recalcitrant Member States did consent to the mechanisms which would enable further supranational constitutionalism. The legal and normative justifications for such a move were elucidated early:

> [I]t is difficult to avoid the view, given the extent to which the system is liable to generate legal rights and duties (and their importance to individuals in terms of human rights) as well as the impact which they will have on clearly EC matters, that they should have been properly integrated into the EC system.[181]

This critique that Justice and Home Affairs should have been incorporated in the First Pillar due to the rights of individuals *qua* judicial objects was a forerunner to contemporary critiques that Member States should not opt out from the AFSJ.[182] The connecting predicate of these critiques is that in an area of vital importance for the pursuit of self-fulfilment of individuals, a central tenet of the EU constitutional order's telos to pursue 'ever closer Union', institutional and normative unity and coherence should be prioritized over pragmatic differentiation to enable vetoes on integration to be overcome.

[179] Jessurun d'Oliveira (n 167) 261.
[180] Peers (n 47) 6.
[181] Curtin (n 143) 26.
[182] Nadine El-Enany, 'The Perils of Differentiated Integration in the Field of Asylum' in Bruno De Witte, Andrea Ott and Ellen Vos (eds), *Between Flexibility and Disintegration* (Edward Elgar Publishing 2017).

V. The Treaty of Amsterdam to the Treaty of Lisbon

i. Schengen

The Treaty of Amsterdam, concluded in 1997 and entering into force on 1 May 1999, fully incorporated the Schengen *acquis* within the supranational constitutional order.[183] The relevant issues are why Schengen was incorporated, why Ireland and the United Kingdom chose to create opt-out Protocols, and why Denmark elected for international law implementation. A further issue is why separate Protocols for Schengen and the AFSJ were created.[184] The constitutional inclusion of Schengen at Amsterdam necessitated the exclusion of the recalcitrant Member States. Georgia Papagianni states that the opt-out Protocols are 'the price to pay for the decision taken by the Heads of State and Government at Amsterdam in order to proceed with the ambition of the project of the "area without internal frontiers"'.[185]

Reform of the Third Pillar was an early topic of debate leading up to the Amsterdam Intergovernmental Conference. The provisions introduced in the Treaty of Maastricht were perceived to be weak.[186] The decision to incorporate the Schengen *acquis* was informed by the 'interdependence between the objective of the elimination of border controls on persons and certain matters covered by the old "Third Pillar" [which] made its partial "communitarisation" . . . indispensable'.[187] Martin Hedemann-Robinson claims that the explicit purpose of enshrining the concept of 'freedom, security and justice' in the Treaties was to provide a 'vehicle for incorporating the body of agreements and measures on immigration and security issues established under the Schengen accords'.[188]

[183] Treaty of Amsterdam amending the Treaty on European Union, the Treaties establishing the European Communities and certain related acts [1997] OJ C 340/1.
[184] See discussion on the Amsterdam Treaty later in this chapter.
[185] Georgia Papagianni, 'Flexibility in Justice and Home Affairs: An Old Phenomenon Taking New Forms' in Bruno De Witte, Dominik Hanf and Ellen Vos (eds), *The Many Faces of Differentiation in EU Law* (Intersentia 2001) 111.
[186] Jörg Monar, 'Justice and Home Affairs in the Treaty of Amsterdam: Reform at the Price of Fragmentation' (1998) 4 European Law Review 320, 321.
[187] Papagianni (n 185) 111.
[188] Martin Hedemann-Robinson, 'The Area of Freedom, Security and Justice with Regard to the UK, Ireland and Denmark: The "Opt-in Opt-Outs" under the Treaty of Amsterdam' in David O'Keefe and Patrick Twomey (eds), *Legal Issues of the Amsterdam Treaty* (Hart Publishing 2000).

The article by a Union official published under the pseudonym 'Helmut Kortenberg' provides an insight into the reasons for the incorporation of Schengen during the opaque negotiations.[189] Kortenberg argues that

> [i]f such a solution had not been found, there was a serious risk of further instances of cooperation along the Schengen model, outside the framework of the Community treaties . . . if these examples of cooperation became numerous, there was a risk that a schism would progressively emerge in the Community, with competition from instances of intergovernmental cooperation developing outside the common institutional framework.[190]

By incorporating Schengen, the executive Masters of the Treaty sought to preserve the integrity of the supranational constitutional order through an 'ordering' of external norms. The substantive telos was the elimination of border controls for individuals, and structurally the objective was to prevent such norms proliferating outside the supranational structures for norm creation and application. Incorporation may be regarded as an action by the constituent powers to preserve the coherence between the quadripartite roles of individuals.

The United Kingdom, Ireland, and Denmark's decisions to opt out may be regarded as a rejection of these objectives. The United Kingdom and Ireland rejected the substantive telos of Schengen, whereas Denmark rejected the process of supranational constitutionalism: '[f]or the United Kingdom, and for Ireland on account of its special links with the United Kingdom, the essential point was to preserve the existence of controls at borders with other Member States. For Denmark, the question was more the avoidance of any new transfer of competences'.[191] The United Kingdom attempted to justify its retention of constituent power by reference to the Declaration affixed to the Single European Act: '[n]othing in these provisions shall affect the right of Member States to take such measures as they consider necessary for the purpose of controlling immigration from third countries'.[192] This declaration is analogous to Protocol (No 30) on the Charter of Fundamental Rights,[193] and may be regarded as a progenitor to Protocols as the mechanism to retain constituent power.

[189] Helmut Kortenberg, 'Closer Cooperation in the Treaty of Amsterdam' (1998) 35 Common Market Law Review 833.

[190] ibid 835.

[191] ibid 836.

[192] General Declaration on Articles 13 to 19 of the Single European Act [1987] OJ L 169/25.

[193] See discussion on the legal status of the Charter 'opt-outs' in the introduction to the chapter above.

There is a consensus that Ireland was effectively compelled to follow the same position as the United Kingdom with regard to border controls. This idea has been expressed most provocatively in Maya Sion-Tzidkiyahu's claim that Ireland's 'veto player' in negotiations was the United Kingdom itself.[194] Similarly, Cyprus has an informal derogation from Schengen because it could not fulfil the obligations to remove frontier controls due to the occupation of its Northern territory.[195] The Common Travel Area is a series of unilateral domestic law provisions which removes border controls for Irish citizens entering the United Kingdom and vice versa.[196] This would be undermined if Ireland removed frontier controls through applying Schengen norms. Following the conclusion of the Good Friday agreement in 1998, this was reinforced by the requirement to ensure no hard border controls between Northern Ireland and the Republic of Ireland.[197] This would emerge as one of the defining issues of the United Kingdom's withdrawal settlement.[198]

The Irish executive made the decision at Amsterdam that ensuring coherence with the United Kingdom's regime of border controls was more important than coherence with the supranational regime. The burdens of passports controls for all individuals *qua* EU citizens were justified by the preservation of peace and security for individuals *qua* nationals of Ireland. The same logic has driven the creation of the Protocol on Ireland/Northern Ireland following the United Kingdom's withdrawal, but with the opposite effects.[199] As the United Kingdom and Ireland did not have opt-outs from customs and internal market norms, the former has been compelled to apply EU law norms in Northern Ireland. Ireland's Schengen and AFSJ opt-outs may be justified on the basis of objective circumstances rather than subjective preferences. This may inform considerations for a model of reform for opt-outs.[200]

Denmark's own 'opt-out' from Schengen was informed not by disagreement with the substance of norms on the abolition of border controls. Instead, the executive contested the supranational form pursued to achieve these aims. Conversely to Ireland opting out to preserve the Common Travel Area, Denmark signed the Schengen Convention in 1996 to preserve the Nordic Passport Union upon the accession of Sweden and Finland to the European

194 Sion-Tzidkiyahu (n 114).

195 ibid.

196 Terry McGuinness and Melanie Gower, 'The Common Travel Area and the Special Status of Irish Nationals in UK Law' (House of Commons Library Briefing Paper No 7661, 9 June 2017).

197 'The Belfast Agreement' (*GOV.UK*, 10 April 1998) <www.gov.uk/government/publications/the-belfast-agreement> accessed 17 April 2020.

198 See discussion in chapter 6.

199 See discussion in chapter 6 on the post-withdrawal fallout.

200 See discussion in chapter 8.

Union.[201] This vindicated nationals *qua* juridical objects by continuing free movement between the territories of these states. Kortenberg argues that '[t]he transfer of competences . . . under the Treaty of Amsterdam . . . was . . . not acceptable, but Denmark did not wish to obstruct such a transfer providing it could be exempted'.[202] He claims that 'Denmark—recalling the difficulties it experienced during the ratification of the Treaty on European Union—simply tried to arm itself against any transfer of competences'.[203]

This accords with Sion-Tzidkiyahu's claim that in Denmark the 'veto player' against levelling up constituent power is the population who voted against Maastricht,[204] and the Eurosceptic parties in Parliament who are able to block the five-sixths majority under Section 20 of the Constitution.[205] The Danish government's policy towards Schengen at Amsterdam was directly influenced by the complications with the levelling up of constituent power experienced at the Maastricht reconstruction. This demonstrates how a pathway dependence of reserved constituent power can develop within a Member State and spill over across constitutional sectors.

Denmark sought to continue its incorporation of the Schengen *acquis* through national and international law methods.[206] The Danish government were subject to a 'volley of unbridled criticism . . . on account of their outright rejection of Community [Union] law and method'.[207] The European Policy Centre clearly articulates this criticism: 'the normal [Union] articles on judicial control will not apply [to Denmark], which represents a serious and unprecedented encroachment on the integrity of the [Union] legal order'.[208] Denmark prioritized the role of its nationals *qua* democratic subjects to the exclusion of all other EU citizens *qua* democratic subjects. Individuals *qua* juridical objects are able to rely on the same norms to avoid border controls when entering Denmark. However, they are unable to vindicate any legal claims before the Court of Justice. The peculiar phenomenon of a Member State exempting itself from supranationalism arises specifically from the incorporation form of opt-out origins. This enables the Member State to retain the previously authoritative international law source of legitimation.

201 Adler-Nissen (n 59) 118.
202 Kortenberg (n 189) 839.
203 ibid 840.
204 See discussion of the Maastricht Treaty and Denmark's opt-outs above.
205 Sion-Tzidkiyahu (n 114).
206 See chapter 3 for explanation of the legal nature of Denmark's opt-outs.
207 Hedemann-Robinson (n 188) 300.
208 European Policy Centre, 'Making Sense of the Treaty of Amsterdam' (1997) para 182.

A final question concerns why separate opt-out Protocols were created for Schengen and the AFSJ in light of the substantive overlap between the two sectors. The ostensible reason is that the Member States chose to use a Protocol attached to the Treaties as the means to incorporate the Schengen norms.[209] Article 1 stated that the contracting parties 'shall be authorised to establish closer cooperation among themselves in areas covered by provisions defined by the Council which constitute the Schengen *acquis*.'[210] This Protocol is connected to the legal bases of the Treaties: '[p]roposals and initiative to build upon the Schengen *acquis* shall be subject to the relevant provisions of the Treaties.'[211] Article 4 delineates the means for participation by Ireland and the United Kingdom in the application of the *acquis*, and Article 5 provides the means for participation by the opt-out Member States in the implementation of the *acquis* through the adoption of further measures.[212] Certain academic commentators have argued that this incorporation was the first usage of the enhanced cooperation mechanism.[213] The Court of Justice has stated that 'Article 4 of the Schengen Protocol ... applies in lieu of Article 331 TFEU within the framework of enhanced cooperation in ... the Schengen *acquis*.'[214] Despite the reference to 'closer cooperation' and the familial resemblance in functioning, the Schengen Protocol is a *sui generis* constitutional mechanism separate from the conditions established by Article 20 TEU.

The Schengen Protocol mandates an endogenous procedure for opt-outs. The Protocol is the vehicle for the validity of both the legal norms and the norms that enable the derogation and iterative opt-ins.[215] By contrast, the AFSJ Protocols are exogenous means to create opt-outs and flexible opt-ins as they pertain to provisions in the main body of the Treaty.[216] Kortenberg

[209] TEU and TFEU, Protocol (No 19) on the Schengen *acquis* integrated into the framework of the European Union.
[210] ibid art 1.
[211] ibid art 5.
[212] ibid arts 4 and 5.
[213] See Thym (n 54) 39; Sebastian Zeitzmann, 'A Rather Strange Animal, This "Enhanced Cooperation"—May It Serve as King of the European Zoonion? Or: Is Enhanced Cooperation Anywhere Near a Constitutional Principle?' in Thomas Giegerich, Desirée C Schmitt and Sebastian Zeitzmann (eds), *Flexibility in the EU and Beyond: How Much Differentiation Can European Integration Bear?* (Hart Publishing/Nomos Verlag 2017) 101 (albeit qualified as 'bogus enhanced co-operation'); Pascale Joannin, 'Elements of Differentiation Within the Schengen Acquis and the Prüm Convention' in Thomas Giegerich, Desirée C Schmitt and Sebastian Zeitzmann (eds), *Flexibility in the EU and Beyond: How Much Differentiation Can European Integration Bear?* (Nomos/Hart 2017) 127.
[214] Case C-44/14 *Spain v European Parliament and Council*, EU:C:2015:554, para 49.
[215] Protocol (No 19) on the Schengen *acquis* integrated into the framework of the European Union, arts 3–4. For detailed analysis of the functioning of these provisions see chapter 3 above.
[216] Specifically, the norms contained in what is now Title V TFEU. See chapter 3 for the legal nature of these Protocols.

emphasizes that this fragmented structure arose from a lack of coordination in the negotiations on the AFSJ Title, the Schengen Protocol, and the AFSJ opt-out Protocols.[217] This was exacerbated by the latter's creation at the end of negotiations.[218] Kortenberg's suggestion to 'straighten things out by harmonizing these regimes on the occasion of a future intergovernmental conference'[219] would go unheeded.

After Amsterdam, the Union institutions and the opt-out Member States clashed over the limits of opting in to Schengen norms without accepting the core obligation to remove internal border controls. The Council adopted two decisions on 20 May 1999 determining the legal basis for each of the provisions that constituted the Schengen *acquis*.[220] The United Kingdom immediately requested to participate in certain measures relating to judicial cooperation in criminal matters, narcotics, and the Schengen Information System.[221] Ireland made its request on 16 June 2000 following the Council's approval of the United Kingdom's participation.[222] The Council authorized the United Kingdom's participation in the requested measures on 29 May 2000 and declared that the United Kingdom 'shall be deemed irrevocably to have notified . . . that it wishes to take part in all proposals and initiatives which build upon the Schengen acquis' in relation to the measures.[223]

In the preamble to the Decision, the Council emphasized the imperative significance of maintaining the coherence of the policy area: '[w]hereas it is the view of the Council that any partial participation by the United Kingdom in the Schengen acquis must respect the coherence of the subject areas which constitute the ensemble of this acquis'.[224] The Council protects the integrity

[217] Kortenberg (n 189) 843.

[218] See further detail on the conclusion of this Treaty amendment later in the chapter.

[219] Kortenberg (n 189) 843.

[220] Council Decision 1999/435/EC of 20 May 1999 concerning the definition of the Schengen *acquis* for the purpose of determining, in conformity with the relevant provisions of the Treaty establishing the European Community and the Treaty on European Union, the legal basis for each of the provisions or decisions which constitute the *acquis* [1999] OJ L 176/1; Council Decision 1999/436/EC of 20 May 1999 determining, in conformity with the relevant provisions of the Treaty establishing the European Community and the Treaty on European Union, the legal basis for each of the provisions or decisions which constitute the Schengen *acquis* [1999] OJ L 176/17.

[221] Commission opinion on the request by the United Kingdom to take part in certain provisions of the Schengen *acquis* [1999] IP/99/550.

[222] Commission opinion on the request by Ireland to take part in some of the provisions of the Schengen *acquis* SEC/2000/1439 final.

[223] Council Decision 2000/365/EC of 29 May 2000 concerning the request of the United Kingdom of Great Britain and Northern Ireland to take part in some of the provisions of the Schengen *acquis* [2000] OJ L 131/43, art 8(2).

[224] Council Decision 2000/365/EC of 29 May 2000 concerning the request of the United Kingdom of Great Britain and Northern Ireland to take part in some of the provisions of the Schengen *acquis* [2000] OJ L 131/43; see discussion in Joannin (n 213) 130–31.

of the supranational constitutional order in its policy towards iterative opt-ins. In the constitutional sectors with uniform application of norms, the role of ensuring coherence and integrity is left to the norm-applying judicial institutions. The Council and Parliament as the co-legislature focus on the policy goals embodied in the creation of norms. Within the Schengen *acquis* and the AFSJ, this coherence insurance function is transferred in the first instance to the Council. Because two of the opt-out Member States were able to choose which norms they wish to apply, the institutional body which mandates this participation must ensure that the holistic integrity of the constitutional order is not undermined.

Disagreements over the opt-out Protocols in the Council can spill over into litigation once the norm-application process commences.[225] The 2007 *UK v Council* case determined that the United Kingdom and Ireland could not participate in the Regulation establishing the FRONTEX border management agency because the Member States did not implement prior measures on removing border controls.[226] The unanimity requirement to enable *de novo* participation by the opt-out Member States would be 'deprived of all effectiveness' if the United Kingdom and Ireland could participate in proposals building upon the Schengen *acquis* even though they had not accepted the relevant provisions or had not been authorized to participate.[227] The Court of Justice preserved the democratic subjecthood of the Council in preserving the integrity of the supranational constitutional order through its decisions to authorize or reject participation by the opt-out Member States.

Kortenberg predicted the *UK v Council* case in 2010.[228] He argued that '[t]he difficulty of distinguishing in the longer term between measures arising from [the AFSJ legal bases], and from the further development of the Schengen *acquis* may be a source of disputes since the legal arrangements are different'.[229] The United Kingdom and Ireland disagreed with the Council over whether a 2008 Decision on consultation of the Visa Information System for the purpose of counter-terrorism fell within Schengen legal bases or the AFSJ legal bases on police cooperation.[230] The Member States participated in the latter but not the former. The Court of Justice found that the Decision must be classified

[225] Case C-77/05 *United Kingdom v Council* [2007] ECR I-11459; Case C-482/08 *United Kingdom v Council* [2010] ECR I-10413.
[226] Case C-77/05 *United Kingdom v Council* (n 225) para 62.
[227] ibid para 67.
[228] Case C-482/08 *United Kingdom v Council* (n 225).
[229] Kortenberg (n 189) 843.
[230] Case C-482/08 *United Kingdom v Council* (n 225) paras 31–41.

as a measure falling within the area of the Schengen *acquis* concerning the common visa policy.[231] A Member State cannot participate in a norm developing the Schengen *acquis* without first adopting the foundational measure, and it cannot circumvent this requirement by citing an AFSJ legal base.[232]

Alberto Miglio argues that the Court of Justice 'aimed to limit fragmentation and to provide an incentive for Ireland and the United Kingdom to join the whole of the Schengen *acquis*'.[233] This is corroborated by the Court's dicta that 'the Schengen Protocol . . . seeks to ensure the maximum participation of all Member States in the Schengen acquis'.[234] The Court of Justice defines and guards the formal limits of the opt-out Protocols. The judicial institution ensures that the reservation of constituent power is properly translated into the functioning of the juridical order. This preserves legal certainty for individuals *qua* juridical objects. This litigation eventually generated attempts to reconstruct the Schengen Protocol during the Lisbon negotiations.[235]

ii. Economic and Monetary Union (EMU)

The UK government triggered its option not to proceed to the Third Stage of EMU after the Maastricht renegotiation. This temporal development is enshrined in the text of the opt-out Protocol: '[g]iven that on 16 October 1996 and 30 October 1997 the UK government notified the Council of its intention not to participate in the third stage of economic and monetary union'.[236] Both Denmark and the United Kingdom grappled with the question of whether to reverse their EMU opt-outs. The 'prepare and decide' policy of the Blair government and the Chancellor Gordon Brown's five economic tests represented a continuation of the economic concerns of the Major era. These factors shaped the political discourse on whether or not to hold a referendum on joining the single currency.[237] The practice of the Labour government of promising

[231] ibid para 57.

[232] ibid para 61.

[233] Alberto Miglio, 'Schengen, Differentiated Integration and Cooperation with the "Outs"' (2016) 1 European Papers 139, 142.

[234] Case C-77/05 *United Kingdom v Council* (n 225) para 67.

[235] See discussion of the Lisbon Treaty later in the chapter.

[236] TEU and TFEU, Protocol (No 15) on certain provisions relating to the United Kingdom of Great Britain and Northern Ireland.

[237] Stuart Smedley, 'A Missed Opportunity? Revisiting the Euro Referendum That Never Was from a Historical Perspective' (*LSE Brexit*, 3 December 2019) <https://blogs.lse.ac.uk/brexit/2019/12/03/a-missed-opportunity-revisiting-the-euro-referendum-that-never-was-from-a-historical-perspective/> accessed 7 April 2020.

a referendum recognized an informal constitutional convention.[238] Denmark held its own unsuccessful referendum on reversing the EMU opt-out in 2000.[239] This may indicate convergence between the opt-out Member States on the legitimate process for reversing all opt-outs. However, this preconception is challenged by the United Kingdom's reversal of the opt-out on Social Policy during the Treaty of Amsterdam negotiations without a popular vote.[240]

The UK executive's prerogative to notify the Council of its intention to adopt the euro was made conditional upon the Chancellor's five economic tests.[241] These tests were 'first, whether there can be sustainable convergence between Britain and the economies of a single currency; secondly, whether there is sufficient flexibility to cope with economic change; thirdly, the effect on investment; fourthly, the impact on our financial services generally; and fifthly, whether it is good for employment'.[242] Andrew Geddes asserts that these economic tests are an indication that the UK executive's contestation of EMU was based upon economic factors rather than constitutional factors: 'there were no constitutional impediments to membership, although a referendum would be required. Brown grounded the case in pragmatic terms: '[i]f a single currency would be good for British jobs, British business, and future prosperity, it is right in principle to join. The constitutional issue is a factor in the decision, but it is not an overriding one'.[243]

Geddes argues that fulfilment of the tests was not insulated from executive preferences:

> The government claimed that any decision to join would be on an economic basis, rather than a political one. In fact, the politics cannot easily be detached from the economics, especially when the 'five economic tests' adopted by Gordon Brown in order to assess British membership allowed a significant margin for interpretation.[244]

[238] Gabriele Ruberto, 'When Does the British Constitution Require a Referendum? V. Bogdanor's Opinion on the Place for the Referendum in the UK' (*The Constitution Unit Blog*, 26 February 2013) <https://constitution-unit.com/2013/02/26/when-does-the-british-constitution-require-a-referendum-v-bogdanors-opinion-on-the-place-for-the-referendum-in-the-uk/> accessed 21 April 2020.
[239] Anders Ravn Sørensen, 'The Danish Euro: Constructing a Monetary Oxymoron in the Danish Euro Debate' (2014) 16 National Identities 31.
[240] TEU and TFEU, Protocol (No 15) on certain provisions relating to the United Kingdom of Great Britain and Northern Ireland.
[241] Ed Potton and Adam Mellows-Facer, 'The Euro: Background to the Five Economic Tests' (House of Commons Library Research Paper 03/53, 4 June 2003)
[242] HC Deb 27 October 1997, vol 299, cols 583–84.
[243] Andrew Geddes, *Britain and the European Union* (Palgrave 2013) 184.
[244] ibid.

The executive retained control through its subjective assessment of the best interests of individuals *qua* juridical objects of economic and monetary policy. The promise of a referendum meant that ostensibly the ultimate decision would be taken by individuals *qua* democratic subjects.

The substantive conditions for a referendum on EMU contrasts with the 2016 referendum on withdrawal. The latter referendum was not predicated upon the fulfilment of any substantive conditions.[245] The 'review of the balance of competences' across all departments of government could have provided conditions analogous to the five economic tests.[246] This discrepancy may indicate that successive UK governments have believed that UK nationals as more likely to revoke their status as EU citizens than strengthen it through adopting the single currency.

The Danish executive actively sought to persuade the electorate to participate in EMU. After the United Kingdom's executive-led adoption of Social Policy, the 2000 Danish referendum could have been the first exercise of popular sovereignty to reverse a reservation of constituent power. The constituted powers of the government and Parliament introduced a Bill in the Danish Parliament providing the national legal authorization to join the Eurozone if the population consented.[247] Attempts were made to reconcile supranational monetary integration and national social policy by claiming the two were mutually compatible.[248] The government sought to synthesize the *teloi* of the two separate constitutional sectors. Adopting the euro was framed as a means to vindicate individuals *qua* nationals rather than individuals *qua* EU citizens: '[t]he ministry [of Economic Affairs] actively sought to frame something as intrinsically novel and supranational as the common currency as nothing but a natural (and national) continuance of Danish monetary history'.[249]

Both Europhile and Eurosceptic voices in the referendum debate presented the same argument that either adopting or rejecting the euro, respectively, was necessary to strengthen the self-determination of individuals *qua* nationals of Denmark. The Danish Minister of Finance argued that 'the euro actually posed a unique opportunity to influence the decisions and policies of the great European powers, rather than flowing with the economic tides, as Denmark had been doing for the past 300 years'.[250] The Danish government moved

[245] See discussion of the legal nature of the referendum in the narrative of disintegration in chapter 6.
[246] 'Review of the Balance of Competences' (*GOV.UK*, 12 December 2012) <www.gov.uk/guidance/review-of-the-balance-of-competences> accessed 22 April 2020.
[247] Sørensen (n 239) 37.
[248] Marcussen (n 98).
[249] Sørensen (n 239) 31.
[250] ibid 42.

beyond the euro's positive economic consequences, and 'eventually sought to promote the euro as a phenomenon closely linked to the nation'.[251] Despite its failure, the Danish government recognized that it was crucial to frame levelling up constituent power in this area as reinforcing the self-determination of individuals *qua* democratic subjects. The mere passive acquisition of economic or other material benefits *qua* juridical objects may have been insufficient to justify levelling up to the supranational level. Sørensen presents the government's proposal to create 'a Danish euro coin' as a 'conceptual oxymoron'.[252] By contrast, the national symbolism of the head of state, in conjunction with the supranational symbol of the twelve stars of the European Union, may have been a microcosmic symbol for the dual supranational and national construction of the European order.

Sørensen identifies three strategies pursued by those who were against the euro: the national currency was presented as a 'symbol of shared historical experiences and the expression of a collective origin'.[253] In functional terms, the Krone was presented as a 'guarantee of the independence and sovereignty of the nation'.[254] The Eurosceptics 'articulated the national currency as a precondition for conducting monetary policy—hence, for the very existence of Denmark as an independent state'.[255] Finally, the retention of national currency and national monetary policy was framed as a 'crucial precondition to the future existence of the Danish welfare model . . . the national currency came to represent not only popular sovereignty but something even more valued: the way Danes have chosen to organise their society'.[256] This interconnection between a substantive macroeconomic policy sector and the capacity for self-determination within Denmark is analogous to the interconnection between the microeconomic and macroeconomic constitutional sectors in the European Union.[257] The arguments to preserve the integrity and autonomy of the role of individual *qua* national in relation to monetary policy won out. The Danish electorate voted by a 53.1 per cent majority to reject the proposal to introduce the euro.

[251] ibid 43.
[252] ibid 46.
[253] ibid 47.
[254] ibid.
[255] ibid.
[256] ibid.
[257] Tuori (n 69).

iii. Area of Freedom, Security and Justice (AFSJ)

The Treaty of Amsterdam reconstructed the Justice and Home Affairs *acquis* as the 'Area of Freedom, Security and Justice'.[258] Funda Tekin argues that this terminology goes beyond window dressing and instead suggests an important balance between these three concepts as objectives of European integration.[259] Peers provides an overview of the holistic nature of the impetus for this reform: 'the objectives of JHA cooperation were not clear; the institutional roles were ill-defined and left in part for future negotiation; the legal effect of the new instruments was ambiguous; and aspects of the third pillar/first pillar borderline were controversial'.[260]

There were two practical limbs to this symbolic move. The first was the incorporation of the Schengen Convention from international law into EU constitutional law. The second limb was the transfer of the legal basis for pre-existing norms on border checks, asylum, and immigration from the intergovernmental Third Pillar to the supranational First Pillar. Police and criminal cooperation remained within the framework of the Third Pillar but with comprehensively amended rules.[261] This was a partial form of the incorporation origin for opt-outs. Supranationalization of the norm-creation and norm-application processes provoked dissidence from Member States that did not believe that this transformation was in the interests of their nationals. The substantive overlap between the chapter on border checks, asylum, and immigration and the Schengen *acquis* can explain the decisions of the United Kingdom and Ireland to opt out at Amsterdam. The reservation of constituent power spilled over between constitutional sectors. When the legal bases on police and judicial cooperation were also incorporated at Lisbon, this led to a far more complex form of opt-out and opt-in legal mechanism due to the United Kingdom's agreement with the policy but resistance to the supranational method.[262]

The Member States chose to dissipate and disaggregate the juridical form of the AFSJ. Symbolically, this was an inauspicious start to the objective of constructing a holistic constitutional area. Beyond the dissipation between the First and Third Pillars, the rules regarding norm creation and norm

[258] Neil Walker (ed), *Europe's Area of Freedom, Security, and Justice* (OUP 2004); Massimo Fichera, *The Foundations of the EU as a Polity* (Edward Elgar Publishing 2018).

[259] Funda Tekin, *Differentiated Integration at Work: The Institutionalisation and Implementation of Opt-Outs from European Integration in the Area of Freedom, Security and Justice* (Nomos Publishers 2012).

[260] Peers (n 47) 8.

[261] ibid 15.

[262] See discussion of the Treaty of Lisbon later in this chapter.

application within these Pillars were subject to caveats, transitional periods, and complexification.[263] Tuytschaever opined that

> [t]he price to be paid for communitarisation . . . is high. It is . . . regrettable that the area of freedom, security and justice is . . . the part of the Treaty which attains a hitherto unequalled level of technical complexity, which is barely understandable for the insider, let alone the ordinary citizen.[264]

The driving force behind this complex disaggregated structure was the contestation of the recalcitrant Member States.[265] The reservation of constituent power complexified the AFSJ even outwith the areas subject to opt-outs. The origins of the AFSJ opt-out Protocols are intimately interconnected with complex depillarization.

As with 'Helmut Kortenberg', Alexander Stubb provides a particular insight as a participant in the negotiations of the Amsterdam Treaty. He validates the hypothesis that complexification was connected to the position of the United Kingdom and Ireland: 'The outcome of the first- or third-pillar question depended to a large extent on what sort of compromise could be struck between the Presidency and the British government'.[266] Stubb illustrates the negotiating logic which drove the United Kingdom's opt-out. He outlines the two possible scenarios in response to the United Kingdom's resistance to integration in the First Pillar. The first was that the United Kingdom would exercise its veto to block the transfer: '[t]his would have led to an unwelcome and pointless crisis and made it more difficult for the United Kingdom to achieve other negotiating aims'.[267]

The alternative was for the United Kingdom to allow this completion of the levelling up of constituent power in the AFSJ and 'seek a formal opt-out from those provisions (i.e. pre-defined flexibility). This would be a satisfactory solution for all, and it would allow the United Kingdom to see solutions in other issues important to its position'.[268] The dichotomy demonstrates the status quo theoretical presumption that opt-outs are created as a necessary compromise to enable the willing Member States to forge forward with deeper integration. The necessary consent of all the nationals of the Member States to level up constituent power is procured through exemption rather than persuasion. Stubb's

[263] Peers (n 47) 11.
[264] Tuytschaever (n 68) 74.
[265] Alexander Stubb, *Negotiating Flexibility in the European Union: Amsterdam, Nice and Beyond* (Palgrave Macmillan 2002); Peers (n 47); Tuytschaever (n 68).
[266] Stubb (n 265) 98.
[267] ibid 99.
[268] ibid.

evidence shows that opt-outs were becoming an accepted feature of Treaty amendment by the time of Amsterdam.

Whereas the opt-outs from the Schengen incorporation were regarded as inevitable, the creation of the concurrent opt-out from the AFSJ was less foreseeable:

> The interesting thing was that no one talked about special arrangements for the United Kingdom, Ireland and Denmark. This is in stark contrast to the Maastricht negotiations where the opt-outs for Britain from EMU and Social Policy were subject to fierce debate, especially during the final stages of negotiations.[269]

Opinions diverge on the predictability of this outcome. Tuytschaever presents the reservation of constituent power as a surprise:

> [T]he technical complexity of the area of freedom, security and justice is a consequence of the fact that a number of Member States, at the very last moment, i.e. at the Amsterdam Summit itself, surprised the other delegations by rejecting the preparatory work . . . and by calling for important exemptions.[270]

By contrast, Stubb presents a certain degree of inevitability:

> This almost indifferent approach indicates that the other member governments had accepted that it would be politically and constitutionally difficult for the United Kingdom, Ireland and Denmark to participate in the issues that were to be transferred from the third to the first pillar . . . These issues would have to be dealt with bilaterally between the Presidency and the government involved.[271]

Stubb highlights the failure of new differentiation mechanisms to accommodate the recalcitrant Member States:

[269] ibid 94.
[270] Tuytschaever (n 68) 74.
[271] Stubb (n 265) 94.

> [I]t had become clear that the enabling clause alone would not be sufficient in third-pillar matters or matters relating to the incorporation of the Schengen Agreement and the new Community provisions on visas, asylum and immigration. The United Kingdom, Ireland and Denmark would have to be dealt with in the traditional way . . . through opt-outs.[272]

Opt-outs were normalized as a constitutional practice following the fierce resistance at Maastricht. A pathway dependence forms once levelling up commences and develops in an area in which a Member State resists. Tuytschaever states that '[a]part from the exemption of the UK and Ireland with respect to Schengen, none of the above exemptions was the subject of any public debate. They were decided behind closed doors at the Amsterdam Summit itself'.[273] The lack of reasoned discourse and argumentation between the representatives in the actual creation of the Protocols is greatly deficient from the perspective of throughput legitimacy, and the full representation of all individuals as nationals of the High Contracting Parties. This is particularly deleterious with regard to the consequences of the flexible AFSJ Protocol for the ordinary legislative procedure.

The road that leads to further Member State opt-outs is paved by the incrementalism of past revisions. Unanimity sets the threshold for future constitutional change at the highest possible level in order to vindicate the sovereignty of dissident Member States. If there is a constituent subject from one or more of the Member States that remains unwilling to level up this power, then it would be illegitimate for the norms to apply within the legal order of the constitutional state. Within this impasse, the representatives of the pro-integration Member States believe that exemption is more expedient than the two alternatives: constitutional paralysis preventing levelling up by any of the constituent powers from the national to the supranational level, or international law being used to enact levelling up by excluding the dissenting Member State, thus causing a *de facto* withdrawal.[274]

[272] ibid 98–99.
[273] Tuytschaever (n 68) 74–75.
[274] See discussion of Denmark after the Maastricht referendum earlier in this chapter.

VI. The Treaty of Lisbon to the New Settlement for the United Kingdom

i. Schengen

The Treaty of Lisbon consolidated the special positions of Denmark, Ireland, and the United Kingdom with regard to the Schengen *acquis*. The amendment of the Protocol responded to the strict application of the meta-norms by the Court of Justice in the *UK v Council* cases.[275] The period after the Treaty ratification saw further judicial determination of the functioning of the opt-outs in *Spain v Parliament and Council*.[276] As the momentum moved from further integration to constitutional disintegration between Lisbon and Brexit, the opt-outs were pushed to their limits by unilateral measures taken by the Danish executive, and the renegotiation of membership by the UK executive.

Schutte details the attempts by the United Kingdom during the Lisbon negotiations to 'try to undo the effects [of the cases] . . . and allow the UK to have a free choice of opting in or staying out of measures that develop the parts of the Schengen *acquis* by which it was bound'.[277] Article 5 of the Protocol was modified to provide the discretion to withdraw a notification of participation within three months.[278] Constitutional replication and complexification are evident in this amendment. The increased discretion for the United Kingdom and Ireland emulates the flexibility of the 'opt-in' procedures provided for in Protocol (No 21) on the AFSJ.[279] Replication creates greater coherence *between* the legal form and operation of different opt-out mechanisms. Complexification results from the desire to maximize executive discretion and avoid legal barriers to political consensus, whilst maintaining a basis in the Treaties. This complex result is a legacy of the different legal sources and forms for the Schengen and AFSJ Protocols. The institutional pathway dependence creates an irrational distinction. Protocols mandating similar procedures within a sector of the constitutional order covering the same substantive norms are not integrated.

The procedure mandated by the Lisbon Treaty for opt-ins affords complete primacy to the institutions representing individuals *qua* nationals to the

[275] See detailed analysis earlier in this chapter.
[276] Case C-44/14 *Spain v European Parliament and Council* (n 214).
[277] Schutte, 'UK v EU' (n 56) 1358.
[278] Protocol (No 19) on the Schengen *acquis* integrated into the framework of the European Union, art 5(2).
[279] See detailed discussion of the creation and operation of the flexible mechanisms in chapter 3 above.

detriment of the supranational institutions and EU citizens. The discretion provided to individual Member States in norm-creation generates uncertainty and opacity. The compromise in the ordinary legislative procedure to accommodate the opt-out Member State's 'interest in participating in measures developing the Schengen *acquis* without being willing to accept the underlying *acquis*'[280] undermines the throughput legitimacy of the norms governing the movement of individuals through the internal space of the Union.

The *Spain v Parliament and Council* case clarified the legal operation of the renegotiated Schengen Protocol. Article 18 of Regulation No 1052/2013 provided for the international law cooperation of the United Kingdom and Ireland in the collection of information through the European Border Surveillance System. The Court of Justice confirmed that the opt-out Protocols are not exempt from the principle that secondary legislation must not contradict primary law: 'the EU legislature cannot validly establish a procedure that differs from . . . Article 4 of the Schengen Protocol, whether in the direction of strengthening or easing that procedure'.[281]

The limited cooperation in the Regulation did not place Ireland or the United Kingdom in a situation equivalent to a Member State, and so did not constitute 'taking part' in Schengen provisions.[282] The factual situation did not fall within the ambit of the Schengen Protocol. The dicta confirm the superior status of the Protocols as primary law even when a Member State is willing to participate in Schengen measures through other means. The positivization of retained constituent power in the Protocols forecloses the use of international law for cooperation mandated therein. EU legality persists even to prevent the fulfilment of the Schengen Protocol's telos to allow 'maximum participation'[283] of all Member States if these attempts are outwith the scope of the Protocol.

The judgment ensured the formal coherence of the EU legal order and the primacy of EU law over public international law. Insistence on the Protocol also ensured that the opt-out Member States cannot enjoy the benefits of certain policies without also accruing the obligations. Otherwise, citizens of the Union *qua* juridical objects would still be subject to the burden of passport checks, whereas individuals *qua* nationals would benefit from the increased security provided by their executive's access to the benefits of security measures that compensate for passport liberalization. The prospect of asymmetric burden-sharing is tempered by the Schengen Protocol's conditions on prior

[280] Schutte, 'Schengen: Its Meaning' (n 45) 1364.
[281] Case C-44/14 *Spain v European Parliament and Council* (n 214) para 31.
[282] ibid paras 42 and 58.
[283] Case C-77/05 *United Kingdom v Council* (n 225) para 67.

participation and consent of the Council. The absence of these features in the AFSJ opt-out Protocol creates asymmetry between the opt-outs and increases the imbalance between individuals *qua* nationals and *qua* EU citizens.[284]

In the early 2010s, the negative consequences of a Member State extricating itself from supranationalism manifested themselves. Rebecca Adler-Nissen claims that Denmark's representatives are not excluded from influencing the norm-creation process by its international law arrangement:

> Denmark has formally abstained from influence but is bound to adopt all decisions taken by the Council of Ministers six months after the other Member States . . . [s]ince Denmark automatically implements all legislation, if only on an intergovernmental basis, and because of the norm of consensus-seeking, Danish representatives are permitted to influence new Schengen measures.[285]

This *de facto* position does not change the discrepancy *de jure* that representatives of individuals *qua* Member State nationals of Denmark are not represented in the creation of Schengen norms. Within Danish territory, individuals *qua* EU citizens have been formally represented in the formulation of the norms, but individuals *qua* nationals have not. Despite this lack of input, the substance of the norms still applies to these individuals on the basis of international and national law. Their representation is reduced to the creation of implementing domestic measures.

There are further consequences for the norm-application process. The Protocol outlines that 'appropriate measures' will be considered if Denmark fails to implement a Council of Ministers decision within the timeframe. Adler-Nissen suggests that this is a 'euphemism' for being 'thrown out of Schengen'.[286] These crude retaliatory sanctions are far removed from the full constitutional jurisdiction of the Court of Justice of the European Union. This adjudicative lacuna was evident in 2011 when border checks were re-established at the border with Germany as part of a concession in forming a coalition government.[287] The threat to the Schengen *acquis* prompted warnings from the President of the Commission that intervention would be pursued if the situation were not remedied.[288] When Denmark and Sweden reinstalled border controls

[284] See the detailed normative critique in chapter 8.
[285] Adler-Nissen (n 59) 136.
[286] ibid.
[287] ibid 134.
[288] Ian Traynor, 'EU Warns Denmark over Border Controls' *The Guardian* (London, 13 May 2011) <www.theguardian.com/world/2011/may/13/eu-denmark-border-controls> accessed 23 April 2020.

again in 2015 in response to the migration crisis, Denmark complied with the norm-specific derogation regime established by the Schengen Border Code on Temporary Reinstatement of Border Controls.[289] The Danish Protocol removes the situation from the enforcement mechanisms of the framing juridical constitution.[290] Any attempts to ensure compliance are limited to non-binding political pressure. The foundations of the Schengen *acquis* in national and international law within Denmark provide weaker foundations to these norms than for the rest of the Member States listed in Article 1 of the Schengen Protocol. As Denmark participates in all Schengen measures in this way, its commitment to Schengen may be regarded as wider but constitutionally shallower than the United Kingdom during its membership and Ireland.

The United Kingdom's February 2016 renegotiation of membership did not explicitly seek to amend Protocol (No 19). However, the amendments proposed to Protocols (No 21) and (No 22) on AFSJ measures sought to address complications that also pertained to the Schengen Protocol.[291] It may also be argued that the United Kingdom's proposed amendments to social benefits and free movement were a spillover from its reservation of constituent power in relation to Schengen. Resistance to removing border controls can be functionally connected to resistance to the free movement of EU citizens into the territory of the United Kingdom. This provides evidence that the reservation of constituent power is an expansive phenomenon.

The Decision proposed the amendment of Regulation No 883/2004 on the coordination of social security systems to provide Member States with an option to index child benefits to the conditions of the Member State where the child resides.[292] The proposal to amend Regulation No 492/2011 on free movement of workers would have seen the creation of an 'emergency brake' mechanism to allow Member States to restrict access to non-contributory in-work benefits for seven years in the event of 'inflow of workers from other Member States of an exceptional magnitude over an extended period of time'.[293]

[289] Alberto Horst-Neidhardt, 'An Ever Looser Union among the Peoples of Europe?' (*European University Institute*, 12 January 2016) <https://me.eui.eu/alberto-horst-neidhardt/blog/an-ever-looser-union-among-the-people-of-europe/> accessed 23 April 2020; temporary reinstatement rules now found in Regulation (EU) 2016/399 of the European Parliament and of the Council of 9 March 2016 on a Union Code on the rules governing the movement of persons across borders (Schengen Borders Code) [2016] OJ L 77/11, arts 25–35.

[290] Tuori (n 69).

[291] See further discussion of these amendments below.

[292] European Council meeting (18 and 19 February 2016)—Conclusions, Annex 1—Decision of the Heads of State or Government, meeting within the European Council, concerning a new settlement for the United Kingdom within the European Union—Brussels 19 February 2016 EUCO 1/16, 22.

[293] ibid 23.

The EU's constitutional legislators, acting in international law, managed to prevent a specific opt-out from the juridical core of EU citizenship for one Member State by instead constructing a general derogation clause. This reverse situation to the negotiation of the EMU opt-out Protocol may be explained by the paradigm shift of an origin for opt-outs arising not from resistance to constitutional innovation, but contestation of the established obligations of the EU legal order. Nevertheless, the boundaries of EU citizenship were pushed in order to appease an uncooperative Member State despite the claim that the re-negotiation would not undermine the 'principles on which the European project is founded'.[294] If these proposals had been enacted, a further legal barrier would have been established for individuals seeking to rely on their EU citizenship to integrate into the society of another Member States. This would have been inimical to the value of free movement as an 'instrument that liberates the individual's mind and body from the domination that the nation-state exerts over it'.[295] The United Kingdom's attempt to reconstruct free movement rights was the logical continuation of its ongoing resistance to the Schengen norms on the removal of border controls. This dissidence is the judicial manifestation of its resistance to the legitimacy of the supranational constituent status of citizenship of the European Union that would eventually culminate in the Member State's withdrawal.

ii. Economic and Monetary Union (EMU)

By the time of the Treaty of Lisbon, the Danish electorate's explicit rejection of the euro, and the procrastination of the UK government over holding a referendum, meant that the EMU Protocols had now become *de facto* temporally unlimited opt-outs. This situation was entrenched further by the traumas of the Eurozone crisis for much of the decade leading up to Brexit.[296] Measures to try and address the crisis in 2011 saw the UK government refuse to level up constituent power for a Treaty amendment that was designed to address

[294] Donald Tusk, 'Letter by President Donald Tusk to the Members of the European Council on His Proposal for a New Settlement for the United Kingdom within the European Union' (*European Council*, 2 February 2016) <www.consilium.europa.eu/en/press/press-releases/2016/02/02/letter-tusk-proposal-new-settlement-uk/> accessed 23 April 2020.

[295] Floris De Witte, 'Freedom of Movement Needs to Be Defended as the Core of EU Citizenship' in Rainer Bauböck (ed), *Debating European Citizenship* (Springer 2019) 98.

[296] See *inter alia* Kaarlo Tuori and Klaus Tuori, *The Eurozone Crisis* (CUP 2014); Thomas Beukers, Bruno De Witte and Claire Kilpatrick, *Constitutional Change through Euro-Crisis Law* (CUP 2017); Mark Dawson and Floris De Witte, 'Constitutional Balance in the EU after the Euro-Crisis' (2013) 76 The Modern Law Review 817.

stability, coordination, and governance in the Eurozone.[297] The objection of the United Kingdom required resort to 'old-style flexibility' and the conclusion of the international Treaty on Stability, Coordination and Governance.[298] This revived the paradigm from Schengen of using international law to overcome Member State reticence. Rather than resistance to a new sector, this was required due to deferred levelling up by the United Kingdom in EMU. The veto also intersected with disintegration as a means to manifest general resistance to European integration in the face of domestic pressure.

The Eurozone crisis drove the demarcation between the spheres of governance of the Eurozone Member States and the opt-out Member States in the February 2016 New Settlement for the United Kingdom. The heads of state or government would have been committed to incorporate the substance of the section into the Treaties at the time of the next revision.[299] The New Settlement reiterated that 'measures, the purpose of which is to further deepen economic and monetary union, will be voluntary for Member States whose currency is not the euro and will be open to their participation wherever feasible'.[300] The opt-out Member States would have committed to not creating obstacles and facilitating such further deepening whilst their rights and competences would have been respected.[301] The declaration would have reiterated that discrimination on the basis of currency was prohibited.[302] In return, Member States whose currency is not the euro would have committed not to impede the implementation of legal acts directly linked to the functioning of the euro area.[303] The application of norms is clarified through the statement that 'Union law on the banking union conferring... authority over credit institutions is applicable only to credit institutions located in Member States whose currency is the euro' or for Member States with a close cooperation agreement with the European Central Bank.[304]

A crucial safeguard would have been provided in the statement that '[e]mergency and crisis measures designed to safeguard the financial stability of the euro area will not entail budgetary responsibility for Member States

[297] 'David Cameron Blocks EU-Wide Deal to Tackle Euro Crisis' (*BBC News*, 9 December 2011) <www.bbc.com/news/uk-16104275> accessed 27 April 2020.

[298] Treaty on Stability, Coordination and Governance of 2 March 2012 T/SCG.

[299] European Council meeting (18 and 19 February 2016)—Conclusions, Annex 1—Decision of the Heads of State or Government, meeting within the European Council, concerning a new settlement for the United Kingdom within the European Union—Brussels 19 February 2016 EUCO 1/16, 15.

[300] ibid 12.

[301] ibid.

[302] ibid 13.

[303] ibid.

[304] ibid.

whose currency is not the euro'.[305] The declarations also sought to preserve the democratic representation of individuals *qua* nationals in relation to economic and monetary policy: 'The informal meetings of the . . . Euro Group shall respect the powers of the Council as an institution upon which the Treaties confer legislative functions and within which Member States coordinate their economic policies'.[306] The throughput legitimacy of the Council is emphasized in the statement that 'all members of the Council participate in its deliberations, even where not all members have the right to vote'.[307]

The declaration may be regarded as reordering the fault line between the Eurozone and non-Eurozone Member States. This demonstrates that the EMU opt-outs established a permanent state of constitutional distinction as opposed to temporal differentiation. This requires principles to ensure the coexistence and equality of individuals *qua* EU citizens despite the material difference in their currency on the basis of their nationality. To this end, 'the Union institutions, together with the Member States, will facilitate the coexistence between different perspectives within the single institutional framework ensuring consistency, the effective operability of Union mechanisms and the equality of Member States before the Treaties'.[308] The withdrawal of the United Kingdom means that this opportunity to clarify constitutional boundaries has been lost.

iii. Area of Freedom, Security and Justice (AFSJ)

The most important development at Lisbon regarding opt-outs was the extension of the scope of Protocol (No 21) and (No 22) to cover judicial and police cooperation. This was a necessary requirement of 'de-pillarisation'[309] with the establishment of the dual-Treaty structure. The abolition of the Third Pillar and the subsequent relocation of the legal bases for police and judicial cooperation brought these measures within the scope of application of the opt-out Protocols. The pathway dependence that had started at Maastricht of application of the full supranational constitutional method despite the resistance of certain Member States had reached its conclusion. Extension in a different dimension was executed through the addition of Article 4a to Protocol (No

[305] ibid 14.
[306] ibid.
[307] ibid.
[308] ibid 12.
[309] Steve Peers, 'In a World of Their Own? Justice and Home Affairs Opt-Outs and the Treaty of Lisbon' (2008) 10 Cambridge Yearbook of European Legal Studies 383; Michael Dougan, 'The Treaty of Lisbon 2007: Winning Minds, Not Hearts' (2008) 45 Common Market Law Review 617.

21). This extended the scope of the opt-out mechanism to include measures amending an existing norm even if the United Kingdom and Ireland had opted in to the original measure. The sub-article addresses the opposite situation of the *UK v Council* cases in which the United Kingdom was prevented from participating in amending measures.[310] The clause provided the opt-out Member States with an even higher degree of flexible discretion, with subsequently greater risk to the internal coherence of the rights and obligations in the AFSJ.

The Lisbon amendments provided a further example of the interconnection between different forms of derogation. Depillarization was tempered by the creation of a transitional regime in Protocol (No 36).[311] Title VII thereof covers AFSJ measures. A continuity clause ensured that all measures adopted before Lisbon remained legally valid. The corollary was that, with respect to police and judicial cooperation measures adopted *before* the entry into force of the Treaty of Lisbon, the Commission's infringement procedure power would not apply and instead the prior consensual regime for Court of Justice adjudication would apply. This represented a gradual embedding of the full architecture of the juridical constitution. The length of this period was established as five years.

This temporal derogation opened the door to a new form of opt-out for the United Kingdom. The Protocol empowered the Member State to notify that it did not accept the new powers of the supranational institutions. Although the initial disapplication of norms did not fall within the executive discretion of the Member State, in the sense that the legal choice was to reject the authority of the supranational institutions, the next paragraph did provide an opt-in discretion.[312] This is analogous to yet distinct from the Protocol (No 21) opt-in mechanism. The United Kingdom was entitled, with the broad temporal discretion indicated by 'any time afterwards', to notify the Council of its wish to participate in the acts which had ceased to apply to it. The United Kingdom exercised this power in 2014 and opted back into a select number of measures.[313] Bruno de Witte notes that

> the privileged treatment which the UK had meted out to itself when signing the Lisbon Treaty consisted not only of having a block *exit* option, but also a selective *re-entry* option for those EU measures that it liked to keep—namely

[310] Case C-77/05 *United Kingdom v Council* (n 225); Case C-482/08 *United Kingdom v Council* (n 225). See discussion earlier in the chapter.
[311] TEU and TFEU, Protocol (No 36) on transitional provisions.
[312] ibid art 10(5).
[313] See chapter 3 on legal form and operation for discussion of the legal conditions for this opt-in.

the ones that seemed most useful from the point of view of the UK's domestic justice and home affairs policy.[314]

The United Kingdom did not provide extensive reasons for its decision to opt in to particular measures under Protocol (No 36). This lack of transparency and accountability has been criticized, and it was left to scholars to reconstruct the reasons for these choices.[315]

Protocol (No 36) provided a *de facto* opt-out from the relevant police and judicial cooperation measures that the United Kingdom did not decide to opt back into. De Witte argues that 'for the first time in the EU's history, it allowed a Member State to free itself from existing EU law obligations'.[316] Although the exact legal power was not to opt out from pre-existing measures, the necessary consequence of a decision to reject supranationalism was that all of the police cooperation and judicial cooperation measures ceased to apply to the Member State.[317] Legally, this blurs the lines between an executive decision to reserve constituent power, and the remedial suspension of legal rights resembling the remedy of reciprocal non-performance of obligations in public international law. Such a 'remedy' is contrary to the EU's self-fulfilling prophecy of constituting a new legal order distinct from international law.[318] It is particularly ironic that such an a-constitutional legal phenomenon was created as part of a grand consolidation of supranational constitutionalism.

This legal construction acted as a smokescreen that obscured innovation in the practice of Member State opt-outs. For the first time, a Member State was given the option to utilize its constituent power to realize the disapplication of binding EU law norms, as opposed to the status quo of securing an exemption from participation in the creation of new norms. A partial justification may be forwarded that, although the substance of the norms had applied to the United Kingdom, the supranational method had not. No norms that had been legitimated by individuals *qua* nationals and *qua* EU citizens were disapplied through the unilateral act of one Member State. The United Kingdom's notification under the Protocol may be regarded as an exercise of deconstructive power rather than mere retention of constituent power. This functions as a

[314] De Witte, 'Variable Geometry and Differentiation' (n 55).

[315] Maria Fletcher, 'EU Criminal Law Flexibility: What Lessons from the UK Protocol No. 36 Saga?' in Valsamis Mitsilegas, Maria Bergström and Theodore Konstadinides (eds), *Research Handbook on EU Criminal Law* (Edward Elgar Publishing 2016); Valsamis Mitsilegas, 'European Criminal Law After Brexit' (2017) 28 Criminal Law Forum 219.

[316] De Witte, 'Variable Geometry and Differentiation' (n 55) 14.

[317] TEU and TFEU, Protocol (No 36) on transitional provisions, art 4(10).

[318] Case 26/62 *Van Gend en Loos v Nederlandse Administratie der Belastingen* [1963] ECR 1.

microcosm of notification under Article 50 TEU. Protocol (No 36) was a theoretical and chronological stepping-stone towards the United Kingdom's eventual withdrawal.

After Lisbon, the United Kingdom sought to enforce the scope of Protocols (No 19) and (No 21) before the Court of Justice of the European Union.[319] This provides further evidence for the importance of the Court in preserving legal certainty when opt-out mechanisms extend into the ordinary legislative functioning of the EU's constitutional order. A series of cases concerned the appropriate legal base for measures concerning Third-Country Nationals.

In *UK v Council* (the EEA case) the United Kingdom argued that legislation extending EU law social security schemes to citizens of the EFTA (European Free Trade Association) states, which was adopted under Article 48 TFEU on freedom of movement for workers, should have been proposed under Article 79 TFEU concerning legally resident Third-Country Nationals.[320] The Court of Justice reiterated the test that the choice of legal basis must rest on 'objective factors amenable to judicial review'. Teleologically, the Court held that the EEA Agreement established a special and privileged relationship for this class of Third-Country Nationals, and endorsed the Decision being adopted under Article 48 TFEU 'so that the internal market established within the European Union is extended to the EFTA States'.[321] The Court of Justice also reinforced its judgment by reference to the telos of Article 79 TFEU: 'the efficient management of migration flows, fair treatment of third-country nationals ... and the prevention of... illegal immigration and trafficking'.[322] None of these objectives pertained to the relationship established within the EEA Agreement, which created a quasi-EU citizenship with full free movement rights. Consequently, it would have been teleologically inappropriate if the United Kingdom were able to opt out from these measures in relation to EEA citizens.

A similar dispute informed the Swiss social security coordination case.[323] The United Kingdom argued, similarly to the above case, that Article 48 TFEU could not be extended to address Third-Country Nationals or economically inactive persons. Again, however, the Court of Justice emphasized the telos behind the Agreement as ensuring free movement for Swiss citizens and EU citizens. It endorsed Article 48 TFEU as the appropriate legal base 'in order to preserve a coherent and correct application of the legal acts of the European

[319] House of Lords European Union Committee, 'The UK's Opt-in Protocol: Implications of the Government's Approach' (House of Lords European Union Committee 2015) Ninth Report of Session 2014-2015 (HL Paper 136).
[320] Case C-431/11 *United Kingdom v Council*, EU:C:2013:589.
[321] ibid para 50.
[322] ibid para 62.
[323] Case C-656/11 *United Kingdom v Council*, EU:C:2014:97.

Union and to avoid administrative and . . . legal difficulties'.[324] Protocol (No 21) plays no part in determining the propriety of this legal base.

The same dispute arose in relation to the extension of social security co-ordination with Turkey.[325] The Court held again that the relationship between the European Union and Turkey was distinct from the general regulation of Third-Country Nationals under Article 79 TFEU. By contrast to the relationship with the EFTA states, however, the Court of Justice held that the principles of the single market did not provide a teleological basis. Article 48 TFEU had to be accompanied by Article 217 TFEU's general competence to conclude agreements with Third Countries. The United Kingdom's strategy to enforce its opt-out Protocol through litigation corrected a legal error by the legislative institutions, albeit without the result for which the United Kingdom argued.

Similar disputes arose in cases outside of the topic of social security co-ordination. In the Philippines case,[326] the Commission sought annulment of a Council Decision to sign a Framework Agreement on Partnership and Cooperation between the European Union and the Philippines. The Commission concluded the agreement under Article 207 TFEU on the Common Commercial Policy and Article 209 TFEU on development cooperation. The Council added additional legal bases, including Article 79(3) TFEU concerning the conclusion of readmission agreements for Third-Country Nationals who do not fulfil conditions for entry or residence in the territory of a Member State. The Court of Justice upheld the Commission's claim, arguing that the predominant telos of development would be promoted by individual clauses on readmission if they served this purpose.[327] The Court of Justice's approach may be regarded as ensuring that AFSJ measures should only be utilized when legislative measures have a predominant telos that concerns this sector of the constitutional order. In turn, this ensures that the scope of the opt-out Protocols is similarly limited and does not creep into measures which seek to uphold objectives outwith the AFSJ.

In the conditional access services case, which concerned the application of the Common Commercial Policy to the Council of Europe Convention on the legal protection of services based on conditional access, the Court of Justice reiterated this approach to the opt-out Protocol, contrary to the interpretation of the United Kingdom.[328] It stated that the opt-in Protocol 'was not capable of

[324] ibid para 62.
[325] Case C-81/13 *United Kingdom v Council*, EU:C:2014:2449.
[326] Case C-377/12 *Commission v Council*, EU:C:2014:1903.
[327] ibid paras 39, 58.
[328] Case C-137/12 *European Commission v Council*, EU:C:2013:675.

having any effect whatsoever on the correct legal basis for the adoption of the Decision'[329] to allow the European Union to sign an international convention. The fact that a provision in the Convention concerned criminal penalties in order to enforce a prohibition did not bring the Council Decision to conclude the Convention under the scope of the AFSJ. This approach would be putting the cart before the horse; the legal basis of the measure determines whether the Protocol should be applied, and not vice versa. This confirmed that the opt-out Protocols are only activated at the point at which the AFSJ legal basis has been confirmed.

The skirmishes over the definition and scope of the United Kingdom's opt-out Protocol revealed the distinction between the reservation of constituent power through opt-outs and the exercise of deconstructive power through withdrawal. With the exception of Denmark's Schengen opt-out, recalcitrant Member States cannot unbind themselves from the overarching formal principles of the constitutional order through the opt-outs. The EU's institutions must have the final say on the exact scope of the legal mechanisms to enshrine these reservations. Only the exercise of deconstructive power and the construction of a new legal relationship in public international law will allow a state to reclaim the sovereignty to determine the formal arrangements governing legal cooperation.

The reforms to the AFSJ opt-out proposed in the New Settlement for the United Kingdom would have addressed the disputes over legal bases:

> The representatives of the Member States in their capacity as members of the Council will ensure that, where a Union measure, in the lights of its aim and content, falls within the scope of [the AFSJ], Protocols No 21 and 22 will apply to it, including when this entails the splitting of the measure into two acts.[330]

This would have expanded the scope of the Protocol to more closely resemble the UK government's interpretation of the opt-out applying to all Justice and Home Affairs relevant legislation. This proposal would have caused further disruption to the ordinary legislative procedure.

Before the United Kingdom's referendum on membership in June 2016, Denmark held another referendum to determine whether the democratic

[329] ibid para 73.

[330] European Council meeting (18 and 19 February 2016)—Conclusions, Annex 1—Decision of the Heads of State or Government, meeting within the European Council, concerning a new settlement for the United Kingdom within the European Union—Brussels 19 February 2016 EUCO 1/16, 18.

subject *qua* national wished to loosen the restrictions on the levelling up of constituent power. On 3 December 2015, a referendum was held on whether to exercise the option afforded under Article 8 of Protocol (No 22).[331] This would have been a necessary condition to enable Denmark to become a full member of the Europol agency. As opposed to the complete reversal of the opt-out envisaged by Article 7, Article 8 mandates the replacement of the complete opt-out with flexible arrangements analogous to the United Kingdom and Ireland's Protocol (No 21). This would also have 'reversed' Denmark's opt-out from the Schengen *acquis*.[332] The condition for the notification is that such a decision is 'in accordance with [the Member State's] constitutional requirements'. This is a standardized condition for the exercise of constituted constituent power within the triptych, and its Protocols which function as off-shoots from Article 48 TEU. The referendum did not provide a case study for the 'reversal' of an opt-out through an exercise of popular sovereignty. The no vote won by 53 per cent and Denmark retained its block opt-out from the AFSJ.[333]

VII. Summary

The Protocols enabling Member State opt-outs result from the retention of constituent power during Treaty amendments. Excavation of the normative foundations of differentiation reveals that opt-outs may be justified when an objective reason distinguishes certain Member State nationals from all other EU citizens. The present conditions for the creation of opt-outs do not require any such justification. Reserved constituent power is positivized through Protocols addended to the Treaties, ensuring control over the legality of derogation by the supranational institutions.

The origins of opt-outs are resistance to incorporation of norms and the creation of new sectors of the supranational constitutional order. From the Single European Act to the Treaty of Maastricht, the opposition of certain Member States required an international agreement to create the Schengen zone of liberalized border controls. EMU was limited to intergovernmental mechanisms with fragmented participation by the opt-out Member States. Justice and Home Affairs cooperation did not have a Treaty base. Cooperation between the Member States instead occurred through international conventions.

331 TEU and TFEU, Protocol (No 22) on the position of Denmark, art 8.
332 ibid art 8(2).
333 Jacobsen (n 36).

The Treaty of Maastricht saw the first creation of opt-out Protocols. Resistance from the United Kingdom and Denmark to the adoption of the euro saw the first official retention of constituent power during a Treaty amendment. Denmark would trigger the option to opt out from the Third Stage of EMU following the initial rejection of the Treaty through a referendum. The United Kingdom also activated its opt-out before the Treaty of Amsterdam. Maastricht also saw the creation of a Treaty base for Justice and Home Affairs in the Third Pillar, with the declared intention of further supranational integration in the future. The Schengen Protocol was incorporated into the supranational constitutional order by the Treaty of Amsterdam. The result of supranational integration was the retention of constituent power by the United Kingdom, Denmark, and Ireland. The reconstruction of Justice and Home Affairs as the AFSJ and the transfer of measures to the First Pillar saw the creation of further opt-out Protocols. Ireland was compelled to secure opt-outs by its unique territorial relationship with the United Kingdom.

Before the Treaty of Lisbon, the UK government prevaricated on holding a referendum on participation in the Third Stage of EMU. The Danish electorate rejected the reversal of the opt-out in a 2000 referendum. The Treaty of Lisbon deepened the opt-outs from the AFSJ in reaction to the depillarization of the Treaties. The adoption of the full supranational method required a transitional regime. This transition created the means for the United Kingdom to reject the authority of the supranational institutions over police and judicial cooperation. The present narrative of disrupted integration transitioned into the narrative of disintegration with the New Settlement for the United Kingdom. The Decision between the heads of state or government in international law would have pre-bound the constituent powers at the next Treaty amendment. Both the form and content of the New Settlement would have pushed the boundaries of the constitutional acceptability of Member State opt-outs. The outcome of the United Kingdom's membership referendum on 23 June 2016, however, transitioned the narrative of disruption into one of disintegration.

5
Article 50 TEU
Telos, Form, and Function

I. Overview of Argument

This chapter introduces the withdrawal clause of Article 50 TEU. The telos of the withdrawal clause is to provide a legitimate means for individuals to exercise deconstructive power over European integration. This legitimacy, as secured through an explicit constitutional clause, distinguishes disintegration through withdrawal from illegitimate means of disintegration, such as judicial determinations that EU values do not apply to the Member State.[1] This purpose is illustrated through a reconstruction of the origins and development of the withdrawal clause, and relevant case law. The first limb of the dual objective of Article 50 TEU ensures a democratic right for individuals *qua* Member State nationals. The second limb ensures that this power respects individuals *qua* EU citizens as juridical objects. This part of the monograph presents Article 50 TEU's operation within the conceptual framework of deconstructive power. This proposes a deconstitutional convention that is conversely analogous to Habermas and Patberg's hypothetical constitutional assemblies, and the actual constitutional assemblies under Articles 48 and 49 TEU. The factual context of the Brexit case study is utilized as it is the only example to date of a Member State withdrawal through Article 50 TEU.

One must reconstruct why individuals as democratic subjects have legitimated norms that will apply to them as juridical objects in order to assess whether such norms are functioning optimally. Telos is crucial to determine exactly why and how individuals have exercised their capacity for individual and collective self-determination in the pursuit of self-fulfilment. In the case of withdrawal, the objective must be to reconstruct why individuals have legitimated a mechanism that will extinguish the norm-creation and norm-application processes

[1] Therefore, this is why arguments regarding 'legal Polexit' differ qualitatively from Brexit. See René Repasi, 'Op-Ed: "Poland's Withdrawal from the 'Community of Law' Is No Withdrawal from the EU"' (*EU Law Live*, 15 October 2021) <https://eulawlive.com/op-ed-polands-withdrawal-from-the-community-of-law-is-no-withdrawal-from-the-eu-by-rene-repasi/> accessed 24 April 2024.

Constitutional Disintegration and Disruption. Oliver Garner, Oxford University Press. © Oxford University Press 2025. DOI: 10.1093/9780198914136.003.0005

for them at the supranational level. Telos is especially relevant to the quadripartite role, as the purpose of deconstructive power to re-establish nationality as the sole constituent status extinguishes the supranational status of citizenship of the European Union.

II. The Origins and Telos of the Withdrawal Clause

i. The partial precedents for withdrawal

Article 50 does not create the legal possibility of withdrawal *ex nihilo*. Instead, it codifies and provides an EU law framework for a pre-existing right in public international law. This international law framework provided the means for the partial precedents for withdrawal of Algeria in 1962 and Greenland in 1985. However, these do not fit the paradigm of a withdrawal under the Vienna Convention on the Law of Treaties because none of these entities were 'parties' to the Treaties.[2] Rather, they are and were territories of Member States. The acceptance by the EEC of the United Kingdom holding a membership referendum in 1975 may be regarded as evidence that the Vienna Convention would have provided the legal means for withdrawal in this case. This consensus may be construed from the renegotiation of membership between the United Kingdom and the EEC before the referendum.[3] Polly Polak argues that, even before the creation of a withdrawal clause,

> [g]iven the special nature of the Union, the correct pre-Lisbon regime for withdrawing under public international law would have . . . been a supranational regime of withdrawal that required certain conditions in more flexible circumstances than under Article 62 VCLT but not an entirely unfettered right as might derive from Article 56 VCLT.[4]

Algeria ceased to be a constituent territory of the EEC upon its independence from France in 1962.[5] The Greenland case was a less dramatic rupture. The territory voted in favour of 'home rule' and greater autonomy from the

[2] VCLT, arts 54 and 56.

[3] Adam Evans, 'Planning for Brexit: The Case of the 1975 Referendum' (2018) 89 The Political Quarterly 127; KR Simmonds, 'The British Referendum' (1975) 12 Common Market Law Review 258.

[4] Polly Polak, *EU Withdrawal as a Supranational Affair: The Case of Brexit* (Brill Nijhoff 2023) 34.

[5] Kiran Klaus Patel, 'Something New under the Sun? The Lessons of Algeria and Greenland' in Benjamin Martill and Uta Staiger (eds), *Brexit and Beyond: Rethinking the Futures of Europe* (UCL Press 2018) 114.

Kingdom of Denmark in 1979. It followed this up with a referendum on 'membership' of the EEC in 1982, after 70 per cent had voted against accession in the Danish nationwide referendum in 1972. Fifty-three per cent voted in favour of leaving the EEC; this was realized through the Greenland Treaty of 1985.[6] Kiran Klaus Patel highlights that in June 1963 a European Community Council of Ministers document noted that Algeria was treated 'de facto as a Member State of the Community'.[7] A further document from 1968 details that relations with Algeria lacked a clear legal basis and that the North African state was treated as if it were part of the common market.[8] The Greenland case provided more legal clarity, as an agreement was negotiated quickly with Protocols providing extensive fishing rights for European Community Member States.[9] Contrary to arguments advanced during the 2003 Convention on the Future of Europe that the Vienna Convention on the Law of Treaties provided an adequate legal framework for withdrawal, the fallout from these partial precedents suggests that a constitutional clause regulating withdrawal is necessary in the interests of legal certainty. Such a mechanism was first proposed at the Convention.

A final counterfactual precedent concerns the position of Denmark after the population rejected the ratification of the Maastricht Treaty. Deirdre Curtin suggests that the other High Contracting Parties considered a form of *de facto* withdrawal for Denmark through concluding a separate treaty excluding the recalcitrant Member State.[10] The rupture in continuity means that this would have represented a form of complete disintegration of the pre-existing treaty basis for the supranational constitutional order and its reconstruction through a *de novo* exercise of constituent power in international law.

ii. The 2003 Convention on the Future of Europe

Article 50 TEU came into force with the Treaty of Lisbon on 1 December 2009.[11] The text of the provision was adopted from the failed draft Treaty establishing a Constitution. The 2003 Convention on the Future of Europe

[6] Treaty amending, with regard to Greenland, the Treaties establishing the European Communities [1985] OJ L 29/1.

[7] Patel (n 5) 116.

[8] ibid 118.

[9] ibid.

[10] Deirdre Curtin, 'The Constitutional Structure of the Union: A Europe of Bits and Pieces' (1993) 30 Common Market Law Review 17, 67–68. See further discussion in chapter 4 regarding Denmark's referendum on Maastricht.

[11] Treaty of Lisbon amending the Treaty on European Union and the Treaty establishing the European Community, signed at Lisbon, 13 December 2007 [2007] OJ C 306/1.

acted as a constitutionalist break from the paradigm of 'Intergovernmental Conferences'.[12] The Convention produced the legal text that would become Article 50 TEU. The process for its creation is the closest approximation to Habermas' hypothetical constitutional convention in the EU's actual history. Documents from the Convention suggest a self-understanding amongst certain Convention members regarding dual representation.[13] The Convention was the most explicit attempt to follow the narrative of constituent power being wielded by representatives of individuals. However, the retention by the High Contracting Parties of the ultimate authority to conclude the Treaty and the international law treaty paradigm remaining the source of the law[14] suggest that the states did not entirely cede their constituent power. Furthermore, Michael Dougan's critique indicates that the specific creation of the withdrawal clause may not have adhered to principles of deliberative exercise of constituent power: 'the relevant proposals were introduced relatively late in the Convention's working life and without having been subject to its standard process of detailed deliberation and debate among dedicated working groups'.[15]

Nevertheless, the Convention structure provides an insight into the intention of the drafters of the withdrawal clause through the publication of deliberations and amendment proposals by the participants. This feature of the Convention coheres with Habermas' method of rational reconstruction. The members of the Convention were invited to submit amendments to draft text prepared by the Praesidium of the Convention. This ensured a confrontation of the presuppositions of individuals as to the normative validity of constitutional provisions. The proposed amendments to the withdrawal clause indicate the perceptions of the constitutional actors. This allows excavation of strategic purposes for the clause beyond its *de jure* constitutional telos.

The withdrawal clause was included within 'Title IX: Union Membership' of the draft Constitution.[16] This title more clearly indicates that these provisions concern the levelling up and levelling down of constructive power than the 'Title VI: Final Provisions' terminology of the Lisbon Treaty. This

[12] TEU, art 48(3).

[13] Alternative Convention member Robert Badinter's contribution to the Convention argued that '[t]wo sources of legitimacy are . . . reunited through the Union: that of the Member States and that of the people of the Union, composed of all its citizens, without any distinction as to nationality': 'Contribution from M Robert Badinter, Alternate Member of the Convention, "A European Constitution" CONV 317/02 CONTRIB 105, Brussels, 30 September 2002 (OR Fr)'.

[14] Bruno de Witte, 'European Union Law: How Autonomous is Its Legal Order?' (2010) 65 Zeitschrift für öffentliches Recht 141, 144.

[15] Michael Dougan, *The UK's Withdrawal from the EU: A Legal Analysis* (OUP 2021) 23.

[16] Draft Treaty Establishing a Constitution for Europe [2003] OJ C 169/1 (hereinafter cited as 'Draft Constitution').

is reinforced by the inclusion of 'Article 57: Conditions of eligibility and procedure for applying for Union membership' in the title.[17] However, the constituted constituent power to amend the Constitution was not included in the title. Instead, the predecessor to Article 7 TEU on enforcing the values of the European Union was included under the title 'Article 58: Suspension of Union membership rights'.[18] The draft text of 'Article 59: Voluntary withdrawal from the Union' of the Constitution was largely reproduced in what would become Article 50 TEU at Lisbon.[19]

Forty-seven amendments proposed by members of the Convention are publicly accessible.[20] These provide valuable insights into the legislative intention behind the clause, and the earliest examples of contestation of the legitimacy of withdrawal. Eight of the amendments proposed the complete deletion of the withdrawal clause. The tenor of these contributions is that explicit legal means to enable disintegration is contrary to the nature and telos of the supranational constitutional order. The amendment moved by Ernâni Lopes and Manuel Lobo argues that 'the nature of the Union is not compatible with such an exit clause' and that 'no one questions their [Member States'] right to withdraw from the Union. The 1969 Vienna Convention on the "Law of Treaties" provides already for this situation.'[21]

The Farnleitner amendment reflected this argument: '[t]he provisions of the Vienna Convention on the Law of Treaties provide a sufficient basis for termination of membership'.[22] In a similar vein GM de Vries and TJAM de

[17] Draft Constitution, art 57.

[18] Draft Constitution, art 58.

[19] Draft Constitution, art 59: '(1) Any Member State may decide to withdraw from the European Union in accordance with its own constitutional requirements. (2) A Member State which decides to withdraw shall notify the Council of its intention; the European Council shall examine that notification. In the light of the guidelines provided by the European Council, the Union shall negotiate and conclude an agreement with that State, setting out the arrangements for its withdrawal, taking account of the framework for its future relationship with the Union. That agreement shall be concluded on behalf of the Union by the Council of Ministers, acting by a qualified majority, after obtaining the assent of the European Parliament. The representative of the withdrawing State shall not participate in the Council's discussions or decisions concerning it. (3) The Constitution shall cease to apply to the State in question from the date of entry into force of the withdrawal agreement or, failing that, two years after the notification referred to in paragraph 2, unless the European Council, in agreement with the Member State concerned, decides to extend this period. (4) If a State which has withdrawn from the Union asks to re-join, its request shall be subject to the procedure referred to in Article 57.'

[20] 'Proposed Amendments to the Text of the Articles of the Treaty Establishing a Constitution for Europe' (*European Convention*, 2003) <https://web.archive.org/web/20220105122837/http://european-convention.europa.eu/EN/amendments/amendmentsdfd1.html?content=46&lang=EN> accessed 3 April 2020.

[21] Ernâni Lopes and Manuel Lobo Antunes, 'Suggestion for Amendment of Article: Article I-59°' (*DORIE—European Commission*, 2003) <https://dorie.ec.europa.eu/en/details/-/card/89825> accessed 3 April 2020.

[22] Hannes Farnleitner, 'Suggestion for Amendment of Article I-59' (*DORIE—European Commission*, 2003) <https://dorie.ec.europa.eu/en/details/-/card/89821> accessed 3 April 2020.

Bruijn, representatives of the Dutch government, argued that 'facilitating the possibility to withdraw from the Union is contrary to the idea of European integration'.[23] The arguments that such a clause was unnecessary and unconstitutional were forwarded further in the amendment proposed by Santer, Fayot, and Schmit. The Luxemburgish representatives claimed that the inclusion of a withdrawal clause would undermine the fundamental engagement that makes the Member States adhere to the Union and the values it represents. They argued that such a clause was also legally unnecessary as nothing impeded a Member State from withdrawing from the Union through international law.[24] Joschka Fischer echoed this argument, by claiming that there is no need for a provision on withdrawal.[25] Jürgen Meyer claimed that individual Member States deciding to leave would be contrary to the idea of a Union based on the solidarity of citizens and states. He also warned of the risk of the clause being misused by anti-Europeans in the Member States.[26]

The arguments in these amendments allude to the strategic purposes underpinning the constitutional project. The detriment to European integration is advanced against 'facilitating' withdrawal. However, the need to fulfil unanimity requirements for Treaty amendment may incentivize the creation of mechanisms to reassure representatives who are reticent about transferring constructive power. In this situation, legal norms may be created not for their ostensible constitutional purpose, but as a means to overcome intergovernmental impasses. Statements by two drafters of the withdrawal clause, John Kerr and Giuliano Amato, corroborate this claim. The latter has stated that the clause was created 'to prevent the British government complaining that there was no way for them to leave the bloc'.[27] He states that the intention was that 'it should be a classic safety valve that was there, but never used'.[28]

[23] GM De Vries and TJAM De Bruijn, 'Suggestion for Amendment of Article: 59' (*European Convention*, 2003) <https://web.archive.org/web/20220121204954/http://european-convention.europa.eu/docs/Treaty/pdf/46/art46vriesEN.pdf> accessed 3 April 2020.

[24] Jacques Santer, Ben Fayot and M Schmit, 'Proposition d'amendement à l'Article: Article 46 (Titre X)' (*DORIE—European Commission*, 2003) <https://dorie.ec.europa.eu/en/details/-/card/89969> accessed 3 April 2020.

[25] Joschka Fischer, 'Suggestion for Amendment of Article: 46' (*DORIE—European Commission*, 2003) <https://dorie.ec.europa.eu/en/details/-/card/90009> accessed 3 April 2020.

[26] Jürgen Meyer, 'Vorschlag für die Änderung von: Art 46, Teil I, Titel X Des Verfassungsentwurfs (CONV 648/03)' (*DORIE—European Commission*, 2003) <https://dorie.ec.europa.eu/en/details/-/card/89975> accessed 3 April 2020.

[27] Christopher Hooton and Jon Stone, 'Brexit: Article 50 Was Never Actually Meant to Be Used, Says Its Author' *The Independent* (London, 26 July 2016) <www.independent.co.uk/news/uk/politics/brexit-eu-referendum-britain-theresa-may-article-50-not-supposed-meant-to-be-used-trigger-giuliano-a7156656.html> accessed 4 April 2020.

[28] ibid.

Kerr imagined that exit may be pursued only by backsliding Member State after the European Union had suspended its voting rights.[29] This functional connection reflects the original situation of Article 7 TEU's predecessor[30] in the same title as the withdrawal clause. Amato's understanding of withdrawal as a strategic safety valve and Kerr's opinion that it would only be used after legal sanctions for values infringement are removed from the *de jure* telos of Article 50 TEU as enshrining a voluntary and unilateral right for any Member State.[31] These strategic intentions may undermine the conception that the existence of the withdrawal clause explicitly guarantees democratic control for nationals of a Member State over the levelling down of constituent power.

iii. Secondary literature on the purpose of withdrawal

Academic scholarship also considers the strategic purposes of Article 50. These analyses draw a connection between disruption through opt-outs and disintegration. Christophe Hillion's analysis corroborates Amato and Kerr's perspective upon withdrawal as a precautionary measure. He argues that withdrawal is a 'safety valve to reassure Member States who would always be allowed to leave, should they be uncomfortable with the integration path envisaged'.[32] Conversely, 'the Member States' choice *not* to leave arguably entails a firm pledge to pursue the "ever closer union" goal'.[33] This suggests that Member States who do not pursue withdrawal should refrain from reserving constituent power at Treaty amendments and disrupting integration. Such a position may regard the possibility of disintegration as providing a resolution for constitutional disruption. Hillion argues that withdrawal 'confirms that participation in the European integration process is essentially voluntary and that the continental vocation of an "ever closer union" cannot trump its democratic foundations'.[34] However, the EU's gesture towards vindicating state sovereignty did not prevent rejection of the draft Treaty establishing a Constitution by the Dutch and French electorates. These strategic narratives present Article 50 as an affirmation of the European Union's democratic grounding. However, the

[29] Andrew Gray, 'Article 50 Author Lord Kerr: I Didn't Have UK in Mind' (*POLITICO*, 28 March 2017) <www.politico.eu/article/brexit-article-50-lord-kerr-john-kerr/> accessed 17 December 2018.
[30] Constitutional Treaty, art 58.
[31] Case C-621/18 *Wightman v Secretary of State for Exiting the European Union*, EU:C:2018:999.
[32] Christophe Hillion, 'This Way, Please! A Legal Appraisal of the EU Withdrawal Clause' in Carlos Closa (ed), *Secession from a Member State and Withdrawal from the European Union: Troubled Membership* (CUP 2017) 230.
[33] ibid.
[34] ibid 231.

ultimate purpose is not the democratic self-determination of individuals *per se*, but the continuation of European integration. One may interpret the 'safety valve' perspective on withdrawal as furthering the self-determination of individuals *qua* EU citizens rather than being a realistic means to enable individuals *qua* Member State nationals to level down constituent power.

Hillion explicates his reading of the relationship between opt-outs and withdrawal: '[t]he right to withdraw may . . . be interpreted as the ultimate elaboration of constitutional devices conceived to cater to the needs of less integrationist states'.[35] Similarly, Carlos Closa argues that '[i]n the EU partial exits (opt-outs) . . . fulfilled the function of alleviating tensions within membership'.[36] Closa warns that, rather than disincentivizing the reservation of constructive power, an explicit withdrawal clause may incentivize the proactive creation of opt-outs outside of amendment. He argues that '[t]he newly formalised exit constructs a different voice[37] mechanism: "voice" acquires the sense of acquiring some right for calling for the renegotiation (meaning *ex post* derogation) of the EU *acquis* and/or terms of membership in the EU'.[38]

Polly Polak presents the withdrawal clause as a full embodiment of the supranational constitutional order:

> Requiring the decision to withdraw to be made by a Member State 'in accordance with its own constitutional requirements' is based on the withdrawal clause proposed by the most constitutionalising contribution of all [to the 2003 Convention] and, therefore, this EU law mandate ordering the Member State to decide to withdraw in a certain manner may be a first restriction to its sovereign exercise of withdrawal.[39]

The contention that 'the right to withdraw is now firmly embedded in the EU legal order and . . . it is therefore governed not only by Article 50 but by the special nature of the legal order it belongs to and by the supranational elements that characterise this system'[40] could suggest that individuals *qua* EU citizens

[35] ibid.

[36] Carlos Closa (ed), *Secession from a Member State and Withdrawal from the European Union: Troubled Membership* (CUP 2017) 2.

[37] Closa utilizes the application of Hirschmann's 'exit, voice, and loyalty' mechanism by JHH Weiler. Crudely, one may propose an analogy between the exercise of 'voice' and the use of constituent power: Carlos Closa, 'Interpreting Article 50: Exit, Voice and . . . What About Loyalty?' in Carlos Closa (ed), *Secession from a Member State and Withdrawal from the European Union: Troubled Membership* (CUP 2017).

[38] ibid 212.

[39] Polak (n 4) 58.

[40] ibid 62.

are, and should be, the dominant constituent players in processes of levelling down constituent power.

Rather than neutralizing the High Contracting Parties' creation of opt-outs at Treaty revisions, Article 50 displaces the contestation that informs such exercises to moments of national constitutional importance. This could explain how Brexit arose in the context of a General Election manifesto promise rather than an EU Treaty amendment. As Closa recognizes, 'withdrawal provisions . . . grant legal certainty (next to facticity) to the full exit option and, because of this, also make it a more credible option.'[41] This reading recognizes that the creation of an explicit withdrawal clause was a decision by the High Contracting Parties wielding constructive power to recognize a legal path for the democratic repudiation of this power.

The strategic perceptions of the withdrawal clause at its origin, and during its development, reflect the dominant paradigm of (disrupted) integration at that time. A more detailed constitutional telos was only recognized after the paradigm shift to disintegration following the Brexit referendum result. This transition from political deterrent to framing an actual process of constitutional deconstruction necessitated this development. The exercise by individuals of their juridical objecthood *qua* EU citizen through court applications regarding the functioning of Article 50 led to the authoritative statement of the provision's dual-constitutional telos in the 2019 *Wightman* judgment.

iv. The dual telos of Article 50 TEU

This subsection excavates a determinative statement of the constitutional telos of Article 50 TEU from the perspective of the quadripartite role of individuals. The authoritative source is Case C-621/18 *Wightman v Secretary of State for Exiting the European Union*.[42] By contrast to the opt-out Protocols discussed in previous chapters, Article 50 applies to the entire supranational constitutional order. This is realized through the statement that 'the Treaties shall cease to apply to the State in question.'[43] The object to which the withdrawal clause applies is the framing purpose of the supranational constitutional order itself. This telos is the extension of the status of democratic subjecthood in the creation of norms, and the status of juridical subject in the reliance thereupon,

[41] Closa (n 37) 207.
[42] *Wightman* (n 31).
[43] TEU, art 50(3).

beyond the boundaries of the constitutional order of nationality through the levelling up of the means to construct norms.[44]

The telos of the withdrawal clause is contradistinct: to enable the repatriation of democratic subjecthood and juridical objecthood through the levelling down of constructive power as regulated by a supranational legal process. The democratic will of any constituent people to cease their participation in European integration is tempered by legal requirements that benefit all individuals *qua* juridical objects. At paragraph 56 of the *Wightman* judgment, the Court of Justice states that:

> Article 50 TEU pursues two objectives, namely, first, enshrining the sovereign right of a Member State to withdraw from the European Union and, secondly, establishing a procedure to enable such a withdrawal to take place in an orderly fashion.[45]

This statement is paradigmatic of the Court's teleological approach towards constructing the EU legal order. At paragraph 44 the Court of Justice reprises the foundational case law that reconstructed the nationals of the Member States as the juridical objects of the supranational constitutional order.[46] The paragraph after provides a succinct overview of the predicative characteristics of the legal order as the EU's juridical 'constitutional identity'.[47] Paragraph 46 derives from these characteristics the conclusion that a holistic approach must be adopted: '[t]he question referred must therefore be examined in the light of the Treaties taken as a whole'.[48] This move broadens the scope of sources to encompass all written and unwritten EU law norms. Paragraph 47 reinforces this move through the delineation of the teleological method of interpretation. The Court of Justice evokes its 'settled case-law' to require account of the wording, objectives, context, and provisions of EU law as a whole.[49] Separately, the Court claims that '[t]he origins of a provision of EU law may also provide information relevant to its interpretation'.[50]

[44] See the discussion of levelling up constituent power in chapter 2.
[45] *Wightman* (n 31) para 56.
[46] ibid para 44, referencing Case 294/83 *Parti écologiste 'Les Verts' v European Parliament* [1986] ECR 1339; Opinion 2/13 on the accession of the EU to the ECHR, EU:C:2014:2454 (Full Court, 18 December 2014).
[47] ibid para 45; see Kaarlo Tuori, 'Crossing the Limits but Stuck behind the Fault Lines?' (2016) 7 Transnational Legal Theory 133.
[48] ibid para 46.
[49] ibid para 47.
[50] ibid.

The Court of Justice thereby empowers itself to use a wide range of sources. The Court makes references to the Treaty declarations that 'indicate that those Treaties have as their purpose the creation of an ever closer union among the peoples of Europe'.[51] This is supplemented by references to liberty and democracy and their Treaty bases; these values are argued to 'form part of the very foundations of the European Union legal order'.[52] These two values, respectively, correspond to the roles of individuals as juridical objects and political subjects. This dichotomy informs the understanding of the telos of Article 50 presented here.

The Court of Justice introduces citizenship of the Union as a component of its holistic method: 'any withdrawal of a Member State from the European Union is liable to have a considerable impact on the rights of all Union citizens, including *inter alia* their right to free movement, as regards both nationals of the Member State concerned and nationals of other Member States'.[53] The final source from EU law as a whole is the 'counterpart'[54] provision of Article 49 TEU, the accession clause.[55] This establishes a juridical connection between the levelling up and levelling down of constituent power. The Court presents this through a public international law framing: '[a]s is apparent from Article 49 TEU . . . the European Union is composed of states which have freely and voluntarily committed themselves to those values [of the EU]'.[56] This 'free and voluntary commitment', as described from an international law perspective, can be understood as the supranational levelling up of constructive power from a constitutional law perspective.

The two objectives of Article 50 TEU are presented as the conclusion of the textual analysis. The first objective is the 'enshrining' of the sovereign right of a Member State to withdraw from the European Union. 'Enshrining' defines an important feature as compared to public international law. Rather than creating *ex nihilo* the legal right of withdrawal, Article 50 replaces the pre-existing public international law power with a specialized supranational framework. This establishes conditions to vindicate the role of individuals. From a public international law perspective, Article 50 TEU operates as *lex specialis* in

[51] ibid para 61.
[52] ibid para 62; referencing Case C-402/05 *Kadi and Al Barakaat International Foundation v Council and Commission* [2008] ECR I-6351, paras 303–4.
[53] *Wightman* (n 31) para 64.
[54] See chapter 2 for the similar conceptualization of Articles 49 and 50 TEU as two limbs of a 'triptych' of constituted constituent power.
[55] *Wightman* (n 31) para 63.
[56] ibid.

relation to the *lex generalis* of the Vienna Convention on the Law of Treaties.[57] From a constitutional perspective, Article 50 constructs a democratic means for individuals *qua* nationals of the Member State to use this power.

The second important feature of the first objective is the language of sovereignty. Armin Cuyvers states that *Wightman* places an 'unusual emphasis on sovereignty'.[58] He notes that this is limited to the 'specific and unique context of withdrawal'.[59] The wording of *Wightman* obscures a specific facet of this background. The language of a 'sovereign right of a Member State' only reflects action on the international plane. This may derive from Article 50(2), which concerns the notification of an intention to withdraw by a Member State to the European Council, being the specific clause in question. This action occurs in the realm of international relations.

The wording misses, however, that the notification communicates a decision to withdraw in accordance with the Member States' 'constitutional requirements'.[60] The Copenhagen criteria for accession ensure that Member States are constitutional democracies. The commitment to the values of democracy and the Rule of Law in Article 2 TEU means that such a decision must be a manifestation of democratic will-formation by individuals *qua* nationals of that Member State.[61] Beyond the sovereign rights of the state in international law, the first objective of Article 50 must also be understood as a means for democratic subjects to initiate legitimate disintegration.[62]

The second objective of an 'orderly procedure' constrains democratic disintegration within a supranational legal procedure. The orderly procedure is conceived of here as a 'deconstitutional convention' that operates analogously to Articles 48 and 49 TEU.[63] This guarantees that withdrawal complies with norms that preserve the position of individuals *qua* juridical objects. Furthermore, the convention also ensures the representation of individuals *qua* democratic subjects by supranational and national institutions. In practice, however, criticism has pointed out that three factors may undermine orderliness: the need for unilateral measures by the European Union and

[57] 'The termination of a Treaty or the withdrawal of a party may take place: (a) in conformity with the provisions of the Treaty; or (b) at any time by consent of all the parties after consultation with the other contracting States': VCLT, art 54.

[58] Armin Cuyvers, 'Wightman, Brexit, and the Sovereign Right to Remain' (2019) 56 Common Market Law Review 1303, 1321.

[59] ibid.

[60] TEU, art 50(1).

[61] Hillion (n 32) 217–18.

[62] Markus Patberg, 'Can Disintegration Be Democratic? The European Union Between Legitimate Change and Regression' (2020) 68 Political Studies 582.

[63] See discussion of the triptych in chapter 2.

withdrawing state to prepare the legal systems; the drafting of Article 50 TEU in 'relatively sketchy terms . . . leaving open various important questions about its correct interpretation and application'; and the possibility of the process ending not in an orderly negotiated settlement but in no deal or revocation of notification.[64]

The telos of Article 50 TEU balances the conflict that emerges between the co-constitutive foundations of democratic will at the Member State level and the Rule of Law at the supranational level.[65] The two objectives also seek to balance the transformation from coexistence to mutual exclusivity between nationality of a Member State and citizenship of the Union.[66] Ultimately, the telos of Article 50 TEU seeks to resolve the conflict between integration and disintegration. The withdrawal clause aims for a compromise whereby neither of these opposing forces obviates its counterpart.

[64] Dougan (n 15) 26. See discussion in chapter 7 for how no deal undermines orderliness and the reform proposals in chapter 8 to address this defect.

[65] Jürgen Habermas, 'On the Internal Relation between the Rule of Law and Democracy' (1995) 3 European Journal of Philosophy 12. See further the discussion in chapter 2.

[66] See the discussion of this relationship in chapter 2.

6
Brexit
A Narrative of Disintegration

I. Article 50 TEU: The Exclusive Means for Withdrawal?

The structure of Article 50 TEU makes provision chronologically for the withdrawal of a Member State. Therefore, this narrative of the UK's use of the clause and the resulting disintegration adopts a structure focusing on the activation and functioning of each provision in the withdrawal clause. The initial legal question is whether Article 50 provides the exclusive means for a legally valid and constitutionally legitimate withdrawal. Possible alternative means are withdrawal through the Vienna Convention on the Law of Treaties and/or domestic measures, or through amendment of the EU Treaties. Neil MacCormick stated that 'one can say with reasonable confidence that this power of repeal [of the European Communities Act 1972], that is of unilateral and valid secession ... subsists in the constitution of the United Kingdom and is exercisable by an Act of Parliament expressly enacted to that end'.[1] MacCormick was writing before the creation of Article 50 TEU. However, arguments for unilateral secession through repeal or amendment of the European Communities Act 1972 were revived during the 2016 referendum campaign.[2] Steve Peers and Darren Harvey consider withdrawal through Treaty amendment: 'it would still be possible for the Member States to provide for the withdrawal of one or more members by amending the Treaties in order to remove references to the withdrawing State from the preamble and other relevant sections of the Treaties'.[3]

These alternative means for withdrawal are deficient from the three perspectives of domestic constitutional law, public international law, and the EU's supranational constitutional order. They fail to ensure that a withdrawal

[1] Neil MacCormick, *Questioning Sovereignty: Law, State, and Nation in the European Commonwealth* (OUP 1999) 88.

[2] John Redwood, 'What Does Brexit Look like? A Lot Better than Staying In' (*John Redwood's Diary*, 1 February 2016) <http://johnredwoodsdiary.com/2016/02/01/what-does-brexit-look-like-a-lot-better-than-staying-in/> accessed 6 April 2020.

[3] Steve Peers and Darren Harvey, 'Brexit: The Legal Dimension' in Catherine Barnard and Steve Peers (eds), *European Union Law* (2nd edn, OUP 2017) 820.

Constitutional Disintegration and Disruption. Oliver Garner, Oxford University Press. © Oxford University Press 2025. DOI: 10.1093/9780198914136.003.0006

decision is legitimate and authoritative for individuals exercising all of the roles as the quadripartite subject. Any proposal to withdraw through the Vienna Convention, including through amendment of the Treaty, would not be valid from the perspective of public international law. The statement in Article 54(b) that a withdrawal may take place by consent of all the parties is the residual condition. The primary condition is that withdrawal occurs 'in conformity with the provisions of the Treaty'.[4] The language of state sovereignty indicates that Article 50 fulfils this function in international law, in addition to national and supranational constitutional law.

Withdrawal via repeal of domestic implementing law would be valid from the national perspective, but not from the international or supranational perspective. Such repeal is a necessary but not sufficient step. The United Kingdom has repealed the European Communities Act 1972 in tandem with the Article 50 deconstitutional convention.[5] Without the supranational procedure, EU law will continue to apply *to* the Member State on the international and supranational planes, even if the norms no longer apply *in* the Member State's constitutional order. The withdrawing Member State would be open to infringement proceedings for breach of the Treaties in such a situation.

These alternative methods of exit from the EU legal order are also constitutionally improper. Exclusively domestic and international means of withdrawal would entail the democratic representation of individuals only as nationals of that constitutional state. Excluding the roles of the European Parliament and the Council would preclude the representation of all individuals *qua* citizens of the European Union and *qua* nationals of the other Member States. When the High Contracting Parties ratified the Treaty of Lisbon, they levelled up the means to level down constituent power. This commitment binds the representatives to follow the process established in Article 50 TEU. The self-determination of individuals in their quadripartite role is guaranteed by this clause: democratic representation is ensured by the relevant Member State and EU institutions, and juridical objecthood is ensured by both domestic courts and the Court of Justice.[6] The following sub-sections will analyse the provisions of Article 50 in depth.

[4] VCLT, art 54(a).

[5] European Union (Withdrawal) Act 2018; European Union (Withdrawal Agreement) Act 2020.

[6] See C-327/18 *PPU—R O*, EU:C:2018:733; Case T-458/17 *Shindler v Council*, EU:T:2018:838; Case C-621/18 *Wightman v Secretary of State for Exiting the European Union*, EU:C:2018:999.

II. Article 50(1) TEU: The Domestic Decision to Repatriate Constituent Power

The two crucial features of Article 50(1) are the provision made for a 'decision' to withdraw, and the condition that the decision must be in accordance with the 'constitutional requirements' of that Member State. This supranational text is declarative of a process that must be internal for the state considering withdrawal. The supranational institutions have no authority to prescribe what these constitutional requirements are, nor what legal or democratic form the 'decision' should take. However, the argument has been made that the EU's own 'constitutional requirements' may overlap conditions upon the Member State's decision:

> [I]t is in no way guaranteed that every EU Member State's constitutional requirements will be up to standards as well as respected if the time comes for one to activate Article 50, thus it is not irrelevant to argue in favour of a state's right to withdrawal being doubly conditional upon its adherence to EU constitutional standards.[7]

This may suggest a residual monitoring role for the EU institutions to vindicate the interests of all individuals *qua* EU citizens. Article 50(1) mandates an exercise of democratic subjecthood by nationals before a bridge is crossed to the supranational order. This leads to an analogy with the initial stage of the levelling up of constituent power being necessarily limited to the national level.[8]

The 'Member State' decision should be understood through the prism of Member State nationals *qua* democratic subjects. Article 50(1) is not addressed exclusively to executive actors, but also to the state's constituent citizens. The assumption is that, for an issue as important as EU membership, the 'constitutional requirements' must enable maximum democratic participation. The constitutional requirements also constrain this will formation to a legal procedure that serves individuals *qua* juridical objects. The reflexive interaction between these two roles has been demonstrated in the Brexit case.

[7] Polly Polak, *EU Withdrawal as a Supranational Affair: The Case of Brexit* (Brill Nijhoff 2023) 110.
[8] See the discussion of levelling up constituent power in chapter 2.

i. The EU Referendum Act 2015

Brexit raises the question of whether the UK's constitutional requirements guaranteed self-determination for nationals *qua* democratic subjects, whilst ensuring certainty of process *qua* juridical objects. Interaction between political and judicial processes informed the decision to withdraw. The Conservative Party 2015 General Election manifesto promised that '[w]e will legislate in the first session of the next Parliament for an in–out referendum to be held on Britain's membership of the EU before the end of 2017'.[9] This promise enabled democratic subjects to use the orthodox process for appointing norm creators—a General Election—to express a preference for the constitutionally unorthodox mechanism of a referendum.[10] The manifesto recognizes this process: 'it is time for the British people—not politicians—to have their say'.[11]

The exercise of direct democracy may conform to Patberg's arguments that constituted powers should be excluded from decisions concerning the levelling up of constituent power.[12] If one accepts that the referendum was a legitimate expression of constituent power, this may address a democratic lag from the Treaty of Maastricht onwards. The delayed ratification of the Treaty precipitated a vote of confidence in the government.[13] This incentivized the Parliamentary majority to continue a Conservative government rather than represent their constituents' interests on EU membership. The delay in ascertaining popular support for European integration continued. In the following years, intimations that the Labour governments of Tony Blair and Gordon Brown would hold referendums on the UK's membership of the euro, the Constitutional Treaty, and the Lisbon Treaty did not come to fruition.[14]

The 2016 referendum was subject to constitutional deficiencies.[15] The authorizing legislation did not confirm whether the vote was legally binding or

[9] 'Conservative Party Manifesto 2015—the Full Pdf' *The Guardian* (London, 14 April 2015) <www.theguardian.com/politics/2015/apr/14/conservative-party-manifesto-2015-the-full-pdf> accessed 7 April 2020.

[10] Michael Gordon, 'Brexit: The Relationship between the UK Parliament and the UK Government' in Michael Dougan (ed), *The UK After Brexit: Legal and Policy Challenges* (Intersentia 2017).

[11] 'Conservative Party Manifesto 2015' (n 9).

[12] Markus Patberg, 'A Systematic Justification for the EU's Pouvoir Constituant Mixte: Principles of Constitutional Politics in Supranational Polities' (2017) 23 European Law Journal 441.

[13] Stephen Goodwin, 'The Vote of Confidence: Major Wins Gamble on Social Chapter Vote' *The Independent* (London, 23 July 1993) <www.independent.co.uk/news/uk/the-vote-of-confidence-major-wins-gamble-on-social-chapter-vote-1486708.html> accessed 7 April 2020.

[14] Stuart Smedley, 'A Missed Opportunity? Revisiting the Euro Referendum That Never Was from a Historical Perspective' (*LSE Brexit*, 3 December 2019) <https://blogs.lse.ac.uk/brexit/2019/12/03/a-missed-opportunity-revisiting-the-euro-referendum-that-never-was-from-a-historical-perspective/> accessed 7 April 2020.

[15] See Jo Shaw, 'The Quintessentially Democratic Act? Democracy, Political Community and Citizenship in and after the UK's EU Referendum of June 2016' (2017) 39 Journal of European

merely politically advisory.[16] The result was dependent upon a simple majority requirement, rather than establishing any further thresholds such as a majority of all the UK's constituent nations.[17] These factors challenge the assumption that the referendum was a legitimate expression of constituent power in a multi-nation state.[18] Opening this new channel for political will expression provoked tension with the constitutional orthodoxy of parliamentary representation.[19]

The unorthodox democratic mechanism had the valid legal base of an Act of Parliament. Section 1 of the European Union Referendum Act 2015 created the obligation that '[a] referendum is to be held on whether the United Kingdom should remain a member of the European Union'.[20] Sections 6 and 7 included duties to publish information on the outcome of renegotiations and membership of the European Union. The Act omitted any statutory obligation for the Prime Minister to notify an intention to withdraw if a leave vote were returned. The legislation was silent on exactly *what* would constitute a decision to withdraw and *how* the constitutional requirements would be fulfilled. A House of Commons Library Briefing Paper suggested that parliamentarians were aware that the referendum was 'pre-legislative or consultative'.[21] The legislation underdetermined the legal nature of the referendum, prompting uncertainty for individuals *qua* juridical objects over the conditions for the initiation of the deconstitutional convention.

A further concern is that the referendum did not enfranchise all individuals who would be affected by the decision as juridical objects. Section 2(1)(a) made those entitled to vote as electors in parliamentary elections the referendum franchise, and section 2(1)(b) extended this franchise to include members of the House of Lords who are usually disqualified from voting. Section 2(1)(c) extended the scope of the franchise to those entitled to vote in European Parliament elections in Gibraltar. Section 2(2) confirms that the franchise included Commonwealth citizens and citizens of the Republic of Ireland. The

Integration 559; AC Grayling, 'The EU Referendum Was Gerrymandered' (*LSE Brexit*, 28 September 2017) <https://blogs.lse.ac.uk/brexit/2017/09/28/the-eu-referendum-was-gerrymandered/> accessed 7 April 2020.

16 European Union Referendum Act 2015.

17 Shaw (n 15).

18 I thank Marise Cremona for reminding me of these points.

19 Oliver Garner, 'After Article 50 and Before Withdrawal: Does Constitutional Theory Require a General Election in the United Kingdom Before Brexit?' (*Verfassungsblog*, 24 March 2017) <https://verfassungsblog.de/after-article-50-and-before-withdrawal-does-constitutional-theory-require-a-general-election-in-the-united-kingdom-before-brexit/> accessed 7 April 2020.

20 European Union Referendum Act 2015, s 1(1).

21 Elise Uberoi, 'European Union Referendum Bill 2015-16' (House of Commons Library Briefing Paper No 07212, 3 June 2015) 25.

franchise omitted EU citizens from other Member States entitled to vote in local and European Parliament elections,[22] and UK citizens who have not been resident within the United Kingdom for more than fifteen years.[23]

Ruvi Ziegler has argued that this franchise was both 'over- and under-inclusive'.[24] The rights that EU citizens have relied upon to settle in the United Kingdom are directly affected by withdrawal, yet these individuals were excluded from participating in the democratic decision. The exclusion of resident EU citizens may be justified as they do not hold the constituent status of national of the Member State which is contemplating withdrawal, and the first stage of this process is limited to the national level. The exclusion of those who do hold this status of nationality, but have been deprived of democratic subjecthood through exercising their EU citizenship *qua* juridical object is harder to justify.

This raises a problem with the analogy to the hypothetical dual-constituent assembly proposed by Habermas and Patberg. At the stage of the initial decision to level up constituent power, individuals act as nationals of constitutional states before their agreement to bestow the new status of EU citizenship upon themselves and nationals of other Member States.[25] In the actual deconstitutional convention, nationals approach the withdrawal decision holding the status of EU citizenship, and decide upon the extinction or retention of the supranational status. This means that the principle of equal constitutional consideration of those holding the same constituent status are also relevant to the initial domestic decision to withdraw. This theoretical consideration manifested itself juridically in the *Shindler* litigation. The UK courts were called upon to determine whether the domestic constitutional requirements for withdrawal were affected by potential detrimental effects on EU law rights.

ii. The *Shindler* judgments on the decision to withdraw

In the absence of legislative clarity, the parameters of the 'decision' and the domestic 'constitutional requirements' for the United Kingdom under Article 50(1) TEU have been determined through individuals exercising their role

[22] European Parliamentary Elections (Franchise of Relevant Citizens of the Union) Regulations 2001; Representation of the People Act 1983.
[23] Representation of the People Act 1985.
[24] Reuven Ziegler, 'GLOBALCIT Report on Political Participation of Mobile EU Citizens: United Kingdom' (2018) Country Report 2018/14, 19.
[25] See the discussion of levelling up constituent power in chapter 2.

as juridical objects before domestic courts. The first example of this litigation occurred before the referendum. In *Shindler v Chancellor of the Duchy of Lancaster*,[26] the claimants argued that their exclusion from the referendum franchise, as they had not been on the UK electoral register for fifteen years, restricted their directly effective EU law rights of freedom of movement.[27] They elaborated that the franchise was 'incompatible with EU law because it . . . discourage[d] them from continuing to exercise their free movement rights by requiring them to return home to the United Kingdom in order to be able to vote in the EU referendum'.[28]

This argument claims that the national withdrawal decision is subject to limitations established by the juridical face of the supranational status of EU citizenship. The UK government counterclaimed that the national decision is untouched by EU law:

> [The defendants] submit that it would be surprising if EU law were to constrain the decision by the United Kingdom whether it wishes to be bound by EU law. Accordingly, they submit that it is only once a decision has been taken to leave the EU that EU law, in the shape of Article 50(2)–(5) TEU applies in order to determine the procedure and timescale for disengagement.[29]

On appeal, the government added that 'the UK cannot sensibly be said to have a sovereign right to decide to withdraw from EU treaties, the exercise of which is constrained by the rule of the very treaties from which it wishes to withdraw'.[30]

The government's perspective is that the text of Article 50(1) is merely declaratory of internal constitutional processes. The supranational constitutional order only becomes relevant after the Member State provides notification under Article 50(2). Article 50(1)'s status—either hermetically sealed within domestic constitutional law, or subject to the supranational constitutional order—determines whether the national decision and constitutional requirements continue to inform the supranational deconstitutional convention until the Treaties cease to apply. The Divisional Court at first instance held that the domestic decision is subject to EU law conditions: 'we do not consider that Article 50(1) . . . confers on a Member State a total exemption from EU law . . . If

[26] *Shindler v Chancellor of the Duchy of Lancaster* [2016] EWHC 957 (Admin).
[27] ibid [2].
[28] ibid [27].
[29] ibid [23].
[30] *Shindler v Chancellor of the Duchy of Lancaster* [2016] EWCA Civ 649.

such a striking departure from established principles of EU law were intended very clear words would be required'.[31]

The Court of Appeal overturned this decision. The Master of the Rolls argued that

> [I]t would have been surprising if the Member States had agreed that a Member who wishes to withdraw from the EU altogether could only do so if the decision to withdraw did not infringe one or more fundamental EU rules . . . If this had been the intention of the Member States, this would surely have been expressly agreed.[32]

Lord Justice Elias supplements this conclusion from a domestic perspective:

> I doubt whether, purely as a matter of domestic law, Parliament would have intended section 2(1) [of the European Communities Act 1972] to apply so as to give primacy to EU law when the very question in issue is whether the UK should remain bound by EU law . . . Parliament agreed to join the EU by exercising sovereign powers untrammelled by EU law and I think it would expect to be able to leave the EU in the exercise of the same untrammelled sovereign power.[33]

Elias LJ concludes, in the alternative, that '[e]ven if it [Article 50] is EU law as a result of section 2(1), the EU has chosen to exercise its power so as to refer sovereignty back exclusively to the UK'.[34]

There are normative reasons to prefer this alternative position that EU law applies but the supranational constitutional order has deferred to the domestic constitutional level. The Court of Appeal rejects the claimant's argument that exclusion from the franchise restricts their juridical free movement rights. It would have been more appropriate to argue that the exclusion restricted not their rights as juridical objects, but as democratic subjects. The UK domestic courts endorse the European Court of Human Rights' dicta that the fifteen-year exclusion rule is a proportionate means to achieve the legitimate objective of 'testing the strength of a citizen's links with the United Kingdom over a significant period of time'.[35] This fails to recognize that General Elections are not

[31] *Shindler* (HC) (n 26) [24].
[32] *Shindler* (CA) (n 30) [16].
[33] ibid [58].
[34] ibid [60].
[35] *Shindler* (HC) (n 26) [43].

only norm-creator processes at the domestic level. These elections also indirectly appoint the members of the Council of Ministers as norm-creator processes for the supranational level. The fifteen-year exclusion may be justified as a bright-line rule to test whether individuals are sufficiently affected by norm application at the *domestic* level. However, it is not justified with regard to the supranational level. Article 20 TFEU only confers the right to vote in local and European Parliament elections in the Member State of residence. The exclusion of these mobile EU citizens from national elections in the state of residence and the state of nationality means they have no representation in the Council, such that they are only represented *qua* EU citizens in the creation of EU law norms to which they are subject. This creates an imbalance whereby individuals may be deprived of participation in norm-creation processes in their role as democratic subject *qua* national due to fully exercising their rights as juridical subject *qua* EU citizen.

The focus on juridical rights misdirected the court's distinction between national elections and the referendum on EU membership:

> [I]f the inability to vote in such [Parliamentary] elections occurring at relatively regular intervals . . . could not reasonably be considered liable to dissuade or deter British citizens from exercising their rights of free movement, it is difficult to see how the inability to vote in a once occurring referendum on membership of the EU could be considered to be capable of having such an effect either.[36]

This prioritizes exclusion from General Elections due to their frequency as opposed to the rarity of an EU referendum. From the perspective of democratic subjecthood, however, this one-off referendum is existentially more important than national elections. It concerns the decision by individuals *qua* nationals to retain or extinguish the supranational constituent status which the concerned individuals have relied upon in pursuit of their life plans. Beyond discrete elections, the referendum decides whether individuals will continue to have the capacity to participate in supranational democratic and judicial processes.

The Divisional Court does state that '[w]e acknowledge the very real and personal interest which these claimants have in the outcome of the EU referendum. If the United Kingdom leaves the European Union, they . . . will certainly be deprived of their EU citizenship and the important rights which

[36] *Shindler* (Admin) (HC) [32].

accompany that status'.[37] The framing of the question around juridical free movement rights, and the silence of Article 50 on EU citizenship, limited the courts to considering whether mobile UK nationals would 'pick up sticks and return'[38] because of the possibility of a referendum. The *Shindler* judgments present the Article 50(1) TEU decision as ungoverned by EU law. Democratic participation is left to the determination of the domestic legislature. This may lead to an arbitrary restriction on who is enfranchised as a democratic subject in the decision. The court's decision resulted from the wording of Article 50 reflecting only the public international law perspective, rather than the supranational constitutional perspective. The reference to the right of a Member State enables the court to conclude that the decision concerns 'untrammelled sovereign power'.[39] This is true regarding the Member State as a High Contracting Party to the foundational Treaties. However, this position fails to capture that, through the same decision, the individuals who hold EU citizenship by virtue of nationality of this Member State will decide whether to retain or to extinguish this constituent status. Withdrawal is a dual process that occurs at the public international level for the state in question, but also at the supranational and national level for constituent individuals. Contra *Shindler*, all those who hold EU citizenship through nationality of the Member State contemplating withdrawal should be able to participate in the democratic decision.

iii. The *Miller* judgment on constitutional requirements

The definition of the domestic 'constitutional requirements' for the decision was touched upon in *Shindler*.[40] This question would re-emerge explosively in the *Miller* litigation after the referendum.[41] The residual ambiguity over the 'decision' to withdraw and its relationship to notification was eventually resolved in the *Webster* judgment.[42] The dicta in *Shindler*, *Miller*, and *Webster* established that there are no conditions established by the juridical constitution of the United Kingdom for a decision to withdraw. The conditions for the decision are determined entirely through democratic processes. This underdetermination

[37] ibid [51].
[38] *Shindler* (CA) (n 30) [45].
[39] ibid [58].
[40] ibid [13].
[41] *R (on the application of Miller) v Secretary of State for Exiting the European Union* [2016] EWHC 2768 (Admin); *R (on the application of Miller) v Secretary of State for Exiting the European Union* [2017] UKSC 5.
[42] *R (on the application of Webster) v Secretary of State for Exiting the European Union* [2018] EWHC 1543 (Admin).

precipitated legal uncertainty over what the constitutional requirements were, whether they had been fulfilled, and what action precisely constituted the decision to withdraw. The practical consequence was an elongated legal vacuum before the United Kingdom provided notification under Article 50(2). This exposed a lacuna within the text of the withdrawal clause.

The Master of the Rolls held in *Shindler* that '[t]he 2015 Act contains part of the constitutional requirements of the UK as to how it may decide to withdraw from the EU. These include the holding of a referendum'.[43] This expression of direct democracy is presented as a contingent feature based on circumstances rather than an immutable predicate:

> In theory, Parliament could decide to withdraw without waiting for the result of the referendum . . . But . . . [t]he reality is that it has decided that it will withdraw only if that course is sanctioned by the referendum [which] . . . is an integral part of the process of deciding to withdraw from the EU.[44]

The Supreme Court in *Miller* held that the referendum had no legal effect: '[b]ut that in no way means it is devoid of effect. It means that, unless and until acted on by Parliament, its force is political rather than legal'.[45] Mark Elliott, Jack Williams, and Alison Young resolve the discrepancy between the cases by arguing that the dicta is cumulative in effect: 'the EU referendum "contains part" of the UK's "constitutional requirements" . . . The *Miller* case concerned the remaining requirements'.[46] Another interpretation is that, whereas *Shindler* concerns the constitutional requirements for a 'decision' under Article 50(1), *Miller* concerns the requirements for the 'notification' thereof under Article 50(2). The *Webster* judgment precluded this interpretation by eliding the decision and the notification into a single legal act.[47]

The ambiguous status of the referendum exemplifies the lack of constitutional codification regarding the levelling up and levelling down of constituent power within the United Kingdom. Parliament remains free to determine the democratic channels, representative or direct, for such a decision. These channels may be altered from decision to decision without any legal requirement for consistency, even if the 1975 in–out referendum informed Parliament's

[43] *Shindler* (CA) (n 30) [13].
[44] ibid [19].
[45] *Miller* (SC) (n 41) [124].
[46] Mark Elliott, Alison L Young and Jack Williams, 'The Miller Tale: An Introduction' in Mark Elliott, Alison L Young and Jack Williams (eds), *The UK Constitution after Miller: Brexit and Beyond* (Hart Publishing 2018) 3.
[47] *Webster* (n 42) [15].

decision to mandate a similar referendum in 2015.[48] Vernon Bogdanor argues that a constitutional convention has arisen through a precedent that referendums are necessary in matters concerning the devolution of power from Westminster, and in matters of particular 'constitutional significance': 'With these referendums—so the argument goes—political actors have created a precedent. They have generated a public expectation that certain pivotal issues of constitutional relevance remain the preserve of popular sovereignty'.[49] This may be regarded as a convention whereby matters concerning the constituent power and status of citizens require referendums. The normative essence of this convention was codified in the 'referendum lock' of the European Union Act 2011 for reconstruction of the supranational constitutional order via Article 48 TEU.[50] This may have been a further influence on the decision to hold a referendum on the deconstruction of EU membership. The privileging of individuals *qua* democratic subjects over individuals *qua* juridical objects is inherent to how the Supreme Court presented the status of EU law in the *Miller* judgment.[51]

The referendum result had no effect in domestic or EU law. An argument could be made that it did have legal consequences in public international law. David Cameron's renegotiation of the UK's membership resulted in a 'Decision of the heads of state or government of the Member States acting through the European Council' in the form of a simplified international Treaty. The condition for that Treaty to come into force is detailed in paragraph 2 of Section E of the European Council conclusions containing the Decision: 'This Decision shall take effect on the same date as the Government of the United Kingdom informs the Secretary-General of the Council that the United Kingdom has decided to remain a member of the European Union'.[52] This may suggest that

[48] Vernon Bogdanor, 'After the Referendum, the People, Not Parliament, Are Sovereign' *Financial Times* (London, FT Weekend 10 December 2016) 14; see further Vernon Bogdanor, *Beyond Brexit: Britain's Unprotected Constitution* (IB Tauris 2019).

[49] Gabriele Ruberto, 'When Does the British Constitution Require a Referendum? V. Bogdanor's Opinion on the Place for the Referendum in the UK' (*The Constitution Unit Blog*, 26 February 2013) <https://constitution-unit.com/2013/02/26/when-does-the-british-constitution-require-a-referendum-v-bogdanors-opinion-on-the-place-for-the-referendum-in-the-uk/> accessed 21 April 2020.

[50] European Union Act 2011, s 6. See Paul Craig, 'Brexit: A Drama in Six Acts' (2016) 41 European Law Review 447, 448–49.

[51] Oliver Garner, 'Conditional Primacy of EU Law: The United Kingdom Supreme Court's Own "Solange (so Long as)" Doctrine?' (*UK Constitutional Law Association*, 31 January 2017) <https://ukconstitutionallaw.org/2017/01/31/oliver-garner-conditional-primacy-of-eu-law-the-united-kingdom-supreme-courts-own-solange-so-long-as-doctrine/> accessed 8 April 2020.

[52] European Council meeting (18 and 19 February 2016)—Conclusions, Annex 1—Decision of the Heads of State or Government, meeting within the European Council, concerning a new settlement for the United Kingdom within the European Union—Brussels 19 February 2016 EUCO 1/16, 24.

the agreement coming into force was predicated upon a remain vote being delivered in the referendum.

However, the referendum result would have been a legally contingent factor. No reference is made to the referendum result in the text; the decision is left to the executive discretion of the Prime Minister. Although politically unfeasible, nothing would have legally prohibited the Prime Minister from making such a notification to the Council even after a leave result.[53] Despite the lack of legal effect, the referendum result and the New Settlement not coming into force may have precipitated the Union institutions' pre-emptive action in preparing the deconstitutional convention before notification.[54]

Both the Divisional Court and the Supreme Court in *Miller* held that the government could not use the prerogative power for the executive to act in foreign affairs in order to notify the intention to withdraw. An Act of Parliament was necessary. Notification through the prerogative would violate the rule that this executive power cannot be used to alter domestic law. This conclusion was predicated upon the conceptualization of EU law as an 'independent and overriding source of domestic law'.[55] The Supreme Court outlines two different perspectives on EU law:

> In one sense, of course, it can be said that the 1972 Act is the source of EU law, in that, without that Act, EU law would have no domestic status. But in a more fundamental . . . and . . . realistic sense, where EU law applies in the United Kingdom, it is the EU institutions which are the relevant source of that law.[56]

This recognizes the different roles that individuals play with regard to EU law. As juridical objects *qua* nationals, EU law applies purely by virtue of the European Communities Act 1972. This statute has been legitimated by individuals *qua* democratic subjects through parliamentary representation. As democratic subjects *qua* EU citizens, however, individuals directly legitimate EU law norms at the supranational level. Furthermore, the standing rules in Article 263 TFEU enable individuals to function *qua* juridical objects of the EU legal order without any mediation through the domestic constitutional order.[57] Academic commentators also claim the significance of supranationalism to the Supreme Court's judgment. Polak argues that 'the UK's main constitutional

[53] I thank Marise Cremona for this argument.
[54] See discussion further below in this chapter.
[55] *Miller* (SC) (n 41) [65].
[56] ibid [61].
[57] See detailed discussion of the role of juridical objects in chapter 2.

requirement in order to exercise the right to withdraw . . . stemmed not only from Britain's constitution and its core principle of Parliamentary sovereignty but, just as importantly, from the special and unparalleled legal nature of the Union'.[58]

The condition for EU law to remain an overriding source of UK law reveals the balance between democratic and juridical requirements in the withdrawal decision. The Supreme Court holds that 'this unprecedented state of affairs will only last so long as Parliament wishes: the 1972 Act can be repealed like any other statute'.[59] The consequence of the ECA 1972 acting as a 'conduit pipe' is 'a dynamic process by which, without further primary legislation . . . EU law . . . actually takes precedence over all domestic sources of UK law, including statutes'.[60] This is conditional acceptance of the Court of Justice's supremacy claims.[61] By contrast to other Member States, however, this conditionality is formal rather than substantive.[62]

The Supreme Court states that, so long as the European Communities Act 1972 remains in force, all EU law will have supremacy over domestic law regardless of its substance. The most prominent example of substantive conditionality is provided by the German Constitutional Court, which has held that EU law will have primacy only so long as its content does not violate numerous predicates of German constitutional identity.[63] These limits were controversially enforced in the 2020 *PSPP* judgment. The UK Supreme Court came close to substantive conditional supremacy in its *HS2* judgment.[64] Lord Mance and Lord Neuberger held that 'there may be fundamental principles, whether contained in other constitutional instruments or recognised at common law, of which Parliament when it enacted the European Communities Act 1972 did not either contemplate or authorise the abrogation'.[65] Perhaps facilitated by the fact that such a possibility could never arise after Brexit, the Supreme Court in *Miller* did not follow this obiter dictum.

[58] Polak (n 7) 110.

[59] *Miller* (SC) (n 41) [60].

[60] Ibid.

[61] Garner, 'Conditional Primacy of EU Law' (n 51).

[62] Oliver Garner, 'The Borders of European Integration on Trial in the Member States: Dansk Industri, Miller, and Taricco' (2017) 9 European Journal of Legal Studies 1.

[63] *Maastricht*, German Constitutional Court Decision of 12 October 1993, BVerfGE 89, 155; *Brunner v European Union Treaty* [1994] 1 CMLR 57; *Lisbon*, Judgment of the Second Senate of 30 June 2009, BVerfG, 2 BvE 2/08.

[64] Mark Elliott, 'Reflections on the HS2 Case: A Hierarchy of Domestic Constitutional Norms and the Qualified Primacy of EU Law' (*UK Constitutional Law Association*, 23 January 2014) <https://ukconstitutionallaw.org/2014/01/23/mark-elliott-reflections-on-the-hs2-case-a-hierarchy-of-domestic-constitutional-norms-and-the-qualified-primacy-of-eu-law/> accessed 8 April 2020.

[65] *R (on the application of HS2 Action Alliance Limited) v Secretary of State for Transport* [2014] UKSC 3, [207].

A corollary to formal conditional supremacy of EU law is that there can be no substantive conditions for the repeal of the UK's authorizing legislation. In Member State constitutional orders that set substantive limits, a violation could be established as a substantive 'constitutional requirement' for an Article 50(1) decision to withdraw. For example, the German legislature could make transgression of the *Maastricht* and *Lisbon* judgment characteristics a constitutional requirement. A determination by the German Constitutional Court of such violation would then be a necessary condition to overcome the Basic Law's commitment to European integration.[66]

The absence of any such substantive limitations in the United Kingdom means that the decision to level down constituent power is determined entirely by individuals *qua* democratic subjects. Domestically, the European Union (Withdrawal) Act 2018 mandated the repeal of the European Communities Act 1972. At the supranational level, the 'decision' was taken through the authorization provided by the EU (Notification of Withdrawal) Act 2017. The UK's decision to withdraw concerned the role of individuals *qua* democratic subjects without any additional legal conditions for the benefit of individuals *qua* juridical objects. Although the *Miller* judgment only led to a salutary conferral of power by Parliament to the Prime Minister on notification, it has been argued that it influenced the manner in which Parliament would assert itself over the process through the European Union (Withdrawal) Act 2018 following the loss of the Conservative majority in the 2017 General Election. Dougan claims that '*Miller* did have an important indirect impact upon the broader legal and political debate about whether the standard constitutional opportunities for parliamentary involvement in the approval and implementation of international agreements were really sufficient in the extraordinary circumstances of the UK's withdrawal from the EU'.[67] This provides further evidence of the reflexive interaction between the quadripartite roles of individuals; an exercise of self-determination by a UK national *qua* juridical object opened up the possibility for greater assertion of authority by the representatives of individuals *qua* democratic subject over the process for levelling down constituent power.

[66] Basic Law for the Federal Republic of Germany in the revised version published in the Federal Law Gazette Part III, classification number 100-1, as last amended by Article 1 of the Act of 28 March 2019 (Federal Law Gazette I p 404), art 23.

[67] Michael Dougan, *The UK's Withdrawal from the EU: A Legal Analysis* (OUP 2021) 86.

v. The EU (Notification of Withdrawal) Act 2017 and the *Webster* judgment

The Article 50(1) process concluded on 29 March 2017 when the Prime Minister exercised the statutory power to notify the European Council of the UK's intention to withdraw from the European Union.[68] The time-lapse of nine months from the referendum is the temporal evidence of a lacuna in Article 50 TEU. The unregulated vacuum between Article 50(1) and Article 50(2) arises through the distinct terminology of 'decision' in the former clause, and 'notification' in the latter. This informed the rejected government submissions during the *Miller* case that using the prerogative power would merely give effect to a decision that had already made in the referendum.

The government continued its logic of treating the referendum as the decision after the Supreme Court judgment compelled it to propose legislation. The two-clause EU (Notification of Withdrawal) Act 2017 provided only the technical means for the Prime Minister to notify the European Council of the UK's intention to withdraw under Article 50(2).[69] There is no textual evidence that the Act, or the exercise of power thereunder, constitutes the Article 50(1) decision to withdraw itself. Commentators recognize the decision-notification lacuna at both the domestic and supranational level. Robert Craig identifies 'a lacuna that was arguably left slightly open in *Miller* . . . who is responsible for dealing with the Article 50 process'.[70] Steve Peers and Darren Harvey highlight that '[Article 50] provides no guidance as to the form (or indeed timing) that this notification must take'.[71]

The paucity of the Notification of Withdrawal Act led to a new judicial review claim that the Prime Minister had acted *ultra vires* in providing notification in the absence of a prior authorizing decision.[72] Lord Justice Gross dispensed with the claim by eliding the 'decision' and 'notification': 'authorisation to the Prime Minister to notify under Art.50(2) . . . plainly contemplated and encompassed the power to take a decision to withdraw and conferred that power expressly on the Prime Minister'.[73] Gross LJ confirms that the Prime

[68] Theresa May, 'Prime Minister's Letter to Donald Tusk Triggering Article 50' (*GOV.UK*, 29 March 2017) <www.gov.uk/government/publications/prime-ministers-letter-to-donald-tusk-triggering-article-50> accessed 8 April 2020.

[69] European Union (Notification of Withdrawal) Act 2017.

[70] Robert Craig, 'New Article 50 Case Resoundingly Rejected by the Divisional Court' (*UK Constitutional Law Association*, 26 June 2018) <https://ukconstitutionallaw.org/2018/06/26/robert-craig-new-article-50-case-resoundingly-rejected-by-the-divisional-court/> accessed 8 April 2020.

[71] Peers and Harvey (n 3) 824.

[72] *Webster* (n 42).

[73] ibid [13].

Minister's letter on 29 March contained 'the language of decision not of notification alone, *in vacuo*, so to speak'.[74] The elision of decision and notification resolves the legal gap in Article 50. The judgment implies that the 'decisions' by the government to hold the referendum and the referendum result were purely political.[75] Therefore, the provisions of Article 50 were not triggered until the Prime Minister's actions on 29 March 2017. The letter constituted both a decision and notification for the purposes of Article 50(1) and (2) respectively. This endorses *Shindler* and insulates the pre-notification exercise of deconstructive power from the purview of the supranational constitutional order.

The ambiguity over the UK's withdrawal decision may prompt a more open-ended interpretation. The wording of the 'intention' to withdraw in the 2017 Act may suggest that the Article 50(1) decision is not fully realized until the 'Treaties cease to apply' at the end of the Article 50 process.[76] The 'Three Knights Opinion' claims that the UK government could have provided a notification that was conditional upon the Article 50(1) 'decision' being Parliament's approval of the final terms of withdrawal.[77]

This moment represents the culmination of levelling down, the extinction of EU citizenship, and the end of the validity of EU law norms within the territory of the withdrawing state.[78] An analogy to the levelling up of constituent power illustrates the contingent nature of the 'decision to withdraw'. Neil Walker presents the supranational limb of the dual-constituent power as existing in an embryonic state of self-construction: '*pouvoir constituant mixte*, made up of individual citizens in their dual identity as members of the already constituted states as well as the in-the-process-of-constituting European Union'.[79] Conversely, withdrawal commences through communication of a decision that does not immediately actualize disintegration, but sets in train a convention to realize the 'in-the-process-of-deconstituting' of the Member State from the Union.

The bridge to the supranational level activates the representation of individuals *qua* EU citizens. The EU institutions have predicated an orderly withdrawal upon preservation of the levels of freedom and equality guaranteed for

[74] ibid [15] (emphasis in original).
[75] Craig (n 70).
[76] TEU, art 50(3).
[77] Sir David Edward and others, 'In the Matter of Article 50 of the Treaty on European Union: Opinion' [2017], paras 39–40.
[78] The 'transition period' creates some uncertainty over this point. See discussion of the Withdrawal Agreement later in this chapter.
[79] Neil Walker, 'Habermas's European Constitution: Catalyst, Reconstruction, Refounding' (2019) 25 European Law Journal 508, 512.

EU citizens *qua* juridical objects.[80] This is conversely analogous to individuals retaining nationality of their Member State in levelling up to preserve these protections.[81] The UK judiciary determined that the decision to withdraw was made by the Prime Minister on 29 March 2017. However, this decision is not ultimately realized until the conclusion of the deconstitutional process under Article 50(3). Developments both exogenous and endogenous mean that this decision may be altered over the course of the two or more years. The judgment that notification may be revoked in *Wightman* recognizes this instability. The fluctuations that occur throughout the deconstitutional process inform the reform proposals in the concluding chapter of this monograph on the legal structure of the Article 50(1) decision.[82]

III. Article 50(2) TEU: The Bridge to the Supranational Deconstitutional Convention

The *Miller* and *Wightman*[83] cases frame the constitutional issues arising from the first sentence of Article 50(2) TEU: '[a] Member State which decides to withdraw shall notify the European Council of its intention'.[84] This clause creates a bridge from the domestic decision to the supranational deconstitutional convention. The *Miller* judgment determined the necessary requirements to legitimate the creation of this bridge. The *Wightman* judgment determined the characteristics of the supranational deconstitutional convention and the requirements to retract the bridge. The judgment on revocation confirmed whether the domestic decision acts as a foundation stone, or whether it is subsumed by the multilateral negotiations. This defines whether the prerogative of the withdrawing Member State's nationals dominates, or whether termination or confirmation of the deconstitutional convention must be executed jointly with all individuals *qua* EU citizens. Following analysis of the two leading judgments, this section concludes with a proposal for an alternative to the *Wightman* reasoning which would have allowed a multilateral process for revocation.

[80] 'European Council (Art. 50) Guidelines for Brexit Negotiations' (*European Council*, 29 April 2017) <www.consilium.europa.eu/en/press/press-releases/2017/04/29/euco-brexit-guidelines/> accessed 17 December 2018.

[81] Jürgen Habermas, *The Crisis of the European Union: A Response* (Polity Press 2013).

[82] See the reform proposals in chapter 8.

[83] *Miller* (SC) (n 41); *Wightman* (n 6).

[84] TEU, art 50(2).

i. *Miller* and notification of intention to withdraw

The dispute in *Miller* may be framed as disagreement over whether notification functions purely in public international law or whether it also has consequences for, and must be regulated by, domestic constitutional law. The former position is endorsed in the minority judgment of Lord Reed.[85] He concludes that the principle of Parliamentary Sovereignty over domestic law

> does not . . . require that Parliament must enact an Act of Parliament before the UK can leave the EU. That is because the effect which Parliament has given to EU law in our domestic law . . . is inherently conditional on the application of the EU Treaties to the UK . . . The Act imposes no requirement, and manifests no intention, in respect of the UK's membership of the EU.[86]

Lord Reed endorses a conception of EU law as a species of public international law rather than supranational constitutional law: '[t]he Act simply creates a scheme under which the effect given to EU law in domestic law reflects the UK's international obligations under the Treaties'.[87] This position rejects the notion that EU law is domestic law: '[i]f the Treaties do not apply to the UK, then there are no rights, powers and so forth which, in accordance with the Treaties, are to be given legal effect in the UK'.[88] This rejects the notion that individuals exercise a role as juridical objects *qua* EU citizens independently of their role as juridical objects *qua* Member State nationals. Lord Reed's interpretation sees the Member States in public international law as the only objects of EU law; legal effects for individuals *qua* nationals only occur through authorizing domestic legislation. This position understands the legal effects of notification as being limited to the international plane between the High Contracting Party of the United Kingdom and the international organization of the European Union as subjects of the public international legal order.

By contrast, the majority judgment is predicated upon the conception of EU law as an 'entirely new, independent and overriding source of domestic law'.[89] Section 2 of the European Communities Act 1972 created a 'conduit pipe' through which EU law is given the status. The Bill of Rights of 1688 establishes the settled constitutional norm that the executive cannot change domestic law

[85] *Miller* (UKSC) (n 41) [153]–[243].
[86] ibid [177].
[87] ibid [187].
[88] ibid [191].
[89] ibid [80].

or the rights flowing from it without parliamentary approval.[90] The executive could not use the foreign affairs prerogative power to provide notification under Article 50(2) as this would change domestic law through rendering the European Communities Act and the rights flowing through it nugatory.

The majority judgment held that 'major change to the UK constitutional arrangements . . . must be effected in the only way that the UK constitution recognises, namely by Parliamentary legislation'.[91] The recognition of the 'independence' of EU law indicates implicit acceptance of the autonomy of EU law regarding the 'more fundamental . . . and . . . realistic sense' in which the EU institutions are the source of law.[92] This position appreciates that individuals can directly fulfil the role of juridical objects of the EU legal order. Notification under Article 50(2) operates not merely as a legal relation between a sovereign state and an international organization, but also as an action in the supranational constitutional order that has direct consequences for all individuals *qua* juridical objects. The regulation of these consequences occurs through the supranational convention mandated by the notification.

The domestic aspect of notification as a constitutional event manifests itself in the legal requirement for an Act of Parliament. For individuals *qua* democratic subjects, the democratically direct deconstructive expression of the referendum is not sufficient. It must be supplemented by a further democratic expression of will by the constituted institution of Parliament. The duplication could only have been avoided if the European Union Referendum Act 2015 had provided a specific legislative power for the Prime Minister to notify in the event of a leave vote. A precedent is provided in Section 8 of the Parliamentary Voting System and Constituencies Act 2011.[93]

The segregated approach to the legislation mandating the referendum and the legislation implementing its result arguably strengthens input legitimacy. Individuals legitimated the decision to withdraw both directly, in the referendum, and indirectly, through the passage of the Act of Parliament providing the power to notify. This extra channel of democratic decision-making also created tension between the constituent will expression and the constituted power of Parliament. Parliament had the discretion to disregard the referendum result and vote against endowing the Prime Minister with the power to

[90] ibid [40]–[45].
[91] ibid [81].
[92] ibid [61].
[93] Parliamentary Voting System and Constituencies Act 2011. Section 8 of the Act created a statutory duty for a Minister to bring into force 'the alternative vote provisions' if more votes had been cast in the referendum on adopting the Alternative Voting system in favour of the answer 'Yes'.

provide notification. This course of action was promoted soon after the referendum by Members of Parliament opposed to Brexit.[94]

This tension evokes Patberg's normative support for separation between constituent power and constituted power in the authorization and de-authorization of supranational levelling up.[95] The underdetermined constitutional status of referendums in the United Kingdom means that it does not include institutions whose only purpose is to facilitate the exercise of constituent power. The conditions for levelling up and levelling down of this power in the United Kingdom are not 'legally codified' beyond Acts of Parliament. The normative desideratum to prevent public authorities from making self-referential constitutional decisions was legally impossible for the notification of intention to withdraw.

The absence of a separation of constituent and constituted power is predicated on popular sovereignty not being the ultimate normative foundation of the UK constitution.[96] The EU referendum returned the first result in such a plebiscite that did not accord with the positions of the constituted powers of the legislature and executive. The referendum opened up a new source of popular sovereignty as a social fact that conflicts with the orthodoxy of Parliamentary Sovereignty as a legal fact.[97] The potential for a clash between these two streams was avoided, however, through the passage of the EU (Notification of Withdrawal) Act 2017.[98]

Despite the lack of formal legal constraints, the executive treated the referendum result as quasi-legal through its political imperative to vindicate the 'will of the people'. This recognizes the priority of democratic subjecthood in the 'political constitution' of the United Kingdom.[99] The House of Commons voted overwhelmingly to endorse the *de minimis* approach in the Bill. This avoided the potential clash between constituted power and constituent will. This tension re-emerged, however, at the point at which Parliament debated and passed the EU (Withdrawal) Act 2018.

Although the purpose of this legislation was to prepare the UK constitution for the juridical situation after withdrawal, the House of Commons included

[94] David Lammy, 'We Need a Second Referendum. The Consequences of Brexit Are Too Grave' *The Guardian* (London, 26 June 2016) <www.theguardian.com/politics/commentisfree/2016/jun/26/second-referendum-consequences-brexit-grave> accessed 9 April 2020.

[95] Patberg (n 12) 452–53.

[96] Martin Loughlin, 'Constituent Power Subverted: From English Constitutional Argument to British Constitutional Practice' in Martin Loughlin and Neil Walker (eds), *The Paradox of Constitutionalism: Constituent Power and Constitutional Form* (OUP 2008).

[97] Garner, 'After Article 50 and Before Withdrawal' (n 19).

[98] EU (Notification of Withdrawal) Act 2017.

[99] JAG Griffith, 'The Political Constitution' (1979) 42 The Modern Law Review 1.

an amendment that the Withdrawal Agreement had to be approved by Parliament in a 'meaningful vote' before coming into force. Such a condition would have been more appropriate in the 2015 Referendum Act or the 2017 Notification Act, as evidenced by the 'meaningful vote' mechanism first being proposed in an amendment to the 2017 Bill by the House of Lords.[100] After numerous failed attempts to pass a Withdrawal Agreement through the 'meaningful vote' mechanism, the European Union (Withdrawal Agreement) Act 2020 repealed the requirement. The passage of the Act came after the General Election in December 2019 returned an overwhelming pro-Brexit majority of Parliamentarians.[101] This resolved the tension between the deconstructive power of the referendum and Parliament through a return to the constitutional orthodoxy of norm-creator processes ending the constitutional impasse.

ii. *Wightman* and revocation of notification

The 'meaningful vote' provided the factual context for the *Wightman* judgment. Parliamentarians sought confirmation of their full range of options beyond approval or rejection of the draft Withdrawal Agreement.[102] The Prime Minister states in the notification letter that 'I am writing to give effect to the democratic decision of the people of the United Kingdom. I hereby notify the European Council in accordance with Article 50(2) . . . of the United Kingdom's intention to withdraw from the European Union'.[103] *Webster* confirmed that '[t]he Prime Minister's letter itself contains a decision; backed by the authority of the 2017 Act, that decision complies with the requirements of *Miller*'.[104] The foreclosure of the domestic level is supplemented by the UK's preferences for resolution at the supranational level. The government implicitly regarded notification to be implicitly irrevocable, as evidenced through the reference to leaving the European Union without an agreement.[105]

This irrevocability assumption was furthered in *Miller*. Academics forwarded arguments that the Supreme Court was obliged to refer the question

[100] 'Lords Examines European Union (Notification of Withdrawal) Bill' (*UK Parliament*, 16 March 2017) <www.parliament.uk/business/news/news-by-year/2017/february/lords-debates-european-union-notification-of-withdrawal-bill/> accessed 9 April 2020.

[101] European Union (Withdrawal Agreement) Act 2020, s 31.

[102] *Andy Wightman MSP v Secretary of State for Exiting the EU* [2018] CSIH 62.

[103] May (n 68).

[104] *Webster* (n 42) [15].

[105] 'If, however, we leave the European Union without an agreement the default position is that we would have to trade on World Trade Organisation terms': May (n 68).

of revocation to the Court of Justice of the European Union. Sanchez-Graells argued that under the *CILFIT*[106] requirements for preliminary references 'it is inconceivable . . . to argue that the . . . (ir)revocability of a notice is irrelevant for the adjudication of this case'.[107] However, the applicants argued that 'when ministers give Notice they will be pulling . . . the trigger which causes the bullet to be fired, with the consequence that the bullet will hit the target and the Treaties will cease to apply'.[108] The government 'did not challenge much if any of the factual basis of these assertions'[109] meaning that there was consensus between the parties on irreversibility.

The Supreme Court did not submit a preliminary reference. The majority stated that 'we are content to proceed on the basis that [the common ground on irreversibility] is correct, without expressing any view of our own on either point'.[110] For the purposes of UK constitutional law, the consequences remained binary: if notice were not revoked then the consequences relied upon would proceed, and if notification were revoked then these consequences would not occur. The Supreme Court considered that these alternatives did not affect the prior question of how exactly these consequences should be initiated.

Rather than the proposition being wrong, the famous analogy of the bullet leaving the chamber is inapposite. A more salient analogy is setting a timer on a bomb that may be defused at any point before the explosion. The possibility of defusing the bomb does not change the fact that only someone with the requisite competence may start the timer. As Jack Williams states, '[t]he triggering of Article 50 sets in motion a series of events which, without more, would result—without Parliamentary authorisation—in statutes being made defunct on the Supreme Court's analysis . . . the foreign relations treaty prerogative cannot be used to have this effect'.[111]

[106] Case 238/81 *Srl CILFIT and Lanificio di Gavardo SpA v Ministry of Health* [1982] ECR 3415.

[107] Albert Sanchez-Graells, 'UK Supreme Court Miller Judgment Seeks to Reassert Parliamentary Sovereignty, but It Does so in Breach of EU Law and in Disservice to the UK Parliament' (*How to Crack a Nut*, 24 January 2017) <www.howtocrackanut.com/blog/2017/1/24/uk-supreme-court-miller-judgment-seeks-to-reassert-parliamentary-sovereignty-but-it-does-so-in-breach-of-eu-law-and-in-disservice-to-the-uk-parliament> accessed 9 April 2020; for the counter-argument see Oliver Garner, 'Referring Brexit to the Court of Justice of the European Union: Why Revoking an Article 50 Notice Should Be Left to the United Kingdom' (*European Law Blog*, 14 November 2016) <www.europeanlawblog.eu/pub/referring-brexit-to-the-court-of-justice-of-the-european-union-why-revoking-an-article-50-notice-should-be-left-to-the-united-kingdom/release/1> accessed 9 April 2020.

[108] *Miller* (UKSC) (n 41) [36].

[109] ibid [37].

[110] ibid [26].

[111] Jack Williams, 'Does Wightman Mean That Miller Was Decided Incorrectly?' (*Monckton Chambers*, 10 December 2018) <www.monckton.com/does-wightman-mean-that-miller-was-decided-incorrectly/> accessed 9 April 2020.

The *Miller* case concerned the internal constitutional requirements of the United Kingdom. The question did not yet fall within the Court of Justice's interpretative authority because the relevant EU law—Article 50 TEU—had not yet been activated.[112] This is justified through the conception that notification is the bridge from the internal constitutional decision to the procedural law governing the supranational deconstitutional convention. Christophe Hillion provides an alternative interpretation: '*formal* compliance with domestic constitutional requirements might not suffice ... if that decision was taken in the midst of internal constitutional turmoil ... and the appropriateness of such requirements was in doubt in relation to EU standards.'[113]

The facts in *Wightman* arose once the bridge from the national to the supranational had been crossed. The crucial question is whether the representation of all individuals *qua* Member State nationals and *qua* EU citizens in the supranational deconstitutional convention means that these individuals should be represented in a revocation decision that nullifies the convention and its output. On 21 September 2018, Scotland's Court of Session sent a preliminary reference to the Court of Justice of the European Union. It asked for confirmation of whether EU law permits notification under Article 50(2) to be revoked unilaterally, and if so subject to what conditions.[114] The first instance judge on 8 June 2018 found that the conditions for a referral under EU law had not been met as the facts were not ascertainable and the issue was hypothetical. The creation of the 'meaningful vote' mechanism when the European Union (Withdrawal) Act received Royal Assent made the issue a live legal reality. Lord Menzies stated that

> [the issues] have been rendered less hypothetical ... as a result of the coming into force of the European Union (Withdrawal) Act 2018, section 13 [of] which sets out the procedures necessary before any withdrawal agreement can be ratified ... it appears to me that it will be legitimate for those who are involved in that vote to know, by means of a judicial ruling, the proper legal meaning of Article 50.[115]

[112] Garner, 'Referring Brexit' (n 107).

[113] Christophe Hillion, 'This Way, Please! A Legal Appraisal of the EU Withdrawal Clause' in Carlos Closa (ed), *Secession from a Member State and Withdrawal from the European Union: Troubled Membership* (CUP 2017) 218 (emphasis in the original).

[114] *Wightman* (n 102).

[115] ibid [37].

The case further illustrates the interconnection between democratic subjecthood and juridical objecthood in illuminating the architecture of withdrawal. The decision by the Parliamentary representatives of democratic subjects to create the meaningful vote mechanism imbued them with sufficient interest *qua* juridical objects to seek clarity on the legal question. The determination by the Court of Justice then clarified the legal situation for all EU citizens *qua* juridical objects. This interaction between legality and democratic will expression is expressed in the petitioner's grounds of appeal:

> In the normal situation, where MPs are voting upon a change in domestic law, issues concerning the legality of their decisions would not arise because of the sovereignty of Parliament. Different considerations arose where EU law was involved. MPs were entitled to know whether their decision to vote, on the basis that the notification could be revoked, was sound in law.[116]

This informed the decision that the matter was not outside of the court's jurisdiction by reason of encroachment upon Parliamentary Sovereignty.

The judgment highlights the failure of Parliament to ensure legal clarity when it empowered the Prime Minister to notify withdrawal in March 2017. This delayed reaction meant that over eighteen months passed after notification before the confirmation of revocability. This period included the General Election in June 2017. The legal ambiguity precluded political parties from offering democratic subjects a legally valid revoke option, as the Liberal Democrats party did in their December 2019 General Election manifesto.[117] The political significance of the judgment prompted the Court of Justice to adopt the expedited procedure for the case.[118] The referring court made this request, as it emphasized 'the two-year timetable . . . which . . . is imposed on that withdrawal procedure, and . . . the fact that the parliamentary consideration and voting on that subject . . . must of necessity take place well in advance of 29 March 2019'.[119] The President of the Court accepted that the grounds 'undeniably' indicated the need to make a ruling before Parliament voted on the Withdrawal Agreement. He also forwarded the general justification that

[116] ibid [12].

[117] 'Liberal Democrat 2019 Manifesto' (*Liberal Democrats*) <www.libdems.org.uk/policy/2019-liberal-democrat-manifesto> accessed 10 April 2020.

[118] *Wightman* (n 6) para 18.

[119] Order of the President of the Court of 19 October 2018 in Case C-621/18 *Andy Wightman v Secretary of State for Exiting the European Union*, EU:C:2018:851, para 8.

'the implementation of Article 50 TEU is of fundamental importance for the United Kingdom and for the constitutional order of the European Union'.[120]

The President fixed the date for the judgment as 10 December 2018, one day before the scheduled 'meaningful vote' in Parliament that was eventually postponed. The expedition demonstrates that the two-year timetable for withdrawal creates a temporal emergency that can necessitate extraordinary constitutional procedures at the domestic and supranational level. These distortions in the United Kingdom became more acute as the deconstitutional convention approached, and then moved past, the initial deadline of 29 March 2019.

The judgment followed the Advocate General's Opinion in finding the preliminary reference admissible. The judgment endorsed the line of case law that confirms that 'questions relating to EU law enjoy a presumption of relevance'.[121] The Court also rejected the argument that the referring court was seeking an advisory opinion, thus circumventing the procedure in Article 218(11) TFEU. The dispute did not concern the compatibility of an international agreement with the Treaties, but instead related to the interpretation of a provision of EU law.[122] The importance of the question for UK nationals *qua* democratic subjects was emphasized:

> [I]t is required to rule on that question of law, which represents a genuine and live issue, of considerable practical importance . . . [and] those Members of the United Kingdom Parliament have an interest in the answer . . . since that answer will clarify the options open to them in exercising their parliamentary mandates.[123]

The Court of Justice's pre-emptive approach to admissibility in *Wightman* should be welcomed. If the legal question were only addressed after any hypothetical attempt to revoke an Article 50 notification then this could cause an accidental withdrawal if the time limit for negotiations were reached in the interim period when a Member State believes it has revoked its notification. The extinction of EU citizenship means that the only means for individuals to remedy this outcome would be the rigorous accession procedures mandated by Article 50(5) TEU. The existential consequences of withdrawal after a limited temporal framework justified the Court's pre-emptive approach. This approach is corroborated by the Advocate General's Opinion: 'the Court is

120 ibid para 11.
121 *Wightman* (n 6) para 27.
122 ibid para 35.
123 ibid para 29.

being asked to give judgment in order to interpret a provision which is actually in the course of being applied and the future legal consequences of which are drawing inexorably closer'.[124] Consequently, 'the relevant time to dispel doubts as to whether the notification ... is revocable is before, not after, Brexit has occurred and the United Kingdom is inexorably immersed in its consequences'.[125]

On the substance, the Court of Justice found that a Member State may revoke an Article 50(2) notification unilaterally. Revocation must be unequivocal and unconditional, and addressed in writing to the European Council. The notice must be sent before a Withdrawal Agreement comes into force, or before the two-year period terminates. The revocation decision must also be in accordance with the state's constitutional requirements.[126] The finding of a sovereign and unilateral right to notify and revoke an intention to withdraw distinguished the legal nature of withdrawal via Article 50 TEU from existing examples of legitimate state secession. The Canadian Supreme Court in *Re Secession of Quebec* conceived of 'unilaterality' as referring only to the capacity for a province to take the steps towards a constitutional amendment to effect secession through a sub-state democratic exercise; it did not extent to 'the right to effectuate secession without prior negotiations with the other provinces and the federal government'.[127] The extent to which Article 50 TEU imposes an obligation to negotiate in good faith has been debated,[128] but the major distinguishing factor is that the residual two-year condition means that withdrawal can be realized without prior agreement of the EU institutions and other Member States. Although the Canadian Supreme Court judgment does not explicitly deal with questions of revocation in its operative paragraphs, the absence of any unilateral right of secession may be regarded as extending to any revocation of the intention to secede also being subject to negotiations.

The judgment may be influenced by a public international law perspective rather than a supranational constitutional one. This is most prevalent in the Advocate General's Opinion. Rather than starting with the text and purpose of Article 50 TEU, the substance of the Opinion commences with the rules of the VCLT, customary rules, and the practice of States on the general right of withdrawal from treaties.[129] The Advocate General only considers later the question of whether the VCLT is applicable to withdrawal of a Member State from

[124] Case C-621/18 *Andy Wightman v Secretary of State for Exiting the European Union*, EU:C:2018:978, Opinion of Advocate General Campos Sánchez-Bordona, point 40.
[125] ibid point 42.
[126] *Wightman* (n 6) para 58.
[127] *Reference re Secession of Quebec* [1998] 2 SCR 217 (Supreme Court of Canada) [86].
[128] Hillion (n 113).
[129] Opinion of AG Campos Sánchez-Bordona (n 124) points 63–76.

the European Union.[130] The Opinion attempts to adopt both the international law and supranational perspectives: '[t]he Treaty on European Union is an international treaty between States and, at the same time, the constituent instrument of an international organisation (the European Union)'.[131] The conflation of the two perspectives is also evident in academic commentary. Auriel Sari argues that the VCLT is relevant as an 'additional basis' because 'the right to revoke a withdrawal notification which the Member States enjoy under customary international law exists and applies in parallel to the corresponding right that they derive from Article 50'.[132]

This leads to the claim in the Opinion that the 'express clause on withdrawal (Article 50 TEU) . . . entails a *lex specialis* in respect of the convention rules (Article 54, 56 and 64 to 68 of the VCLT) of international law on the subject'.[133] Although such statements may be true from a public international law perspective, it is inappropriate for a representative of a supranational institution to adopt this perspective when addressing a lacuna in the autonomous legal order. The Advocate General's discussion of state practice in relation to other treaties is particularly insensitive to the specific telos of Article 50.[134]

The Court of Justice's final judgment ostensibly adopts an explicitly constitutional approach. Polly Polak argues that

> [t]he result is that the *Wightman* ruling is fully based on the need to preserve the process of integration: allowing a Member State to remain in the Union even after having notified its intention to withdraw is the only result consistent with the aims and values of the Treaties, their purpose of creating an ever closer union and the fact that their subjects are not only the states but also the citizens.[135]

The judgment reiterates that the founding Treaties 'constitute the basic constitutional charter of the European Union'.[136] This is supplemented by recognition of the 'autonomy of EU law with respect both to the law of the Member States and to international law'.[137] These paragraphs delineate the predicative

[130] ibid point 77.
[131] ibid point 78.
[132] Aurel Sari, 'Reversing a Withdrawal Notification under Article 50 TEU: Can a Member State Change Its Mind?' [2017] European Law Review 451.
[133] Opinion of AG Campos Sánchez-Bordona (n 124) point 81.
[134] ibid points 68–70.
[135] Polak (n 7) 75.
[136] *Wightman* (n 6) para 44.
[137] ibid para 45.

characteristics of the Court's conception of the constitutional identity of the European Union. The Full Court only considers the public international law sources in the more appropriate context of persuasive authority in order to 'corroborate' the conclusions derived from the supranational constitutional sources.[138] Nevertheless, the residue of the public international law perspective utilized by the Advocate General remains. This is epitomized by notification and revocation being presented as 'sovereign' decisions by the withdrawing Member State.[139] The *ratio decidendi* of the case emerges prematurely without detailed argumentation following the delineation of the two objectives of Article 50: '[a]s the Advocate General stated in points 94 and 95 of his Opinion, the sovereign nature of the right of withdrawal . . . supports the conclusion that the Member State concerned has a right to revoke'.[140]

One may infer two predominant grounds for the judgment. The first is a coherence argument. In light of Article 50's silence on revocation, the Court constructs a position that most closely coheres to the framework for the original action of notification: '[i]n the absence of an express provision governing revocation of the notification of the intention to withdraw, that revocation is subject to the rules laid down in Article 50(1) TEU for the withdrawal itself'.[141] This adopts the Advocate General's conception of the deconstitutional convention whereby notification functions as the predicative foundation stone for negotiations:

> [If] the Member State's initial decision is reversed and the judicial and constitutional basis on which it was sustained subsequently disappears . . . the first phase of the procedure loses its foundation . . . Logically, the second phase of the procedure must also be affected, since the premiss upon which it is based has fallen away.[142]

The Points of the Opinion that the Court cites show that an emphasis on Member State sovereignty informs this conception: 'unilateral revocation would . . . be a manifestation of the sovereignty of the departing Member State . . . the unilateral nature of the first phase extends also . . . to the second stage of the Article 50 procedure'.[143]

[138] ibid para 70.
[139] ibid paras 50, 59, 72.
[140] ibid para 57.
[141] ibid para 58.
[142] Opinion of AG Campos Sánchez-Bordona (n 124) points 105–106.
[143] ibid points 94–95.

The Advocate General's focus on sovereignty only emphasizes the constitutional role of individuals *qua* nationals. This democratic subjecthood is expressed through the external sovereign will of the Member State executive. Eleni Frantziou and Piet Eeckhout argue that '[t]he reference to constitutional requirements in Article 50(1) suggests that, in order to revoke the notification, the withdrawing State would simply need to show that the decision to withdraw is no longer compatible with its constitutional requirements in that a new decision has been taken'.[144] This position provides a domestic constitutional perspective upon the unilateral revocation argument. Rather than the sovereign will of the state in public international law being the predicate for the deconstitutional convention, the continuing fulfilment of the domestic constitutional requirements functions as the foundation stone.

The Advocate General recognizes that the Member State's sovereign will may be mitigated by the multilateral nature of the deconstitutional convention: '[i]t is true, however, that in that second phase that unilateral nature appears to be counteracted by the EU institutions' actions'.[145] The Commission and the Council presented an alternative conception of the Article 50 assembly in their submissions: 'In their view . . . the intermediate phase (the negotiation) is bilateral or multilateral in nature, so that the powers of the EU institutions take precedence. As soon as the second phase is activated, the notifying Member State loses control over the procedure'.[146] Prior academic arguments for multilateral revocation support the EU institutions' position. Stephen Weatherill argues that '[t]he primary concern which underpins Article 50 is to ensure that, once a Member State has chosen to submit its notification of intention to withdraw, the interests of the 27 Member States and the EU institutions then come to the forefront and are protected'.[147] Stijn Smismans states that '[t]he power balance created by Article 50 implies that the UK has no right to revoke but will depend on the willingness of the other Member States to allow such revocation'.[148]

The Court of Justice's rejection of this conception was predicated upon the second normative ground for its decision: 'that requirement [for unanimous

[144] Piet Eeckhout and Eleni Frantziou, 'Brexit and Article 50 TEU: A Constitutionalist Reading' (2017) 54 Common Market Law Review 695, 712–13.

[145] Opinion of AG Campos Sánchez-Bordona (n 124) point 95.

[146] ibid point 119.

[147] Stephen Weatherill, 'EU Law Analysis: Can an Article 50 Notice of Withdrawal from the EU Be Unilaterally Revoked?' (*EU Law Analysis*, 16 January 2018) <http://eulawanalysis.blogspot.com/2018/01/can-article-50-notice-of-withdrawal.html> accessed 13 April 2020.

[148] Stijn Smismans, 'About the Revocability of Withdrawal: Why the EU (Law) Interpretation of Article 50 Matters' (*UK Constitutional Law Association*, 29 November 2016) <https://ukconstitutionallaw.org/2016/11/29/stijn-smismans-about-the-revocability-of-withdrawal-why-the-eu-law-interpretation-of-article-50-matters/> accessed 13 April 2020.

approval of the European Council for revocation] would transform a unilateral sovereign right into a conditional right subject to an approval procedure . . . [this] would be incompatible with the principles . . . that a Member State cannot be forced to leave the European Union against its will'.[149] The Court concludes that 'in those circumstances, given that a state cannot be forced to accede to the European Union against its will, neither can it be forced to withdraw from the European Union against its will'.[150] The judgment corroborates this argument with the rejection of amendments during the 2003 Convention advocating expulsion of Member States.[151]

The voluntary nature of the levelling down of constituent power is crucial for it to be an exercise of democratic self-determination. The Council and Commission arguments identify situations in which there is no genuine will to reverse withdrawal. Their submissions raise concerns over revocation as a negotiating strategy rather than a reversal of the process: 'the Member State concerned could use its right of revocation shortly before the end of the period . . . and notify a new intention to withdraw . . . the Member State would enjoy, de facto, a right to negotiate its withdrawal without any time-limit'.[152] The further claim is made that 'a Member State could at any time use its right of revocation as leverage in negotiations . . . it could threaten to revoke its notification and thus put pressure on the EU institutions in order to alter the terms of the agreement to its own advantage'.[153] Through the lens of these arguments the extensive discretion afforded to a notifying Member State may undermine Article 50's objectives. Revocation may not reflect the 'sovereign will' of individuals *qua* nationals. The consequences may impinge upon the second objective of certainty for all EU citizens over the structure and outcome of the process.

The Advocate General recognizes abuse of the procedure as 'the most substantial argument in support of the position that unilateral revocation is not possible'.[154] However, he dismisses the concerns: 'the possibility that a right may be abused or misused is, generally speaking, not a reason to deny the existence of that right. Rather the abuse must be prevented through the use of the appropriate legal instruments'.[155] The general principle that EU law cannot be relied on for abusive or fraudulent ends is advanced as this instrument.[156] The

[149] *Wightman* (n 6) para 72.
[150] ibid para 65.
[151] See discussion of the origins of the withdrawal clause in chapter 6.
[152] *Wightman* (n 6) para 40.
[153] ibid para 41.
[154] Opinion of AG Campos Sánchez-Bordona (n 124) point 151.
[155] ibid point 152.
[156] ibid point 153.

Advocate General also claims that the principles of good faith and sincere co-operation impose limits on revocation.[157] Regarding tactical revocations, the Advocate General indicates that 'the obligation that a revocation must be carried out in accordance with the Member State's constitutional requirements is . . . a filter which acts as a deterrent in order to prevent abuse', because these legal and political requirements mean that it would be 'extremely difficult for tactical revocations to proliferate'.[158]

The final judgment does not muse upon preventing abuse or tactical revocations. The Court concludes that an approval procedure would be incompatible with the principle that a Member State cannot be forced to leave the European Union against its will. Michael Dougan comments that 'it is unfortunate that the ruling in *Wightman* failed to elaborate any further on the precise nature of or process for this Union law safeguard against potential abuse of the power to revoke'.[159] The only echo of the Advocate General's argument in the judgment is that revocation must be 'unequivocal and unconditional . . . the purpose of that revocation is to confirm the EU membership of the Member State concerned under terms that are unchanged as regards its status as a Member State, and that revocation brings the withdrawal procedure to an end'.[160]

The Advocate General's approach runs into practical and legal problems. First, a revoking Member State may use *Wightman*'s extraordinary emphasis on its sovereignty as a shield to repel the jurisdiction of the Court of Justice if claims were made on the basis of general principles of EU law. Second, the problem of accidental withdrawal arises again. The Advocate General indicates correctly that 'any abuse could occur only when a *second* notification of the intention to withdraw is submitted, but not by unilaterally revoking the first'.[161] A determination that revocation was invalid could mean that an unintentional and disorderly withdrawal had already occurred. Finally, the constitutional requirements filter argument has less force for the United Kingdom. Constitutional minimalism means that a simple majority vote of parliamentarians may be sufficient. Such legislation could also be passed extremely quickly. The emergency situation of impending Brexit deadlines saw Acts of Parliament on Article 50 extension passed in under a day through unorthodox procedural arrangements.[162]

[157] TEU, art 4(3).
[158] Opinion of AG Campos Sánchez-Bordona (n 124) point 156.
[159] Dougan, *The UK's Withdrawal* (n 67) 45.
[160] *Wightman* (n 6) para 74.
[161] Opinion of AG Campos Sánchez-Bordona (n 124) point 155.
[162] European Union (Withdrawal) Act 2019; European Union (Withdrawal) (No 2) Act 2019.

The *Wightman* judgment mimics the requirements for notification in order to provide a coherent solution to a lacuna within Article 50 TEU. This approach underplays the objective of orderliness. The representative role of the EU institutions after notification is subordinate to the sovereign will of the withdrawing Member State. Individuals *qua* withdrawing Member State national are prioritized over individuals *qua* EU citizens in the revocation decision. The deconstitutional convention is a norm-creation process as the Withdrawal Agreement functions as EU law. Supranational norm creation requires legitimation by representatives of the dual subject. Arguably the termination of this process should also require input by all individuals *qua* Member State nationals and EU citizens.

iii. A multilateral alternative to *Wightman*?

A role for the Union institutions in revocation would enable *ex ante* regulation of its authenticity in the service of all individuals *qua* EU citizens. The *Wightman* decision overemphasizes the objective of enshrining the sovereign right of a Member State to withdraw to the detriment of the second objective of an orderly procedure. Subjecting withdrawal to a constitutional clause seeks to ensure a legally certain process to mitigate the seismic consequences of disintegration. The withdrawing Member State's capacity to terminate the deconstitutional convention unilaterally through a simple notification to the European Council undermines this orderliness. An alternative approach could provide a coherent legal answer whilst ensuring that a Member State cannot be expelled against its will. Instead of merely seeking to cohere with Article 50(1) on notification, the Court could have constructed revocation through analogy to Article 50 TEU as a whole.

Notification of the intention to withdraw is an inherently unilateral action. The process it mandates is multilateral, and the primary condition for the conclusion of negotiations is a multilateral agreement. Withdrawal at the end of the two-year period if this multilateral agreement cannot be reached ensures that the original unilateral intention is ultimately vindicated. The notification of an *intention* to revoke could also initiate a multilateral process whereby the Union institutions assess the authenticity of the notification and make provision for an orderly termination of the deconstitutional convention. This negotiated revocation would determine how actions taken in anticipation of withdrawal, such as a missed Presidency of the Council, may be rectified.

To prevent judicial construction of institutional requirements, a minimalist approach would use Article 50 to determine the requirements for a multilateral revocation. One option is the requirement of unanimity in the European Council to issue the negotiation guidelines. This may be sufficient for symmetry between the conclusion of the deconstitutional convention and its commencement. The alternative is the approval by Qualified Majority Voting in the Council and consent of the European Parliament that is necessary for a Withdrawal Agreement. This would ensure symmetry with Article 50 as a whole, and it would also ensure the representation of individuals as both nationals and EU citizens in the revocation decision.

If multilateral agreement cannot be reached, the end of the Article 50 two-year period could be the point at which revocation takes place unilaterally. This would operate as a 'no deal revocation' and a reversion to the status quo of membership in contrast to a 'negotiated revocation'. This alternative approach to revocation would impose constraints upon the sovereign will of the Member State, but it would ensure greater orderliness and democratic representation than the *Wightman* judgment. The representation in the European Parliament would also include nationals of the withdrawing Member States, a point missed in the emphasis on state sovereignty in the *Wightman* Opinion and judgment. The reform proposals in the final chapter of this monograph will consider more extensive revision of the architecture of revocation in tandem with amendment of the decision process under Article 50. The reconstructive process of Treaty amendment would be free from the constraints that were placed upon the Court of Justice in determining the question to this legal gap in *Wightman*.

IV. Article 50(2) and Article 50(4) TEU: The Structure of the Deconstitutional Convention

Habermas recognizes the significance of the supranational procedure for withdrawal: 'the modalities which must be taken into account before the decision to leave comes into effect show that the right of exit is not founded on a 'supreme constitutional authority beholden to no other law than its own free choice'.[163] The withdrawal negotiations are therefore conceptualized as a 'deconstitutional convention'. The deconstitutional convention should mirror the principles informing the hypothetical constitutional conventions in the dual-constituent

[163] Habermas (n 81) 40–41.

theories.[164] The convention should therefore ensure the expression of political self-determination of democratic subjects *qua* Member State nationals and EU citizens, on formally equal terms, with pluralistic representation, and within a forum that enables discursive interaction to determine the orderly withdrawal of a Member State. In practice, however, a number of deficiencies arose including the usurpation of roles by the institutions without explicit authorization. Michael Dougan identifies that the under-determination of Article 50 TEU opened the space for this executive entrepreneurialism: 'The fact that the Treaty framework governing withdrawal was both novel and underdeveloped would therefore inevitably compel the Union institutions to make the choices and decisions necessary to convert Article 50 TEU into a genuinely operational legal process and properly effective legal basis'.[165]

i. The roles of the supranational institutions

The opening of the deconstitutional convention requires the consent of the representatives of the nationals of all the High Contracting Parties acting through the European Council. This reflects the primacy afforded to individuals *qua* Member State nationals in supranational construction, reconstruction, and deconstruction.[166] Polak goes further and argues that the notification to open the deconstitutional convention must also comply with supranational requirements: 'this act is in fact subject to the double compliance of being in line with EU law and case law or, more specifically, with the EU's fundamental values enshrined in Article 2 TEU as interpreted by the Court'.[167] The mandate of the European Council is sufficient to legitimate the action of the other Union institutions within the boundaries of the Article 50 procedure. Extension of the two-year framework, however, requires reactivation of the European Council mandate.[168] The European Council guidelines ensure that the political communities of all the Member States are represented in formally equal terms, and that the deconstitutional procedure is established on the basis of a discursive exchange of reasons.[169]

[164] See the discussion of these theories in chapter 2.
[165] Dougan, *The UK's Withdrawal* (n 67) 33.
[166] See the discussion of the triptych in chapter 2.
[167] Polak (n 7) 115.
[168] See further discussion on extension of the Article 50 period later in this chapter.
[169] See discussion of the principles of levelling up constituent power in chapter 2.

One feature of the Brexit deconstitutional convention was the initiative seized by the institutions that represent individuals *qua* EU citizens. The Commission established itself as the Union negotiator despite no explicit references to the institution in Article 50 TEU. This role was confirmed even before the formal processes commenced through notification by the United Kingdom. Following notification, the European Parliament issued a resolution with its own guidelines for the negotiations.[170]

The Commission's actions during deconstruction are a manifestation of its role as the 'guardian of the Treaties'. Whereas this role benefits all individuals in their quadripartite role, the European Parliament exclusively represents individuals *qua* EU citizens. It focused on the protection of the status and rights of EU citizens *qua* juridical objects during negotiations.[171] This developed the minimal obligation under Article 50(2) that the European Parliament must consent to the Withdrawal Agreement. To execute this protective role, the European Parliament pursued the claim that it must be kept informed of the progress of the negotiations.

The European Parliament's own guidelines and self-empowerment ensured that the deconstitutional convention outcomes were an expression of self-determination by EU citizens on the basis of formal equality through European Parliament plenary, steering group, and committee sessions. Article 50(4) TEU excludes representatives of the withdrawing Member State from Council and European Council deliberations. The distinction between the democratic roles of individuals for withdrawing state nationals continues even during the process of extinguishing EU citizenship. The European Parliament continues to represent these individuals *qua* EU citizens up to the point that the Treaties cease to apply. Despite these roles, the secondary condition for withdrawal of the two-year 'guillotine clause' means that the supranational institutions may not be involved at all in the final withdrawal. This vindicates the individual *qua* national as having ultimate residual control over withdrawal from the Union.

Supranationality was also reinforced by the practice adopted that Article 50 TEU provided its own special exclusive competence that allowed any relevant matter to be encompassed by the Withdrawal Agreement. This also excluded the possibility that national parliaments as representatives of individuals *qua*

[170] European Parliament resolution of 5 April 2017 on negotiations with the United Kingdom following its notification that it intends to withdraw from the European Union [2017] OJ C 252/201.
[171] ibid paras 16–20.

nationals of a constitutional state would be required to approve the agreement. Michael Dougan outlines the

> Council's decision (taken relatively early in the entire Article 50 TEU process) to exclude any possibility that the withdrawal agreement should call not only for approval by the Union's own institutions—the first concrete indication that Article 50 TEU was to be treated as an exceptional competence or legal basis, capable of deviating from some of the ordinary principles once would expect to follow under constitutional law.[172]

ii. The pre-notification actions

The EU's institutions commenced preparations for the supranational deconstitutional convention before the United Kingdom had provided official notification. Both the legal basis for these actions and their constitutional legitimacy are questionable. On 29 June 2016, there was an 'informal meeting at 27' of the Heads of State or Government of the 27 Member States and the Presidents of the European Council and European Commission in Brussels.[173] The catalyst for this communication may have been a response to the condition for the Decision concerning the UK's New Settlement to come into force. Following the referendum result, notification that the United Kingdom would remain a Member State was not forthcoming. The communique was a pre-emptive political statement by the heads of state or government who hold legal authority under Article 50(2) TEU. This provided an early indication that withdrawal is a process concerning the exercise of constructive and deconstructive power of the supranational order. Representatives of individuals *qua* Member State nationals assert their primacy, and the supranational institutions play supplementary roles.

The statement from the informal meeting clarified some of the framework principles of the convention before their confirmation in the European Council guidelines. The communication outlines the commitment to this procedure: 'Once the notification has been received, the European Council will adopt guidelines for the negotiations of an agreement with the UK. In a further process, the European Commission and the European Parliament will play

[172] Dougan, *The UK's Withdrawal* (n 67) 48; see 56–60 for detailed legal discussion of the debate.

[173] EU-27, 'Informal Meeting at 27—Brussels, 29 June 2016—Statement' (*European Council*, 29 June 2016) <www.consilium.europa.eu/en/press/press-releases/2016/06/29/27ms-informal-meeting-statement/> accessed 13 April 2020.

their full role in accordance with the Treaties'.[174] This summarizes the interaction between the institutions representing individuals *qua* nationals and *qua* EU citizens in the deconstitutional process.

The communication asserted that '[u]ntil the UK leaves the EU, EU law continues to apply to and within the UK, both when it comes to rights and obligations'.[175] This political statement of the continuing status of UK nationals *qua* juridical objects, and the UK legal order as territory for the application of these norms, was confirmed by the Court of Justice in Case C-327/18 *PPU*, *Minister for Justice and Equality v RO*.[176] The EU-27 communique planted the seeds for the judicial confirmation of the objectives of Article 50: 'There is a need to organise the withdrawal of the UK from the EU in an orderly fashion'.[177] An initial attempt was made to ameliorate disorderliness by addressing the lacuna between the democratic yet legally unbinding decision in the referendum and formal notification: 'It is up to the British government to notify the European Council of the UK's intention to withdraw from the Union. This should be done as quickly as possible. There can be no negotiations of any kind before this notification has taken place'.[178]

The final sentence confirms that the levelling down of constituent power can only take place legitimately through prescribed legal means. This distinguishes disintegration theoretically and pragmatically from the reservation of constituent power contained within opt-outs. The latter are not expressly regulated by a provision of primary supranational constitutional law.[179] The statement distinguishes the withdrawal process from the pre-referendum negotiations on the 'New Settlement' for the United Kingdom.[180] This was a prior agreement on the reservation of constituent power conducted extraneously from, and in anticipation of, the amendment procedure of Article 48 TEU.[181]

In the same breath that the EU-27 insist on compliance with Article 50, they risk undermining the Article 50(2) notification process. The political pressure placed upon the UK government to notify 'as quickly as possible' goes beyond prospectively stating the Article 50 legal framework. The *Miller* judgment shows that if the UK government had acquiesced to such pressure in June 2016

[174] ibid para 3.
[175] ibid para 1.
[176] C-327/18 *PPU—R O* (n 6).
[177] EU-27 (n 173) para 2.
[178] ibid.
[179] See the discussion of the triptych of constituted constituent power in chapter 2.
[180] European Council meeting (18 and 19 February 2016)—Conclusions, Annex 1—Decision of the Heads of State or Government, meeting within the European Council, concerning a new settlement for the United Kingdom within the European Union—Brussels 19 February 2016 EUCO 1/16.
[181] See further discussion of the New Settlement in chapter 5.

then it would have issued a legally invalid notification. The communication risked illegitimate influence before the proper stage at which the institutions fulfil their constitutional role. As Christophe Hillion makes clear: 'as long as such a message [of notification] has not been conveyed to the EU, and so long as the Member State continues to fulfil its membership obligations completely, the withdrawal process cannot be deemed to have been triggered'.[182]

Despite the potential constitutional impropriety of the EU-27 statement, its legal validity as a political statement does not seem to be in question. Graver concerns may be raised over the Commission's appointment as the Union negotiator before notification. On 27 July 2016, a press release confirmed that the Commission President had appointed Michel Barnier as the Chief Negotiator in charge of the Preparation and Conduct of the negotiations with the United Kingdom.[183] The negotiator would 'report directly to the President'[184] of the Commission, hold the status of Director-General, and would be advised by a group of Director-Generals comprising the Commission Taskforce for the Preparation and Conduct of the Negotiations with the United Kingdom under Article 50 TEU (Taskforce Article 50).

Both the Council and the European Parliament also commenced internal preparations before notification. Brigid Laffan details that '[w]ithin two days of the referendum, the Council appointed . . . [the] Head of the Council's Brexit Task Force'.[185] The European Parliament established a Brexit Steering Group of six members on 8 September 2016.[186] Laffan argues that 'the creation of the [Council] Task Force was initially regarded as a pre-emptive strike by the Council to retain control over the negotiations. In fact, it contributed to the ease of engagement between the Council and the Commission and to the effectiveness of EU negotiations'.[187] The Council and European Parliament's internal preparations, although pre-dating notification, may be justified on the basis of the defined roles of both institutions under Article 50. The Council's early action is particularly appropriate as it needs to adopt a decision to open negotiations. The extent to which the European Parliament's Brexit Steering Group extended the confirmatory role of the European Parliament will be considered further below.

[182] Hillion (n 113) 219.

[183] 'President Juncker Appoints Michel Barnier as Chief Negotiator in Charge of the Preparation and Conduct of the Negotiations with the United Kingdom under Article 50 of the TEU' (*European Commission*, 27 July 2016) <https://ec.europa.eu/commission/presscorner/detail/en/IP_16_2652> accessed 14 April 2020.

[184] ibid.

[185] Brigid Laffan, 'How the EU27 Came to Be' (2019) 57 Journal of Common Market Studies 13, 18–19.

[186] ibid 19.

[187] ibid.

By contrast, the Commission appears to have authorized itself to act as Union negotiator without any explicit legal basis. Article 50 TEU merely states that 'the Union' shall negotiate the agreement. Furthermore, no institution is authorized to act before notification to the European Council other than the Member State which makes the decision to withdraw. The Commission Press Release appointing the negotiator refers to the informal meeting on 29 June 2016 in the 'Background' section:

> In line with the principle of 'no negotiation without notification', the task of the Chief Negotiator in the coming months will be to prepare the ground internally for the work ahead. Once the Article 50 process is triggered, he will take the necessary contacts with the UK authorities and all other EU and Member State interlocutors.[188]

The only textual basis authorizing such a role for the Commission is found in the statement by the EU-27 that 'the European Commission . . . will play [its] full role in accordance with the Treaties'.[189] The reference to the Treaties as a whole rather than Article 50 TEU specifically would justify its position as withdrawal negotiator as a manifestation of its role as 'guardian of the Treaties'. Article 50(2)'s appropriation of the general framework for the conclusion of international agreements under Article 218 TFEU could provide the basis for the Commission exercising the same role in relation to withdrawal. Article 218(3) states that '[t]he Commission . . . shall submit recommendations to the Council, which shall adopt a decision authorising the opening of negotiations and . . . nominating the Union negotiator or the head of the Union's negotiating team'.[190] The reference to 'the Treaties' in the 29 June 2016 statement could be a reference to this provision.

Adam Łazowski endorses this position: 'A cross-reference to Article 218(3) TFEU suggests that this [the key role of the European Commission] was the intention of the drafters'.[191] Even on this reading the Commission's unilateral decision on 27 June would still have pre-empted the discretion of the Council to nominate the Union negotiator. The Commission should have limited itself to the narrower permission to submit 'recommendations' to the European

[188] European Commission (n 183).
[189] EU-27 (n 173).
[190] TFEU, art 218(3).
[191] Adam Łazowski, 'Be Careful What You Wish for: Procedural Parameters of EU Withdrawal' in Carlos Closa (ed), *Secession from a Member State and Withdrawal from the European Union: Troubled Membership* (CUP 2017) 242.

Council including the recommendation that it should be appointed negotiator. This reading is supported by Hillion's statement that '[t]he reference to Article 218(3) TFEU indicates that . . . the Commission could be involved in drafting the negotiating mandate alongside the European Council, and entrusted by the Council with the task of negotiating the withdrawal agreement, or, at the very least, be part of the negotiating team'.[192]

The Commission was still not explicitly approved as the Union negotiator in the European Council guidelines. The only possible reference is the broad statement that '[t]he Union will approach the negotiations with unified positions, and will engage with the United Kingdom exclusively through the channels set out in these guidelines and in the negotiating directives'.[193] The Commission's role was finally confirmed in the Council Decision authorizing the opening of negotiations on 15 May 2017: 'The Commission is hereby authorised to open negotiations, on behalf of the Union, for an agreement . . . and is hereby nominated as the Union negotiator'.[194] At the very most this legal act, adopted nearly a year after the Commission's initial decision, is *ex post facto* validation of an exercise of executive discretion.

The actions of the EU-27 and the Commission could have prejudiced the initial exercise of deconstructive power by the United Kingdom. The exhortation to send notification as soon as possible and the decision to prepare a negotiating team could have compelled the UK government to commence the process before legal permission was enacted through an Act of Parliament. This could have undermined the first objective of Article 50 TEU to vindicate the sovereign right of a Member State to commence withdrawal unilaterally. In reality, the UK government treated the referendum result as democratically binding in the same way as the European Union institutions. It is unlikely that these actions had a material effect on the domestic Brexit position.

The pre-emptive actions of the supranational institutions did have a material effect on their roles during the deconstitutional convention. The Commission arguably contravened the text of Article 218(3) TFEU. In turn, this undermined the second objective of Article 50 to ensure an orderly withdrawal. A prerequisite for orderliness is that the EU institutions comply with the withdrawal clause's prescriptions. The irony is that the Commission's 'a-legal' approach occurred within the context of statements to the United Kingdom that the legal

[192] Hillion (n 113) 225.

[193] European Council (n 80).

[194] Council Decision authorising the opening of negotiations with the United Kingdom of Great Britain and Northern Ireland for an agreement setting out the arrangements for its withdrawal from the European Union, Brussels, 15 May 2017 XT 21016/17 LIMITE BXT 24, art 1.

process must be followed. The Commission ensured a centralized withdrawal process that provided a monolithic conception of the EU's interests in order to guide negotiations. From the quadripartite perspective, this ensured disintegration was conditioned upon the interests of individuals *qua* EU citizens, rather than allowing the interests of individuals *qua* particular Member States to guide the process as may have happened if, for example, the European Council had adopted the negotiating role.

iii. The European Council guidelines and the European Parliament resolution

The deconstitutional convention officially commenced with the notification letter delivered by the United Kingdom to the European Council on 29 March 2017. The European Council fulfilled its mandated role under Article 50 by issuing guidelines for the negotiations on 29 April 2017.[195] The guidelines established the substantive principles, and some of the structural framework which is not regulated by Article 50, that guided the negotiations. This added substantive flesh to the procedural bones of Article 50 TEU. As Hillion suggests, 'the TEU only sets out the basic elements of the withdrawal process. Much had indeed to be clarified once the process was activated'.[196] This procedural scarcity prompted the criticism from Hannes Hofmeister that 'the procedural provisions lack clarity and—perhaps even worse—are incomplete'.[197] The European Council was left with the task of not only defining the EU's substantive priorities, but also providing for the 'detailed procedural legal framework' that Hofmeister argues is 'essential to avoid the risk of deadlock'.[198]

The guidelines state in their introduction that 'the Union's overall objective in these negotiations will be to preserve its interests, those of its citizens, its businesses and its Member States'.[199] The guidelines may provide evidence that the two objectives of Article 50 identified in *Wightman* are chronologically ordered. Once the prior objective of enabling the sovereign right of withdrawal is enabled by the operation of Article 50(1) and the first sentence of Article 50(2) TEU, the second objective of ensuring an orderly withdrawal comes to the fore.

[195] European Council (n 80).
[196] Hillion (n 113) 226.
[197] Hannes Hofmeister, '"Should I Stay or Should I Go?"—A Critical Analysis of the Right to Withdraw from the EU' (2010) 16 European Law Journal 589, 595.
[198] ibid 594.
[199] European Council (n 80).

This is evidenced further by the statement in the guidelines that '[t]he main purpose of the negotiations will be to ensure the United Kingdom's orderly withdrawal so as to reduce uncertainty and, to the extent possible, minimise disruption caused by this abrupt change'.[200]

The Union institutions' desire to preserve the unity of the constitutional order may be inferred as a driving consideration. The core principles of the European Council's draft guidelines detail that '[p]reserving the Single Market excludes participation on a sector-by-sector approach. A non-member of the Union, that does not live up to the same obligations as a member, cannot have the same rights and enjoy the same benefits as a member'.[201] The further objectives of the first phase of the negotiations are outlined as settling the disentanglement of the United Kingdom from the Union and from all of its rights and obligations, and to provide as much clarity and legal certainty as possible to citizens, businesses, stakeholders, and international partners. This may be regarded as a negotiating objective to ensure the preservation of the supranational constitutional order at this moment of seismic upheaval. This is further bolstered by the statement that '[t]he Union will preserve its autonomy as regards its decision-making as well as the role of the Court of Justice of the European Union'.[202]

The guidelines' arrangements for an orderly withdrawal establish the three substantive principles that would drive the EU's position in the negotiations: the protection of EU citizens' rights,[203] a single financial settlement to cover the UK's liabilities, and solutions to avoid a hard border between Northern Ireland and Ireland.[204] The guidelines also establish the structural principle that drove the deconstitutional convention of a 'phased approach to negotiations' which meant that 'an agreement on a future relationship between the Union and the United Kingdom as such can only be finalised and concluded once the United Kingdom has become a third country'.[205] This demarcated the Withdrawal Agreement as a *sui generis* form of EU international agreement distinct from the traditional agreements with Third Countries regulated by Articles 208, 217, and 218 TFEU. This is predicated upon the retention of the constituent status of EU citizenship for UK nationals up to the date of its extinction when the Treaties cease to apply.

[200] ibid para 4.
[201] ibid para 1.
[202] ibid.
[203] ibid para 8.
[204] ibid para 11.
[205] ibid paras 4–7.

The protection of EU citizens, and thus the supranational constitutional order they generate, may be regarded as the telos of the European Council's approach. The objective concerning citizens' rights seeks to address the specific situation of EU citizens *qua* juridical objects in the territory of the United Kingdom, and UK nationals *qua* former EU citizens in the territory of the European Union. The European Parliament, as the direct representative of these individuals, also explicitly made their protection its objective in negotiations through a resolution on 5 April 2017.[206] The resolution goes further than the European Council guidelines as it

> [t]akes note that many citizens of the United Kingdom have expressed strong opposition to losing the rights they currently enjoy pursuant to Article 20 of the Treaty on the Functioning of the European Union [and] proposes that the EU-27 examine how to mitigate this within the limits of Union primary law whilst fully respecting the principles of reciprocity, equity, symmetry and non-discrimination.[207]

Beyond the preservation of citizens' rights in the Withdrawal Agreement,[208] this opposition to the loss of EU citizenship would also eventually lead to the 'Amsterdam case' in which a claim was made for the preservation of the supranational status despite withdrawal.[209]

The European Council managed to avoid deadlock by establishing clear structural principles and substantive objectives for the negotiations. Michael Dougan claims that 'the solution adopted by the European Council was instrumental in structuring the conduct of the negotiations and . . . proved decisive in promoting their eventual success—at least judged by the objective of delivering a negotiated, orderly withdrawal'.[210] These choices have implications for the objectives of Article 50 TEU. In order to ensure that the objective of an orderly withdrawal was not undermined, sequencing required a transition period and the Protocol on Ireland/Northern Ireland.[211] Such transitional arrangements were unforeseen in the drafting of the text of Article 50 TEU. An international agreement between the withdrawing Member State and the EU cannot be

[206] European Parliament (n 170).
[207] ibid para 27.
[208] See discussion of Part II of the Withdrawal Agreement later in the chapter.
[209] *C/13/640244/KG ZA 17-1327* of the Rechtbank Amsterdam. See detailed analysis of the case later in this chapter.
[210] Dougan, *The UK's Withdrawal* (n 67) 96.
[211] See detailed discussion of the transition period and the Northern Ireland Protocol later in this chapter.

legally concluded before the Treaties cease to apply. Article 50(3) TEU does not, however, require the resolution of all withdrawal issues before any discussions on the framework for future relations. This was a political decision taken by the European Council and agreed upon by the UK government.

The EU enforced this phased approach by making 'sufficient progress' a condition for movement to the discussions of the future relationship. The only regulation of this condition is found in the guidelines: 'The European Council will monitor progress closely and determine when sufficient progress has been achieved to allow negotiations to proceed to the next phase'.[212] This was achieved in the joint report of the United Kingdom and the European Union in December 2017. The sequencing of negotiations fell within the legal discretion of the European Council under Article 50(2). The legitimacy of this discretion may be questioned with regard to a lack of sufficient clarity over the conditions for 'sufficient progress', and the exclusion of input from the European Parliament.

Polly Polak recognizes that '[t]he ordering of the withdrawal negotiations—either in parallel or in phases—was immensely relevant for the balance of power within them, especially as the phased approach favoured by the institutions included a selection of material issues that, although not determined either by Article 50, were also imposed by the EU'.[213] Dennis Dixon argues more critically that a phased approach to negotiations creates a hostile environment for the withdrawing Member State, and undermines the objective to enable a sovereign decision.[214] This analysis misses the practical point that the UK government made no attempt to reach internal consensus on the future relationship until the 'Chequers proposal' in July 2018.[215] This plan led to great fractures amongst the government and the resignations of the Foreign Secretary and the Secretary of State for Exiting the European Union. The hostile environment for withdrawal negotiations was generated as much by internal UK disunity as external imposition by the supranational institutions. Early political consensus on the model for a future relationship could have enabled clarity on the Irish border arrangements. Certainty over the sovereign preferences of the United Kingdom could have ensured a smoother transition to discussions of the future relationship.

[212] European Council (n 80) para 4.

[213] Polak (n 7) 139.

[214] Dennis Dixon, 'Article 50 and Member State Sovereignty' (2018) 19 German Law Journal 901, 903.

[215] 'The Future Relationship between the United Kingdom and the European Union' (*GOV.UK*, 17 July 2018) <www.gov.uk/government/publications/the-future-relationship-between-the-united-kingdom-and-the-european-union> accessed 16 April 2020.

Rather than sequencing *per se*, the legitimacy problem is the discretion of the European Council to determine and regulate the phases of the negotiations. The EU institutions must necessarily identify the substantive areas for resolution as these are not prescribed in Article 50 TEU. There is less clarity on the permissible boundaries for the EU institutions in determining the procedure for negotiations within their discretion under the withdrawal clause. Greater clarity could be enshrined on the procedure for the negotiations, and what institutions are legitimated to enforce the conditions of this procedure, in the text of the withdrawal clause.

Sequencing may also be challenged by the wording whereby negotiations should be conducted 'taking account of the framework for . . . future relations'.[216] The hasty conclusion and renegotiation of a 'Political Declaration'[217] at the end of the second phase of negotiations may call into question the extent to which the negotiation of the Withdrawal Agreement itself took this framework into account. If one interprets 'taking account' to require a constant process of determining separation issues with regard to the framework for future relations, then the Political Declaration falls short. This interpretation would require the creation of the framework at the onset of the negotiations. Such an interpretation would also preclude the political option of sequencing negotiations. This is a feasible but not necessary interpretation of the wording 'taking account'. In the Brexit case, there was no challenge to the legal validity of the conclusion of such a Political Declaration before the point at which the Treaties ceased to apply.

V. Article 50(3) TEU: The *Finalité* of Withdrawal

Article 50(3) TEU states the *finalité* of the withdrawal process: 'the Treaties shall cease to apply to the State in question'. The primary condition is 'the date of entry into force of the withdrawal agreement', and the secondary residual condition is 'two years after the notification referred to in paragraph 2' if the primary condition is unfulfilled. These withdrawal conditions are qualified by the derogative clause 'unless the European Council, in agreement with the Member State concerned, unanimously decides to extend this period'.[218]

[216] TEU, art 50(2).

[217] 'New Withdrawal Agreement and Political Declaration' (*GOV.UK*, 19 October 2019) <www.gov.uk/government/publications/new-withdrawal-agreement-and-political-declaration> accessed 16 April 2020.

[218] TEU, art 50(3).

i. The primary and secondary conditions

The primary condition ensures that the EU institutions represent the interests of all individuals *qua* nationals and *qua* EU citizens through shaping the content of a Withdrawal Agreement.[219] Although the initial domestic decision may be insensitive to the interests of any individuals beyond the Member State nationals, the final implementation of this decision is multilateral and may preserve the interests of the remaining constituent subjects of the supranational constitutional order. The negotiating guidelines of the European Council[220] and the resolution of the European Parliament[221] emphasize this objective.

The residual two-year condition has been interpreted as a 'cooling-off period' which provides the withdrawing Member State with an opportunity to reverse its decision before it is made final.[222] This comparison to withdrawal clauses in other international treaties has been forwarded as an argument for unilateral revocation of notification.[223] An alternative purpose of the two-year period is to ensure that withdrawal cannot be delayed indefinitely by a failure to find consensus with the Union institutions. This vindicates the ultimate self-determination of the constituent subjects of the withdrawing state if there is an absolute failure to negotiate an orderly withdrawal.

This period may only be extended with the agreement of the withdrawing Member State, further vindicating the self-determination of its nationals. The unanimity requirement in the European Council ensures the representation of the nationals of the High Contracting Parties as individual peoples. A more rigorous standard is applied for extension than the conclusion of a Withdrawal Agreement, which is effected by Qualified Majority Voting in the Council. This discrepancy is justified because a decision to extend the period is an amendment to the fundamental framework for the negotiations, whereas the Withdrawal Agreement is a natural conclusion to the course set by the guidelines established through unanimity. The ordinary rules of representation of all individuals *qua* Member State nationals in the Council suffices for the former, whereas amendment of the structure of the deconstitutional convention requires legitimation by every High Contracting Party. It could be argued

[219] See Hillion (n 113); Łazowski (n 191).
[220] European Council (n 80) para 8.
[221] European Parliament (n 170) para 18.
[222] Carlos Closa, 'Interpreting Article 50: Exit, Voice and...What About Loyalty?' in Carlos Closa (ed), *Secession from a Member State and Withdrawal from the European Union: Troubled Membership* (CUP 2017).
[223] Carlos Closa, 'Is Article 50 Reversible? On Politics Beyond Legal Doctrine' (*Verfassungsblog*, 4 January 2017) <https://verfassungsblog.de/is-article-50-reversible-on-politics-beyond-legal-doctrine/> accessed 16 April 2020.

that the reconstruction of the Brexit deconstitutional convention following extensions after 29 March 2019 provided the necessary legitimacy for the renegotiation of the Irish Protocol in October 2019.

ii. The Withdrawal Agreement: Transforming the quadripartite role

The legal nature of the Withdrawal Agreement manifests the hybrid nature of the levelling down of constituent power as a transformation of relations from supranational to international. Polak argues that 'supranationality will most certainly trespass into the actual content of any withdrawal agreement'.[224] It is an international agreement but it is imbued with characteristics of supranational constitutionalism such as primacy and direct effect.[225] Dougan notes, however, that 'the governance provisions of the Withdrawal Agreement are entirely familiar from standard international practice'.[226] The Withdrawal Agreement may be regarded as creating a simulacrum of the EU Treaties, whilst also reflecting the content of other EU international agreements with third countries. Part One defines common provisions, including definitions and interpretation; Part Two covers citizens' rights; Part Three regulates separation provisions including goods, customs, intellectual property, and police cooperation; Part Four establishes the transition period; Part Five settles the financial provisions, known as the 'divorce settlement'; and Part Six sets the institutional and final provisions including preliminary reference to the Court of Justice under Part Two, the intergovernmental governance institutions, and the dispute settlement procedure. The Withdrawal Agreement is governed by a Joint Committee that is co-chaired by a UK Minister and a Vice-President of the European Commission.[227] This transforms the basis for exercise of democratic subjectivity from supranational constitutionalism and dual legitimation to representation only be members of the executive in the international place. Dispute settlement beyond citizens' rights is similarly intergovernmental with an arbitration panel being composed of nominations from both parties.[228]

[224] Polak (n 7) 187.

[225] Agreement on the withdrawal of the United Kingdom of Great Britain and Northern Ireland from the European Union and the European Atomic Energy Community [2019] OJ C 384/1, art 4 (hereafter 'EU–UK Withdrawal Agreement').

[226] Dougan, *The UK's Withdrawal* (n 67) 188.

[227] Oliver Garner, 'Written Evidence Submitted to the House of Commons Committee on the Future Relationship with the European Union: The EU–UK Joint Committee' (*Bingham Centre for the Rule of Law*, 15 May 2020) <https://binghamcentre.biicl.org/publications/written-evidence-submitted-to-the-house-of-commons-committee-on-the-future-relationship-with-the-european-union-the-eu-uk-joint-committee> accessed 20 October 2023.

[228] EU–UK Withdrawal Agreement, arts 167–81.

This transforms the role of individual as juridical object to only the state of the United Kingdom and the international organization of the European Union exercising this role. There are three Protocols concerning territorial issues with EU Member States—Ireland and Northern Ireland, sovereign bases in Cyprus, and Gibraltar, and nine Annexes including rules of procedure.

Part Two transformed the quadripartite role of individuals in its substantive provisions covering citizens' rights and the means created to vindicate democratic subjecthood and juridical objecthood. Parts of the new legal regime function as a microcosm of the supranational constitutional order. The substance and relational structure of legal norms are replicated. However, the method for their creation and maintenance, and the basis for the validity, of these norms has been transformed from supranational constitutionalism to public international law. Dougan criticizes Part Two of the Withdrawal Agreement for too closely replicating EU law rather than being sensitive to the Brexit context: 'the Union itself adopted an essentially legalistic and formalistic approach . . . rather than recognizing the need for a more generous system that would reflect the more complex and fluid realities of so many individual lives'.[229]

The preamble to the Agreement establishes the purpose of the citizens' right chapter: to provide reciprocal protection of the exercise of free movement rights by UK and EU citizens before a date set by Agreement and to ensure that the rights are enforceable and based on the principle of non-discrimination. The temporal starting point for protection is that free movement rights have been exercised before the end of the transition period. However, this is complicated by additional temporal exceptions provided for in the text, in addition to the complexities of the scope of who is protected.

The Withdrawal Agreement defines 'Union citizen' and 'United Kingdom national' separately.[230] The former is defined paradigmatically as 'any person holding the nationality of a Member State',[231] and the list of Member States excludes the United Kingdom.[232] The latter is defined by reference to the New Declaration by the UK Government of 31 December 1982 on the definition of nationals, together with the Treaty of Lisbon's Declaration No 63.[233] The provision disaggregates nationals of the United Kingdom from the wider class of EU citizens. This is the first definition of the juridical objects of the new

229 Dougan, *The UK's Withdrawal* (n 67) 350.
230 EU–UK Withdrawal Agreement, art 2.
231 ibid art 2(c).
232 ibid art 2(b).
233 ibid art 2(d).

regime of public international law created between the Union and a former Member State.

Defining these objects preserves a semblance of legal 'ordering' around the new normative point governing EU and UK relations. In specific areas, this is achieved by reference to the formerly authoritative EU legal regime. For example, Title III of Part Two on the coordination of social security systems defines one class of 'persons covered' as 'United Kingdom nationals who are subject to the legislation of a Member State at the end of the transition period, as well as their family members and survivors'.[234] UK nationals are transformed from quadripartite subjects of the supranational constitutional order to residual juridical objects.

Part Two of the Agreement addresses the issue of citizens' rights that had been identified as a predicate for an orderly withdrawal. The provisions preserve a partial version of EU citizenship as a juridical status. Withdrawal extinguishes the right to free movement for UK citizens into and through EU territory, and for EU citizens into UK territory. Legal protection is limited to preserving the rights of individuals who have already exercised free movement to be present within either UK territory or the territory of a Member State. The only partial rights of movement preserved for UK nationals are for those who fulfil the definition of 'frontier worker'.[235] The rights are limited to this territory, which means that UK citizens do not retain free movement rights to other EU Member States other than their state of residence. Part Two preserves the legacy rights for individuals, and a limited category of current and future family members, in order to vindicate the guarantees of EU citizenship that individuals had relied upon before the UK's withdrawal. This protection is limited to juridical rights; Part Two does not preserve the voting rights that enable political self-determination *qua* EU citizen.

The Withdrawal Agreement duplicates the text of supranational legal sources. Part Two, Title II, Chapter 1 replicates the provisions of Directive 2004/38 on citizens' free movement and residence rights,[236] Chapter 2 transposes Regulation No 492/2011 on the free movement of worker,[237]and Chapter 3 covers Directive 2005/36/EC on the recognition of professional

[234] ibid art 30(1)(b).

[235] ibid art 9(b).

[236] Directive 2004/38/EC of the European Parliament and of the Council of 29 April 2004 on the right of citizens of the Union and their family members to move and reside freely within the territory of the Member States [2004] OJ L 158/77.

[237] Regulation (EU) No 492/2011 of the European Parliament and of the Council of 5 April 2011 on freedom of movement for workers within the Union [2011] OJ L 141/1.

qualifications.[238] Title III is dedicated to duplicating Regulation No 883/2004 on the coordination of social security systems.[239] The degree of replication is so extensive that Stijn Smismans has used the term 'copy and paste'.[240] These Chapters partially preserve the substance and objectives of EU law within the new source of an international treaty. A particular moment of the UK's nationals' constitutional input into the development of these norms is ossified. The formerly dynamic process of development of the rights of juridical objects is converted into a static legal source with a predefined expiration. This is the external analogue to the ossification of 'retained EU law' in the UK's constitutional order.[241] The Withdrawal Agreement and the domestic legislation are the juridical means to repatriate constituent power to the domestic level. The termination of EU citizenship as a democratic and juridical status means that the processes of norm-formulation and alteration become the exclusive domain of UK institutions at the domestic and international level.

The definition of 'host State'[242] establishes the new default temporal grounding for the retention of residence rights. The exercise of these rights must have come before the end of the transition period, and residence must continue thereafter. Periods of legal residence or work in accordance with Union law both before and after the end of the transition period are included in the calculation of the qualifying period of five years that is necessary to acquire a right of permanent residence.[243] Certain categories of individuals will be protected by the provisions even if they exercise their rights after the end of the transition period.[244] These are direct relations of an EU national in the United Kingdom or a UK national in the European Union who resided outside the host State before the end of the transition period and who fulfil the conditions in Directive 2004/38,[245] and individuals who are born to or legally adopted by covered individuals after the end of the transition period.

This functions as a generational clause which ensures the continuing protection of the offspring of affected citizens. This ensures the continuity of legal rights in order to preserve family unity for those who have utilized their EU citizenship to pursue their life plans. Article 39 confirms that '[t]he persons

[238] Directive 2005/36/EC of the European Parliament and of the Council of 7 September 2005 on the recognition of professional qualifications [2005] OJ L 255/22.
[239] Regulation (EC) No 883/2004 of the European Parliament and of the Council of 29 April 2004 on the coordination of social security systems [2004] OJ L 166/1.
[240] Smismans (n 148).
[241] European Union (Withdrawal) Act 2018, s 6.
[242] EU–UK Withdrawal Agreement, art 9(c).
[243] ibid art 15.
[244] ibid art 10(e)(ii).
[245] Directive 2004/38 (n 236), art 2(2).

covered by this Part shall enjoy the rights provided for in the relevant Titles of this Part for their lifetime, unless they cease to meet the conditions set out therein'.[246] The rights may only be revoked if the restrictions on the rights of residence and entry are fulfilled. This confirms that the hereditary nature of citizenship rights, whereby family members inherit rights regardless of their acquisition of EU citizenship,[247] is henceforth terminated.

The Withdrawal Agreement protects the juridical objecthood of the new status for individuals. The judicial architecture of the supranational constitutional order is extended beyond the date of withdrawal. UK courts may send preliminary references to the Court of Justice of the European Union for cases that commenced at first instance within a period of eight years after the end of the transition period.[248] A new independent 'Authority' is established within the United Kingdom to monitor the implementation and application of Part Two.[249] This authority has powers equivalent to the European Commission to conduct enquiries, receive complaints from affected individuals, and bring legal actions before a competent court.[250] The 'Authority' may only be disbanded by a decision of the Joint Committee overseeing the Agreement. The Withdrawal Agreement establishes a specialized Committee on Citizens' Rights as one of the constituent parts of this Joint Committee overseeing the 'interpretation and application' of the Agreement meeting at least once a year.[251] Finally, Part Two is exempt from the remedy of temporary suspension of obligations by one of the parties to the Agreement following a failure to implement a ruling of the Joint Committee.[252] The protection of citizens' rights forms the substantive 'core' of the new legal regime established by the Withdrawal Agreement. Its purpose is to vindicate the self-actualization of individuals who have relied upon their EU citizenship for as long as possible. Accordingly, these provisions must be afforded comprehensive judicial protection and cannot be the subject of coercive remedial measures in public international law, which should be targeted at states rather than individuals.

The Withdrawal Agreement does not preserve the political rights to vote and stand as candidates in European Parliament and municipal elections.[253] UK nationals, therefore, lose their democratic subjecthood *qua* EU citizens,

[246] EU–UK Withdrawal Agreement, art 39.
[247] Case C-34/09 *Gerardo Ruiz Zambrano v Office national de l'emploi (ONEm)* [2011] ECR I-1177.
[248] EU–UK Withdrawal Agreement, art 158.
[249] ibid art 159.
[250] See European Union (Withdrawal Agreement) Act 2020, sch 2 for the domestic implementation of the Independent Monitoring Authority.
[251] EU–UK Withdrawal Agreement, art 165(1)(a).
[252] ibid art 178(2)(a).
[253] TFEU, arts 20(2)(b) and 22.

and EU citizens lose this democratic capacity within the territory of the United Kingdom. The state that has withdrawn from the European Union has a discretion whether to enfranchise EU nationals in local elections, and individual EU Member States have the discretion to enfranchise UK nationals to vote in local elections as Third Country Nationals. The silence of the Withdrawal Agreement on political rights may reinforce the conception of the status as one that individuals utilize for the passive acquisition and exercise of legal rights, rather than a status that empowers individuals to engage in self-determination through participation in democratic procedures.

The termination of EU citizenship as a democratic status may create a practical problem beyond this theoretical deficiency. A lacuna may arise in Northern Ireland.[254] All UK nationals born in Northern Ireland have the option to adopt the nationality of Ireland by virtue of the Good Friday Agreement[255] and subsequent amendments to the Irish Constitution.[256] UK nationals born in this territory can retain their EU citizenship through this channel. Theoretically, all national residents in Northern Ireland could be EU citizens, but unable to vote in European Parliament elections within their territory of residence. This situation would be analogous to that of citizen residents of Gibraltar who, before the *Matthews* decision,[257] were not enfranchised in European Parliament elections despite holding EU citizenship. This could prompt litigation and may require further unilateral or bilateral legislative action beyond the scope of the Withdrawal Agreement before the next European Parliament elections.

The Withdrawal Agreement does not preserve the status of EU citizenship for UK nationals. Both the UK and EU negotiators relied implicitly on an interpretation that the withdrawal of a Member State automatically leads to the extinction of EU citizenship for those holding the nationality of that state.[258] This position assumes that the termination of the condition for the acquisition of EU citizenship—nationality of a Member State—functions as the condition for its revocation. In 2018 this assumption was challenged in an application

[254] Reuven Ziegler, 'Part I Mini-Symposium on EU Citizenship in the Shadow of Brexit: The Brexit Effect—European Parliamentary Elections in the UK' (*European Law Blog*, 19 December 2018) <https://web.archive.org/web/20190827213516/https://europeanlawblog.eu/2018/12/19/part-i-mini-symposium-on-eu-citizenship-in-the-shadow-of-brexit-the-brexit-effect-european-parliamentary-elections-in-the-uk/> accessed 16 April 2020.

[255] 'The Belfast Agreement' (*GOV.UK*, 10 April 1998) <www.gov.uk/government/publications/the-belfast-agreement> accessed 17 April 2020.

[256] Nineteenth Amendment to the Constitution Act 1998.

[257] *Matthews v United Kingdom* (1999) 28 EHRR 361 (ECHR).

[258] For full argumentation see Oliver Garner, 'Does Member State Withdrawal from the European Union Extinguish EU Citizenship? C/13/640244 / KG ZA 17-1327 of the Rechtbank Amsterdam (The Amsterdam Case)' (*European Law Blog*, 19 February 2018) <www.europeanlawblog.eu/pub/does-member-state-withdrawal-from-the-european-union-extinguish-eu-citizenship-c13640244-kg-za-17-1327-rechtbank-amsterdam-the-amsterdam-case/release/1> accessed 17 April 2020.

before the Dutch courts for a preliminary reference to the Court of Justice to determine whether EU citizenship is necessarily lost with Member State withdrawal or not.[259]

The first instance preliminary reference request was reversed on appeal due to the issue being 'insufficiently concrete' and hypothetical. The legal claim became live again when the Withdrawal Agreement came into force in February 2020. This possibility was recognized by the General Court in its dismissal of the claim that the European Council's recommendation for a decision to commence withdrawal negotiations did not directly affect the legal situation of UK citizens.[260] The Court of Justice states that '[i]t is only at the end of the procedure laid down in Article 50 TEU that the rights of the applicants are liable to be affected, to an extent which is not, however, possible to predict'.[261] On 30 March 2020 and 23 April 2020 further legal actions challenging the loss of EU citizenship as a result of the Withdrawal Agreement were filed before the Court of Justice of the European Union.[262] A preliminary reference arising from the claim of a UK citizen who had been removed from the electoral roll for municipal elections in France was sent to the Court of Justice on 9 December 2020, resulting in the *EP* judgment on 9 June 2022.[263] The Court held that 'there is an inseparable and exclusive link between possession of the nationality of a Member State and not only the acquisition, but also the *retention*, of the status of citizen of the Union'.[264] Sergii Lashyn notes that '[t]he judgment finally provides a definitive answer to the issue of the loss of EU citizenship and evinces the Court's departure from its expansive interpretation of the provisions on Union citizenship'.[265] In reference to the referendum, Lashyn argues that 'no democratic process is enough legal justification for an *en masse* revocation of the citizenship status'.[266] Whilst recognizing the distinction between EU citizenship and nationality of a Member State, he states that 'it has

[259] *C/13/640244/KG ZA 17-1327* of the Rechtbank Amsterdam (n 209).
[260] Case T-458/17 *Shindler v Council* (n 6).
[261] ibid para 23.
[262] Julien Fouchet, 'DON'T TOUCH MY EU CITIZENSHIP' (*CrowdJustice*) <www.crowdjustice.com/case/dont-touch-my-european-citizenship/> accessed 17 April 2020; Stephen Hocking, David Harrison and Alexandra von Westernhagen, 'DAC Beachcroft Files Landmark Case with General Court of the EU on Behalf of a Group of UK Nationals' (*DAC Beachcroft*, 23 April 2020) <https://web.archive.org/web/20200501213655/https://www.dacbeachcroft.com/en/gb/news/2020/april/dac-beachcroft-files-landmark-case-with-general-court-of-the-eu-on-behalf-of-a-group-of-uk-nationals/> accessed 25 April 2020.
[263] Case C-673/20 *EP v Préfet du Gers and Institut national de la statistique et des études économiques (INSEE)* EU:C:2022:449.
[264] ibid 48 (emphasis added).
[265] Serhii Lashyn, 'Sacrificing EU Citizenship on the Altar of Brexit' (2022) 29 Maastricht Journal of European and Comparative Law 736, 739.
[266] ibid 742.

the same essence of a durable legal bond'.[267] This normative position underplays the extent to which EU citizenship is a unique supranational species of this genre that is ultimately dependent upon the prior status of nationality of a Member State for its existence. The decision in *EP* confirmed unequivocally that this status cannot persist for nationals of a Member State that had made the decision to withdraw from the Union. The democratic mischief in the case may be regarded as resulting from the previously discussed under-inclusivity of the franchise for the referendum result, which excluded citizens such as the claimant in *EP* who had been outside of the territory of the United Kingdom for fifteen years despite the existential consequences of the result of the referendum for these individuals.

iii. The Protocol on Ireland/Northern Ireland

The Protocol on Ireland/Northern Ireland nuances the status of UK nationals *qua* juridical objects after withdrawal.[268] The Protocol addresses the substantive goal in the negotiations to find 'flexible and imaginative solutions . . . with the aim of avoiding a hard border [in Ireland]'.[269] It ensures an orderly withdrawal by protecting the Good Friday settlement and the integrity of the EU internal market. Michael Dougan outlines that the price to achieve orderliness was compromises on both sides:

> For the Union, the Protocol means accepting that part of the EU's own external frontiers will essentially be policed and enforced by authorities and officials of a third country. For the British, the Protocol provides for Northern Ireland to be subject to different customs and regulatory arrangements from the rest of the UK and consequently for the erection of various barriers to trade in goods with Great Britain.[270]

The Protocol mandates a substantial continuation of the Union legal order within a devolved territory of a former Member State. A broad range of EU

[267] ibid.
[268] These paragraphs reproduce extracts from Oliver Garner, 'The New Irish Protocol Could Lead to the Indefinite Jurisdiction of the EU Court of Justice within the UK' (*LSE Brexit*, 23 October 2019) <https://blogs.lse.ac.uk/brexit/2019/10/23/the-new-irish-protocol-could-lead-to-the-indefinite-jurisdiction-of-the-court-of-justice-of-the-european-union-within-the-united-kingdom/> accessed 17 April 2020.
[269] European Council (n 80) para 11.
[270] Dougan, *The UK's Withdrawal* (n 67) 257–58.

internal market law, customs law, state aid law, and VAT and excise law is applicable within Northern Ireland by virtue of the Protocol.[271] The Protocol that was originally agreed in 2018 would have achieved this by continuing the application of the EU customs union to the entirety of Great Britain and Northern Ireland. By contrast, the renegotiated Protocol of October 2019 no longer mandates a single customs territory between the whole of the United Kingdom and the European Union. Instead, the application of customs duties in Northern Ireland is dependent on the condition that 'a good is at risk of subsequently being moved into the Union, whether by itself or forming part of another good following processing'.[272]

The previous Protocol operated as an insurance policy in the event that no satisfactory arrangements were established for the Irish border in a future relationship: '[T]he Union and the United Kingdom shall use their best endeavours to conclude, by 31 December 2020, an agreement which supersedes this Protocol in whole or in part'.[273] By contrast, the new Protocol merely states that 'any subsequent agreement between the Union and the United Kingdom shall indicate the parts of this Protocol which it supersedes'.[274] Following extensive calls to renegotiate the Protocol throughout 2021 and 2022 and unilateral derogations by the UK government, such an agreement was concluded in the 'Windsor Framework' in February 2023.[275] The Protocol operates as the default mode of regulating the relationship between Northern Ireland and the European Union after the transition period at least until a decision is made by the Northern Ireland Assembly before the end of 2024 either to maintain or scrap the Protocol under the Article 18 'democratic consent mechanism'.

The Protocol also maintains the EU's juridical architecture for norm application. EU institutions have the power conferred upon them by Union law in relation to the Protocol.[276] This article states that 'in particular, the Court of Justice of the European Union shall have the jurisdiction provided for in the Treaties in this respect'.[277] This confirms that the Article 267 TFEU preliminary reference procedure shall apply to and in the United Kingdom by virtue of the Protocol. There are only two means to terminate this jurisdiction: the

[271] EU–UK Withdrawal Agreement (n 225), Protocol on Ireland/Northern Ireland [2019] OJ C 384 I/92, annex 5.

[272] ibid art 5.

[273] Protocol on Ireland/Northern Ireland, Draft Agreement on the withdrawal of the United Kingdom of Great Britain and Northern Ireland from the European Union and the European Atomic Energy Community, as agreed at negotiators' level on 14 November 2018 TF50 (2018) 55, art 2(1).

[274] New Protocol on Ireland/Northern Ireland (n 271) art 13.

[275] 'The Windsor Framework' (*GOV.UK*, 30 January 2024) <www.gov.uk/government/publications/the-windsor-framework> accessed 30 April 2024.

[276] New Protocol on Ireland/Northern Ireland (n 271) art 12.

[277] ibid.

Northern Irish Assembly may refuse to consent to the ongoing operation of the Protocol, or a future relationship agreement may supersede the Protocol. If neither of these conditions comes to pass, the Court of Justice of the European Union will have indefinite jurisdiction within the United Kingdom in relation to the actions of UK nationals *qua* juridical objects within the scope of the Protocol.

The Protocol on Ireland/Northern Ireland preserves the juridical objecthood of individuals in relevant situations. The UK's withdrawal may not be regarded as a full and unconditional restoration of nationality as a constituent status because a sub-set of nationals remain objects of EU norms without retaining democratic subjecthood. Rather than continual input into the creation of applicable norms through representation in the EU legislative institutions, democratic self-determination becomes a one-off event four years after the end of the transition period when the Northern Irish Assembly will be asked to consent to the continuing operation of the Protocol.[278] This raises the unique situation of the final decision over the application of a simulacrum of EU law norms resting with individuals *qua* democratic subjects of a sub-state devolved region.

This preservation of juridical objecthood may be justified by the unique relationship between the United Kingdom, Northern Ireland, and Ireland and their respective constituent statuses. This is recognized by the preamble to the Protocol 'having regard to the historic ties and enduring nature of the bilateral relationship between Ireland and the United Kingdom'.[279] This relationship has been a crucial feature of disrupted integration as well as disintegration. The same concerns relating to the border between Ireland and Northern Ireland that have driven Schengen and AFSJ opt-outs are the drivers behind the Protocol.[280] The opt-out of both Member States from the Schengen zone, in favour of their own regime of border-liberalization in the Common Travel Area,[281] explains why the Protocol is limited to the triggering condition of free movement of goods.

The continuation of juridical objecthood in Northern Ireland may be justified by the unique constituent status of individuals in this region. People born in Northern Ireland can choose whether to be citizens of the United Kingdom, citizens of Ireland, or citizens of both states.[282] All these individuals have the

[278] ibid art 18.

[279] New Protocol on Ireland/Northern Ireland (n 271).

[280] See further discussion on the origins of Ireland opt-outs in chapter 5.

[281] Graham Butler, 'Europe's "Other" Open-Border Zone: The Common Travel Area under the Shadow of Brexit' (2018) 20 Cambridge Yearbook of European Legal Studies 252.

[282] The Belfast Agreement (n 255); Nineteenth Amendment to the Constitution Act 1998.

inherent capacity to continue their status as EU citizens following Brexit. Their status as continuing juridical objects of EU law can, therefore, be legitimated by their status as potential nationals of the Irish state and as potential EU citizens, albeit without the capacity to vote in Northern Ireland itself in European Parliament elections. The actions of the Irish government in support of the border solution throughout the deconstitutional convention were also legitimate to protect individuals who are already nationals of the state, and individuals in Northern Ireland who are potential nationals.

The resolution of the Irish border issue was a key substantive objective in the initiation of the deconstitutional convention. This made Ireland a unique constituent player amongst the High Contracting Parties. Ireland exercised this role in the determination of 'sufficient progress' to move on to Phase 2 of the withdrawal negotiations in December 2018,[283] and in breaking the impasse on the renegotiation of the Protocol in October 2019.[284] The Protocol on Ireland/Northern Ireland is a caveat to the theoretical purity of the model of withdrawal as levelling down constituent power. This exceptional disintegrative phenomenon arises from the practical exigencies of the UK's internal constitutional status. Nevertheless, the Protocol benefits from the input legitimacy of the governments of Ireland and the United Kingdom in the deconstitutional convention. Output legitimacy is evidenced through the protection of the juridical rights of individuals in the territories of Ireland and Northern Ireland. Finally, the explicit inclusion in the European Council guidelines of the Irish border as a key issue for resolution in the Withdrawal Agreement generates throughput legitimacy.

iv. The future relationship

Article 50 TEU only regulates the future relationship between the EU and the Withdrawing Member State to the extent that it imposes an obligation for the parties to agree the 'framework for [the] future relationship'.[285] The EU and the Theresa May government fulfilled this originally through the conclusion of a

[283] Kevin O'Rourke, *A Short History of Brexit: From Brentry to Backstop* (Pelican 2019).

[284] Department of the Taoiseach, 'Joint Statement by Taoiseach Leo Varadkar and Prime Minister Boris Johnson' (*Gov.ie*, 10 October 2019) <https://gov.ie/en/press-release/e3a113-joint-statement-by-an-taoiseach-leo-varadkar-and-prime-minister-bori/> accessed 17 April 2020.

[285] See discussion earlier in the chapter for extent to which the United Kingdom and the European Union fulfilled the obligation of 'taking account' of this framework in their negotiation of the Withdrawal Agreement.

'Political Declaration', which was subsequently renegotiated by Boris Johnson and published in its final form on 12 November 2019.[286] Michael Dougan opined that the 'text foresees only a relatively shallow relationship between the two parties—certainly as compared to the years of UK membership . . . but even when set against other models for third country relations that had been proposed and discussed during the referendum campaign and thereafter'.[287] The introduction emphasizes that the autonomy of the European Union and the sovereignty of the United Kingdom must be ensured. Part I outlines the initial provisions including core values and rights as the basis for cooperation and the areas of shared interest; Part II details the objectives and areas for the economic partnership, including the need for a level playing field for open and fair competition; Part III outlines the aims for the security partnership, including law enforcement and judicial cooperation in criminal matters—the area that was previously subject to the UK's opt-in Protocol concerning the AFSJ; Part IV details the objectives for institutional and other horizontal arrangements; and Part V details the aspirations for the forward process.

The United Kingdom refused to entertain the option for the Joint Committee to extend the transition period by a period of either one or two years that expired on 1 July 2020 despite the COVID-19 pandemic.[288] The Trade and Cooperation Agreement (TCA) was subsequently concluded between the European Union and the United Kingdom on 31 December 2020.[289] The TCA was concluded as an EU only agreement under Article 217 TFEU as an Association Agreement. Polak argues that this is a 'remarkable decision' as 'its comprehensive scope . . . clearly covers areas of shared competence'.[290] She concludes that this has 'further supranationalised the process of withdrawal, including its final phase of negotiating a new trade relationship with the ex-Member State turned third country'.[291] Part One of the TCA establishes the common and institutional provisions; Part Two governs trade, transport, fisheries and other arrangements, including Title XI on the level playing field for

[286] Political Declaration setting out the framework for the future relationship between the European Union and the United Kingdom of Great Britain and Northern Ireland [2019] OJ C 384I/178.

[287] Dougan, *The UK's Withdrawal* (n 67) 302.

[288] David Duguid MP and The Rt Hon Allister Jack MP, 'UK Government Will Not Be Seeking an Extension to the EU Exit Transition Period' (*GOV.UK*, 12 June 2020) <www.gov.uk/government/news/uk-government-will-not-be-seeking-an-extension-to-the-eu-exit-transition-period> accessed 30 April 2024.

[289] Trade and Cooperation Agreement between the European Union and the European Atomic Energy Community, of the one part, and the United Kingdom of Great Britain and Northern Ireland, of the other part [2021] OJ L 149/10 (hereafter 'EU–UK TCA').

[290] Polak (n 7) 255.

[291] ibid.

open and fair competition and sustainable development;[292] Part Three covers law enforcement and judicial cooperation in criminal matters; Part Four outlines thematic cooperation in the areas of health security and cyber security; Part Five governs the UK's participation in Union programmes, financial management, and financial provisions; Part Six concerns dispute settlement and horizontal provisions; Part Seven outlines final provisions; forty annexes cover technical details such as appointment rules and rules of procedure; three Protocols cover combating fraud in VAT, mutual administrative assistance in customs, and social security coordination; and fifteen declarations pertain to areas such as exchange and protection of classified information.[293]

The overall tenor of the TCA may be regarded as 'new old intergovernmentalism' with the exclusion of supranational institutions and the exclusion of the role of individuals as either democratic subjects or juridical objects beyond the national level with states and international organizations acting as the only constituent parties.[294] Similarly to the Withdrawal Agreement Joint Committee, the TCA establishes a Partnership Council[295] co-chaired by a UK Minister and a Vice-President of the Commission. Therefore individuals are only represented in decision-making as democratic subjects by members of the executive exercising their prerogative in international law. An intriguing innovation in the TCA is the creation of a Parliamentary Partnership Assembly.[296] The Assembly is composed of representatives of the UK Parliament and the European Parliament, and has the prerogative to request information regarding the implementation of the TCA, must be kept informed of the decisions and recommendations of the Partnership Council, and may make recommendations thereto. Although the role of parliamentarians may only extend to advice and not decision-making, this has echoes of normative proposals for 'republican intergovernmentalism' as a means to ensure non-domination in European integration.[297] Time will tell whether the TCA could function as a challenger model to supranational constitutionalism,

[292] Polly Polak argues that these level playing field requirements continue supranationalism as 'these continue to place especially significant restrictions on the UK's sovereignty post-withdrawal': ibid 241.
[293] For a detailed analysis of the TCA see Federico Fabbrini (ed), *The Law & Politics of Brexit: Volume III: The Framework of New EU–UK Relations* (OUP 2021).
[294] Oliver Garner, 'Part Three of the EU–UK TCA—From a "Disrupted" Area of Freedom, Security and Justice to "New Old" Intergovernmentalism in Justice and Home Affairs?' (DCU Brexit Institute 2021) Brexit Institute Working Paper Series No 1/2021.
[295] There are also various sub-committees for thematic areas, perhaps echoing the different configurations of the Council of the EU.
[296] EU–UK TCA, art 11.
[297] Richard Bellamy, *A Republican Europe of States* (CUP 2019).

particularly for the Member States that have engaged in persistent resistance to the EU's foundational values.[298]

v. The residual conditions for withdrawal: transition, extension, and no deal

Article 50(3) TEU defines the residual conditions for withdrawal. Failing the entry into force of a Withdrawal Agreement, the Treaties shall cease to apply 'two years after the notification referred to in paragraph 2, unless the European Council, in agreement with the Member State concerned, unanimously decides to extend this period'.[299] The constitutional propriety of the two-year time limit, no deal withdrawal, and the legitimacy of extension have all been challenged by the Brexit case study. The transition period from 31 January to 31 December 2020 was a creature of the Withdrawal Agreement rather than Article 50(3)'s residual conditions for withdrawal. Nevertheless, it is analysed here due to its relationship with extension and no deal. The transition period is a mechanism that obviates a prolonged extension period in which the United Kingdom would remain a Member State. In turn, the telos of extension is to avoid the constitutional disorder of withdrawal without an agreement upon the conclusion of the Article 50 time period.

Part Four of the Withdrawal Agreement provides the legal basis for the transition period. Article 126 states that '[t]here shall be a transition or implementation period, which shall start on the date of entry into force of this Agreement and end on 31 December 2020'.[300] Article 132 confirms that 'the Joint Committee may, before 1 July 2020, adopt a single decision extending the transition period for up to 1 or 2 years', but this option was not exercised by the European Union and the United Kingdom.[301] Some ambiguity arises over the temporal limits of transition due to the reference in Article 132(2)(c) to an extension that is 'not a multiple of 12 months'.[302] Article 127(1) outlines that 'Union law shall be applicable to and in the United Kingdom during the transition period'.[303] Paragraph 3 clarifies that 'Union law . . . shall produce in respect of and in the United Kingdom the same legal effects as those which it

[298] See further discussion at the end of chapter 8.
[299] TEU, art 50(3).
[300] EU–UK Withdrawal Agreement, art 126.
[301] ibid art 132.
[302] ibid art 132(2)(c).
[303] ibid art 127(1).

produces within the Union and its Member States, and shall be interpreted and applied in accordance with the same methods and general principles as those applicable within the Union.'[304] Article 128 further confirms that the United Kingdom will not retain 'institutional rights . . . to submit proposals, initiatives or requests to the institutions.'[305] Transition preserves juridical objecthood without continuing democratic subjecthood, thus creating an imbalance in the role of UK nationals.

The national authorization for the continuing application of EU law during the transition period was provided by the European Union (Withdrawal Agreement) Act 2020. This was achieved by extending the validity of the 'conduit pipe' of the European Communities Act 1972 until the end of the transition period, thus creating an 'after-life'[306] for this constitutional statute following its repeal by the European Union (Withdrawal) Act 2018. The explicit use of an Act of Parliament to provide for the continuation of the application of EU law to individuals as juridical objects means that this norm-application was legitimated by individuals as nationals in their role as democratic subjects represented by the Parliament as well as the executive during the Withdrawal Agreement negotiations.

Article 127 confirms that EU law within the scope of the opt-out Protocols[307] remains inapplicable during transition. This is a form of 'differentiated disintegration'[308] that preserves the constitutional status quo. However, the United Kingdom does not retain its capacity to opt in to AFSJ and Schengen measures during the transition period.[309] The only new norms that will apply in these areas are those that amend, replace, or build upon a measure which the United Kingdom opted in to before the Withdrawal Agreement came into force. The exclusion of the United Kingdom from enhanced cooperation further confirms

[304] ibid art 127(3).
[305] ibid art 128.
[306] Kenneth Armstrong, 'Reincarnation and Resurrection—the Afterlife of the European Communities Act 1972 in the Withdrawal Bill' (*divergence*, 22 October 2019) <https://divergence.blog/2019/10/22/reincarnation-and-resurrection-the-afterlife-of-the-european-communities-act-1972-in-the-withdrawal-bill/> accessed 30 April 2024.
[307] TEU and TFEU, Protocol (No 15) on certain provisions relating to the United Kingdom of Great Britain and Northern Ireland 15; TEU and TFEU, Protocol (No 19) on the Schengen *acquis* integrated into the framework of the European Union; TEU and TFEU, Protocol (No 20) on the application of certain aspects of Article 26 of the Treaty on the Functioning of the European Union to the United Kingdom and to Ireland; TEU and TFEU, Protocol (No 21) on the position of the United Kingdom and Ireland in respect of the area of freedom, security and justice; TEU and TFEU, Protocol (No 36) on transitional provisions.
[308] Frank Schimmelfennig, 'Brexit: Differentiated Disintegration in the European Union' (2018) 25 Journal of European Public Policy 1154.
[309] EU–UK Withdrawal Agreement, art 127(5).

that the UK's differentiation during this period is disintegrative and does not enable participation in further deepening of integration.[310]

Article 128(2) states that '[f]or the purposes of the Treaties, during the transition period, the parliament of the United Kingdom shall not be considered to be a national parliament of a Member State'.[311] This confirms the removal of the representative institutions of individuals *qua* nationals of the United Kingdom from the supranational constitutional order. Therefore UK nationals were deprived of input over norms created during this period that would be applied to them as juridical objects.[312] The transition period replicates the juridical but not the democratic constitutional functions of the European Union. Article 128 on supervision and enforcement confirms the functioning of the juridical mechanisms:

> [T]he institutions, bodies, offices and agencies of the Union shall have the powers conferred upon them by Union law in relation to the United Kingdom and natural and legal persons residing or established in the United Kingdom. In particular, the Court of Justice of the European Union shall have jurisdiction as provided for in the Treaties. The first paragraph shall also apply as regards the interpretation and application of this Agreement.[313]

One may conceptualize transition in two ways. First, these provisions may be seen as an extension of the supranational constitutional order to the United Kingdom for a limited time period. Alternatively, one may argue that the transition period creates a simulacrum of EU law *de novo*. This would be analogous to the EEA Agreement.[314] This interpretation is supported in the UK's domestic implementation of the Withdrawal Agreement, which creates a new source of 'relevant separation agreement law'.[315] This has primacy over other domestic law by virtue of the 'after-life' of the European Communities Act 1972.[316] Conceptualizing the source of law that applies to and within the United Kingdom during transition is relevant for determination of whether the transition period complies with Article 50's text and objectives.

[310] ibid art 127(4).
[311] ibid art 128(2).
[312] See chapter 7 for further elaboration of this criticism.
[313] EU–UK Withdrawal Agreement, art 128.
[314] Agreement on the European Economic Area [1994] OJ L 1/3. I thank Marise Cremona for this analogy.
[315] European Union (Withdrawal Agreement) Act 2020.
[316] Armstrong (n 306).

Michael Dougan conceptualizes transition as a 'wholesale extension of EU law' to a third country.[317] Extending EU law to a withdrawn state would contravene the explicit wording of Article 50 that the 'the Treaties cease to apply'. Dougan argues that the European Union and the United Kingdom have used a 'hierarchically inferior' instrument to amend the operation of the Treaties.[318] Dougan observes that 'the range of possible dates upon which the Treaties should cease to apply to the UK has been clearly identified by Article 50 TEU and could only be amended by changing the Treaties themselves'.[319] It is crucial that political outcomes are realized through orthodox legal provisions rather than secondary law constructions that do not have an explicit primary law base. If one accepts that the transition period continues the application of primary law, then this undercuts the requirement of unanimity for Article 50 extension as only a Qualified Majority is required for the conclusion of the Withdrawal Agreement.

The alternative conceptualization of transition as a simulacrum of EU law provides a counter-argument. On this reading, the transition period serves a different qualitative objective to extension. The crucial predicate is that transition operates *after* the Treaties cease to apply. The disqualification of UK nationals from input into the creation of norms distinguishes the new source of law from the supranational constitutional order. Domestically, democratic subjecthood over this law is limited to the national level and the creation of the implementing legislation of the European Union (Withdrawal Agreement) Act 2020. From the international perspective, the former Member State's transformation into a third country means that this period can be used for the negotiation and finalization of a future relationship agreement. The simulacrum concept illustrates how transition operates as the initial transformation for EU–UK relations from supranational constitutional law to the public international law source of the Withdrawal Agreement. This source can then be replaced by the more distinct Future Relationship Agreement(s), which represents the move to traditional public international law-creation and maintenance. Form preceded substance, as the norms contained within EU law were maintained in the international law form of the Withdrawal Agreement before new substantive rules could be created to regulate EU–UK regulations in the Trade and Cooperation Agreement.

[317] Michael Dougan, 'An Airbag for the Crash Test Dummies? EU–UK Negotiations for a Post-Withdrawal "Status Quo" Transitional Regime under Article 50 TEU' (2018) 55 Common Market Law Review 57.
[318] ibid.
[319] ibid 93.

Regardless of how transition is conceptualized, the reality is that it affords great discretion to the EU institutions over determination of to whom EU law applies and who may participate in its creation. Michael Dougan argues that

> even an exceptional power [the exclusive competence of Article 50 TEU] must have limits. A transitional regime based on the direct and wholesale (even if only temporary) extension of the Union legal order to the territory of a third country represents a highly expansive conception of the competences conferred by Article 50 TEU [which] is . . . difficult to square with the explicit telos of Article 50 TEU itself.[320]

The transition period also provided time for adjustment before the substance of EU law norms ceased to apply to the former Member State. This function may encroach upon the purposes of extension. If the United Kingdom had applied for an early extension of the Article 50 period for this explicit purpose, the normative problems of numerous extension requests to avoid a no deal exit could have been avoided.[321]

The transition period's inclusion in the draft Withdrawal Agreement could not prevent extension of the Article 50 period due to the repeated rejections of the treaty by the House of Commons. This compelled the Theresa May government to seek extensions in March and April 2019. Following Boris Johnson's ascent to the position of Prime Minister, in September 2019 a final further extension from 31 October 2019 to 31 January 2020 was imposed upon the executive through Members of Parliament taking control of the House of Commons standing orders.[322]

The only legal conditions for extension are procedural: the unanimous agreement of the European Council heads of state or government, and the agreement of the withdrawing Member State. The ostensible justification for this legal regime is symmetry with the conditions for the opening of the deconstitutional convention: unanimity within the European Council in issuing the guidelines for negotiations. There is complete discretion for the European Council to decide how long an extension may last. The European

[320] Dougan, *The UK's Withdrawal* (n 67) 203.

[321] See Federico Fabbrini and Rebecca Schmidt, 'The Extension of UK Membership in the EU: Causes and Consequences' [2019] European Journal of Legal Studies 87. Also see Dougan, who in highlighting the same point argues '[b]ut for its essentially domestic political reasons, the UK chose not to rely on those explicit mechanisms—or at least, relied on them only partially and even then with great reluctance': Dougan, *The UK's Withdrawal* (n 67) 203.

[322] Oliver Garner, 'The Benn–Burt Extension Act: A Roadblock to a No-Deal Brexit?' (*UK Constitutional Law Association*, 13 September 2019) <https://ukconstitutionallaw.org/2019/09/13/oliver-garner-the-benn-burt-extension-act-a-roadblock-to-a-no-deal-brexit/> accessed 13 April 2022.

Council is also free to determine what conditions may be imposed on the withdrawing Member State, so long as these are in accordance with the Treaties.[323] Fabbrini and Schmidt outline that Article 50(3) 'provides a fairly rudimentary framework and . . . does not clearly indicate the possible purposes of an extension'.[324] Furthermore, it is 'silent on the substantive regulation of extension'.[325] The only constraints are political. For example, if an extremely long extension were proposed with politically sensitive conditions, it seems likely that the withdrawing Member State would withhold its consent.

The discretion of the European Council over extension means that individuals are represented only in their role as nationals through their elected heads of state or government. There is no representation of individuals in their role as EU citizens because the European Parliament has no role in the extension decision. This institution may only exercise a political role through expressing its opinion on extensions, as it did in its September 2019 resolution on the progress of negotiations.[326] The opaque intergovernmental working methods of the European Council mean that there is no transparency, no obligation to provide reasons, and no opportunity for scrutiny of this executive decision by national parliaments or the European Parliament.

These deficiencies in input and throughput legitimacy are exacerbated by the output legitimacy implications of extension. The European Council has the unilateral power to decide the timeframe for the application of EU law within a domestic constitutional order, the continuing application of obligations and rights to a state, and the continuation of EU citizenship for individuals holding the nationality of the withdrawing state. The ordinary constitutional mechanisms for deciding on the territory for the application of EU law and the class of individuals who hold EU citizenship are Articles 49 and 48 TEU.[327] These provisions mandate a complex procedure with specific functions for all the EU institutions representing individuals in their multiple roles. Therefore, it seems incongruous that the European Council alone exercises an analogous role under Article 50 TEU.

Extension also has the potential to distort the functioning of the EU's constitutional order. Federico Fabbrini and Rebecca Schmidt have identified short-term consequences for the European Union arising from the two Brexit

[323] Fabbrini and Schmidt (n 321).
[324] ibid 5.
[325] ibid.
[326] European Parliament resolution of 18 September 2019 on the state of play of the UK's withdrawal from the European Union [2021] OJ C 171/2.
[327] See discussion of the triptych of constituted constituent power in chapter 2.

extensions in spring 2019. The second extension to 31 October 2019 was subject to the condition that the United Kingdom hold European Parliament elections on 23–25 May.[328] If it did not, the Decision stipulated that the United Kingdom would automatically withdraw on 31 May 2019. The European Parliament had adopted a new decision on the configuration of the European Parliament in 2018 whereby the number of seats was reduced, and the UK's seats were redistributed to other Member States.[329] The consequence of the UK's participation in the 2019 European Parliament elections was that the fall-back clause had to be employed whereby the configuration for the 2015 election was used.

This meant that the mandates of the twenty-seven MEPs elected to replace the UK MEPs were held in abeyance, and the mandates of the seventy-three UK MEPs terminated at the point that the Treaties ceased to apply on 31 January 2020. This has consequences for the balance between supranational representatives and the executive institutions. The Commission is directly approved by the European Parliament. A relationship of accountability and confidence exists with the institution that endows the unelected College of Commissioners with its democratic legitimacy. Fabbrini and Schmidt argued that 'modifying the composition of the EP in the course of the 9th term . . . would unsettle the inter-institutional relation between the EP and the Commission, potentially affecting the confidence in the Commission itself'.[330]

The termination of the mandate of the UK MEPs also poses problems for the dual-legitimation thesis. The European Council, and the Council are constituted through the representation of individuals as nationals of the Member States. This preserves the intergovernmental limb of the supranational constitutional order. By contrast, the European Parliament is elected directly by EU citizens who have the right to vote and stand in elections held in any Member State. This is reflected by Article 50's non-exclusion of representatives elected within the withdrawing Member State in the European Parliament. The logic of the mandate of UK representatives being automatically terminated does not apply as clearly to the European Parliament as it does to the institutions representing nationals. A similar issue was raised in relation to the mandate of the UK Advocate General at the Court of Justice of the European Union,[331]

328 European Council Decision taken in agreement with the United Kingdom extending the period under Article 50(3) TEU Brussels, 11 April 2019 (OR en) EUCO XT 20013/19 BXT 38.

329 European Council Decision (EU) 2018/937 of 28 June 2018 establishing the composition of the European Parliament [2018] OJ L 165 I/1.

330 Fabbrini and Schmidt (n 321) 19.

331 Benedikt Pirker and others, 'In Support of the EU Rule of Law and Advocate General Eleanor Sharpston—An Open Letter' (*European Law Blog*, 18 March 2020) <https://web.archive.org/web/202

eventually leading to a Court of Justice decision endorsing the termination that has been criticized for undermining the independence of the court and prioritizing the whims of the Member States.[332]

The UK's allocation of MEPs is also legitimated by the votes of nationals from other Member States who qualify to vote in the United Kingdom by virtue of residence. These individuals retain their EU citizenship and role as democratic subject after withdrawal. The allocation of a withdrawing Member State also may consist of MEPs who hold the nationality of other Member States and thus retain their EU citizenship.[333] The text of the European Council Decision on the composition of the European Parliament potentially clashes with Article 14 TEU. Article 2 of the Decision states that 'once the UK's withdrawal from the Union becomes legally effective, the number of representatives in the European Parliament elected in each Member State shall be the one provided for in paragraph 1 of this Article.'[334] However, Article 14(3) TEU states that 'the members of the European Parliament shall be elected for a term of five years by direct universal suffrage in a free and secret ballot.'[335] This suggests that MEPs elected in the United Kingdom had a Treaty right to execute a mandate term of five years. Arguably, at the point when the 'Treaties cease to apply' to the United Kingdom, this provision had already been executed and continued to have effect until the end of the legislature in 2024.

The Decision refers to Article 10 TEU, which details that the 'functioning of the Union shall be founded on representative democracy.'[336] Fabbrini and Schmidt argue that the text of the Decision may also undermine this statement. The termination of the mandate of MEPs in the United Kingdom who are EU citizens and/or represent EU citizens could undermine the statement that 'every citizen shall have the right to participate in the democratic life of the Union.'[337] These consequences may flow from the framing of withdrawal. The condition for withdrawal being the 'Treaties ceasing to apply' presents a public international law perspective. This neglects the supranational perspective on

00408190341/https://europeanlawblog.eu/2020/03/18/in-support-of-the-eu-rule-of-law-and-advocate-general-eleanor-sharpston-an-open-letter/> accessed 18 April 2020.

[332] Dimitry Kochenov and Graham Butler, 'Independence of the Court of Justice of the European Union: Unchecked Member States Power after the Sharpston Affair' (2022) 28 European Law Journal 262.

[333] TFEU, art 22.

[334] European Council Decision (EU) 2018/937 of 28 June 2018 establishing the composition of the European Parliament [2018] OJ L 165 I/1.

[335] TEU, art 14(3).

[336] TEU, art 10.

[337] TEU, art 10(3).

the constitutional order and its constituent subjects.[338] The absence of any reference to the termination of EU citizenship in the withdrawal clause leads to the ambiguities discussed above. Extension is not only deficient regarding democratic input and the process; it also has deleterious consequences for the functioning of the EU constitutional order. The ultimate cause of these distortions is the emergency situation that is created by the deadline of two years.

The deadline also distorted constitutional processes at the domestic level within the United Kingdom. The two-year period insulated the parliamentarians who voted for the notification of Article 50 from the immediate consequences of this action.[339] This provided full discretion to the government to negotiate and finalize the Withdrawal Agreement. As the 29 March deadline drew nearer, the House of Commons inserted a 'meaningful vote' condition for ratification of the Agreement.[340] The three rejections by the House of Commons of the eventual draft Withdrawal Agreement starkly contrasted with the overwhelming majority for notification in 2017. As the deadline of a no deal withdrawal approached, the usual constitutional proceedings were distorted by the temporal emergency artificially constructed by Article 50(3). These distortions included innovations such as the House of Commons taking control of the executive's role of proposing legislation to create the Act of Parliament that requested an extension of membership.[341] This led to a threat to the Rule of Law at the national level as government ministers intimated that they would not comply with this legislation in September 2019.[342] Shortly thereafter, the government were found by the Supreme Court to have acted unlawfully in proroguing Parliament for an extended period in an apparent attempt to curtail any attempts by MPs to frustrate withdrawal.[343] Constitutional orthodoxy was only restored by the usual channels of a General Election in December 2019. These phenomena arguably undermine the objective of Article 50 TEU to vindicate the sovereign right of the Member State. The original purpose of the two-year period to prevent a Member State's withdrawal being delayed had unintended negative consequences in the domestic order.

The cliff-edge of automatic withdrawal without an agreement exposes a disequilibrium between the two objectives of Article 50. All EU law ceasing to

[338] See the discussion in chapter 2.

[339] European Union (Notification of Withdrawal) Act 2017.

[340] European Union (Withdrawal) Act 2018, s 13.

[341] European Union (Withdrawal) (No 2) Act 2019.

[342] Murray Hunt, 'In a Democracy the Rule of Law Means Parliament Is Supreme over the Executive' (*Bingham Centre for the Rule of Law*, 3 September 2019) <https://binghamcentre.biicl.org/comments/57/in-a-democracy-the-rule-of-law-means-parliament-is-supreme-over-the-executive> accessed 30 April 2024.

[343] *R (on the application of Miller) v The Prime Minister/Cherry and others v Advocate General for Scotland* [2019] UKSC 41, [2019] 3 WLR 589.

apply to and within the withdrawing Member State upon the expiry of the two-year period means that the democratic sovereign decision ultimately obviates the orderly regulation of disintegration. The legal vacuum and political emergency that this creates would require the extensive exercise of executive power to maintain order. Michael Dougan recognizes that 'a collapse in the Article 50 TEU negotiations leading to a disorderly withdrawal posed a serious risk that the UK might experience outright legislative, regulatory, and administrative malfunction.'[344] In the United Kingdom, extensive use of delegated legislation to cope with no deal contingencies, along with the possible use of the powers contained within the Civil Contingencies Act 2004, were mooted.[345] The principles of accountability and proper legislative scrutiny are restricted through the time-pressure on the legal regulation needing to come into force. The Commission's no deal Brexit communication of 4 September 2019 stated that '[t]he Commission calls on the co-legislators to ensure the swift adoption of the proposed legislative acts so that, where necessary, they are in force by the date of the withdrawal of the United Kingdom.'[346]

No deal withdrawal may be an existential threat to the values of the European Union,[347] and its commitment to promote these values in external relations.[348] The operation of Article 50(3) could lead to dire consequences for a state and for individuals that have only just ceased to be constituent partners in European integration.[349] No deal undermines the functional potential to secure an orderly withdrawal. Its extreme consequences mean that on three separate occasions both the United Kingdom and the European Union were unwilling to countenance this scenario. This led to repeated requests for and grants of extensions, as discussed above. The cliff-edge of no deal, in concert with the potential for extension, restricts the likelihood of orderly withdrawal through a Withdrawal Agreement coming into force. Contestation over domestic ratification in the United Kingdom led to extension, which in turn

[344] Dougan, *The UK's Withdrawal* (n 67) 39.

[345] Civil Contingencies Act 2004.

[346] Communication from the Commission to the European Parliament, the European Council, the Council, the European Central Bank, the European Economic and Social Committee, the Committee of the Regions and the European Investment Bank Finalising preparations for the withdrawal of the United Kingdom from the European Union on 1 November 2019 Brussels, 4.9.2019 COM (2019) 394 final.

[347] TEU, art 2.

[348] TEU, art 21.

[349] 'Operation Yellowhammer HMG Reasonable Worst Case Planning Assumptions As of 2 August 2019' <https://assets.publishing.service.gov.uk/government/uploads/system/uploads/attachment_data/file/831199/20190802_Latest_Yellowhammer_Planning_assumptions_CDL.pdf> accessed 5 May 2020; 'No Deal Brexit: Issues, Impact, Implications' (*UK in a Changing Europe*, 3 September 2019) <https://ukandeu.ac.uk/research-papers/no-deal-brexit-issues-impact-implications/> accessed 18 April 2020.

incentivized attempts to revise the agreement and new contestation and extension requests in a vicious cycle that was only solved through a change in the composition of representatives of individuals.

By contrast to the detailed procedure to conclude a Withdrawal Agreement, there is no procedure for what happens in a no deal scenario and no provision is made for the role of the supranational institutions. This is a particular vacuum for legal orderliness as there is no adjudicative forum for the resolution of disputes. Although the European Union would probably insist on the jurisdiction of the Court of Justice in a no deal scenario, the United Kingdom would not be bound to recognize this jurisdiction. If no alternative dispute resolution can be agreed, the final forum which might be called upon to resolve issues such as the UK's financial obligations to the EU could be the International Court of Justice. This threatens the EU's self-understanding of autonomy as precluding any other body from ruling upon the interpretation and application of EU law. Reform should seek to ameliorate the dire consequences of no deal withdrawal for individuals by addressing this procedural and substantive lacuna.

VI. Article 50(5) TEU: Reauthorizing the Levelling Up of Constituent Power

Article 50(5) TEU states that '[i]f a State which has withdrawn from the Union asks to rejoin, its request shall be subject to the procedure referred to in Article 49'.[350] This guarantees the complete levelling down of constituent power from the supranational level to the national level. Article 50(3)'s confirmation that the 'Treaties cease to apply' to the withdrawing Member State is not merely a statement that the Member State and its constituent individuals cease to function as juridical objects of EU law. It also confirms the extinction of the status of the Member State and its citizens as constituent subjects of the supranational constitutional order. The reference to the levelling up limb of the triptych, Article 49 TEU, confirms that a withdrawn Member State reverts to the status of a Third Country that is entitled to apply for accession as a European state. Proposals forwarded by Markus Patberg and Peter Niesen to reform this guarantee of the levelling down of constituent power are considered in the later chapter on reform.[351]

[350] TEU, art 49.

[351] Markus Patberg, 'Can Disintegration Be Democratic? The European Union Between Legitimate Change and Regression' (2020) 68 Political Studies 582; Markus Patberg and Peter Niesen, 'After Brexit, the UK Should Have a Democratic Right of Return' (*LSE Brexit*, 30 October 2018) <https://blogs.lse.

Reactivation of membership requires the full constitutional process for levelling up constituent power, and the approval of this process at the supranational level. This has implications for the hard case of the EU membership of regions of Member States that secede and become independent European states.[352] If secession occurs outside of the frame of withdrawal, the Article 48 amendment process can be utilized to enable continuing membership of the independent state, so long as this mechanism is created before independence is finalized.[353] Revisionary constituent power could even be used to construct such an inheritance mechanism if secession occurs during the withdrawal of a Member State. Both of these situations are legitimate as the constituent subjects of the seceding state will hold EU citizenship through nationality of the existing Member State.

However, after the Treaties cease to apply in accordance with Article 50(3) TEU, the extinction of Member State nationality and EU citizenship in conjunction with Article 50(5) TEU means that the membership of an independent state after a future secession would require re-accession to the European Union through the normal constitutional procedure for levelling up constituent power contained within Article 49 TEU.

Michael Dougan reflects upon the possibility of future re-accession by the United Kingdom, or accession by an independent Scotland. He speculates that if such an application sought to 'resurrect old British membership privileges' then 'the Union would have to make its own essentially political choice about whether and how far to accommodate those demands for special treatment'.[354] The emergency of the possibility of 'differentiated accession' with regard to Ukraine could create 'an appropriate legal vehicle'[355] for any such attempt to re-accede on the terms of disrupted membership. *Prima facie*, however, the prescription in Article 50(5) that any such re-accession attempts must be subject to Article 49 TEU militates in favour of the candidate process operating *a novo* for any Member State that has withdrawn from the Union.

ac.uk/brexit/2018/10/30/after-brexit-the-uk-should-be-able-to-re-enter-the-eu-if-it-wishes-to-do-so/ > accessed 24 January 2020.

352 For further consideration of the inter-relation between Member State withdrawal and state secession see Carlos Closa (ed), *Secession from a Member State and Withdrawal from the European Union: Troubled Membership* (CUP 2017).

353 The Scottish Government, 'Scotland's Future' (*gov.scot*, 26 November 2013) <www.gov.scot/publications/scotlands-future/> accessed 24 January 2020.

354 Dougan, *The UK's Withdrawal* (n 67) 353.

355 ibid.

VII. Summary

Withdrawal from the European Union was regulated by the international law of treaties before the 2003 Convention on the Future of Europe. The rejected Constitutional Treaty proposed a specific constitutional clause to regulate disintegration through Member State withdrawal. Proposed amendments to the clause revealed the opinions of certain Convention members that a withdrawal clause was constitutionally inappropriate. Statements made by the drafters suggest that the clause was promulgated for the strategic purpose of reassuring recalcitrant Member States. The triggering of Article 50 TEU has required the Court of Justice to delineate the dual telos of the withdrawal clause. Article 50 enshrines a sovereign right of withdrawal whilst ensuring an orderly process. The text and telos of Article 50 TEU reflect a predominantly international rather than supranational perspective.

The clauses of the withdrawal clause are conceptualized as a deconstitutional convention. The first example of the operation of Article 50 has arisen with the Brexit case study. Article 50(1) TEU mandates a domestic constitutional decision by the nationals of a Member State to repatriate constituent power. The under-determination of the 'constitutional requirements' of the United Kingdom has prompted litigation to resolve legal uncertainty. The *Shindler* decision established that the franchise for the membership referendum was a sovereign prerogative of the UK legislature. *Miller* confirmed that an Act of Parliament is necessary as a constitutional requirement for the decision. *Webster* elided the legal effect and consequences of decision and notification under Article 50(2). Article 50(2) TEU functions as a bridge between the national deconstructive decision and the supranational deconstitutional convention. The *Wightman* judgment established that the foundation for the deconstitutional convention is the sovereign will of the withdrawing Member State. The Article 50 process can be extinguished by a unilateral revocation in accordance with the constitutional requirements of the withdrawing Member State.

Article 50(2) and (4) TEU define the conditions for initiating the supranational deconstitutional convention. The roles of the institutions representing Member State nationals and EU citizens are defined as are the rules determining decision-making. The European Council's guidelines for the negotiations defined the procedure and substantive issues that shaped negotiations. Article 50(3) TEU defines the *finalité* of the deconstitutional convention. The EU Treaties ceased to apply to the United Kingdom on 31 January 2020 after the Withdrawal Agreement came into force. This Withdrawal Agreement confirmed the extinction of the constituent status of UK nationals, and the transformation of the status of EU citizens within the territory of the United Kingdom. The peculiarities of the United Kingdom and Ireland's relationship required a Protocol to define a special regime on the island of Ireland. The Withdrawal Agreement also created a transition period that overlaps in telos with the mechanisms of extension of the Article 50 period. The three extensions agreed upon by the United Kingdom and the European Union exposed the extensive discretion for the European Council to determine the continuing application of EU law to and within a withdrawing Member State. The residual condition for withdrawal is the expiry of the two-year period without an agreement. Preparations for this eventuality in the Brexit case study indicate the deleterious consequences of this outcome. Article 50(5) confirms the extinction of supranational constituent power as a result of withdrawal. A former Member State is subject to the full requirements of Article 49 TEU in order to re-establish the levelling up of constituent power to the supranational level.

7

The Normative Failings of Opt-Outs and Withdrawal

I. Normative Deficiencies of Opt-Outs

The prevalence of opt-outs in the supranational constitutional order violates the quadripartite role of individuals.[1] The creation of these legal Protocols recognizes the retention of supranational constituent power, which is then legitimated by all of the High Contracting Parties through the ratification of the Treaty amendments. This use of this power to carve out sectors of the EU legal order extends the function of the constitutional states as guarantors of their nationals' self-determination into encroachment upon the ordinary functioning of the supranational constitutional order. These opt-outs reveal an irritation in the 'levelling up' of constituent power whereby Member States contest the legitimacy of certain norms being created at the supranational level. The European Parliament has argued that 'opt-outs for individual Member States endanger the uniform application of EU law, lead to excessive complexity in terms of governance, jeopardise the cohesion of the Union and undermine solidarity among its citizens'.[2]

The manifestation of opt-outs in practice poses challenges to the validity of the dual-legitimation thesis as an explanatory theory of European integration. The opt-outs violate the normative principles of equality between individuals *qua* democratic subjects. They provide evidence that, in the critical processes of establishing the primary law norms that will apply and will not apply to individuals as juridical objects, the executive representatives of individuals *qua* nationals of a Member State remain the dominant constituent power. The representatives of individuals *qua* EU citizens, the Members of the European Parliament, are excluded from the processes of discursive deliberation that

[1] This chapter develops the text in Oliver Garner, 'Reforming Withdrawal and Opt-Outs from the European Union: A Dual-Constituent Perspective' (DCU Brexit Institute 2018) DCU Brexit Institute Working Paper N.11 2018 <https://papers.ssrn.com/abstract=3303938> accessed 29 March 2020.

[2] European Parliament resolution of 16 February 2017 on possible evolutions of and adjustments to the current institutional set-up of the European Union [2018] OJ C 252/201.

Constitutional Disintegration and Disruption. Oliver Garner, Oxford University Press. © Oxford University Press 2025. DOI: 10.1093/9780198914136.003.0007

produce the Protocols enabling opt-outs. Their role is relegated to either approving or disapproving the entire negotiated text with no specific influence over whether or not opt-out Protocols should be included or not. Furthermore, once created, the operation of these opt-outs is also indicative of the continuing constituent dominance of the Member States, in particular with regard to the iterative 'opt-in' mechanisms provided for in the AFSJ.

These opt-outs undermine the co-equivalence between individuals *qua* nationals of a Member State and *qua* citizens of the Union because individuals from an opt-out Member State are represented in the creation of norms in the latter role, but not in the former role. Further inequality is created between individuals *qua* democratic subject and *qua* juridical object. The asymmetric territorial application of norms to individuals undermines the equality of representation in the creation of these norms. For individuals from the non-opt-out Member States there is territory of the European Union in which they are disconnected from the norms that they have legitimated. Conversely, individuals who are from the opt-out Member States will be subjected to norms within the territory of other Member States that they have legitimated in only one of their democratic subject personae.

The current opt-outs pose specific challenges to the supranational constitutional order. With regard to the opt-outs from EMU, the legislative institutions that represent democratic subjects in their dual roles have been fragmented by the informal Eurogroup that represent the Member States of the Eurozone.[3] This is exacerbated by the executive body of the European Central Bank, which is predominantly empowered to act only with regard to the Eurozone Member States.[4] Both the creation processes for opt-outs and the actions of Member States derogating from EMU have increased the propensity for the High Contracting Parties to revert to 'satellite Treaties' as a tool of European integration.[5] The Edinburgh Agreement that bound the Member States to implement opt-outs for Denmark after the Maastricht ratification failure was an international Treaty between the heads of state or government.[6] This precedent

[3] Deirdre Curtin and Cristina Fasone, 'Differentiated Representation: Is a Flexible European Parliament Desirable?' in Bruno De Witte, Andrea Ott and Ellen Vos (eds), *Between Flexibility and Disintegration: The Trajectory of Differentiation in EU Law* (Edward Elgar Publishing 2017).

[4] Chiara Zilioli and Martin Selmayr, *The Law of the European Central Bank* (Hart Publishing 2001); Chiara Zilioli and Martin Selmayr, 'The Constitutional Status of the European Central Bank' (2007) 44 Common Market Law Review 355.

[5] Bruno De Witte, 'The Law as Tool and Constraint of Differentiated Integration' (European University Institute 2019) Working Paper EUI RSCAS, 2019/47 <http://cadmus.eui.eu//handle/1814/63604> accessed 26 April 2020.

[6] 'Edinburgh European Summit—Conclusions of the Presidency—December 1992' (*European Parliament*, 11–12 December 1992) <www.europarl.europa.eu/summits/edinburgh/default_en.htm> accessed 17 December 2018. See discussion of Denmark in chapter 5.

was followed for the United Kingdom's renegotiation in February 2016, which was concluded as an international agreement binding between the 'Heads of State or Government, meeting within the European Council'.[7]

Between these two instances, the objection of the United Kingdom during the Article 48 amendment process to the 'Fiscal Compact', despite the fact its opt-out meant that it would not be bound by all of the obligations contained therein, led to the conclusion of the international Treaty on Stability, Coordination and Governance.[8] The resort to international law sidelines the supranational institutions in the creation of norms even if it explicitly assigns roles for them in its application. This undermines the capacity for individuals *qua* EU citizens to exercise democratic subjecthood due to the exclusion of the European Parliament.

Denmark's 'opt-out' from the Schengen *acquis* raises a unique challenge for supranational constitutionalism. The substance of these norms is the same for individuals *qua* juridical objects within the territory of Denmark. However, the norms are created and apply through national and international law. Only individuals *qua* nationals of the state are represented in the creation of these norms. The supranational judicial architecture for the application of these norms is unavailable for individuals *qua* juridical objects. The flexible opt-outs from Schengen and the AFSJ have different yet particularly egregious consequences for the supranational constitutional order. The retention of the constituent power of the state spills over into the supranational creation of legislation within the Council. This undermines the principles that underpin the functioning of this institution.[9] The spillover of the constituent power function is also evident in the wholesale opt-out and opt-in procedures mandated by Protocol (No 36). This Protocol crossed the Rubicon because it enabled the de-enforcement of norms that already applied to and within the opt-out Member State. Notification under the Protocol by the United Kingdom may be understood as a forerunner to the exercise of deconstructive power under Article 50 TEU.[10]

The iterative opt-in mechanisms for Schengen and AFSJ may undermine the holistic integrity of these constitutional sectors. The opt-out Member States

[7] European Council meeting (18 and 19 February 2016)—Conclusions, Annex 1—Decision of the Heads of State or Government, meeting within the European Council, concerning a new settlement for the United Kingdom within the European Union—Brussels 19 February 2016 EUCO 1/16. See discussion of the New Settlement in chapter 5.

[8] Treaty on Stability, Coordination and Governance of 2 March 2012 T/SCG. See discussion of these developments in chapter 5.

[9] See the discussion of these principles in chapter 2.

[10] See the discussion in chapter 5.

have been left with the executive discretion to opt in to measures which they believe will support their own domestic justice and home affairs policies.[11] Nadine El-Enany observes that 'the UK has opted-out of nearly all proposals concerning visas, borders and legal migration, but it has opted into all proposals concerning asylum and civil law and nearly all proposals concerning illegal immigration'.[12] These latter measures have been conceptualized as 'compensatory measures'[13] that compensate the Member States for removal of internal frontiers. The opt-out Member States can benefit from added rights without undertaking the initial duties. El-Enany argues that a Member State 'neither has to justify its asylum regime choices as reasonable, sensible, moral or defensible, nor must it compromise on its individual preferences'.[14] The selective participation of Member States in the supranational legislative process undermines the principles whereby the interests of individuals *qua* nationals are represented on the basis of an exchange of persuasive reasons.

The reasons for the creation of Ireland's Schengen and AFSJ opt-outs may indicate normative justifications. The executive was compelled to follow the reservation of constituent power of the United Kingdom in order to ensure the legal regime of border controls between the two states was maintained.[15] The interests of Irish nationals *qua* juridical objects in the preservation of internal security provided an objective difference to nationals of other Member States without the unique context of relations between the United Kingdom and Ireland. This distinction outweighed the importance of a uniform regime of border controls for all individuals *qua* EU citizens on the island of Ireland.

II. Normative Deficiencies of Withdrawal

Disintegration has more deleterious consequences for individuals *qua* democratic subjects and *qua* juridical objects than disrupted integration. The normative paradox is that withdrawal is a more acceptable phenomenon from the perspective of the integrity of the supranational constitutional order than opt-outs. Disrupted integration takes an *ad hoc* legal form that accommodates the

11 See the discussion of the functioning of the UK and Ireland opt-outs in chapter 4.

12 Nadine El-Enany, 'The Perils of Differentiated Integration in the Field of Asylum' in Bruno De Witte, Andrea Ott and Ellen Vos (eds), *Between Flexibility and Disintegration* (Edward Elgar Publishing 2017) 365.

13 Steve Peers, *EU Justice and Home Affairs Law: EU Justice and Home Affairs Law: Volume I: EU Immigration and Asylum Law* (4th edn, OUP 2016).

14 El-Enany (n 12) 365.

15 See the discussion of the Irish opt-outs in chapter 5.

executive discretion of Member State governments during Treaty amendments when supranational constraints are inapplicable. By contrast, disintegration is prospectively mandated by a supranational clause with express roles for the institutions that represent individuals in their quadripartite role and a clearly defined juridical outcome. The normative critique concerns whether the dual objective of Article 50 TEU has been fully realized during Brexit as the first manifestation of Member State disintegration.

Withdrawal cleaves apart the quadripartite role of individuals. The status of citizenship of the European Union is severed from the status of nationality of the Member State that has withdrawn.[16] Former EU citizens lose the rights to vote in European Parliament and local elections throughout the European Union that form the core of the status as a means to exercise supranational democratic subjecthood.[17] They also lose the core of the juridical rights contained within EU citizenship of free movement between different Member State territories.[18] The status of EU citizenship as the unique reserve for these rights is evidenced by their omission from Part II on citizens' rights in the Withdrawal Agreement.[19] Individuals *qua* nationals of a former Member State revert back to a special transitional sub-category of Third Country National as a residual juridical object within the territory of the European Union's Member States.

Within the Member State that has withdrawn the supranational source of EU law norms is disapplied. In the United Kingdom the creation of a replacement domestic constitutional source for these norms means that their continuing application is left within the discretion of domestic legislative and executive bodies.[20] For sedentary nationals of the state who have not relied upon the core democratic and juridical rights of EU citizenship, norms that they may have relied upon domestically for their life plans will be left exposed to domestic alteration or disapplication without supranational protection.[21] The architecture for the application of EU law norms within the territory of the former Member State will be conditionally dismantled.[22] For nationals of other Member States who continue to hold EU citizenship, the territory within

[16] For a categorical overview of the juridical consequences of withdrawal see Oliver Garner, 'After Brexit: Protecting European Citizens and Citizenship from Fragmentation' (European University Institute 2016) EUI Law Department Working Paper No 2016/22 4–7 <https://papers.ssrn.com/abstract=2871404> accessed 1 February 2017.

[17] See explication of this status in chapter 2.

[18] See the discussion of juridical objecthood in chapter 2.

[19] See the discussion of the Withdrawal Agreement in chapter 6.

[20] See the mechanisms for retention and alteration of 'retained EU law' in the United Kingdom's European Union (Withdrawal) Act 2018.

[21] Garner (n 16) 6–7.

[22] See discussion of the Withdrawal Agreement for the exceptions in which the preliminary reference procedure will continue to apply in chapter 6.

which they can exercise their democratic subjecthood and juridical objecthood contracts. Their presence within the territory moves from supranational regulation to determination through national and international law measures. The enfranchisement of EU citizens in local and national elections has become the prerogative of the former Member State due to an absence of regulation by the Withdrawal Agreement and the Trade and Cooperation Agreement.

Legitimate disintegration through Article 50 TEU explodes the dialectic tension between nationality of a Member State and citizenship of the European Union as co-equivalent constituent statuses. The relationship transforms from constant balancing leading to tensions, as exemplified by disrupted integration, to the complete destruction of EU citizenship and the re-establishment of nationality of a constitutional state as the exclusive constituent status in the former Member State. Certain authors have criticized this dialectic resolution as democratically illegitimate.[23] Legal claims have been pursued arguing that the extinction of EU citizenship by the Withdrawal Agreement is juridically invalid.[24] So long as the wording 'the Treaties cease to apply' is held to revoke EU citizenship this remains a juridically mandated consequence of disintegration. Furthermore, the capacity for the nationals of a Member State to control the levelling down of constituent power is a precept for the dual-constituent foundations of the European Union.[25] The extinction of the status and rights of EU citizenship is not a normative deficiency of withdrawal, but a necessary consequence of disintegration. Normative deficiencies may be assessed by considering whether the process to realize these consequences complies with the dual telos of Article 50 TEU to enshrine a sovereign right of withdrawal, and to subject the exercise of the right to an orderly process.

The overarching deficiency concerns the framing of the first objective of Article 50. The Court of Justice of the European Union defined this objective as 'enshrining the sovereign right of a Member State to withdraw from the European Union'.[26] This presents a public international law perspective of withdrawal from an international treaty, rather than a supranational constitutional

[23] Hauke Brunkhorst, *Solidarity: From Civic Friendship to a Global Legal Community* (MIT Press 2005) 167–68; Tore Vincents Olsen and Christian F Rostbøll, 'Why Withdrawal from the European Union Is Undemocratic' (2017) 9 International Theory 436. See detailed discussion further below in the chapter.

[24] *C/13/640244/KG ZA 17-1327* of the Rechtbank Amsterdam; Stephen Hocking, David Harrison and Alexandra von Westernhagen, 'DAC Beachcroft Files Landmark Case with General Court of the EU on Behalf of a Group of UK Nationals' (*DAC Beachcroft*) <https://web.archive.org/web/20200501213655/https://www.dacbeachcroft.com/en/gb/news/2020/april/dac-beachcroft-files-landmark-case-with-general-court-of-the-eu-on-behalf-of-a-group-of-uk-nationals/> accessed 25 April 2020.

[25] See the establishment of this conceptual framework in chapter 2.

[26] Case C-621/18 *Wightman v Secretary of State for Exiting the European Union*, EU:C:2018:999, para 56.

law perspective on the levelling down of constituent power.[27] This framing is evident throughout the wording of the withdrawal clause. The subject of the clause is defined as the 'Member State'. No reference is made to the 'nationals of the Member State', despite the implicit inclusion of these individuals *qua* democratic subjects in the reference to 'constitutional requirements'.[28] The 'Member State' may decide to withdraw, and the 'Member State' notifies the intention to the Council. The condition for withdrawal is defined as 'the Treaties shall cease to apply to the State',[29] rather than ceasing to apply within the state, and to the nationals of the Member State *qua* juridical objects. The absence of a supranational perspective is evident in the omission of any reference to EU citizenship in the conditions to initiate and finalize withdrawal. There is no reference to the decision to withdraw as a decision by nationals of a Member State to extinguish the co-constituent status of EU citizenship. There is no reference to the extinction of this status as a consequence of the Treaties ceasing to apply.

Withdrawal is presented in the Treaties as an action that occurs on the plane of international relations between states rather than the constitutional plane between individuals. This framing has contributed to the legal ambiguities of withdrawal that have generated litigation. The omission of a right of revocation in the wording of Article 50 is a deficiency in itself. The consequences were that the UK government engaged in the deconstitutional convention for over a year whilst ignorant of the right of nationals of the United Kingdom to reverse the process. The United Kingdom submitted its notification under Article 50(2) on the basis of an improper understanding of the law due to the presumption of irreversibility in the *Miller* case.[30] The international law framing of Article 50 may have contributed towards the Court of Justice in *Wightman* emphasizing sovereignty in establishing unconditional revocation, rather than considering the supranational constitutional interests of individuals represented by the Council and the European Parliament.[31] The silence on EU citizenship has led the Court of Justice to hold that this status is extinguished upon the Treaties ceasing to apply.[32] The international law framing enabled the court in *Shindler* to hold that the franchise for a referendum on membership is a matter of untrammelled Member State sovereignty. This enabled the exclusion of certain Member State nationals from the decision.[33] The international law

27 See critique in the discussion of *Wightman* in chapter 6.
28 TEU, art 50(1).
29 TEU, art 50(3).
30 See the detailed discussion of the case in chapter 6.
31 See the analysis of the judgment in chapter 6.
32 See discussion of the recent cases in chapter 6.
33 See discussion of this judgment in chapter 6.

perspective may also have incentivized the UK government to regard the prerogative power for the conduct of treaty relations to be a sufficient legal basis for notification, leading to the *Miller* litigation.

Miller exposed the United Kingdom's domestic deficiencies in its manifestation of withdrawal. No explicit definition of the 'constitutional requirements' of the United Kingdom was provided before the 2016 referendum. There was an absence of clarity on the exact procedure for the decision and notification, which led to a debate over whether an Act of Parliament was necessary or executive powers were sufficient. The result was uncertainty for individuals *qua* juridical objects. There was no attempt to elaborate substantive conditions to justify a decision to withdraw, despite the balance of competences review that had been recently concluded.[34] The ambiguous status of the referendum also caused disputes as to whether the vote was a genuine expression of self-determination that legitimated the United Kingdom's withdrawal.[35] This deficiency did not derive from the text of Article 50, but from the realization of its requirements by a Member State. The Brexit case study provides a cautionary tale for any Member States considering withdrawal in the future. The explicit prior definition of constitutional requirement is a necessary prerequisite to ensure that disintegration results from a legitimate expression of self-determination by nationals *qua* democratic subjects.[36]

Discrepancies in the wording between Article 50(1) and 50(2) can be blamed for further judicial disputes in the United Kingdom. Whereas Article 50(1) refers to a decision to withdraw, Article 50(2) refers to notification of an intention to withdraw. Domestically the legal meaning and effects of decision and intention were elided by the courts.[37] Nevertheless, legitimate debate may persist over what exact legal act constituted the United Kingdom's decision to withdraw. The disconnect between Article 50(1) and Article 50(2) also exposes a lacuna in the temporal operation of the withdrawal clause. Once a decision is made under Article 50(1), there is no indication of when notification must be submitted to the European Council under Article 50(2). The United Kingdom provided notification on 29 March 2017, over nine months after the referendum decision on 23 June 2016. The vacuum opens up the possibility of

[34] 'Review of the Balance of Competences' (*GOV.UK*, 12 December 2012) <www.gov.uk/guidance/review-of-the-balance-of-competences> accessed 22 April 2020.

[35] See discussion of the legislation establishing the referendum in chapter 6.

[36] See reform proposals in chapter 8.

[37] *R (on the application of Webster) v Secretary of State for Exiting the European Union* [2018] EWHC 1543 (Admin). See discussion of the judgment in chapter 6.

a Member State indefinitely postponing notification following a decision in accordance with its constitutional requirements.[38]

The period of uncertainty between the referendum and notification provided the conditions for pre-emptive actions by the supranational institutions in relation to the deconstitutional convention. The United Kingdom's presidency of the Council was abolished, and the Commission appointed itself as the Union negotiator before the Article 50 process had officially commenced. The latter action arguably did not comply with the Treaty procedure for the nomination of an institution to conduct negotiations.[39] The actions of the supranational institutions during the intermission between referendum and negotiation could have prejudiced the United Kingdom's sovereign right whether to provide notification or not. The ambiguous legal basis for these actions jeopardized the objective to ensure that disintegration follows an orderly process in accordance with the Rule of Law.

The institutional discretion afforded to the European Council to determine the initiation and extension of the deconstitutional convention has provoked further normative criticism. The argument has been made that the European Council's decision to sequence negotiations in order to ensure that all of the withdrawal priorities were resolved before discussion of the future relationship prejudiced the sovereignty of the withdrawing Member State.[40] Sequencing arguably generated the externalities of the transition period and the Protocol on Ireland/Northern Ireland in the Withdrawal Agreement as mechanisms to regulate issues provisionally before a future relationship could be negotiated.[41]

The discretion of the European Council over the extension of the two-year period for negotiations in the deconstitutional convention is a clearer example of a normative deficiency for individuals as quadripartite subjects.[42] A decision to continue the status of individuals as co-constituent democratic subjects and juridical objects of the order, and to continue the operation of EU law norms in the territory of a state, is left purely to the determination of the heads of state or government. No supranational representation of individuals through the Commission or the European Parliament is provided. In addition to input legitimacy concerns, the throughput legitimacy of this decision is deficient due

[38] For discussion of this possibility and responses see Christophe Hillion, 'This Way, Please! A Legal Appraisal of the EU Withdrawal Clause' in Carlos Closa (ed), *Secession from a Member State and Withdrawal from the European Union: Troubled Membership* (CUP 2017).

[39] See detailed analysis in chapter 6.

[40] Dennis Dixon, 'Article 50 and Member State Sovereignty' (2018) 19 German Law Journal 901. See detailed discussion of sequencing in chapter 6.

[41] See the discussion of these dynamics in chapter 6.

[42] See detailed discussion of this discretion in chapter 6.

to the opacity of the European Council and the absence of any need to provide justifications for the decision. Article 50 does not constrain how long the European Council may decide to continue the extension of the application of the Treaties, nor does it specify what substantive conditions it may impose. The primacy of the intergovernmental institution of the European Council, with its working methods predicated in the paradigm of diplomatic international relations, is a further example of the withdrawal clause's international law framing of disintegration.

The final normative deficiency of Article 50 TEU is no deal withdrawal. The automatic cessation of the application of the Treaties if no Withdrawal Agreement is concluded seeks to vindicate the first objective of Member State sovereignty. The realization of this objective would completely obviate the second objective of ensuring an orderly withdrawal. This suggests a misbalancing in the teloi of Article 50. The immediate disapplication of EU law that is binding on and within the withdrawing Member State would lead to dramatic negative consequences.[43] Such material consequences resulting from the automatic operation of EU law would call into question the extent to which Article 50 TEU realizes the EU's foundational values.

[43] See detailed discussion of these possible consequences in chapter 6.

8

Reforming the Opt-Out Protocols and Article 50 TEU

I. Introduction: The Argument for Reform

Brexit provides an opportunity to assess the functioning of opt-outs and withdrawal and consider reform. After two decades of disrupted integration, the European Union has experienced the phenomenon of disintegration for the first time. The operation of Article 50 TEU in practice allows assessment of whether it fulfils its telos of providing for a sovereign right of withdrawal and an orderly procedure. Schimmelfennig and Winzen claim that 'Denmark and other countries with a comparatively high level of differentiation are unlikely to follow the UK out of the EU'.[1] It should be added that Member States such as Poland and Hungary that have engaged in existential values clashes with the supranational institutions are also unlikely to trigger Article 50.[2] This unlikelihood may be regarded as a success for the deterrent strategy of preventing further disintegration pursued by the supranational institutions during Brexit negotiations. Nevertheless, withdrawal remains a sovereign right of all the Member States and should be designed to operate optimally regardless of whether its use is likely.

The withdrawal of the United Kingdom also means that the main protagonist of disrupted integration will no longer participate in reconstructions of the supranational constitutional order. The Protocols enabling opt-outs will no longer fully apply. Schimmelfennig and Winzen predict that 'Brexit may ... not only reduce the probability of further differentiation in future treaty negotiations and legislation. It may also create pressures on peripheral countries to

[1] Frank Schimmelfennig and Thomas Winzen, 'Differentiated EU Integration: Maps and Modes' (European University Institute 2020) EUI RSCAS Working Paper 2020/24 21 <http://cadmus.eui.eu//handle/1814/66880> accessed 27 April 2020.

[2] For the alternative argument that the conduct of the Hungarian and Polish governments constitutes an intention to withdraw under Article 50(1) TEU see Christophe Hillion, 'Poland and Hungary are Withdrawing from the EU' (*Verfassungsblog*, 27 April 2020) <https://verfassungsblog.de/poland-and-hungary-are-withdrawing-from-the-eu/> accessed 27 April 2020.

Constitutional Disintegration and Disruption. Oliver Garner, Oxford University Press. © Oxford University Press 2025. DOI: 10.1093/9780198914136.003.0008

reconsider and reduce their opt-outs from monetary union, interior policies and defence'.[3]

This chapter considers the arguments for reform of the Protocols and Article 50 TEU at the next EU Treaty amendment. The objective is not to remove the possibility of withdrawal or opt-outs, but instead to ensure that the legal mechanisms function in a manner that is more normatively consistent with the supranational constitutional order. These reforms are considered through the specific normative lens of vindicating the role of individuals as both nationals of the Member States and citizens of the Union in their roles as democratic subject and juridical object.

II. Amending Amendment?

The amendment limb of the triptych of constituted constituent power procedure may need to be amended itself to allow reform of opt-outs and withdrawal that would vindicate individuals *qua* quadripartite subjects. Proposals to remove unanimity in certain politically sensitive areas, such as Common Foreign and Security Policy, have emerged in the last years.[4] This has been exacerbated by the exercise of veto powers by Hungary inhibiting the EU's response to Russia's invasion of Ukraine.[5] Increasing restriction of veto power, and the possibility of constraints upon the unbound control of the High Contracting Power over the amendment procedure, could facilitate an unintended consequence of increasing the possibility of disintegration in reaction to the foreclosure of disruption through opt-outs.

Rather than analysing the minutiae of Article 48 TEU,[6] this section considers briefly whether proposals for a new dual-constituted institutional body are necessary for the reform of opt-outs and withdrawal.[7] For withdrawal, greater representation of individuals *qua* EU citizens may be necessary to enable a more supranational framing of the withdrawal clause. Amending revisionary

[3] Schimmelfennig and Winzen (n 1) 21.

[4] See eg Max Griera, 'EU Parliament Draws up Plan for Countries to Overcome Unanimity' (*Euractiv*, 12 July 2023) <https://web.archive.org/web/20230712043842/www.euractiv.com/section/politics/news/eu-parliament-draws-up-plan-for-countries-to-overcome-unanimity/> accessed 30 April 2024.

[5] Lorne Cook and Samuel Petrequin, 'EU Agrees to $54 Billion Ukraine Aid Package despite Hungary's Threat' (*AP News*, 1 February 2024) <https://apnews.com/article/ukraine-war-russia-hungary-eu-summit-budget-6d0f11bc16b4b21073f92925de2046e4> accessed 30 April 2024.

[6] See Bruno De Witte, 'Treaty Revision Procedures after Lisbon' in Andrea Biondi, Piet Eeckhout and Stefanie Ripley (eds), *EU Law after Lisbon* (OUP 2012).

[7] See the proposal in Markus Patberg, 'A Systematic Justification for the EU's Pouvoir Constituant Mixte: Principles of Constitutional Politics in Supranational Polities' (2017) 23 European Law Journal 441.

constituent power is most significant for opt-outs because the Protocols derive from the capacity for a Member State to reserve the levelling up of constituent power. After the multilateral Convention under Article 48(3) TEU, the only constraints upon the conference of representatives of the Member State are the requirements of state consent and domestic ratification.[8]

There is currently no legal way to prevent the creation of opt-outs except through the diplomatic means of other Member State executives refusing to accept these Protocols in negotiations. The only democratic input for individuals *qua* nationals beyond the representation by their government is the refusal to ratify this Treaty amendment in representative or direct democratic procedures at the domestic level. After the Convention individuals *qua* EU citizens are not represented at all in the final execution of the reconstruction. Unlike Article 218 TFEU in relation to international agreements,[9] there is no mechanism for the Court of Justice of the European Union to issue an Opinion on the suitability of the revisions for individuals *qua* juridical objects. The representatives of the government are ostensibly free to reconstruct or deconstruct any feature of the supranational constitutional order.

The present procedure for constitutional amendment within the European Union does not sufficiently enable individuals in their dual-legitimation role to exercise self-determination through representative institutions. Exercises of reconstructive constituent power should be expressions of self-determination of the political communities involved, and such representation should represent a plurality of positions from the state demoi.[10] Critique of opt-outs by opposition political parties can only be expressed through acceptance or rejection of the ratification of a Treaty. This is not a true opportunity for will formation because in the case of opt-outs the contestation may be precisely against decisions not to bind the state to obligations created in the Treaty amendment.[11] This was the case during the United Kingdom's ratification of the Maastricht Treaty. The opposition Labour party opposed the Social Policy opt-out. The remedy of rejecting ratification of the Treaty itself to protest against these opt-outs is self-defeating. Furthermore, if a simple democratic majority suffices for ratification rather than a super-majority then the votes of opposition parties will have no effect. A simple majority has been sufficient to ratify Treaty amendments in the United Kingdom. The democratic lock requirements of the European Union Act 2011 were never put into effect.[12] This contrasts to the

[8] See the discussion of the triptych in chapter 2.
[9] TFEU, art 218.
[10] See the discussion of the principles in chapter 2.
[11] See discussion of the ratification of the Treaties and creation of opt-out Protocols in chapter 6.
[12] European Union Act 2011.

super-majority of five-sixths of parliament, or a referendum, that has been necessary in Denmark.[13]

The only democratic input for individuals *qua* citizens to reject these opt-outs would be through the European Parliament. This role could only be exercised through the institution refusing to consent to the consensus recommendation of the Convention to the conference.[14] The historical precedent of the text of opt-outs being proposed at the later stages of the conference displaces the European Parliament's earlier filtering role in the Convention. The role of the European Parliament in supranational reconstructions is diminished compared to the supranational legislative process, and even supranational disintegration through Article 50 TEU. This falls short of the principles whereby constitutional decisions are expressions of the political self-determination of individuals *qua* EU citizens, and these EU citizens interact on formally equal terms *qua* democratic subjects.[15]

Patberg concludes his explication of the principles for supranational politics by proposing reforms to the amendment procedure: 'the executive-centred mode of EU Treaty making should be replaced with procedures and institutions that enable the citizens to exercise constituent power, that is, to shape the supranational polity without the involvement of constituted powers'.[16] The re-situation of Habermas' hypothetical original constituent convention in the processes of amendment of the constitutional Treaties is expressly envisaged by Patberg: 'while I have developed these normative standards through the thought experiment of a process of founding, they apply to processes of reform as well'.[17] He proposes a permanent elected constitutional convention at the EU level consisting of two 'chambers' that would each be composed of representatives elected from different lists and by different national and European constituencies. The different channels of representation 'would allow the citizens to determine the common good from the standpoints of Member State citizens and EU citizens'.[18] The proposal bears a resemblance to Deirdre Curtin's response to the Maastricht amendment: 'What is needed is either a constituent assembly (involving both the members of the European Parliament and of national parliaments . . .) or a new Committee of (non-political) Experts to prepare a revised Constitution'.[19] Patberg's reform would

[13] The Constitutional Act of Denmark of 5 June 1953, s 20.
[14] TEU, art 48(3).
[15] See outline of these principles in chapter 2.
[16] Patberg, 'A Systematic Justification' (n 7) 453.
[17] ibid.
[18] ibid.
[19] Deirdre Curtin, 'The Constitutional Structure of the Union: A Europe of Bits and Pieces' (1993) 30 Common Market Law Review 17, 69.

extinguish the reconstructive constituent power of the state as a constituted power in international law. Constituent power would be limited to the initial decision to accede to the EU, deconstructive decisions to withdraw from the Treaty structure, or a decision by all the High Contracting Parties to disintegrate the European Union. Decisions to opt out from EU law would be reallocated to the dual-constituent convention.

If EU Treaty amendment were subject to a dual-constituent convention it may make reform of opt-outs and withdrawal more likely. It is not, however, a necessary condition. Within the current paradigm it is not possible to preclude entirely the continuing creation of opt-outs through Protocols addended to Treaty revisions. However, the creation of an explicit clause to regulate opt-outs may incentivize the High Contracting Parties to prevent extra-constitutional means of retaining constituent power. The reforms of opt-outs and withdrawal below may be considered from this ideal paradigm of a dual-constituted amendment power or from the current paradigm of executive-led Treaty amendment. In both situations the holders of revisionary constituent power would need to agree upon the best balance between individuals *qua* national citizens and *qua* EU citizens with regard to the conditions to enable Member States to cease partially or completely to apply the Treaties.

III. Reforming Opt-Outs

Reform proposals would constrain constituent power by limiting the discretion for Member States to opt out from EU law. Member States should only reserve constituent power when their residual function as guarantors of the freedom and security of nationals would be threatened by participation in the supranational constitutional order. After considering alternatives, this subsection will argue for the creation of a new limb of the triptych of constituted constituent power to accompany Articles 48, 49, and 50 TEU.[20] The reconstructed quadriptych would ensure that opt-outs are subject to clear constitutional rules and supranational oversight akin to amendment, accession, and withdrawal rather than the iterative anomaly of Protocols with *ad hoc* and discrete rules for creation and maintenance.

The most radical reform proposal is to abolish opt-outs entirely. The President of the Commission stated in 2017 his hope that 'Europeans will wake up to a Union . . . [w]here being a full member of the euro area, the Banking

[20] See chapter 2 for the outline of the triptych of constituted constituent power.

Union and the Schengen area has become the norm for all'.[21] The European Parliament proposed in the same year that 'the next revision of the Treaties should rationalise the current disorderly differentiation by ending, or at least drastically reducing, the practice of opt-outs, opt-ins and exceptions for Member States at EU primary-law level'.[22] Abolition would require a constitutional decision by the individuals *qua* nationals of Denmark and Ireland to revoke these Protocols.[23] Representatives of these Member States, in either a hypothetical dual-constituent convention or in the Article 48 TEU conference, could forward compelling reasons for why the complete abolition of their opt-outs might undermine the capacity for self-determination of their nationals. These constitute elaborations of the principle whereby the content of the constitutional order is determined on the basis of an exchange of genuine reasons.[24]

Irish representatives could argue, with regard to the opt-outs from Schengen and the AFSJ, that the preservation of the Common Travel Area with the United Kingdom is fundamental to guarantee the freedom and security of Irish nationals. This necessity has been exacerbated by the withdrawal of the United Kingdom; the prevention of a hard border between Ireland and Northern Ireland was a crucial sticking point in the Brexit negotiations.[25] Ireland finds itself in an analogous situation to Cyprus whereby its territorial connection to a Third Country makes it incapable of participation in the Schengen *acquis*.[26]

For Denmark, the reversal of opt-outs is predicated upon the conditions of Article 20 of the Constitution.[27] Representatives of Danish nationals could argue that a supranational decision to abolish Denmark's opt-out Protocols would violate the principle whereby Article 20 functions as an autonomous elaboration of the right of individuals to participate in revisions of the constitution or processes of supra-state constitutional politics.[28] The complete abolition of opt-outs would not vindicate individuals *qua* Member State nationals

[21] Jean-Claude Juncker, 'State of the Union Address 2017' (*European Commission*, 13 September 2017) <https://ec.europa.eu/commission/presscorner/detail/en/SPEECH_17_3165> accessed 27 April 2020.

[22] European Parliament resolution of 16 February 2017 on possible evolutions of and adjustments to the current institutional set-up of the European Union [2018] OJ C 252/201, para 10.

[23] See chapter 4 for the conditions for revocation of the opt-out Protocols.

[24] See chapter 2 for the outline of these principles.

[25] See discussion in chapter 6 for detailed discussion of the negotiations on the Irish border.

[26] Maya Sion-Tzidkiyahu, 'Comparing Opt-Outs: How Different Is Differentiated Integration' in Thomas Giegerich, Desirée C Schmitt and Sebastian Zeitzmann (eds), *Flexibility in the EU and Beyond: How Much Differentiation Can European Integration Bear?* (Hart Publishing; Nomos Verlag 2017).

[27] The Constitutional Act of Denmark of 5 June 1953, s 20.

[28] See chapter 2 for the elaboration of these principles.

in the process of supranational reconstruction. The reasons that may justify Denmark and Ireland's opt-outs may arise again in the future. In the parlance of the European Parliament reform proposals would need to 'rationalise' disrupted integration rather than abolish it entirely.[29] The reconstructed regime for opt-outs needs to respect the genuine reasons why Member States believe they cannot level up constituent power whilst better preserving the integrity of supranational norm-creation and norm-application.

Fritz W. Scharpf and R. Daniel Kelemen have both proposed mechanisms to manage Member State opt-outs. The former is grounded in the norm-creation process, whereas the latter focuses on opt-outs arising from the norm-application process. Like Habermas, Scharpf grounds his rules for a multilevel European democracy in a hypothetical scenario.[30] Rather than an imagined historical foundation, Scharpf envisages a major future crisis that disrupts the present foundations of European integration. He proposes a complex regime that would resituate the capacity to opt out from primary law revisions to the secondary legislative process. The first rule is that individual Member States should have the right to opt out from ordinary legislation.[31] This is qualified by the rule that legislation may propose the exclusion of opt-outs, but this must be adopted by an absolute majority in Parliament and by a qualified majority in the Council.[32]

Scharpf's purpose is to 'enlarge, at the same time, the action spaces of national and European political processes'.[33] The objective to 'facilitate political action and opportunities for politicisation and democratic accountability at the European level' is balanced against the need to 'respond to *demoicratic* aspirations for Member State autonomy'.[34] National opt-outs would protect the 'legitimate diversity' of Member States that would be challenged by a move to a simple majoritarian legislative process. This would protect the democratic and juridical interests of individuals *qua* nationals against the majority preferences of EU citizens *qua* democratic subjects. The exception of legislation without opt-outs attempts to preserve the uniformity of EU law for individuals *qua* juridical objects only when it would be considered essential by democratic subjects. This reverses the status quo whereby uniformity is the default position and derogation is the exception.

[29] European Parliament resolution of 16 February 2017 (n 22).

[30] Fritz W Scharpf, 'After the Crash: A Perspective on Multilevel European Democracy' (2015) 21 European Law Journal 384.

[31] ibid 401.

[32] ibid.

[33] ibid 404.

[34] ibid 400.

Opt-outs as a default possibility in the norm-creation process undermines the equality between individuals *qua* nationals and *qua* EU citizens. In the process of will formation the 'citizens of the . . . supranational polity' would not interact on formally equal terms.[35] After the majority vote of the European Parliament, the ultimate decision on the application of the norms would rest with each individual Member State in the Council. This would replicate the representation deficits in the Article 48 TEU Convention and conference structure. Retention of constituent power as the default position would also undermine equality in the representation of Member State nationals in the Council. The exceptional situation for the United Kingdom and Ireland under the AFSJ Protocol would become the supranational constitutional default.

Scharpf's 'demoicratic' perspective neglects the autonomous status of EU citizenship.[36] Demoicracy holds that the different peoples of the Member States are all individually *pouvoirs constituants* without any admixture.[37] Scharpf explicitly distinguishes his position from Habermas' dual-constituent thesis.[38] A default regime of opt-outs can only be justified by recognizing nationals of the Member States as the sole constituent subject. Scharpf recognizes the consequences of his proposal for EU citizenship as a status of democratic subjecthood: 'As different majorities are likely to form in different issue areas, they would not necessarily strengthen the sense of common identity and the democratic legitimacy of the European polity'.[39] The perspective of the dual-constituted supranational constitutional order could not allow Member States to opt out from secondary legislation as a default. Within Patberg's hypothetical institution it may be hypothesized that the chamber representing EU citizens would reject the proposal.

Kelemen envisages a route to create opt-outs through juridical processes. This concerns the role of national constitutional courts and the Court of Justice in preserving the autonomy of individuals *qua* juridical objects.[40] Kelemen argues that the primacy of EU law means that the only remedy for national

[35] See chapter 2 for the detailed outline of these principles.

[36] For the distinction between demoicracy and the dual-constituent thesis see Peter Niesen, 'The "Mixed" Constituent Legitimacy of the European Federation' (2017) 55 Journal of Common Market Studies 183.

[37] Francis Cheneval, Sandra Lavenex and Frank Schimmelfennig, 'Demoi-Cracy in the European Union: Principles, Institutions, Policies' (2015) 22 Journal of European Public Policy 1. See discussion of demoicracy in chapter 2.

[38] 'In this regard, demoicracy differs from the position of Habermas . . . He also asserts a dual identity of individuals as citizens of their respective states and of the Union, but in his view this dualism justifies majoritarian democracy at the European level in order to break the strangle-hold of intergovernmental veto players under present rules of the Community Method': Scharpf (n 30) n 51.

[39] ibid n 56.

[40] See the elaboration of individuals as juridical objects in chapter 2.

constitutional courts when EU institutions threaten constitutional identity is to declare membership in the European Union to be unconstitutional.[41] He argues that '[t]his approach would compel governments to either amend their constitutions, to work through the EU political process to change the EU legal norms in question or secure an opt-out or, if necessary, to withdraw from the Union altogether'.[42]

If this observation were repurposed as an exclusive model for the creation of opt-outs it would show more deference to EU citizenship than Scharpf's proposal. Opt-outs would only be available if the application of EU law threatened the capacity for Member States to guarantee self-determination in the domestic constitutional sphere. The problem is that, whereas the other remedial measures Kelemen proposes have the clear procedural routes of Article 48 and Article 50 TEU, there is no generalized procedure whereby a Member State claiming a constitutional identity infringement could claim an opt-out. Outside of Treaty amendments, the simplified international treaty of the United Kingdom's New Settlement was necessary for pre agreement on opt-outs. Even beyond the normative problem of using international law to pre-bind the exercise of reconstructive power, the agreement could only envisage the actual creation of opt-outs at the time of the next Treaty amendment. The proposal for an opt-out clause below will attempt to address the mischief that Kelemen raises whilst also constitutionalizing the situation that led to the United Kingdom's renegotiation.

The triptych of constituted constituent power of Articles 48, 49, and 50 TEU should be complemented by a specific limb concerning the reservation of constituent power. The anomalous Protocols would be replaced by a fourth limb of the newly reconstituted quadriptych. This would enable the supranational institutions to assess claims for opt-outs and provide explicit authorization or rejection. Opt-outs would no longer be a side-effect of the failure to level up constituent power through the amendment procedures. Instead, the legitimacy and authority of opt-outs would be predicated upon a supranational constitutional mechanism. To avoid the legitimacy defects of the existing opt-outs, the creation of an opt-out under the new mechanism would be subject to strict conditions. The precedent for such regulation of differentiation is already provided by Article 20 TEU and Articles 329–334 TFEU on enhanced cooperation.[43] The former provides that the Council is the institution that adopts a

[41] R Daniel Kelemen, 'On the Unsustainability of Constitutional Pluralism: European Supremacy and the Survival of the Eurozone' (2016) 23 Maastricht Journal of European and Comparative Law 136, 149.
[42] ibid.
[43] See discussion in chapter 3.

decision to authorize the cooperation. A crucial initiating condition is that the Council determine that it is 'a last resort, when it has established that the objectives of such cooperation cannot be attained within a reasonable period by the Union as a whole'.[44] A new Treaty article on opt-outs could similarly determine such a predicative qualitative condition for when opt-outs would be available. Article 329 TFEU confirms that areas of exclusive competence are excluded from enhanced cooperation; similarly, an opt-out mechanism could ring-fence certain areas of the Treaty. The Commission, and the Council in cases of CFSP (Common Foreign and Security Policy), is given a monitoring role by Article 331 TFEU in determining that conditions for participation have been fulfilled and also must also ensure the consistency of activities under Article 334 TFEU. The institutions could fulfil a similar role with regard to the conditions for the creation of opt-outs, with the inclusion of the European Parliament as representative of EU citizens.

The activation of the reservation limb could be strictly time-limited to the period between the conclusion of the Treaty amendment and its coming into force. This would provide a separate constitutional forum for considering the merits of disruption disentangled from the wider discussions over the substance of the Treaty amendment. In the ideal theory of Patberg's dual-constituted assembly, this body would make the decision to approve or reject an opt-out. In the current status quo, both the Council and the European Parliament should be required to approve the opt-out by analogy to their roles in the ordinary legislative procedure and in approving or rejecting a Withdrawal Agreement under Article 50 TEU. The need to persuade representatives of all Member State nationals and EU citizens would require an exchange of reasons. The recalcitrant Member State's representatives would need to convince its peers about why the levelling up of constituent power would undermine the capacity for self-determination of its nationals due to specific conditions that make the Member State a distinct case. If their concerns are, by contrast, general then these should be ventilated through resistance during the amendment itself. The disentanglement of the creation of opt-outs from the process of Treaty amendment could also provide the space for a Court of Justice Opinion mechanism equivalent to Article 218 TFEU. This would allow the Court to provide a prospective overview of the consequences of the opt-out for individuals if a constituent player requests an Opinion.

The maintenance of the opt-out should be subjected to a review process that is conducted periodically by the supranational institutions. This would contrast

[44] TEU, art 20.

with the accountability mechanisms existing solely at the national level for the present opt-outs. As was seen with the United Kingdom in relation to Protocol (No 21),[45] this incentivizes the Member State government to pursue only the interests of individuals *qua* Member State nationals with no incentive to consider the position of all individuals *qua* EU citizens.[46] Representatives of the supranational institutions in the proposed mandated review process would ensure that these justifications to maintain the opt-out were balanced against the interests of individuals *qua* EU citizens.

The review mechanism for the maintenance of opt-outs could draw inspiration from secondary legislation that enables Member State derogations. The Directive on voting in municipal elections by EU citizens residing in other Member States is clear that derogations 'must be warranted . . . by problems specific to a Member State' and that any derogation 'must, by its very nature, be subject to review'.[47] The legislation mandates derogations that are available to all Member States that fulfil these conditions.[48] The preamble recognizes a specific derogation for Belgium comparable to the primary law opt-outs. This is predicated upon characteristics of the constitutional identity of that state:

> Whereas the Kingdom of Belgium is characterized by specific features and balance linked to the fact that . . . its Constitution provide[s] for three official languages and a territorial division into regions and communities, as a result of which full application of this Directive . . . might have effects such as to necessitate providing for the possibility of derogation . . . in order to take account of those specific features and balances.[49]

This provides a clear example of the form in which Member States should present claims that opt-outs are necessary in order to justify the reservation of constituent power. Ideally, a Member State would identify why the full application of EU law could affect the defined 'specific features' of its constitutional order.

The scheme of derogations in the Directive on municipal voting also provides a model for a primary law review mechanism for opt-outs. Article 12(4)

[45] See analysis of the functioning of the opt-in mechanism at the end of chapter 3.

[46] See the outline of these dynamics in chapter 5.

[47] Council Directive 94/80/EC of 19 December 1994 laying down detailed arrangements for the exercise of the right to vote and to stand as a candidate in municipal elections by citizens of the union residing in a member state of which they are not nationals [1994] OJ L 368/38.

[48] Voting of non-national EU citizens may be restricted to those who have been resident for a minimum period if 20 per cent of the total number of EU citizens of voting age are not nationals: ibid art 12.

[49] Belgium may apply the conditions of the derogation to a limited number of local government units in addition to the total electorate: ibid art 12(2).

mandates the Commission to submit reports to the European Parliament and the Council every six years to 'check whether the grant to the Member States concerned of a derogation . . . is still warranted and shall propose any necessary adjustments be made'.[50] A similar review mechanism could be incorporated into the new constitutional mechanism mandating the reservation of constituent power. This would ensure that the objective justifications for the opt-out persist and can be verified by the supranational institutions. This contrasts to the stagnation in the current regime of opt-outs regarding justification. For example, the United Kingdom's ostensibly temporary deferral of a constituent decision on EMU became permanent due to the lack of sufficient conditions imposed upon the executive. The national and supranational conditions for the revocation of the opt-outs could be explicitly tied to the outcome of the periodic reviews. A creation and review process involving the European Parliament and the Council would rekindle symmetry within the quadripartite role by ensuring that individuals *qua* EU citizens and *qua* all Member State nationals are represented in decisions whether to maintain or extinguish opt-outs. This ensures that all individuals affected by the opt-outs *qua* juridical objects can express their political subjecthood regarding the legitimacy of such disrupted integration.

IV. Reforming Withdrawal

This section will first consider radical proposals to reform withdrawal. These reforms are rejected on the basis that they would undermine the telos of Article 50 TEU. In turn, they would jeopardize the balance between individual *qua* nationals and individuals *qua* EU citizens. The section will then conclude by proposing reforms to the operation of Article 50 that would preserve the telos of a sovereign right of withdrawal in an orderly fashion but would ensure greater vindication of the self-determination of individuals in their quadripartite role.

i. Radical proposals for reform

Radical proposals for reform would alter two dimensions of the operation of Article 50 TEU: its unconditionality and its unilaterality. The former considers the setting of conditions for withdrawal at the supranational level. The latter

[50] ibid art 12(4).

considers the representation of all those holding EU citizenship in the process of decision, rather than only those who hold the constituent status of nationality of the Member State contemplating withdrawal. These proposals will be explicated below before being critiqued on the basis of their (in)compatibility with the dual-legitimation thesis.

This first proposal may be deduced from the criticisms of the withdrawal clause offered by Hauke Brunkhorst,[51] and Christian F. Røstboll and Tore Vincents Olsen.[52] These build upon the criticisms advanced during the 2003 Convention that the withdrawal clause would undermine the purpose of 'ever closer union'.[53] These criticisms are predicated upon the significance of citizenship as a constituent status. Brunkhorst argued at the time of the creation of the withdrawal clause that its use would be 'inadmissible because regardless of their national citizenship the citizens of the European Union have rights within the whole territory of the European Union, and thus in all of the member countries'.[54] Røstboll and Olsen develop this position to argue that the United Kingdom's decision to withdraw was undemocratic. They advance the thesis of the 'all affected status principle' whereby 'people whose status as free and equal is mutually dependent ought to be included and remain in common democratic decision-making'.[55] Unilateral decisions to withdraw do not live up to this principle because 'they exclude people from participating in a decision that affects their status as rights holders and co-rulers, and hence, they do not rule themselves'.[56]

If one extracts a prescriptive reform from Røstboll and Olsen's criticisms, beyond the absolute abolition of withdrawal, it is the shackling of deconstructive power to strict supranational conditions:

> our argument is not directed at the right to withdrawal but concerns the democratic credentials of its use. Regarding the latter, we do not deny that there might be conditions under which the right could be used as a remedy against domination, but only that normally this is not the case.[57]

This resonates with Hofmeister's argument before the first use of Article 50 that 'withdrawal should only be possible under exceptional circumstances that

[51] Hauke Brunkhorst, *Solidarity: From Civic Friendship to a Global Legal Community* (MIT Press 2005).
[52] Tore Vincents Olsen and Christian F Rostbøll, 'Why Withdrawal from the European Union Is Undemocratic' (2017) 9 International Theory 436.
[53] See discussion of the origins of withdrawal in chapter 6.
[54] Brunkhorst (n 51) 167–68.
[55] Olsen and Rostbøll (n 52) 445.
[56] ibid 461.
[57] ibid.

would need to be clearly defined'.[58] Withdrawal as a remedy against 'domination' may be understood in the same terms as the proposal for the reform of opt-outs explicated above. One could make an argument whereby withdrawal could only be made available in the event of a complete failure to resolve a situation in which a Member State has claimed that the capacity for individuals *qua* nationals of that Member State to exercise self-determination has been violated by participation in the supranational constitutional order.

This would positivize within the Treaties Kelemen's argument that, if necessary, Member States should withdraw in the event of a fundamental constitutional conflict.[59] Article 50(1)'s necessary condition that a decision is an exercise of self-determination by individuals *qua* nationals would be supplemented by the complementary 'constitutional requirements' of the EU's constitutional order. The objective would be to preserve insofar as possible the self-determination of individuals *qua* EU citizens. This would be achieved by limiting the possibility to extinguish the constituent status of EU citizenship and the contraction of the constitutional territory in which it is effective to a last resort. The conditions established by the German Constitutional Court for the protection of constitutional identity and thus the areas in which the government would be barred from levelling up constituent power[60] could be transposed to the supranational level as the explicit conditions for when withdrawal would be legitimate. This would enshrine that withdrawal from the supranational order would only be possible if it had violated the constitutional identity of a Member State.

An alternative or supplement to strict supranational conditionality would be reform of the unilaterality of the exercise of deconstructive power. This could draw inspiration from the multilateral nature of secession established by the Canadian constitution whereby the federal House of Commons must approve the negotiation settlement arising from the exercise of popular will

[58] Hannes Hofmeister, '"Should I Stay or Should I Go ?" A Critical Analysis of the Right to Withdraw from the EU' (2010) 16 European Law Journal 589, 599.

[59] See outline of this argument earlier in this chapter.

[60] 'European integration may neither lead to an erosion of the democratic system of government in Germany . . . nor may the supranational public authority fail to adhere to basic democratic requirements'; 'European integration on the basis of a Treaty-based union of sovereign states cannot be realised in such a way that the Member States are left without sufficient political latitude to address economic, cultural and social conditions. This applies in particular to matters that shape the citizens' living conditions and, above all, their private area of autonomy and of personal and social security, which is protected by fundamental rights; it also applies to political decisions that are especially reliant on prior cultural, historical and linguistic concepts and unfold in the sphere of party politics and of parliamentary decision-making, in the context of political discussion': *Lisbon*, Judgment of the Second Senate of 30 June 2009, BVerfG, 2 BvE 2/08, paras 244 and 209.

at the sub-federal level.[61] Conditionality protects the self-determination of EU citizens *qua* juridical objects by ensuring their legal rights may only be rescinded as a last resort to preserve the self-determination of individuals *qua* Member State nationals. Expanding the scope of those entitled to make the decision would enfranchise EU citizens *qua* democratic subjects in a determination about the contraction of the territory in which they can exercise their status *qua* juridical objects. Such a transformation in the effective utility of the constituent status of EU citizenship would be legitimated through the democratic consent of all those who hold it. This would necessitate an amendment whereby a decision to withdraw would be made not only by individuals *qua* nationals of that state, through the fulfilment of the domestic 'constitutional requirements', but also by all individuals *qua* EU citizens. Røstboll and Olsen reject the argument that the enfranchisement of all individuals *qua* EU citizens in a decision to withdraw would legitimate the process: 'even a multilaterally agreed decision to allow an individual nation to withdraw from the EU is undemocratic because of its detrimental consequences for future democracy'.[62]

The representation of all individuals *qua* EU citizens regardless of their nationality could be achieved through representative democratic channels by making the European Parliament a necessary decision-maker in the Article 50(1) TEU process. A more ambitious direct democratic channel would be a European-wide referendum. An alternative demoicratic model of decisions by national parliaments and governments would be more problematic on the basis that their main representative interest is towards individuals *qua* nationals of the individual Member States. A withdrawal decision by all EU citizens would represent the political vindication of the judicial dicta that EU citizenship is a status of political and legal equality throughout the territory of the Union. It would also recognize the negative effects of withdrawal for the nationals of remaining Member States due to the change of status within a former territory of the Union. If a decision to withdraw were dependent upon the consent of all EU citizens, then the government proposing withdrawal would be incentivized to protect the rights of these individuals in order to secure their support. This would vindicate the normative democratic principle of the representation of the 'all affected status'.[63]

[61] *Reference re Secession of Quebec* [1998] 2 SCR 217 (Supreme Court of Canada) [91]; An Act to give effect to the requirement for clarity as set out in the opinion of the Supreme Court of Canada in the Quebec Secession Reference S.C. 2000, c. 26 Assented to 2000-06-29. See discussion in chapter 2.

[62] Olsen and Rostbøll (n 52) 461.

[63] ibid.

From the dual-legitimation perspective, the criticisms which form the basis for such reform proposals over-emphasize the importance of citizenship of the Union as a constituent status. Røstboll and Olsen argue that 'if the conditions of citizens are determined by factors beyond the control of national (state) institutions, the value of self-determination is seriously reduced . . . under current conditions, sovereign self-determination is illusory and hence not a cogent idea.'[64] This ignores the fact that, although the conditions of citizens as democratic subjects and juridical objects are determined beyond the boundaries of the national constitutional orders, the levelling up process means that this is not beyond the control of national institutions. Instead, they are the crucial co-player in the process. Furthermore, these criticisms conflate EU citizenship as a role of juridical objecthood and as a role of democratic subjecthood. The normative premise of the argument is a conceptualization of the status as one of absolute equality. This reflects the judicial construction of a fundamental status of juridical equality.[65] This misses the material reality that there is no absolute equality due to the fact that prior nationality of a Member State underpins acquisition of the status, and these national citizenships are heterogenous.

The potential for a Member State to withdraw from the European Union is one of the key tenets in the dual-legitimation thesis. The retention of the capacity for individuals *qua* Member State nationals to disengage from the process of levelling up constituent power is the ultimate means to ensure that the freedom-guaranteeing function of the constitutional state is not undermined by European integration. This retention of sovereignty through the constituent status of nationality distinguishes unilateral supranational withdrawal from the multilateral and conditional nature of secession in the Canadian constitution.[66] As Habermas explicates: 'although the Union was not founded for a definite duration, every member state is free to *regain* the degree of sovereignty it enjoyed before joining the Union.'[67] This sentiment is expressed in the judicial determination of the telos of Article 50 TEU as 'enshrining the sovereign right of a Member State to withdraw from the European Union.'[68] This sovereign right should be understood in supranational democratic terms as the capacity for individuals exclusively *qua* nationals to level down constituent power without interference in their initial decision. This mirrors the position

[64] ibid 454.
[65] See the discussion of juridical objecthood in chapter 2.
[66] See *Re Secession of Quebec* (n 61) and discussion in chapter 2 and chapter 6.
[67] Jürgen Habermas, *The Crisis of the European Union: A Response* (Polity Press 2013) 40.
[68] Case C-621/18 *Wightman v Secretary of State for Exiting the European Union*, EU:C:2018:999, para 56. See discussion of the case in chapter 6.

whereby the initial decision to level up constituent power and either participate in the co-creation of the supranational polity or accede thereafter is also a decision purely for individuals *qua* nationals.

Reform proposals to constrain withdrawal to supranational conditions or to enfranchise all individuals *qua* EU citizens are not compatible with this limb of the dual objective of Article 50 TEU. Even if such conditions were promulgated in accordance with the principles for supranational constitutional politics, they would still undermine the entire basis of *pouvoir constituant mixte*:

> Entry and exit would still be matters to be decided by each Member State autonomously. There is no contradiction in demanding, on the one hand, that procedures for shaping the EU polity should conform to the standard of dual-constituent power and insisting, on the other hand, that the Member States have the right to unilaterally decide whether they want to (continue to) be part of the EU. Nothing in the rational reconstruction of polity formation implies that the *pouvoir constituant mixte* should become the final authority on the question of membership.[69]

The dual-constituent thesis recognizes that the ultimate authority on the question of membership, both accession under Article 49 TEU and withdrawal under Article 50 TEU, is the primordial constituent subject of 'national of a constitutional state'. The principles that determine the exercise of this authority are the first stage of the hypothetical constitutional convention before any levelling up is enacted.[70] The principle that enables the 'levelling up' of constituent power at the domestic level must also enable the 'levelling down' of this power, through the operation of the 'constitutional requirements' of Article 50(1) TEU. This principle is the predicate upon which the supranational functions of Member State nationals and EU citizens is legitimated. To subject the 'levelling down' of constituent power to conditions established at the supranational level, or to enfranchise individuals beyond the original constituent subjects who have authorized 'levelling up', would violate the initial premises of supranational integration.

Patberg and Niesen's own proposal to reform withdrawal falls foul of this interpretation of withdrawal as 'levelling down' constituent power. They recommend that 'Article 50 . . . be amended to allow for the re-entry of former Member States, by referendum or act of parliament, or, if this cannot be achieved, by

[69] Patberg, 'A Systematic Justification' (n 7) 453.
[70] ibid 448–49. See chapter 2 for elaboration of the principles.

providing an identical re-entry clause in the withdrawal agreement'.[71] The normative basis is that the current configuration of Article 50(5), whereby a Member State that withdraws can only reapply for membership through the accession procedure of Article 49 TEU, undermines the self-determination of that state's nationals: 'its citizens will not have a definitive say in the outcome as they do now. They will be treated as petitioners, not co-sovereigns, no different from the nationals of first-time applicants'.[72] This proposal reframes Member State withdrawal in relation to the constituent process. It is not a process of 'levelling down' that repatriates constituent power exclusively to the domestic constitutional level. Instead, Article 50 would hold the levelling up of constituent power in abeyance in the ultimate extension of disrupted integration. This constituent power could be reactivated at any time by an exercise of self-determination by the national democratic subject. As the piece concludes, '[f]ormer EU citizens would not fall back to the status of third-country nationals but encounter current EU citizens as co-citizens "on standby"'.[73] This challenges the notion that the 'levelling up' of constituent power can be completely extinguished by the domestic constituent subject and so could undermine the autonomy of nationality as the base constituent status.

The only arena that would be acceptable for reforms to unilaterality and unconditionality is the domestic constitutional level. The proposals to establish conditions for withdrawal and to enfranchise all individuals *qua* EU citizens can be repurposed for the domestic 'constitutional requirements'.[74] It would be desirable for all Member States, even if they do not intend to make a decision under Article 50(1), to clarify proactively the procedural conditions for how the constitutional requirements would be fulfilled, and the substantive conditions that would justify a decision to withdraw. The former process could draw inspiration from permanent domestic law provisions such as the Canadian Clarity Act of 2000 which sets the procedure for the secession of Quebec.[75]

[71] Markus Patberg and Peter Niesen, 'After Brexit, the UK Should Have a Democratic Right of Return' (*LSE Brexit*, 30 October 2018) <https://blogs.lse.ac.uk/brexit/2018/10/30/after-brexit-the-uk-should-be-able-to-re-enter-the-eu-if-it-wishes-to-do-so/> accessed 24 January 2020. See also Markus Patberg, 'Can Disintegration Be Democratic? The European Union Between Legitimate Change and Regression' (2020) 68 Political Studies 582.

[72] Patberg and Niesen (n 71).

[73] ibid.

[74] This draws upon Oliver Garner, 'Why All Member States Should Clarify Their Constitutional Requirements for Withdrawing from the EU' (*Verfassungsblog*, 2 November 2016) <https://verfassungsblog.de/why-all-member-states-should-clarify-their-constitutional-requirements-for-withdrawing-from-the-eu/> accessed 18 December 2018.

[75] An Act to give effect to the requirement for clarity as set out in the opinion of the Supreme Court of Canada in the Quebec Secession Reference (n 61).

The latter could draw inspiration from the clarification of the conditions for Germany's continuing commitment to European integration established by the German Constitutional Court,[76] which are now enshrined in the conditional commitment under Article 23(1) of the Basic Law.[77]

Prospective procedural conditions would ensure that the legal uncertainty surrounding Article 50's activation in the United Kingdom would not be repeated.[78] Nationals *qua* democratic subject could exercise deconstructive power with complete clarity regarding the reasons why and methods for how a withdrawal decision would be made. The domestic 'constitutional requirements' could be transformed to mandate a dual decision. Individuals would decide to revoke the membership of their state *qua* nationals, and to revoke explicitly their status *qua* citizens of the Union. This would ensure that individuals are fully aware that the consequence of their decision is not only the withdrawal of their state from a treaty on the international plane, but also the extinction of their constituent capacity to determine the nature and functioning of a supranational constitutional order. This reform would address the criticism that the withdrawal process in Article 50 TEU is delineated in international law rather than supranational constitutional terms.

ii. Reforms to the text of Article 50 TEU

Transforming the unconditionality and unilaterality of the withdrawal decision would undermine the telos of Article 50 TEU of providing a sovereign right to the nationals of a Member State. Therefore, reform should focus on the second limb of the dual objective of ensuring that the process of withdrawal is orderly. A range of specific amendments may be proposed to the operation of Article 50 TEU. These seek to address the normative failings of the clause

[76] *Lisbon* (n 60), paras 244 and 249.

[77] Basic Law for the Federal Republic of Germany in the revised version published in the Federal Law Gazette Part III, classification number 100-1, as last amended by Article 1 of the Act of 28 March 2019 (Federal Law Gazette I p. 404), art 23(1).

[78] See the analysis of this uncertainty in chapter 6.

during the Brexit negotiations.[79] The overarching objective is to provide a supranational rather than international framing for the withdrawal clause.[80]

A. Proposal 1: The double-decision lock

This reform would retain the initial decision by a Member State in accordance with its constitutional requirements to express the *intention* to withdraw. For the Treaties to cease to apply, however, a Member State would need to make a second final confirmatory decision to withdraw at the end of negotiations. This addresses the changes of circumstances that may occur between expression of the intention to withdraw and the conditions of Article 50 being fulfilled. This was evidenced in the Brexit case study. There was a paucity of discussion of the Irish border during the referendum campaign before this became the most important issue during the withdrawal negotiations.[81] Over a period of time individuals *qua* democratic subject may change their mind regarding exercises of self-determination as circumstances become clearer. Michael Dougan discusses the possibility of such a conditional notification within the current framework of Article 50: '[s]uch conditionality could be explicit . . . if the relevant State were to notify its intention to withdraw, provided that its national parliament later . . . approved . . . ex ante conditionality could, in some cases, even be treated as implicit in the relevant State's original notification of intention to withdraw'.[82] This reform proposal would make such a framework the legal default rather than a hypothetical possibility.

The double-decision lock would also resolve the remaining uncertainty over whether there is a distinction between the notification of the 'intention' to withdraw, and the eventual 'decision' to withdraw itself.[83] Within the new structure, the first instruction in accordance with the constitutional requirements would represent the expression of the 'intention' to withdraw. The second instruction would be the 'decision' once the outcome of the deconstitutional convention is clear. This encourages symmetry with the accession limb of the constituted constituent power triptych.[84] Article 49 TEU first vindicates the intention to accede to the European Union through candidate state status, before this intention is realized through the formal conclusion of the accession treaty and

[79] See the summary of the failings in chapter 7.
[80] For a more detailed elaboration of these proposals, see Oliver Garner, 'Seven Reforms to Article 50 TEU' [2021] European Law Review 784.
[81] See the analysis of the negotiations in chapter 6.
[82] Michael Dougan, *The UK's Withdrawal from the EU: A Legal Analysis* (OUP 2021) 39.
[83] See analysis of this ambiguity in chapter 6.
[84] See the elaboration of these limbs in chapter 2.

the acquisition of Member Statehood. The formal confirmation of a final decision requirement would constitutionalize *de jure* what happened *de facto* in the Brexit case study. The orthodox will-expression of the General Election in 2019 was necessary to realize the popular expression of will in 2016 due to resistance within the constituted institution of Parliament. A supranational condition of a final decision would ensure that the ordinary constitutional functioning of the domestic order is not distorted by the need to make *de facto* decisions on withdrawal.

B. Proposal 2: Revocation replaced by a fast-tracked second decision

The unwritten right to revoke notification of an intention to withdraw would be reformed into a right to bring forward the final confirmatory decision to any point during negotiations. The establishment of a two-stage process for withdrawal would obviate the necessity of a unilateral right of revocation. Instead, the telos that *Wightman* recognized—to ensure that the withdrawal decision is a voluntary expression of democratic will by the nationals of the Member State—would be upheld by enabling the final decision to be taken at any time during the negotiation of a Withdrawal Agreement.

This reform to fast-track the final decision could also address the issues concerning the constitutional propriety of the *Wightman* judgment. The United Kingdom conducted negotiations over withdrawal from March 2017 to December 2018 without full cognizance of the extent of its sovereign power to initiate and reverse the levelling down of constituent power. In contrast to the Brexit case study, a future Member State would have clarity and certainty over the exact procedural parameters of their withdrawal, and their capacity to request an expedited conclusion to this process.

The opportunity for the constituent powers of the Member States and the supranational institutions to address the textual lacuna means that a mechanism could be constructed that involves the representation of the supranational institutions. The mechanism for a fast-track request could replicate the multilateral structure of withdrawal itself.[85] Rather than a unilateral decision, the Member State could have the right to request taking a final decision. This would then need to be approved by the supranational institutions. Such approval is justified by an early decision constituting alteration of the deconstitutional convention. If the institutions decide not to approve this request, the sovereign right to withdrawal would not be undermined, but deferred until the conclusion of the negotiations.

[85] See alternative to *Wightman* as discussed in chapter 6.

C. Proposal 3: A time limit on renotification of withdrawal

The *Wightman* judgment left many of the practical concerns expressed by the EU institutions regarding strategic revocation unanswered. The Court of Justice instead merely established the condition that revocations must be in good faith and unconditional to ameliorate the possibility of abuse.[86] The amendment of Article 50 would provide the constituent powers and the supranational institutions with the opportunity to address these concerns proactively. A strong means to achieving this would be a bright-line condition that, if a Member State makes a final confirmatory decision to revoke its intention to withdraw and remain a Member State, then a time limit would be imposed before it could choose to send a new notification of an intention to withdraw.

D. Proposal 4: The reform of no deal withdrawal

Within the new double-decision structure, the withdrawing Member State would still have the option not to adopt a Withdrawal Agreement and to leave without a deal. However, the current paradigm in which the Treaties immediately cease to apply undermines the telos of ensuring an orderly withdrawal. The dramatic consequences of a no deal exit arguably violate the EU's values in its relations with third countries in its neighbourhood. In order to avoid these consequences, a reform proposal would amend no deal exit so that it would operate as a graduated process. Following a final decision not to adopt a Withdrawal Agreement, a withdrawing Member State would move through stages of Treaty de-application. As opposed to a cliff-edge, the levelling down of constituent power would operate analogously to a parachute landing.

This would promote further symmetry with the process of levelling up constituent power. The current regime established for accession to the European Union ensures that a candidate state is able to apply the sectors of the *acquis communautaire* through a monitoring process before the accession treaty is concluded.[87] By analogy, a graduated no deal withdrawal would involve a monitoring process whereby the withdrawn Member State and the supranational institutions would ensure that the former is in a position not to apply EU law within particular sectors before the Treaties are finally de-applied.

The amendment of no deal withdrawal into a graduated process would also constitutionalize the purposes of the *ad hoc* mechanism of the transition period established in the Withdrawal Agreement but in the event that there is no such agreement. A graduated no deal withdrawal would ensure sufficient time

[86] ibid.
[87] See the summary of Article 49 TEU in chapter 2.

to preserve the interests of individuals *qua* juridical objects of EU law in the transition to becoming solely objects of the national legal order. The graduated process would also enshrine *de jure* the purpose behind the contingency legislation proposed by the European Commission to continue the application of EU law to the United Kingdom in the event of a no deal withdrawal.[88] By contrast to these emergency measures, the graduated process would ensure a sustainable process with a clear legal base in the withdrawal clause.

E. Proposal 5: The reform of the time limit and extension for withdrawal negotiations

The double-decision structure would obviate the requirement for a two-year time limit for negotiations. The time period for negotiations would be made contingent on a decision by the withdrawing Member State and the supranational institutions in the guidelines that commence the deconstitutional convention. This would provide further coherence with accession as Article 49 TEU does not impose time limits for accession. The original telos of the time limit was to ensure that a Member State's sovereign intention to withdraw could not be frustrated by interminable negotiations. This purpose would be served by the capacity to make a final withdrawal decision. If a fast-tracked decision request were refused, sovereignty would be ensured through the final decision at the expiry of the time period for negotiations agreed upon with the European Union.

The removal of the two-year time limit in the text of Article 50 would also remove the executive-driven extension mechanism.[89] Instead, two separate means for extending the negotiation period may be provided to address different justifications. The first instance is when the withdrawing Member State rejects the outcome of the negotiations, but also does not wish to reverse its decision to withdraw. In this situation, one of the options available for the final decision in accordance with the constitutional requirements should be to re-initiate the negotiation period, with the agreement of the supranational institutions. In order to avoid the interminable repetition of withdrawal negotiations, the supranational institutions should have the power to reject this request. This would require the Member State to decide either to reverse the withdrawal or withdraw without an agreement.

The second situation in which extension may be required covers the 'technical' extensions that may be necessary to finalize ratification of a Withdrawal

[88] ibid.
[89] See discussion and critique in chapter 7.

Agreement. Any such extensions after a final decision to withdraw should be limited to situations of necessity for national and EU ratification procedures. This can be provided for prospectively in the determination of the time limits at the start of the negotiations, or iteratively following a final decision to withdraw.

F. Proposal 6: The roles of the EU institutions and the sequencing of negotiations

The ambiguity over the sequencing of the withdrawal negotiations and the necessity of a two-agreement solution should be clarified in the text of Article 50. This would include clarifying the role of the Commission as the institution responsible for conducting the negotiations.[90] The wording of Article 218(3) TFEU that clarifies the Commission's role in submitting recommendations to the Council before the nomination of the Union negotiator could be replicated. Clarification of the institutional roles would ensure coherence with the EU's general framework for negotiating international agreements.

A possible further amendment is that the 'framework for future relations' should be replaced by a legally binding mandate for future relationship negotiations. This reform would ensure that the negotiations actually take account of the future relationship, as opposed to a political declaration that is concluded at the end of negotiations as an afterthought.[91] A hard reform to the text of the Treaty could make the conclusion of a treaty on future relations in simplified form a condition for the Treaties to cease to apply. A softer reform would be a commitment for any hypothetical future withdrawal negotiations guidelines to work on separation and future issues in tandem. Provision should also be made for a mandate to be concluded and for negotiations on a future relationship to commence as an integral component of a staggered no deal withdrawal. This would constitutionalize the situation in the Irish Protocol whereby replacement of the transitional regime by a future relationship agreement is explicitly mandated.[92]

G. Proposal 7: EU Citizenship in the withdrawal clause

A major deficiency in Article 50 TEU is the lack of explicit recognition that an automatic effect of withdrawal from the European Union is the extinction of the status of EU citizenship for nationals of that Member State. The text

[90] See criticism in chapter 7 and summary in chapter 8.
[91] See discussion in chapter 7 of the political declaration regarding the future relationship.
[92] See the discussion of the dynamics during Brexit in chapter 7.

should be amended to make it clear not only that a Member State may withdraw through a decision in accordance with its constitutional requirements, but that the necessary consequence of this decision is that individuals *qua* nationals will extinguish their status as EU citizens. The reformed wording would reflect the character of the European Union as a creature of both international treaty law and supranational constitutional law. Primary law confirmation would also resolve the ambiguity that prompted challenges to the Withdrawal Agreement's removal of EU citizenship for UK nationals.[93]

The withdrawal clause should also constitutionalize the protection of citizens' rights. Polak argues that already in the current regime '[citizens] must also be protected by the other institutions in charge of the [withdrawal] process'[94] and that 'it is now impossible to imagine any Article 50 withdrawal agreement from the EU not containing a preferential section dedicated to citizens' rights with specific judicial guarantees'.[95] This proposal would confirm this through explicit confirmation of such protection in Article 50 TEU. Guaranteed protection would reinforce the 'orderliness' of withdrawal for individuals *qua* juridical objects who are exposed to uncertainty over their legal and political status. At present, there is no guarantee of the preservation of citizenship rights beyond the political will of negotiators for bilateral solutions and national legislatures to provide unilateral protection. The extensive legal protection provided by Part Two of the Withdrawal Agreement would have been rendered null by a no deal withdrawal.

This idea could be constitutionalized in primary law by establishing agreement on the holistic protection of citizens' rights as a condition for withdrawal. Although this would not ameliorate the risk of a withdrawing state retreating from such international agreement after finalizing its withdrawal, it would provide far more certainty than the present situation. A more radical proposal would provide for the retention of a status equivalent to EU citizenship by nationals of a withdrawing Member State for the rest of their lifetime. By contrast to the Withdrawal Agreement, this would ensure that individuals from the former Member State also retain their rights as democratic subjects to vote in local and European Parliament elections in an EU Member State. An alternative indirect method to ensure the retention of EU citizenship for former Member State nationals would be to provide a legal competence for fast-track naturalization in the Member State of residence. This would respect

[93] ibid.
[94] Polly Polak, *EU Withdrawal as a Supranational Affair: The Case of Brexit* (Brill Nijhoff 2023) 203.
[95] ibid 238.

the principle that nationality of a Member State is the predicate for holding and retaining EU citizenship. Such a proposal may be controversial due to nationality laws being a last bastion of Member State sovereignty that has not been 'pooled' at the European level. Implementing legislation at the national level would be necessary. Therefore, it may only be realistic to secure a political commitment from the Member State governments that they will legislate to create a special status for former EU citizens in the acquisition of nationality.

If this radical option were feasible, Article 50 could be amended to provide an option either to rely on the protections of the legal status that mimics EU citizenship, akin to the EU–UK Withdrawal Agreement, or instead to enjoy a right to fast-track naturalization in the state of residence. Individuals may choose the former option because they do not feel a sufficiently genuine connection to the Member State that they are resident in to become a national citizen. Furthermore, they may wish to rely upon rights of family reunification that are only available to EU citizens residing in a different Member State which they would lose upon naturalization. Alternatively, naturalization would enable retention of EU citizenship as a status of democratic self-determination rather than just the protection of legal rights. Former Member State nationals could continue to exercise self-determination *qua* EU citizens in local and European Parliament elections, in addition to electing their representatives in the Council *qua* nationals through participation in the national elections of their state of residence. The protection of citizens' rights became an immutable requirement *de facto* for an EU–UK Withdrawal Agreement.[96] Constitutionalizing protection as the default scenario regardless of negotiations ensures certainty for individuals *qua* juridical objects and democratic subjects.

V. Reforming the European Union?

The holistic consideration of the effects of disruption and disintegration for the EU's constitutional order, and the reforms proposed to address these effects, prompts broader consideration of whether the European Union as a whole needs to be reformed. Brexit, the COVID-19 pandemic, the Rule of Law backsliding crisis, the refugee crisis, and now the Ukrainian–Russian war

[96] See discussion of the negotiations leading to the conclusion of the Withdrawal Agreement in chapter 6.

and the question of accession have renewed interest in the topic. The French President Emmanuel Macron has recently raised the existential fate of Europe in the face of these challenges.[97] The Conference on the Future of Europe concluded in 2022[98] and has been followed by an independent Franco–German group report on reforming and enlarging the Union.[99] Proposals that are directly relevant to the triptych of constituted constituent power and the legitimation roles of individuals include changes to the unanimity rules in certain areas, and suggestions to adjust the Article 49 TEU accession process to accommodate the unique situation of a candidate state that finds itself embroiled in armed conflict.

Developments external to the borders of the EU, and the supranational organization's response thereto, may militate in favour of a more intergovernmental and geopolitical conceptualization of European integration that coheres to the 'international treaty' challenger model.[100] By contrast, however, the EU's own internal ruminations upon its future have adopted language and methods that have parallels to the exercise of constituent power and may indicate movement towards the 'federal' model.[101] Regarding external phenomena, the acceptance of Ukraine as a candidate state for EU accession in February 2022 has been conceptualized as a shift to 'integration through war'.[102] This unique context has seen proposals for adaptation of the Article 49 TEU accession process, ranging for a call for immediate accession of Ukraine,[103] to recent exploration of whether differentiation could be introduced into the accession process with major derogations after membership had been confirmed rather

[97] Gérard Araud, '"Our Europe Is Mortal. It Can Die." Decoding Macron's Sorbonne Speech' (*Atlantic Council*, 29 April 2024) <www.atlanticcouncil.org/blogs/new-atlanticist/our-europe-is-mortal-it-can-die-decoding-macrons-sorbonne-speech/> accessed 3 May 2024.

[98] 'Conference on the Future of Europe—Report on the Final Outcome' (*European Parliament*, 2022) <www.europarl.europa.eu/resources/library/media/20220509RES29121/20220509RES29121.pdf> accessed 23 January 2024.

[99] Franco–German Working Group on EU Institutional Reform, 'Sailing on High Seas: Reforming and Enlarging the EU for the 21st Century' (*France Diplomatie–Ministère de l'Europe et des Affaires étrangères*, 2023) <www.diplomatie.gouv.fr/IMG/pdf/20230919_group_of_twelve_report_updated14.12.2023_cle88fb88.pdf> accessed 23 January 2025.

[100] See discussion in chapter 2.

[101] See discussion in chapter 2.

[102] Roman Petrov, 'Applying for EU Membership in Time of War: "Accession through War" of Ukraine' (*IAI Istituto Affari Internazionali*, 3 May 2023) <www.iai.it/en/pubblicazioni/applying-eu-membership-time-war-accession-through-war-ukraine> accessed 24 April 2024.

[103] Dimitry Kochenov, 'Immediate EU Membership for Ukraine? In Conversation with Dimitry Kochenov' (*Review of Democracy*, 20 April 2022) <https://revdem.ceu.edu/2022/04/20/immediate-eu-membership-for-ukraine-in-conversation-with-dimitry-kochenov/> accessed 24 April 2024.

than strict requirements to adapt the entire *acquis communautaire* during candidature.[104]

The resurgence of armed conflict on the European continent has also seen the resuscitation of the 'European Political Community' (at least terminologically), which would have created a deeper political union if it had not been vetoed internally by the French legislature in the 1950s. The rebranded European Political Community would seem to function as a geopolitical alliance on foreign affairs, perhaps bolstering the concept of the European Union as a means of pooling intergovernmental resources on issues that cannot be addressed solely within state borders. This would provide support to the challenger model to supranational constitutionalism of the European Union as intergovernmentalist cooperation.[105]

Internally, by contrast, the 'Conference on the Future of Europe' has pursued the methods and rhetoric of popular sovereignty through the formation of citizens' assemblies in various locations throughout the EU's Member States. Its conclusions have produced numerous recommendations that would further constitutionalize the European Union, including introducing Qualified Majority Voting for the Common Foreign and Security Policy. The institution representing individuals in their role as EU citizens—the European Parliament—has sought to parlay the conclusions into formal revision of the EU Treaties via Article 48 TEU. Further suggestions that the citizens' assemblies that were constituted *ad hoc* for the Conference could be made a permanent feature of the European Union through institutionalization[106] bear striking similarities to Markus Patberg's prescriptions for a Permanent Constituent Assembly to represent individuals in their role as EU citizens.[107] The acceleration of developments concerning the composition of the European Union—both in response to external developments and resulting from internal consideration—suggests a re-opening within intellectual circles of how we theorize European integration and the part that individuals play therewithin. The adoption of the methods and rhetoric of constitutionalism within political circles may suggest a volta in the 'Overton window' with

[104] Sophia Besch and Eric Ciaramella, 'Ukraine's Accession Poses a Unique Conundrum for the EU' (*Carnegie Endowment for International Peace*, 24 October 2023) <https://carnegieendowment.org/2023/10/24/ukraine-s-accession-poses-unique-conundrum-for-eu-pub-90838> accessed 1 May 2024.

[105] See discussion of supranational constitutionalism and its challenger models in chapter 2.

[106] Enrico Letta, 'Much More than a Market: Speed, Security, Solidarity—Empowering the Single Market to Deliver a Sustainable Future and Prosperity for All EU Citizens' (*European Council*, 2024) <www.consilium.europa.eu/media/ny3j24sm/much-more-than-a-market-report-by-enrico-letta.pdf> accessed 31 January 2025.

[107] Markus Patberg, *Constituent Power in the European Union* (OUP 2020).

regard to future development of the Union at Treaty revisions, following the 'de-constitutionalization' at Lisbon that occurred following the failure of the Constitutional Treaty in 2005.

The greatest internal challenge to the European Union during and following Brexit has been the values crisis with Hungary and Poland. The election results that brought Donald Tusk back to power in Poland in 2023 and the success of his government will be a litmus test for whether resistance to the EU's foundational values can be resolved purely through domestic democratic processes.[108] Reforms proposed to opt-outs and withdrawal in the previous sections may be instrumentalized to confront the ongoing challenge of resistance to the EU values by Member States. Proposals published elsewhere to transform Article 7 TEU into a deliberative mechanism may be connected to the reformed opt-out and withdrawal clauses.[109] If the rhetoric of the Fidesz government in Hungary and the Law and Justice government in Poland when it was in power are regarded as grounded in genuine ideological disagreement, then the argument can be made that Article 7 TEU is not the only mechanism to cope with such a situation. The sanctioning mechanism is relevant to breaches of Article 2 TEU values, but the disagreements with supranational constitutionalism that underpin these nationalist actions should be the subject of deliberation during amendment under Article 48 TEU, with the safety valve for failures to resolve disagreement being opt-outs, and withdrawal via Article 50 TEU as a final resort in the case of complete dialogical breakdown.

The United Kingdom's disrupted integration had the potential to mutate into a form of illegitimate constitutional resistance akin to Poland and Hungary, as demonstrated by its legal arguments regarding the illegitimacy of the abolition of border controls in the 1980s.[110] However, the United Kingdom had the opportunity to debate these issues and ultimately secure opt-outs during the four treaty amendments in the fifteen years between 1986 and 2001. By contrast, there have been no ordinary revision procedures for Poland and Hungary to ventilate their own disagreements since the Treaty of Lisbon in 2007, which was concluded three years before Viktor Orbán came to power in Hungary and eight years before Law and Justice took office in Poland. A reform to Article 7 TEU to create a pathway to the mechanisms in the triptych that deal with

[108] Marcin Szwed, 'Rebuilding the Rule of Law: Three Guiding Principles' (*Verfassungsblog*, 29 April 2024) <https://verfassungsblog.de/rebuilding-the-rule-of-law/> accessed 3 May 2024.

[109] Oliver Garner, 'Bridging Brexit and the Values Crisis: From Constitutional Resistance to Deliberation?' (2024) Forum Transregionale Studien 33/2024 re:constitution Working Paper <www.reconstitution.eu/fileadmin/bilder/re_constitution/33-2024_WP_reconstitution_Garner_finalDOI.pdf> accessed 31 January 2025.

[110] ibid 15.

challenge and change—Articles 48 and 50 TEU—could create a new means of addressing values backsliding.

If a deliberative process to deal with constitutional resistance were to lead to discussions on opt-outs, then the reformed mechanism proposed in this chapter means that the other Member States would have control over imposing strict forms of conditionality including the need to demonstrate defined threats to constitutional identity. The context would also be distinct from the situations in which the United Kingdom, Ireland, and Denmark were granted their opt-outs because this Article 48 TEU process would have been commenced purely to deal with the situation of the resistant Member State rather than seeking to deepen integration, and therefore these Member States would not have a veto power over the preferences of the other High Contracting Parties.

If attempts at accommodation failed, the new double-decision structure for the withdrawal clause proposed earlier in this chapter means that it could be used to apply pressure on the resistant Member States. The deferral of a final withdrawal decision means that the other Member States could seek to pressure these states to make a political commitment to decide in accordance with their constitutional requirements whether there is an intention to withdraw. This could induce a zero-sum game whereby if the resistant Member State cannot persuade its constituent partners to adapt European integration to its vision then it should either cease its resistance, or go to its citizens to make a choice whether to cease participation in the European project. The double-decision structure means that the nationals of that Member State would then be plunged into a constituent debate as to whether they value more their participation in European integration, or the aspects of constitutional identity that their government has claimed are inimical to the supranational order.

Enabling debate over the realization of the EU's Article 2 TEU values with resistant Member States could open up a Pandora's Box of intergovernmentalist challenger models to supranational constitutionalism. The lack of salience of the Conference on the Future of Europe may provide definitive proof that even attempts at bottom-up deliberative reform of the European Union will not succeed in bridging the gap of constituent ownership of the integration project. Amendment procedures, and the opt-outs arising therefrom, have demonstrated that the High Contracting Parties remain in control of the law that will apply to EU citizens as juridical objects. The United Kingdom's withdrawal from the European Union demonstrates that EU citizenship may be extinguished through simple majoritarian exercises of democratic subjecthood at the national level. This may make the status too precarious to act as a sustainable base for individuals to exercise constituent power at the supranational level in order to reform the European Union. Any genuine attempt to go beyond the status quo of European integration may need to focus first on transforming citizenship of the European Union into a genuine standalone status of first and last resort for individuals to exercise self-determination.[111]

[111] Liav Orgad and Jules Lepoutre (eds), 'Should EU Citizenship Be Disentangled from Member State Nationality?' (European University Institute 2019) Working Paper EUI RSCAS 2019/24 <https://cadmus.eui.eu/handle/1814/62229> accessed 1 May 2024.

9
Conclusion

The Treaty of Rome represented an exercise of constituent power in international law by the High Contracting Parties to create a supranational constitutional order. This order is a new species of constitutionalism because individuals retain their nationality as their primordial constituent status whilst constructing the new coexistent constituent status of citizenship of the European Union. These roles are co-equivalent in the EU's ordinary norm-creation process as an exercise of democratic subjecthood. Individuals also fulfil the role of juridical objects in the application of EU law. The High Contracting Parties created a triptych of primary law in order to constitutionalize the exercise of constituent power. The triptych ensures a legitimate means to reconstruct the supranational constitutional order without the need to resort to complete disintegration by dissolving the international treaty basis of the European Union. Article 49 TEU enables the extension of the constituent statuses to new individuals, Article 48 TEU mandates the reconstruction of the order, and Article 50 TEU mandates the repatriation of constituent power by a particular class of Member State nationals.

Member State withdrawal functions as a means of regulated partial disintegration of the supranational constitutional order as the territory for the application of norms contracts, and a class of state nationals lose their supranational citizenship. The capacity for a Member State's nationals to repatriate constituent power is a necessary precept of the retention of nationality as the dominant constituent status. The withdrawal clause provides a prescribed constitutional procedure for disintegration that vindicates the sovereign decision of the Member State nationals whilst providing an orderly supranational procedure. Member State opt-outs, by contrast, are not a necessary component of the dual-constituent basis of the supranational constitutional order. This phenomenon of disrupted integration is a product of the particular design of the amendment procedure in Article 48 TEU. The initial Convention involves supranational institutions representing individuals as Member State nationals and EU citizens. The conference that adopts the final amendment, however, is composed solely of the heads of state or government of the High Contracting

Constitutional Disintegration and Disruption. Oliver Garner, Oxford University Press. © Oxford University Press 2025. DOI: 10.1093/9780198914136.003.0009

Parties. The unravelling of the EU legal order during reconstruction enables particular Member State executives to reserve the levelling up of constituent power. Protocols addended to the treaties, rather than a dedicated supranational clause, are utilized to enshrine exemption for certain constituent partners from the creation and application of EU law norms.

Article 50 TEU was created to supranationalize the pre-existing right of Member States to withdraw from the European Union. It enshrined a specialized procedure that is distinct from the residual public international law on treaty exit. Strategically, the clause may have been promulgated to reassure the Member States that were reluctant about further integration. The actual use of the clause may not have been envisaged by the original drafters. The United Kingdom's eventual withdrawal on 31 January 2020 has provided the first case study of the operation of Article 50. The deficiencies during this period may be agglomerated under a general critique that, despite the novelty of a specialized EU Treaty provision, the withdrawal clause still frames disintegration as a process in public international law, rather than a phenomenon that has effects within a supranational constitutional order. The specific problems were the United Kingdom's underdetermination of its 'constitutional requirements' for the decision to withdraw; the ambiguous relationship between this 'decision' to withdraw and 'notification' thereof to the European Council; the temporal vacuum that was opened up between these two actions; the executive discretion for the European Council to determine the initiation and extension of the deconstitutional convention, and the deleterious consequences of no deal withdrawal for the balance between the teloi of Article 50 TEU. The unconditionality and unilaterality of withdrawal at the supranational level are necessary to ensure the dual-constituent foundations of European integration. A number of alterations to the text of Article 50 TEU may enable the withdrawal clause to realize more fruitfully its teloi to provide a sovereign right for the nationals of a Member State *qua* democratic objects to repatriate constituent power, whilst also ensuring an orderly supranational process for this partial disintegration in the interests of all EU citizens *qua* juridical objects.

Member State opt-outs have arisen more haphazardly over two decades as a form of disrupted integration. This phenomenon is not as easy to conceptualize neatly within the framework of the dual-constituent thesis. This exposes the disjuncture between the hypothetical device of an original founding exercise of dual-constituent power, and the reality of the incremental development of the European Union from intergovernmental cooperation to a (predominantly) supranational constitutional order. The decision to bypass reluctant Member States and use international law to establish the Schengen *acquis* on border liberalization set disrupted integration in motion. The other form of origin arose at the Treaty of Maastricht through resistance to the creation of the new constitutional sector of EMU. This confirmed Protocols addended to the Treaties as the legal mechanism to enshrine reserved constituent power. When the Member States sought to incorporate the Schengen *acquis* into the supranational constitutional order during the Treaty of Amsterdam negotiations, the excluded Member States continued their resistance by reserving their constituent power and creating further opt-outs. The opt-outs from the AFSJ represent a mid-point between these two forms of origin and provide further evidence that the incremental reality of European integration has driven disruption. The transfer of competences from the intergovernmental former Third Pillar to the supranational First Pillar at Amsterdam prompted the further reservation of constituent power. This resistance was deepened further when the Pillars were abolished all together at the Treaty of Lisbon.

The opt-out Protocols lead to asymmetry in the quadripartite role of individuals. Territory is demarcated within which EU law does not apply, and certain individuals legitimate these norms solely in their role EU citizens *qua* democratic subjects without any representation *qua* nationals. The flexible opt-in provisions in the AFSJ and Schengen Protocols distort the supranational legislative process by enabling executive discretion over participation in the ordinary creation and application of norms. The Danish opt-out from Schengen undermines supranational constitutionalism by enabling national and international law means of participation. Reform of the Treaties in order to create a new limb of a reconstructed quadriptych of constituted constituent power to mandate and regulate opt-outs would address these asymmetries.

These specific deficiencies mean that disrupted integration through opt-outs is, contrary to expectations, more detrimental to supranational constitutionalism than partial disintegration through withdrawal. This seems paradoxical as the output legitimacy consequences of Member State withdrawal are more dramatic for individuals than the partial disapplication of norms through opt-outs. From the perspective of input and throughput legitimacy, however, withdrawal is subject to a prescribed supranational process rather than the *ad hocism* of the opt-out Protocols. Withdrawal also serves to protect the integrity of the supranational constitutional order from recalcitrant Member States. The United Kingdom's renegotiation of membership in February 2016 threatened inroads into the juridical rights of EU citizenship in addition to the telos of 'ever closer union'. This Decision demonstrated a Member State that was not only symbolically closer to disintegration, but also practically through the condition that the pre-binding of the constituent powers could only come into force upon notification of a decision to remain in the European Union.

Opt-outs have been presented as a means to prevent Member State withdrawal, and the possibility of Member State withdrawal has been presented as an incentive to prevent opt-outs. The withdrawal of the Member State that has been the leading protagonist in reserving constituent power prompts a reconsideration of the relationship between disrupted integration and disintegration. The material conditions within which the nationals of a Member State decided to repatriate constituent power were shaped by a sustained strategy of reserving constituent power as an executive preference with minimal input from individuals *qua* democratic subjects. The result has been a distinctly disconnected experience for United Kingdom nationals *qua* juridical objects. Opt-outs from Schengen, the AFSJ, and EMU distanced the United Kingdom from the experience of the Eurozone and migration crises in the last decade. Supranational constitutional innovation generated contestation, which in turn generated the deconstitutional innovations of disruption and disintegration. This innovation has been presented as a restoration of the status quo of national constitutionalism to reverse supranational mutations for which UK nationals never provided their consent.

This experience was distinct from the other opt-out Member States of Ireland and Denmark. The Irish government were compelled to pursue an opt-out strategy in order to ensure harmonization with the United Kingdom's legal regime on border controls. Post-withdrawal, this relationship has generated 'differentiated disintegration' with the continuing application of EU law in the UK territory of Northern Ireland. Denmark's retention of constituent power had been legitimated and re-legitimated by nationals *qua* democratic subjects through clearly mandated national constitutional procedures. This continuing discourse on levelling up constituent power was born out of the possibility of a *de facto* withdrawal from the European Union following the Maastricht treaty referendum rejection by the Danish electorate. This provides a converse dynamic in the relationship between disintegration and disrupted integration in comparison to the United Kingdom.

The emergence of disintegration through Brexit may also require a reappraisal of the consequences and value of differentiated integration in the European Union. The withdrawal of the key proponent of opt-outs means that a phenomenon that was regarded as a temporal form of disrupted or deferred integration at the time of the Treaty amendments may now more properly be considered to be deferred disintegration. The debates during the 2016 referendum campaign concerning sovereignty took the same form as the arguments during the Maastricht ratification and the creation of the first example of an opt-out Protocol. The United Kingdom's experience suggests a relational dialectic between European integration and disintegration. Differentiation creates a legitimacy deficit through the lack of consent of a subset of constituent nationals. This deficit is repaid when attempts at supranational uniformity are made at future Treaty amendments. A precarious state of disrupted (dis)integration can only persist for so long before it needs to be resolved in favour of one outcome or the other. This relation may inform the future development of Ireland and Denmark's participation in European integration. Those who propose further differentiated integration as a solution to the EU's current challenges should also take heed. The short-term success of overcoming Member State vetoes to secure a Treaty amendment ratification can gestate a long-term legacy of disintegration.

The dual-constituent thesis can be used to explain and critique disrupted integration and disintegration, but these phenomena also challenge the explanatory and normative validity of the thesis. The fact that the Member States dominate the Article 48 TEU process with a diminished role for the supranational institutions representing citizens of the Union has enabled the retention of constituent power. The prerogative of Member State nationals to extinguish EU citizenship for themselves is enshrined in Article 50 TEU. Withdrawal is the ultimate rejection by a Member State population of the idea that constituent power should be shared with a supranational subject. Opt-outs are the symptoms of the malaise. Disruption and disintegration are evidence that nationality of a Member State remains the dominant constituent status in Europe. Rather than a co-equivalent means to exercise a *pouvoir constituant mixte*, citizenship of the European Union is a parasitic status that is precariously dependent on the democratic will of nationals. Entirely domestic exercises of simple majoritarian democracy can completely extinguish EU citizenship as a means for democratic and juridical self-determination. Disintegration has exposed the precarity of EU citizenship. It remains to be seen whether the extinction of the status for a class of former Member State nationals may prompt a counter-reaction whereby individuals who do regard EU citizenship as a fundamental constituent status engage in an exercise of emancipatory constituent power to protect its continuing existence against future disintegration.

Since the existential membership crisis of Brexit, the European Union has faced the further material crises of COVID-19 and the Russian invasion of Ukraine. These short-term irruptions are framed by the longer perspective of climate catastrophe as the greatest threat to the well-being of Europeans and the rest of the world's citizens. As a mirror image to the conceptual disruption of opt-outs eventually leading to the United Kingdom's withdrawal, the total material disruption of armed invasion has resulted in Ukraine's application for accession to the Union. The dire consequences of loss of life from both pandemic and man-made violence may have provided perspective upon the real costs of Brexit—although the potential human disruption that could arise from the new international law footing for relations should not be underplayed, particularly in the tenuous resolution found for the Irish border. The dynamic of the European Parliament elections of 2019 being framed as a battle for the soul of Europe between nationalists and supranationalists may only be exacerbated in the 2024 elections, the first to be held without the participation of the United Kingdom. Ultimately, the future of supranational constitutionalism and the viability of the quadripartite role that individuals play therein may depend upon whether political actors can more successfully persuade the citizens of Europe that the appropriate level for the resolution of the threats to Europe's existential security lies within the borders of the nation-state or beyond.

Bibliography

I. Secondary literature

R Adler-Nissen, *Opting Out of the European Union: Diplomacy, Sovereignty and European Integration* (CUP 2014)

G Agamben and S Wakefield, 'What Is a Destituent Power?' (2014) 32 Environment and Planning D: Society and Space 65

KJ Alter, 'Who Are the "Masters of the Treaty"? European Governments and the European Court of Justice' (1998) 52 International Organization 121

S Anglesey, 'Does Geert Wilders's Election Mean Nexit Is on the Horizon?' (*The New European*, 25 November 2023) <www.theneweuropean.co.uk/does-geert-wilderss-election-mean-nexit-is-on-the-horizon/> accessed 1 December 2023

G Araud, '"Our Europe Is Mortal. It Can Die". Decoding Macron's Sorbonne Speech' (*Atlantic Council*, 29 April 2024) <www.atlanticcouncil.org/blogs/new-atlanticist/our-europe-is-mortal-it-can-die-decoding-macrons-sorbonne-speech/> accessed 3 May 2024

H Arendt, *On Revolution* (Penguin Classics 2009)

H Arendt, *The Origins of Totalitarianism* (Penguin Classics 2017)

K Armstrong, 'Reincarnation and Resurrection—the Afterlife of the European Communities Act 1972 in the Withdrawal Bill' (*divergence*, 22 October 2019) <https://divergence.blog/2019/10/22/reincarnation-and-resurrection-the-afterlife-of-the-european-communities-act-1972-in-the-withdrawal-bill/> accessed 30 April 2024

A Aust, 'Treaties, Termination' in *Max Planck Encyclopaedia of International Law* (Oxford Public International Law 2006) <https://opil.ouplaw.com/display/10.1093/law:epil/9780199231690/law-9780199231690-e1491> accessed 30 March 2020

L Azoulai, 'Transfiguring European Citizenship: From Member State Territory to Union Territory' in Dimitry Kochenov (ed), *EU Citizenship and Federalism* (CUP 2017)

R Badinter, 'Contribution from M. Robert Badinter, Alternate Member of the Convention, "A European Constitution" CONV 317/02 CONTRIB 105, Brussels, 30 September 2002 (OR. Fr)'

P Bárd and VZ Kazai, 'Enforcement of a Formal Conception of the Rule of Law as a Potential Way Forward to Address Backsliding: Hungary as a Case Study' (2022) 14 Hague Journal on the Rule of Law 165

S Bardutzky and E Fahey (eds), *Framing the Subjects and Objects of Contemporary EU Law* (Edward Elgar Publishing 2017)

C Barnard, 'The "Opt-Out" for the UK and Poland from the Charter of Fundamental Rights: Triumph of Rhetoric over Reality?' in Stefan Griller and Jacques Ziller (eds), *The Lisbon Treaty: EU Constitutionalism without a Constitutional Treaty?* (Springer 2008)

JP Beetz, 'From Practice to Principle and Back: Applying a New Realist Method to the European Union's Democratic Deficit' (2018) 66 Political Studies 339

R Bellamy, *A Republican Europe of States* (CUP 2019)

R Bellamy and S Kröger, 'A Demoicratic Justification of Differentiated Integration in a Heterogeneous EU' (2017) 39 Journal of European Integration 625

R Bellamy and S Kröger, 'Differentiated Integration as a Fair Scheme of Cooperation' (European University Institute 2019) Robert Schuman Centre for Advanced Studies Research Paper No RSCAS 2019/27

S Besch and E Ciaramella, 'Ukraine's Accession Poses a Unique Conundrum for the EU' (*Carnegie Endowment for International Peace*, 24 October 2023) <https://carnegieendowment.org/2023/10/24/ukraine-s-accession-poses-unique-conundrum-for-eu-pub-90838> accessed 1 May 2024

T Beukers, B De Witte and C Kilpatrick, *Constitutional Change through Euro-Crisis Law* (CUP 2017)

J Black, 'From Mood to Movement: English Nationalism, the European Union and Taking Back Control' (2019) 32 Innovation: The European Journal of Social Science Research 191

V Bogdanor, 'Why the People Should Have a Vote on Maastricht: The House of Lords Must Uphold Democracy and Insist on a Referendum, Says Vernon Bogdanor' *The Independent* (London, 8 June 1993) <www.independent.co.uk/voices/why-the-people-should-have-a-vote-on-maastricht-the-house-of-lords-must-uphold-democracy-and-insist-1490346.html> accessed 21 April 2020

V Bogdanor, 'After the Referendum, the People, Not Parliament, Are Sovereign' *Financial Times* (London, FT Weekend 10 December 2016) 14.

V Bogdanor, *Beyond Brexit: Britain's Unprotected Constitution* (IB Tauris 2019)

T van den Brink and V Passalacqua (eds), *Balancing Unity and Diversity in EU Legislation* (Edward Elgar Publishing 2024)

H Brunkhorst, *Solidarity: From Civic Friendship to a Global Legal Community* (MIT Press 2005)

T Bryant, 'How the British Conception of Sovereignty Makes EU Membership Untenable' (*BrexitCentral*, 27 September 2019) <https://brexitcentral.com/how-the-british-conception-of-sovereignty-makes-eu-membership-untenable/> accessed 2 April 2020

G Butler, 'Europe's "Other" Open-Border Zone: The Common Travel Area under the Shadow of Brexit' (2018) 20 Cambridge Yearbook of European Legal Studies 252

C Calliess and G van der Schyff (eds), *Constitutional Identity in a Europe of Multilevel Constitutionalism* (CUP 2019)

F Cheneval, *The Government of the Peoples: On the Idea and Principles of Multilateral Democracy* (Palgrave Macmillan 2011)

F Cheneval, S Lavenex and F Schimmelfennig, 'Demoi-Cracy in the European Union: Principles, Institutions, Policies' (2015) 22 Journal of European Public Policy 1

'Clarity Act | Canadian History' (*Britannica*) <www.britannica.com/topic/Clarity-Act> accessed 23 April 2024

HD Clarke, M Goodwin and P Whiteley, *Brexit: Why Britain Voted to Leave the European Union* (CUP 2017)

C Closa, 'Is Article 50 Reversible? On Politics Beyond Legal Doctrine' (*Verfassungsblog*, 4 January 2017) <https://verfassungsblog.de/is-article-50-reversible-on-politics-beyond-legal-doctrine/> accessed 16 April 2020

C Closa, 'Interpreting Article 50: Exit, Voice and ... What About Loyalty?' in Carlos Closa (ed), *Secession from a Member State and Withdrawal from the European Union: Troubled Membership* (CUP 2017)

C Closa (ed), *Secession from a Member State and Withdrawal from the European Union: Troubled Membership* (CUP 2017)

C Closa and D Kochenov (eds), *Reinforcing Rule of Law Oversight in the European Union* (CUP 2016)

JL Cohen, *Globalization and Sovereignty: Rethinking Legality, Legitimacy, and Constitutionalism* (CUP 2012)

'Conference on the Future of Europe—Report on the Final Outcome' (*European Parliament*, 2022) <www.europarl.europa.eu/resources/library/media/20220509RES29121/20220509RES29121.pdf> accessed 25 January 2025

'Conservative Party Manifesto 2015—The Full Pdf' *The Guardian* (London, 14 April 2015) <www.theguardian.com/politics/2015/apr/14/conservative-party-manifesto-2015-the-full-pdf> accessed 7 April 2020

L Cook and S Petrequin, 'EU Agrees to $54 Billion Ukraine Aid Package despite Hungary's Threat' (*AP News*, 1 February 2024) <https://apnews.com/article/ukraine-war-russia-hungary-eu-summit-budget-6d0f11bc16b4b21073f92925de2046e4> accessed 30 April 2024

P Craig, 'Brexit: A Drama in Six Acts' (2016) 41 European Law Review 447

R Craig, 'New Article 50 Case Resoundingly Rejected by the Divisional Court' (*UK Constitutional Law Association*, 26 June 2018) <https://ukconstitutionallaw.org/2018/06/26/robert-craig-new-article-50-case-resoundingly-rejected-by-the-divisional-court/> accessed 8 April 2020

D Curtin, 'The Constitutional Structure of the Union: A Europe of Bits and Pieces' (1993) 30 Common Market Law Review 17

D Curtin and C Fasone, 'Differentiated Representation: Is a Flexible European Parliament Desirable?' in Bruno De Witte, Andrea Ott and Ellen Vos (eds), *Between Flexibility and Disintegration: The Trajectory of Differentiation in EU Law* (Edward Elgar Publishing 2017)

A Cuyvers, 'Wightman, Brexit, and the Sovereign Right to Remain' (2019) 56 Common Market Law Review 1303

'David Cameron Blocks EU-Wide Deal to Tackle Euro Crisis' *BBC News* (9 December 2011) <www.bbc.com/news/uk-16104275> accessed 27 April 2020

M Dawson and F De Witte, 'Constitutional Balance in the EU after the Euro-Crisis' (2013) 76 The Modern Law Review 817

M Dawson and F De Witte, 'Self-Determination in the Constitutional Future of the EU' (2015) 21 European Law Journal 371

G De Búrca, 'Differentiation within the Core: The Case of the Internal Market' in Gráinne De Búrca and Joanne Scott (eds), *Constitutional Change in the EU: From Uniformity to Flexibility?* (Hart Publishing 2000)

G De Búrca and Jo Scott (eds), *Constitutional Change in the EU: From Uniformity to Flexibility?* (Hart Publishing 2000)

GM De Vries and TJAM De Bruijn, 'Suggestion for Amendment of Article: 59' (*European Convention*, 2003) <https://web.archive.org/web/20220121204954/http://european-convention.europa.eu/docs/Treaty/pdf/46/art46vriesEN.pdf> accessed 3 April 2020

B De Witte, 'Old-Fashioned Flexibility: International Agreements between Member States of the European Union' in Gráinne de Búrca and Joanne Scott (eds), *Constitutional Change in the EU: From Uniformity to Flexibility?* (Hart Publishing 2000)

B De Witte, 'European Union Law: How Autonomous is its Legal Order?' (2010) 65 Zeitschrift für öffentliches Recht 141

B De Witte, 'Treaty Revision Procedures after Lisbon' in Andrea Biondi, Piet Eeckhout and Stefanie Ripley (eds), *EU Law after Lisbon* (OUP 2012)

B De Witte, 'Variable Geometry and Differentiation as Structural Features of the EU Legal Order' in Bruno De Witte, Andrea Ott and Ellen Vos (eds), *Between Flexibility and Disintegration: The Trajectory of Differentiation in the EU* (Edward Elgar Publishing 2017)

B De Witte, 'The Law as Tool and Constraint of Differentiated Integration' (European University Institute 2019) Working Paper EUI RSCAS, 2019/47 <http://cadmus.eui.eu//handle/1814/63604> accessed 26 April 2020

B De Witte, 'The Legal Feasibility and Constitutional Acceptability of Differentiated Integration' (Kick-off Meeting H2020 Project InDivEU Integrating Difference in the European Union, European University Institute, 24 January 2019)

B De Witte, 'EU Law: Is It International Law?' in Catherine Barnard and Steve Peers (eds), *European Union Law* (3rd edn, OUP 2020)

B De Witte, D Hanf and E Vos, *The Many Faces of Differentiation in EU Law* (Intersentia 2001)

B De Witte, A Ott and E Vos, *Between Flexibility and Disintegration: The Trajectory of Differentiation in EU Law* (Edward Elgar Publishing 2017)

F De Witte, 'Freedom of Movement Needs to Be Defended as the Core of EU Citizenship' in Rainer Bauböck (ed), *Debating European Citizenship* (Springer 2019)

J Delors, 'Report on Economic and Monetary Union in the European Community by Committee for the Study of Economic and Monetary Union Presented 17 April 1989' (1989) EU Commission—Working Document

Department of the Taoiseach, 'Joint Statement by Taoiseach Leo Varadkar and Prime Minister Boris Johnson' (*Gov.ie*, 10 October 2019) <https://gov.ie/en/press-release/e3a113-joint-statement-by-an-taoiseach-leo-varadkar-and-prime-minister-bori/> accessed 17 April 2020

D Dixon, 'Article 50 and Member State Sovereignty' (2018) 19 German Law Journal 901

M Dougan, 'The Treaty of Lisbon 2007: Winning Minds, Not Hearts' (2008) 45 Common Market Law Review 617

M Dougan, 'An Airbag for the Crash Test Dummies? EU–UK Negotiations for a Post-Withdrawal "Status Quo" Transitional Regime under Article 50 TEU' (2018) 55 Common Market Law Review 57

M Dougan, *The UK's Withdrawal from the EU: A Legal Analysis* (OUP 2021)

D Duguid and A Jack, 'UK Government Will Not Be Seeking an Extension to the EU Exit Transition Period' (*GOV.UK*, 12 June 2020) <www.gov.uk/government/news/uk-government-will-not-be-seeking-an-extension-to-the-eu-exit-transition-period> accessed 30 April 2024

G Duke, 'European Constitutionalism and Constituent Power' (2019) 44 European Law Review 49

'Dutch Say "No" to EU Constitution' (*BBC News*, 2 June 2005) <http://news.bbc.co.uk/1/hi/4601439.stm> accessed 23 January 2020

R Dworkin, *Law's Empire* (Harvard UP 1986)

K Dyson and K Featherstone, *The Road To Maastricht: Negotiating Economic and Monetary Union* (OUP 1999)

'Edinburgh European Summit—Conclusions of the Presidency' (*European Parliament*, 11–12 December 1992) <www.europarl.europa.eu/summits/edinburgh/default_en.htm> accessed 17 December 2018

SD Edward and others, 'In the Matter of Article 50 of the Treaty on European Union: Opinion' [2017]

P Eeckhout and E Frantziou, 'Brexit and Article 50 TEU: A Constitutionalist Reading' (2017) 54 Common Market Law Review 695

P Eleftheriadis, *A Union of Peoples* (OUP 2020)
N El-Enany, 'The Perils of Differentiated Integration in the Field of Asylum' in Bruno De Witte, Andrea Ott and Ellen Vos (eds), *Between Flexibility and Disintegration* (Edward Elgar Publishing 2017)
BL Elliott, W Hutton and J Wolf, 'September 17 1992: Pound Drops out of ERM' *The Guardian* (London, 17 September 1992) <www.theguardian.com/business/1992/sep/17/emu.theeuro> accessed 27 January 2020
M Elliott, 'Reflections on the HS2 Case: A Hierarchy of Domestic Constitutional Norms and the Qualified Primacy of EU Law' (*UK Constitutional Law Association*, 23 January 2014) <https://ukconstitutionallaw.org/2014/01/23/mark-elliott-reflections-on-the-hs2-case-a-hierarchy-of-domestic-constitutional-norms-and-the-qualified-primacy-of-eu-law/> accessed 8 April 2020
M Elliott, AL Young and J Williams, 'The Miller Tale: An Introduction' in Mark Elliott, Alison L Young and Jack Williams (eds), *The UK Constitution after Miller: Brexit and Beyond* (Hart Publishing 2018)
C Enders, 'Human Dignity in Germany' in Paolo Becchi and Klaus Mathis (eds), *Handbook of Human Dignity in Europe* (Springer 2018)
'EU Solidarity with Ukraine—European Commission' (26 February 2022) <https://eu-solidarity-ukraine.ec.europa.eu/index_en> accessed 1 May 2024
EU-27, 'Informal Meeting at 27—Brussels, 29 June 2016—Statement' (*European Council*, 29 June 2016) <www.consilium.europa.eu/en/press/press-releases/2016/06/29/27ms-informal-meeting-statement/> accessed 13 April 2020
European Central Bank, 'European Monetary Cooperation Fund (1973-93)' (*European Central Bank*) <www.ecb.europa.eu/ecb/access_to_documents/archives/emcf/html/index.en.html> accessed 27 January 2020
European Commission, 'Accession Criteria' (*European Neighbourhood Policy And Enlargement Negotiations—European Commission*, 6 December 2016) <https://ec.europa.eu/neighbourhood-enlargement/policy/glossary/terms/accession-criteria_en> accessed 17 December 2018
European Commission, 'President Juncker Appoints Michel Barnier as Chief Negotiator in Charge of the Preparation and Conduct of the Negotiations with the United Kingdom under Article 50 of the TEU' <https://ec.europa.eu/commission/presscorner/detail/en/IP_16_2652> accessed 14 April 2020
European Council, 'European Council (Art. 50) Guidelines for Brexit Negotiations' (*European Council*, 29 April 2017) <www.consilium.europa.eu/en/press/press-releases/2017/04/29/euco-brexit-guidelines/> accessed 17 December 2018
European Council, 'European Council – Nice, 7–10 December 2000: Conclusions of the Presidency' <www.europarl.europa.eu/summits/nice1_en.htm> accessed 27 January 2020
European Policy Centre, 'Making Sense of the Treaty of Amsterdam' (1997)
A Evans, 'Planning for Brexit: The Case of the 1975 Referendum' (2018) 89 The Political Quarterly 127
F Fabbrini, 'Enhanced Cooperation under Scrutiny: Revisiting the Law and Practice of Multi-Speed Integration in Light of the First Involvement of the EU Judiciary' (2013) 40 Legal Issues of Economic Integration 197
F Fabbrini, *Brexit and the Future of the European Union: The Case for Constitutional Reforms* (OUP 2020)
F Fabbrini (ed), *The Law & Politics of Brexit: Volume III: The Framework of New EU–UK Relations* (OUP 2021)

F Fabbrini and O Pollicino, 'Constitutional Identity in Italy' in Christian Calliess and Gerhard van der Schyff (eds), *Constitutional Identity in a Europe of Multilevel Constitutionalism* (CUP 2019)

F Fabbrini and R Schmidt, 'The Extension of UK Membership in the EU: Causes and Consequences' [2019] European Journal of Legal Studies 87

H Farnleitner, 'Suggestion for Amendment of Article I-59' (*DORIE—European Commission*, 2003) <https://dorie.ec.europa.eu/en/details/-/card/89821> accessed 3 April 2020

M Fichera, *The Foundations of the EU as a Polity* (Edward Elgar Publishing 2018)

J Fischer, 'Suggestion for Amendment of Article: 46' (*DORIE—European Commission*, 2003) <https://dorie.ec.europa.eu/en/details/-/card/90009> accessed 3 April 2020

M Fletcher, 'EU Criminal Law Flexibility: What Lessons from the UK Protocol No 36 Saga?' in Valsamis Mitsilegas, Maria Bergström and Theodore Konstadinides (eds), *Research Handbook on EU Criminal Law* (Edward Elgar Publishing 2016)

J Fontanella-Khan, 'Geert Wilders Outlines Case for a Dutch "Nexit" from the EU' *Financial Times* (The Hague, 7 February 2014) 3

J Fouchet, 'DON'T TOUCH MY EU CITIZENSHIP' (*CrowdJustice*) <www.crowdjustice.com/case/dont-touch-my-european-citizenship/> accessed 17 April 2020

T Fournier, 'From Rhetoric to Action, a Constitutional Analysis of Populism' (2019) 20 German Law Journal 362

Franco–German Working Group on EU Institutional Reform, 'Sailing on High Seas: Reforming and Enlarging the EU for the 21st Century' (*France Diplomatie–Ministère de l'Europe et des Affaires étrangères*, 2023) <www.diplomatie.gouv.fr/IMG/pdf/20230919_group_of_twelve_report_updated14.12.2023_cle88fb88.pdf>

'French Say Firm "No" to EU Treaty' (*BBC News*, 30 May 2005) <http://news.bbc.co.uk/1/hi/world/europe/4592243.stm> accessed 23 January 2020

O Garner, 'After Brexit: Protecting European Citizens and Citizenship from Fragmentation' (European University Institute 2016) EUI Law Department Working Paper No 2016/22 <https://papers.ssrn.com/abstract=2871404> accessed 1 February 2017

O Garner, 'Why All Member States Should Clarify Their Constitutional Requirements for Withdrawing from the EU' (*Verfassungsblog*, 2 November 2016) <https://verfassungsblog.de/why-all-member-states-should-clarify-their-constitutional-requirements-for-withdrawing-from-the-eu/> accessed 18 December 2018

O Garner, 'Referring Brexit to the Court of Justice of the European Union: Why Revoking an Article 50 Notice Should Be Left to the United Kingdom' (*European Law Blog*, 14 November 2016) <https://europeanlawblog.eu/2016/11/14/referring-brexit-to-the-court-of-justice-of-the-european-union-why-revoking-an-article-50-notice-should-be-left-to-the-united-kingdom/> accessed 9 April 2020

O Garner, 'The Borders of European Integration on Trial in the Member States: Dansk Industri, Miller, and Taricco' (2017) 9 European Journal of Legal Studies 1

O Garner, 'Conditional Primacy of EU Law: The United Kingdom Supreme Court's Own "Solange (so Long as)" Doctrine?' (*UK Constitutional Law Association*, 31 January 2017) <https://ukconstitutionallaw.org/2017/01/31/oliver-garner-conditional-primacy-of-eu-law-the-united-kingdom-supreme-courts-own-solange-so-long-as-doctrine/> accessed 8 April 2020

O Garner, 'After Article 50 and Before Withdrawal: Does Constitutional Theory Require a General Election in the United Kingdom Before Brexit?' (*Verfassungsblog*, 24 March 2017) <https://verfassungsblog.de/after-article-50-and-before-withdrawal-does-constitutional-theory-require-a-general-election-in-the-united-kingdom-before-brexit/> accessed 7 April 2020

O Garner, 'Does Member State Withdrawal from the European Union Extinguish EU Citizenship? C/13/640244 / KG ZA 17-1327 of the Rechtbank Amsterdam ("The Amsterdam Case")' (*European Law Blog*, 19 February 2018) <https://europeanlawblog.eu/2018/02/19/does-member-state-withdrawal-from-the-european-union-extinguish-eu-citizenship-c13640244-kg-za-17-1327-rechtbank-amsterdam-the-amsterdam-case/> accessed 17 April 2020

O Garner, 'The Existential Crisis of Citizenship of the European Union: The Argument for an Autonomous Status' (2018) 20 Cambridge Yearbook of European Legal Studies 116

O Garner, 'Reforming Withdrawal and Opt-Outs from the European Union: A Dual-Constituent Perspective' (DCU Brexit Institute 2018) DCU Brexit Institute Working Paper N.11 2018 <https://papers.ssrn.com/abstract=3303938> accessed 29 March 2020

O Garner, 'The Benn-Burt Extension Act: A Roadblock to a No-Deal Brexit?' (*UK Constitutional Law Association*, 13 September 2019) <https://ukconstitutionallaw.org/2019/09/13/oliver-garner-the-benn-burt-extension-act-a-roadblock-to-a-no-deal-brexit/> accessed 13 April 2022

O Garner, 'The New Irish Protocol Could Lead to the Indefinite Jurisdiction of the EU Court of Justice within the UK' (*LSE Brexit*, 23 October 2019) <https://blogs.lse.ac.uk/brexit/2019/10/23/the-new-irish-protocol-could-lead-to-the-indefinite-jurisdiction-of-the-court-of-justice-of-the-european-union-within-the-united-kingdom/> accessed 17 April 2020

O Garner, 'Written Evidence Submitted to the House of Commons Committee on the Future Relationship with the European Union: The EU–UK Joint Committee' (*Bingham Centre for the Rule of Law*, 15 May 2020) <https://binghamcentre.biicl.org/publications/written-evidence-submitted-to-the-house-of-commons-committee-on-the-future-relationship-with-the-european-union-the-eu-uk-joint-committee> accessed 20 October 2023

O Garner, 'Seven Reforms to Article 50 TEU' [2021] European Law Review 784

O Garner, 'Part Three of the EU-UK TCA—From a "Disrupted" Area of Freedom, Security and Justice to "New Old" Intergovernmentalism in Justice and Home Affairs?' (DCU Brexit Institute 2021) Brexit Institute Working Paper Series, No 1/2021 <https://papers.ssrn.com/abstract=3778183> accessed 4 February 2021

O Garner, 'Bridging Brexit and the Values Crisis: From Constitutional Resistance to Deliberation?' (2024) Forum Transregionale Studien 33/2024 re:constitution Working Paper <www.reconstitution.eu/fileadmin/bilder/re_constitution/33-2024_WP_reconstitution_Garner_finalDOI.pdf> accessed 31 January 2025

A Geddes, *Britain and the European Union* (Palgrave 2013)

P Genschel and M Jachtenfuchs (eds), *Beyond the Regulatory Polity? The European Integration of Core State Powers* (OUP 2013)

T Giegerich, 'Treaties, Multilateral, Reservations To' in *Max Planck Encyclopaedia of International Law* (Oxford Public International Law 2010) <https://opil.ouplaw.com/view/10.1093/law:epil/9780199231690/law-9780199231690-e1680> accessed 30 March 2020

A Gliszczyńska-Grabias and W Sadurski, 'Is It Polexit Yet? Comment on Case K 3/21 of 7 October 2021 by the Constitutional Tribunal of Poland' (2023) 19 European Constitutional Law Review 163

M Goldoni and MA Wilkinson, 'The Material Constitution' (2018) 81 The Modern Law Review 567

S Goodwin, 'The Vote of Confidence: Major Wins Gamble on Social Chapter Vote' *The Independent* (London, 23 July 1993) <www.independent.co.uk/news/uk/the-vote-of-confidence-major-wins-gamble-on-social-chapter-vote-1486708.html> accessed 7 April 2020

M Gordon, 'Brexit: The Relationship between the UK Parliament and the UK Government' in Michael Dougan (ed), *The UK After Brexit: Legal and Policy Challenges* (Intersentia 2017)

HM Government, 'The Windsor Framework' (*GOV.UK*, 30 January 2024) < www.gov.uk/government/publications/the-windsor-framework> accessed 30 April 2024

A Gray, 'Article 50 Author Lord Kerr: I Didn't Have UK in Mind' (*POLITICO*, 28 March 2017) < www.politico.eu/article/brexit-article-50-lord-kerr-john-kerr/> accessed 17 December 2018

A Grayling, 'The EU Referendum Was Gerrymandered' (*LSE Brexit*, 28 September 2017) <https://blogs.lse.ac.uk/brexit/2017/09/28/the-eu-referendum-was-gerrymandered/> accessed 7 April 2020

M Griera, 'EU Parliament Draws Up Plan for Countries to Overcome Unanimity' (*Euractiv*, 12 July 2023) <https://web.archive.org/web/20230712043842/www.euractiv.com/section/politics/news/eu-parliament-draws-up-plan-for-countries-to-overcome-unanimity/> accessed 30 April 2024

JAG Griffith, 'The Political Constitution' (1979) 42 The Modern Law Review 1

D Grimm, M Wendel and T Reinbacher, 'European Constitutionalism and the German Basic Law' in Anneli Albi and Samo Bardutzky (eds), *National Constitutions in European and Global Governance: Democracy, Rights, the Rule of Law: National Reports* (TMC Asser Press 2019)

JH Haahr, '"Our Danish Democracy": Community, People and Democracy in the Danish Debate on the Common Currency' (2003) 38 Cooperation and Conflict 27

J Habermas, 'Citizenship and National Identity: Some Reflections on the Future of Europe' (1992) 12 Praxis International 1

J Habermas, 'On the Internal Relation between the Rule of Law and Democracy' (1995) 3 European Journal of Philosophy 12

J Habermas, *Between Facts and Norms: Contributions to a Discourse Theory of Law and Democracy* (new edn, Polity Press 1997)

J Habermas, *The Crisis of the European Union: A Response* (Polity Press 2013)

J Habermas, 'Citizen and State Equality in a Supranational Political Community: Degressive Proportionality and the *Pouvoir Constituant Mixte*' (2017) 55 Journal of Common Market Studies 171

TC Halliday, *Transnational Legal Orders* (CUP 2016)

HLA Hart, *The Concept of Law* (3rd edn, OUP 2012)

M Hedemann-Robinson, 'The Area of Freedom, Security and Justice with Regard to the UK, Ireland and Denmark: The "Opt-in Opt-Outs" under the Treaty of Amsterdam' in David O'Keefe and Patrick Twomey (eds), *Legal Issues of the Amsterdam Treaty* (Hart Publishing 2000)

LE Hill, CE Butler and SA Lorenzen, 'Inflation and the Destruction of Democracy: The Case of the Weimar Republic' (1977) 11 Journal of Economic Issues 299

C Hillion, 'This Way, Please! A Legal Appraisal of the EU Withdrawal Clause' in Carlos Closa (ed), *Secession from a Member State and Withdrawal from the European Union: Troubled Membership* (CUP 2017)

C Hillion, 'Poland and Hungary are Withdrawing from the EU' (*Verfassungsblog*, 27 April 2020) <https://verfassungsblog.de/poland-and-hungary-are-withdrawing-from-the-eu/> accessed 27 April 2020

S Hocking, D Harrison and A von Westernhagen, 'DAC Beachcroft Files Landmark Case with General Court of the EU on Behalf of a Group of UK Nationals' (*DAC Beachcroft*) <https://web.archive.org/web/20200501213655/https://www.dacbeachcroft.com/en/

gb/news/2020/april/dac-beachcroft-files-landmark-case-with-general-court-of-the-eu-on-behalf-of-a-group-of-uk-nationals/> accessed 25 April 2020

H Hofmeister, '"Should I Stay or Should I Go?" A Critical Analysis of the Right to Withdraw from the EU' (2010) 16 European Law Journal 589

C Hooton and J Stone, 'Brexit: Article 50 Was Never Actually Meant to be Used, Says its Author' *The Independent* (London, 26 July 2016) <www.independent.co.uk/news/uk/politics/brexit-eu-referendum-britain-theresa-may-article-50-not-supposed-meant-to-be-used-trigger-giuliano-a7156656.html> accessed 4 April 2020

M Höpner, 'Should Sweden Adopt the Euro?' (Swedish Institute for European Policy Studies) Issue 2017: 12epa <https://sieps.se/en/publications/2017/should-sweden-adopt-the-euro/> accessed 23 April 2024

T Horsley, *The Court of Justice of the European Union as an Institutional Actor: Judicial Lawmaking and Its Limits* (CUP 2018)

A Horst-Neidhardt, 'An Ever Looser Union among the Peoples of Europe?' (*European University Institute*, 12 January 2016) <https://me.eui.eu/alberto-horst-neidhardt/blog/an-ever-looser-union-among-the-people-of-europe/> accessed 23 April 2020

House of Commons Hansard Debate on Economic and Monetary Union, 27 October 1997, cols 583–4

House of Commons Hansard Debates for 20 November 1991, vol 199, col 274

House of Commons Hansard Debates for 23 July 1993, vol 229, cols 625–724

House of Lords European Union Committee, 'The UK's Opt-in Protocol: Implications of the Government's Approach' (House of Lords European Union Committee 2015) Ninth Report of Session 2014-2015 (HL Paper 136)

M Hunt, 'In a Democracy the Rule of Law Means Parliament Is Supreme over the Executive' (*Bingham Centre for the Rule of Law*, 3 September 2019) <https://binghamcentre.biicl.org/comments/57/in-a-democracy-the-rule-of-law-means-parliament-is-supreme-over-the-executive> accessed 30 April 2024

'Ireland Rejects Nice Treaty' *The Guardian* (London, 8 June 2001) <www.theguardian.com/world/2001/jun/08/eu.politics> accessed 18 April 2020

'Is the US Constitution Voluntary? Can Any State Opt Out of It When They Wish?' (*Quora*) <www.quora.com/Is-the-US-Constitution-voluntary-Can-any-state-opt-out-of-it-when-they-wish> accessed 23 April 2024

H Jacobsen, 'Denmark Rejects Further EU Integration in Referendum' (*Euractiv*, 4 December 2015) <www.euractiv.com/section/justice-home-affairs/news/denmark-rejects-further-eu-integration-in-referendum/> accessed 23 January 2020

HU Jessurun d'Oliveira, 'Expanding External and Shrinking Internal Borders: Europe's Defence Mechanisms in the Area of Free Movement, Immigration and Asylum' in David O'Keeffe and Patrick M Twomey (eds), *Legal Issues of the Maastricht Treaty* (John Wiley & Sons 1994)

P Joannin, 'Elements of Differentiation Within the Schengen Acquis and the Prüm Convention' in Thomas Giegerich, Desirée C Schmitt and Sebastian Zeitzmann (eds), *Flexibility in the EU and Beyond: How Much Differentiation Can European Integration Bear?* (Nomos/Hart 2017)

J-C Juncker, 'State of the Union Address 2017' (*European Commission*, 13 September 2017) <https://ec.europa.eu/commission/presscorner/detail/en/SPEECH_17_3165> accessed 27 April 2020

I Kant, *Critique of Pure Reason* (Bohn 1855)

RD Kelemen, 'On the Unsustainability of Constitutional Pluralism: European Supremacy and the Survival of the Eurozone' (2016) 23 Maastricht Journal of European and Comparative Law 136

H Koch, 'Grundlovsstridige EU-Folkeafstemninger (Unconstitutional EU Referenda)' in Henning Koch (ed), *Politik og jura. Festskrift til Ole Espersen* (Forlaget Thomson 2004)
D Kochenov, 'EU Citizenship and Withdrawals from the Union: How Inevitable Is the Radical Downgrading of Rights?' in Carlos Closa (ed), *Secession from a Member State and Withdrawal from the European Union: Troubled Membership* (CUP 2017)
D Kochenov, 'Immediate EU Membership for Ukraine? In Conversation with Dimitry Kochenov' (*Review of Democracy*, 20 April 2022) <https://revdem.ceu.edu/2022/04/20/immediate-eu-membership-for-ukraine-in-conversation-with-dimitry-kochenov/> accessed 24 April 2024
D Kochenov and G Butler, 'Independence of the Court of Justice of the European Union: Unchecked Member States Power after the Sharpston Affair' (2020) 28 European Law Journal 262
A Kölliker, *Flexibility and European Unification: The Logic of Differentiated Integration* (Rowman & Littlefield 2006)
H Kortenberg, 'Closer Cooperation in the Treaty of Amsterdam' (1998) 35 Common Market Law Review 833
D Kosař and L Vyhnánek, 'Constitutional Identity in the Czech Republic' in Christian Calliess and Gerhard van der Schyff (eds), *Constitutional Identity in a Europe of Multilevel Constitutionalism* (CUP 2019)
S Kröger and R Bellamy, 'Beyond a Constraining Dissensus: The Role of National Parliaments in Domesticating and Normalising the Politicization of European Integration' (2016) 14 Comparative European Politics 131
H Krunke, 'From Maastricht to Edinburgh: The Danish Solution' (2005) 1 European Constitutional Law Review 339
'David Cameron Blocks EU-Wide Deal to Tackle Euro Crisis' *BBC News* (9 December 2011) <www.bbc.com/news/uk-16104275> accessed 27 April 2020
M Kumm, 'Institutionalising Socratic Contestation: The Rationalist Human Rights Paradigm, Legitimate Authority and the Point of Judicial Review' (2007) 1 European Journal of Legal Studies 153
B Laffan, 'How the EU27 Came to Be' (2019) 57 Journal of Common Market Studies 13
D Lammy, 'We Need a Second Referendum. The Consequences of Brexit Are Too Grave' *The Guardian* (London, 26 June 2016) <www.theguardian.com/politics/commentisfree/2016/jun/26/second-referendum-consequences-brexit-grave> accessed 9 April 2020
S Lashyn, 'Sacrificing EU Citizenship on the Altar of Brexit' (2022) 29 Maastricht Journal of European and Comparative Law 736
A Łazowski, 'Be Careful What You Wish For. Procedural Parameters of EU Withdrawal' in Carlos Closa (ed), *Secession from a Member State and Withdrawal from the European Union: Troubled Membership* (CUP 2017)
E Letta, 'Much More than a Market: Speed, Security, Solidarity—Empowering the Single Market to Deliver a Sustainable Future and Prosperity for All EU Citizens' (*European Council*, 2024) <www.consilium.europa.eu/media/ny3j24sm/much-more-than-a-market-report-by-enrico-letta.pdf> accessed 31 January 2025
D Leuffen, B Rittberger and F Schimmelfennig, *Differentiated Integration: Explaining Variation in the European Union* (Palgrave 2012)
'Liberal Democrat 2019 Manifesto' (*LibDems.org*) <www.libdems.org.uk/policy/2019-liberal-democrat-manifesto> accessed 10 April 2020
J Lindeboom, 'Why EU Law Claims Supremacy' (2018) 38 Oxford Journal of Legal Studies 328
S Lindroos-Hovinheimo, 'There Is No Europe: On Subjectivity and Community in the EU' (2017) 18 German Law Journal 1229

E Lopes and M Lobo Antunes, 'Suggestion for Amendment of Article: Article I-59 º' (*DORIE—European Commission*, 2003) <https://dorie.ec.europa.eu/en/details/-/card/89825> accessed 3 April 2020

'Lords Examines European Union (Notification of Withdrawal) Bill' (*UK Parliament*, 16 March 2017) <www.parliament.uk/business/news/news-by-year/2017/february/lords-debates-european-union-notification-of-withdrawal-bill/> accessed 9 April 2020

M Loughlin, 'Constituent Power Subverted: From English Constitutional Argument to British Constitutional Practice' in Martin Loughlin and Neil Walker (eds), *The Paradox of Constitutionalism: Constituent Power and Constitutional Form* (OUP 2008)

M Loughlin, *The British Constitution: A Very Short Introduction* (OUP 2013)

J Lourie, 'The Social Chapter' (House of Commons Library 1997) Research Paper 97/102 <http://researchbriefings.files.parliament.uk/documents/RP97-102/RP97-102.pdf> accessed 27 January 2020

N MacCormick, *Questioning Sovereignty: Law, State, and Nation in the European Commonwealth* (OUP 1999)

A MacDowall, 'Voters Back Viktor Orbán's Rejection of EU Migrant Quotas' (*POLITICO*, 2 October 2016) <www.politico.eu/article/hungary-referendum-eu-migration-viktor-orban/> accessed 23 January 2020

MR Madsen, HP Olsen and U Šadl, 'Competing Supremacies and Clashing Institutional Rationalities: The Danish Supreme Court's Decision in the Ajos Case and the National Limits of Judicial Cooperation' (2017) 23 European Law Journal 140

MP Maduro, *We the Court: The European Court of Justice and the European Economic Constitution: A Critical Reading of Article 30 of the EC Treaty* (Hart Publishing 1998)

J Major, 'Mr Major's Speech to the Lord Mayor's Banquet—11 November 1991' (*Sir John Major KG CH*, 11 November 1991) <www.johnmajorarchive.org.uk/1991/mr-majors-speech-to-the-lord-mayors-banquet-11-november-1991/> accessed 20 April 2020

M Marcussen, 'EMU: A Danish Delight and Dilemma' in Kenneth Dyson (ed), *European States and the Euro: Europeanization, Variation, and Convergence* (OUP 2002)

T May, 'Prime Minister's Letter to Donald Tusk Triggering Article 50' (*GOV.UK*, 29 March 2017) <www.gov.uk/government/publications/prime-ministers-letter-to-donald-tusk-triggering-article-50> accessed 8 April 2020

H McDonald and A Stratton, 'Irish Voters Reject EU Treaty' *The Guardian* (13 June 2008) <www.theguardian.com/world/2008/jun/13/ireland> accessed 18 April 2020

T McGuinness and M Gower, 'The Common Travel Area and the Special Status of Irish Nationals in UK Law' (House of Commons Library Briefing Paper No 7661, 9 June 2017)

Member States of the European Community, 'Resolution on the Achievement by Stages of Economic and Monetary Union in the Community' (European Parliament—Committee on Institutional Affairs 1982)

J Meyer, 'Vorschlag für die Änderung von: Art. 46, Teil I, Titel X Des Verfassungsentwurfs (CONV 648/03)' (*DORIE—European Commission*, 2003) <https://dorie.ec.europa.eu/en/details/-/card/89975> accessed 3 April 2020

A Miglio, 'Schengen, Differentiated Integration and Cooperation with the "Outs"' (2016) 1 European Papers 139

D Miller, *National Responsibility and Global Justice* (OUP 2012)

Ministry of Justice and Home Office, 'Report to Parliament on the Application of Protocols 19 and 21 to the Treaty on European Union (TEU) and the Treaty on the Functioning of the European Union (TFEU) ("the Treaties") in Relation to EU Justice and Home Affairs Matters (1 December 2010–30 November 2011)' (2012)

Ministry of Justice and Home Office, 'Fifth Annual Report to Parliament on the Application of Protocols 19 and 21 to the Treaty on European Union (TEU) and the Treaty on the

Functioning of the European Union (TFEU) ("the Treaties") in Relation to EU Justice and Home Affairs (JHA) Matters (1 December 2013–30 November 2014)' (2015)
V Mitsilegas, 'European Criminal Law After Brexit' (2017) 28 Criminal Law Forum 219
K Möller, 'From Constituent to Destituent Power beyond the State' (2018) 9 Transnational Legal Theory 32
C Möllers, '"We Are (Afraid of) the People": Constituent Power in German Constitutionalism' in Martin Loughlin and Neil Walker (eds), *The Paradox of Constitutionalism: Constituent Power and Constitutional Form* (OUP 2008)
R Momtaz, 'French Far Right Wants to Scrap European Commission' (*POLITICO*, 15 April 2019) <www.politico.eu/article/marine-le-pen-national-rally-french-far-right-wants-to-scrap-european-commission/> accessed 23 January 2020
J Monar, 'Justice and Home Affairs in the Treaty of Amsterdam: Reform at the Price of Fragmentation' (1998) 4 European Law Review 320
A Moravcsik, *The Choice for Europe: Social Purpose and State Power from Messina to Maastricht* (Cornell UP 1998)
K-P Nanz, 'The Schengen Agreement: Preparing the Free Movement of Persons in the European Union' in Roland Bieber and Jörg Monar (eds), *Justice and Home Affairs in the European Union* (European Interuniversity Press 1995)
PJ Neuvonen, 'Retrieving the "Subject" of European Integration' (2019) 25 European Law Journal 6
K Nicolaidis, 'The Idea of European Demoicracy' in Julie Dickson and Pavlos Eleftheriadis (eds), *Philosophical Foundations of European Union Law* (OUP 2012)
P Niesen, 'The "Mixed" Constituent Legitimacy of the European Federation' (2017) 55 Journal of Common Market Studies 183
P Niesen, 'Reframing Civil Disobedience: Constituent Power as a Language of Transnational Protest' (2019) 15 Journal of International Political Theory 31
'No Deal Brexit: Issues, Impact, Implications' (UK in a Changing Europe, 3 September 2019) <https://ukandeu.ac.uk/research-papers/no-deal-brexit-issues-impact-implications/> accessed 18 April 2020
D O'Keeffe and PM Twomey (eds), *Legal Issues of the Maastricht Treaty* (John Wiley & Sons 1994)
TV Olsen and CF Rostbøll, 'Why Withdrawal from the European Union Is Undemocratic' (2017) 9 International Theory 436
'Operation Yellowhammer HMG Reasonable Worst Case Planning Assumptions as of 2 August 2019' <https://assets.publishing.service.gov.uk/government/uploads/system/uploads/attachment_data/file/831199/20190802_Latest_Yellowhammer_Planning_assumptions_CDL.pdf> accessed 5 May 2020
L Oppenheim, *International Law: A Treatise* (Longmans, Green, & Co 1905)
K O'Rourke, *A Short History of Brexit: From Brentry to Backstop* (Pelican 2019)
G Papagianni, 'Flexibility in Justice and Home Affairs: An Old Phenomenon Taking New Forms' in Bruno De Witte, Dominik Hanf and Ellen Vos (eds), *The Many Faces of Differentiation in EU Law* (Intersentia 2001)
M Patberg, 'Constituent Power beyond the State: An Emerging Debate in International Political Theory' (2013) 42 Millennium 224
M Patberg, 'Supranational Constitutional Politics and the Method of Rational Reconstruction' (2014) 40 Philosophy & Social Criticism 501
M Patberg, 'Against Democratic Intergovernmentalism: The Case for a Theory of Constituent Power in the Global Realm' (2016) 14 International Journal of Constitutional Law 622

M Patberg, 'The Levelling Up of Constituent Power in the European Union' (2017) 55 Journal of Common Market Studies 203

M Patberg, 'Constituent Power: A Discourse-Theoretical Solution to the Conflict between Openness and Containment' (2017) 24 Constellations 51

M Patberg, 'A Systematic Justification for the EU's Pouvoir Constituant Mixte: Principles of Constitutional Politics in Supranational Polities' (2017) 23 European Law Journal 441

M Patberg, 'After the Brexit Vote: What's Left of "Split" Popular Sovereignty?' (2018) 40 Journal of European Integration 923

M Patberg, 'Can Disintegration Be Democratic? The European Union Between Legitimate Change and Regression' (2020) 68 Political Studies 582

M Patberg, *Constituent Power in the European Union* (OUP 2020)

M Patberg and P Niesen, 'After Brexit, the UK Should Have a Democratic Right of Return' (*LSE Brexit*, 30 October 2018) <https://blogs.lse.ac.uk/brexit/2018/10/30/after-brexit-the-uk-should-be-able-to-re-enter-the-eu-if-it-wishes-to-do-so/> accessed 24 January 2020

KK Patel, 'Something New under the Sun? The Lessons of Algeria and Greenland' in Benjamin Martill and Uta Staiger (eds), *Brexit and Beyond: Rethinking the Futures of Europe* (UCL Press 2018)

L Pech and KL Scheppele, 'Illiberalism Within: Rule of Law Backsliding in the EU' (2017) 19 Cambridge Yearbook of European Legal Studies 3

S Peers, 'In a World of Their Own? Justice and Home Affairs Opt-Outs and the Treaty of Lisbon' (2008) 10 Cambridge Yearbook of European Legal Studies 383

S Peers, *EU Justice and Home Affairs Law: EU Justice and Home Affairs Law: Volume I: EU Immigration and Asylum Law* (4th edn, OUP 2016)

S Peers and D Harvey, 'Brexit: The Legal Dimension' in Catherine Barnard and Steve Peers (eds), *European Union Law* (2nd edn, OUP 2017)

V Perju, 'The Asymmetries of Pouvoir Constituant Mixte' (2019) 25 European Law Journal 515

R Petrov, 'Applying for EU Membership in Time of War: "Accession through War" of Ukraine' (*IAI Istituto Affari Internazionali*, 3 May 2023) <www.iai.it/en/pubblicazioni/applying-eu-membership-time-war-accession-through-war-ukraine> accessed 24 April 2024

B Pirker and others, 'In Support of the EU Rule of Law and Advocate General Eleanor Sharpston—An Open Letter' (*European Law Blog*, 18 March 2020) <https://web.archive.org/web/20200408190341/https://europeanlawblog.eu/2020/03/18/in-support-of-the-eu-rule-of-law-and-advocate-general-eleanor-sharpston-an-open-letter/> accessed 18 April 2020

P Polak, *EU Withdrawal as a Supranational Affair: The Case of Brexit* (Brill Nijhoff 2023)

'Political Declaration Political Declaration setting out the framework for the future relationship between the European Union and the United Kingdom of Great Britain and Northern Ireland [2019] OJ C 384I/178.

E Potton and A Mellows-Facer, 'The Euro: Background to the Five Economic Tests' (House of Commons Library Research Paper 03/53, 4 June 2003)

'Proposed Amendments to the Text of the Articles of the Treaty Establishing a Constitution for Europe' (*European Convention*, 2003) <https://web.archive.org/web/20220105122837/http://european-convention.europa.eu/EN/amendments/amendmentsdfd1.html?content=46&lang=EN> accessed 3 April 2020

'Recovery and Resilience Facility' <https://economy-finance.ec.europa.eu/eueconomyexplained/recovery-and-resilience-facility_en> accessed 1 May 2024

J Redwood, 'What Does Brexit Look Like? A Lot Better than Staying In.' (*John Redwood's Diary*, 1 February 2016) <http://johnredwoodsdiary.com/2016/02/01/what-does-brexit-look-like-a-lot-better-than-staying-in/> accessed 6 April 2020

R Repasi, 'Op-Ed: "Poland's Withdrawal from the 'Community of Law' Is No Withdrawal from the EU"' (*EU Law Live*, 15 October 2021) <https://eulawlive.com/op-ed-polands-withdrawal-from-the-community-of-law-is-no-withdrawal-from-the-eu-by-rene-repasi/> accessed 24 April 2024

'Review of the Balance of Competences' (*GOV.UK*, 12 December 2012) <www.gov.uk/guidance/review-of-the-balance-of-competences> accessed 22 April 2020

S Reynolds, 'May We Stay? Assessing the Security of Residence for EU Citizens Living in the UK' in Michael Dougan (ed), *The UK After Brexit: Legal and Policy Challenges* (Intersentia 2017)

M Rosenfeld, 'Constitutional Identity' in András Sajó and Michel Rosenfeld (eds), *The Oxford Handbook of Comparative Constitutional Law* (OUP 2012)

G Ruberto, 'When Does the British Constitution Require a Referendum? V. Bogdanor's Opinion on the Place for the Referendum in the UK' (*The Constitution Unit Blog*, 26 February 2013) <https://constitution-unit.com/2013/02/26/when-does-the-british-constitution-require-a-referendum-v-bogdanors-opinion-on-the-place-for-the-referendum-in-the-uk/> accessed 21 April 2020

W Sadurski, *Poland's Constitutional Breakdown* (OUP 2019)

A Sajó, 'Emotions in Constitutional Design' (2010) 8 International Journal of Constitutional Law 354

A Sajó, 'Emotions in Constitutional Institutions' (2016) 8 Emotion Review 44

A Sanchez-Graells, 'UK Supreme Court Miller Judgment Seeks to Reassert Parliamentary Sovereignty, but It Does so in Breach of EU Law and in Disservice to the UK Parliament' (*How to Crack a Nut*, 24 January 2017) <www.howtocrackanut.com/blog/2017/1/24/uk-supreme-court-miller-judgment-seeks-to-reassert-parliamentary-sovereignty-but-it-does-so-in-breach-of-eu-law-and-in-disservice-to-the-uk-parliament> accessed 9 April 2020

J Santer, B Fayot and M Schmit, 'Proposition d'amendement à l'Article: Article 46 (Titre X)' (*DORIE—European Commission*, 2003) <https://dorie.ec.europa.eu/en/details/-/card/89969> accessed 3 April 2020

A Sari, 'Reversing a Withdrawal Notification under Article 50 TEU: Can a Member State Change Its Mind?' [2017] European Law Review 451

FW Scharpf, *Governing in Europe: Effective and Democratic?* (OUP 1999)

FW Scharpf, 'After the Crash: A Perspective on Multilevel European Democracy' (2015) 21 European Law Journal 384

'Schengen: MEPs Angry at Council Attack on Democratic Powers' (*European Parliament*, 12 June 2012) <https://web.archive.org/web/20220901050749/https://www.europarl.europa.eu/news/en/headlines/security/20120612STO46654/schengen-meps-angry-at-council-attack-on-democratic-powers> accessed 23 January 2020

KL Scheppele, DV Kochenov and B Grabowska-Moroz, 'EU Values Are Law, After All: Enforcing EU Values through Systemic Infringement Actions by the European Commission and the Member States of the European Union' (2020) 39 Yearbook of European Law 3

F Schimmelfennig, 'Brexit: Differentiated Disintegration in the European Union' (2018) 25 Journal of European Public Policy 1154

F Schimmelfennig and T Winzen, 'Instrumental and Constitutional Differentiation in the European Union' (2014) 52 Journal of Common Market Studies 354

F Schimmelfennig and T Winzen, 'Differentiated EU Integration: Maps and Modes' (European University Institute 2020) EUI RSCAS Working Paper 2020/24 <http://cadmus.eui.eu//handle/1814/66880> accessed 27 April 2020

F Schimmelfennig and T Winzen, *Ever Looser Union? Differentiated European Integration* (OUP 2020)

J Scholtes, *The Abuse of Constitutional Identity in the European Union* (OUP 2023)

J Schutte, 'Schengen: Its Meaning for the Free Movement of Persons in Europe' (1991) 28 Common Market Law Review 549

J Schutte, 'UK v EU: A Continuous Test Match' (2011) 34 Fordham International Law Journal 1346

R Schütze, *From Dual to Cooperative Federalism: The Changing Structure of European Law* (OUP 2009)

European Commission, 'President Juncker Appoints Michel Barnier as Chief Negotiator in Charge of the Preparation and Conduct of the Negotiations with the United Kingdom under Article 50 of the TEU' <https://ec.europa.eu/commission/presscorner/detail/en/IP_16_2652> accessed 14 April 2020

The Scottish Government, 'Scotland's Future' (*gov.scot*, 26 November 2013) <www.gov.scot/publications/scotlands-future/> accessed 24 January 2020

J Shaw, 'The Quintessentially Democratic Act? Democracy, Political Community and Citizenship in and after the UK's EU Referendum of June 2016' (2017) 39 Journal of European Integration 559

Z Sheftalovich, 'Nigel Farage: June 23 Should Be Britain's "Independence Day" Holiday' (*POLITICO*, 24 June 2016) <www.politico.eu/article/nigel-farage-june-23-should-be-britains-independence-day-holiday-leave-eu-brexit/> accessed 23 April 2024

'Should EU Citizenship Be Disentangled from Member State Nationality?' (European University Institute 2019) Working Paper EUI RSCAS, 2019/24 <https://cadmus.eui.eu/handle/1814/62229> accessed 1 May 2024

R Simeon, 'Opting-Out' (*The Canadian Encyclopedia*, 7 February 2006) <www.thecanadianencyclopedia.ca/en/article/opting-out> accessed 23 April 2024

B Simma and D Pulkowski, 'Of Planets and the Universe: Self-Contained Regimes in International Law' (2006) 17 European Journal of International Law 483

KR Simmonds, 'The British Referendum' (1975) 12 Common Market Law Review 258

M Sion-Tzidkiyahu, 'Comparing Opt-Outs: How Different Is Differentiated Integration' in Thomas Giegerich, Desirée C Schmitt and Sebastian Zeitzmann (eds), *Flexibility in the EU and Beyond: How Much Differentiation Can European Integration Bear?* (Hart Publishing; Nomos Verlag 2017)

I Sirbiladze and E Ventura, 'The EU's Eastern Enlargement and Differentiated Democracy Support' (*Carnegie Europe*, 11 September 2023) <https://carnegieeurope.eu/2023/09/11/eu-s-eastern-enlargement-and-differentiated-democracy-support-pub-90488> accessed 24 April 2024

S Smedley, 'A Missed Opportunity? Revisiting the Euro Referendum That Never Was from a Historical Perspective' (*LSE Brexit*, 3 December 2019) <https://blogs.lse.ac.uk/brexit/2019/12/03/a-missed-opportunity-revisiting-the-euro-referendum-that-never-was-from-a-historical-perspective/> accessed 7 April 2020

S Smismans, 'About the Revocability of Withdrawal: Why the EU (Law) Interpretation of Article 50 Matters' (*UK Constitutional Law Association*, 29 November 2016) <https://ukconstitutionallaw.org/2016/11/29/stijn-smismans-about-the-revocability-of-withdrawal-why-the-eu-law-interpretation-of-article-50-matters/> accessed 13 April 2020

B Smulders and L Prete, 'The Coming of Age of Infringement Proceedings' (2010) 47 Common Market Law Review 9

AR Sørensen, 'The Danish Euro: Constructing a Monetary Oxymoron in the Danish Euro Debate' (2014) 16 National Identities 31

E Stein, 'Lawyers, Judges, and the Making of a Transnational Constitution' (1981) 75 American Journal of International Law 1

M Stothard, 'Could France's Marine Le Pen Deliver Frexit?' *Financial Times* (Paris, 15 March 2017) 3

A Stubb, 'A Categorization of Differentiated Integration' (1996) 34 Journal of Common Market Studies 283

A Stubb, *Negotiating Flexibility in the European Union: Amsterdam, Nice and Beyond* (Palgrave Macmillan 2002)

A Stubb, 'Stubb: "Europe Is a Rational Choice, but It Needs to Feel Good"' (*@alexstubb*, 12 October 2018) <www.twitter.com/alexstubb/status/1050707810605039618> accessed 23 January 2020

M Szwed, 'Rebuilding the Rule of Law: Three Guiding Principles' (*Verfassungsblog*, 29 April 2024) <https://verfassungsblog.de/rebuilding-the-rule-of-law/> accessed 3 May 2024

F Tekin, *Differentiated Integration at Work: The Institutionalisation and Implementation of Opt-Outs from European Integration in the Area of Freedom, Security and Justice* (Nomos Publishers 2012)

M Thatcher, 'House of Commons Statement: Rome European Council, Hansard HC 178/869-92 ("No No No")' (*Margaret Thatcher Foundation*, 30 October 1990) <www.margaretthatcher.org/document/108234> accessed 1 April 2020

M Thatcher, 'Press Conference after Madrid European Council' (*Margaret Thatcher Foundation*, 27 June 1989) <www.margaretthatcher.org/document/107711> accessed 27 January 2020

'The Difficulties of the Monetary Snake and the EMCF—Research Corpora' (*CVCE.eu by Uni.lu*) <www.cvce.eu/en/collections/unit-content/-/unit/56d70f17-5054-49fc-bb9b-5d90735167d0/2d84f078-672e-4ae9-92d5-b4969911442a> accessed 27 January 2020

'The ERM and the Single Currency' (*UK Parliament*) <www.parliament.uk/about/living-heritage/evolutionofparliament/legislativescrutiny/parliament-and-europe/overview/britain-joins-erm-to-introduction-of-single-currency/> accessed 27 January 2020

'The European Monetary System—Historical Events in the European Integration Process (1945–2009)' (*CVCE.eu by Uni.lu*) <www.cvce.eu/en/education/unit-content/-/unit/02bb76df-d066-4c08-a58a-d4686a3e68ff/1040d119-5eba-4c7b-a850-ed254556c43c> accessed 27 January 2020

'The Future Relationship between the United Kingdom and the European Union' (*GOV.UK*, 17 July 2018) <www.gov.uk/government/publications/the-future-relationship-between-the-united-kingdom-and-the-european-union> accessed 16 April 2020

'The Snake—Historical Events in the European Integration Process (1945–2009)' (*CVCE.eu by Uni.lu*) <www.cvce.eu/en/education/unit-content/-/unit/02bb76df-d066-4c08-a58a-d4686a3e68ff/1b3433df-a25b-455a-b872-dec04270f820> accessed 27 January 2020

D Thym, '"United in Diversity": The Integration of Enhanced Cooperation into the European Constitutional Order' in Philip Dann and Michał Rynkowski (eds), *The Unity of the European Constitution* (Springer 2006)

D Thym, 'Competing Models for Understanding Differentiated Integration' in Bruno De Witte, Andrea Ott and Ellen Vos (eds), *Between Flexibility and Disintegration: The Trajectory of Differentiation in EU Law* (Edward Elgar Publishing 2017)

I Traynor, 'EU Warns Denmark over Border Controls' *The Guardian* (London, 13 May 2011) <www.theguardian.com/world/2011/may/13/eu-denmark-border-controls> accessed 23 April 2020

K Tuori, *European Constitutionalism* (CUP 2015)

K Tuori, 'Crossing the Limits but Stuck behind the Fault Lines?' (2016) 7 Transnational Legal Theory 133

K Tuori and K Tuori, *The Eurozone Crisis* (CUP 2014)

D Tusk, 'Letter by President Donald Tusk to the Members of the European Council on His Proposal for a New Settlement for the United Kingdom within the European Union' (*European Council*, 2 February 2016) <www.consilium.europa.eu/en/press/press-releases/2016/02/02/letter-tusk-proposal-new-settlement-uk/> accessed 23 April 2020

F Tuytschaever, *Differentiation in European Union Law* (Hart Publishing 1999)

P Twomey and D O'Keefe, *Legal Issues of the Amsterdam Treaty* (Bloomsbury 1999)

E Uberoi, 'European Union Referendum Bill 2015-16' (House of Commons Library Briefing Paper No 07212, 3 June 2015)

S Van Kessel, 'Geert Wilders Is No Longer so Keen on Pushing for a "Nexit"—and It's Because Dutch People Don't Want It' (*EUROPP*, 2 March 2017) <https://blogs.lse.ac.uk/europpblog/2017/03/02/nexit-evolving-euroscepticism-geert-wilders/> accessed 23 January 2020

D Vincenti, 'MEPs launch counterattack against Schengen deal' (*Euractiv*, 13 June 2012) <www.euractiv.com/section/justice-home-affairs/news/meps-launch-counterattack-against-schengen-deal/> accessed 15 October 2024

N Walker (ed), *Europe's Area of Freedom, Security, and Justice* (OUP 2004)

N Walker, 'The EU's Constitutional Overabundance?' (University of Edinburgh 2016) Edinburgh School of Law Research Paper No 2016/14 <https://papers.ssrn.com/abstract=2776800> accessed 28 January 2020

N Walker, 'Habermas's European Constitution: Catalyst, Reconstruction, Refounding' (2019) 25 European Law Journal 508

S Wall, *A Stranger in Europe: Britain and the EU from Thatcher to Blair* (OUP 2008)

S Weatherill, 'EU Law Analysis: Can an Article 50 Notice of Withdrawal from the EU Be Unilaterally Revoked?' (*EU Law Analysis*, 16 January 2018) <http://eulawanalysis.blogspot.com/2018/01/can-article-50-notice-of-withdrawal.html> accessed 13 April 2020

D Webber, *European Disintegration? The Politics of Crisis in the European Union* (Red Globe Press 2018)

JHH Weiler, 'Van Gend En Loos: The Individual as Subject and Object and the Dilemma of European Legitimacy' (2014) 12 International Journal of Constitutional Law 94

P Werner, 'Report to the Council and the Commission on the Realisation by Stages of Economic and Monetary Union in the Community ("Werner Report")' (1970) Supplement to Bulletin II-1970 of the European Communities

J Williams, 'Does Wightman Mean That Miller Was Decided Incorrectly?' (*Monckton Chambers*, 10 December 2018) <www.monckton.com/does-wightman-mean-that-miller-was-decided-incorrectly/> accessed 9 April 2020

T Worre, 'First No, Then Yes: The Danish Referendums on the Maastricht Treaty 1992 and 1993' (1995) 33 Journal of Common Market Studies 235

S Zeitzmann, 'A Rather Strange Animal, This "Enhanced Cooperation"—May It Serve as King of the European Zoonion? Or: Is Enhanced Cooperation Anywhere Near a Constitutional Principle?' in Thomas Giegerich, Desirée C Schmitt and Sebastian Zeitzmann (eds), *Flexibility in the EU and Beyond: How Much Differentiation Can European Integration Bear?* (Hart Publishing/Nomos Verlag 2017)

R Ziegler, 'GLOBALCIT Report on Political Participation of Mobile EU Citizens: United Kingdom' (2018) Country Report 2018/14

R Ziegler, 'Part I Mini-Symposium on EU Citizenship in the Shadow of Brexit: The Brexit Effect—European Parliamentary Elections in the UK' (*European Law Blog*, 19 December 2018) <https://web.archive.org/web/20190827213516/https://europeanlawblog.eu/2018/12/19/part-i-mini-symposium-on-eu-citizenship-in-the-shadow-of-brexit-the-brexit-effect-european-parliamentary-elections-in-the-uk/> accessed 16 April 2020

C Zilioli and M Selmayr, *The Law of the European Central Bank* (Hart Publishing 2001)

C Zilioli and M Selmayr, 'The Constitutional Status of the European Central Bank' (2007) 44 Common Market Law Review 355

II. Cases

Andy Wightman MSP and others v Secretary of State for Exiting the EU [2018] CSIH 62

C/13/640244/KG ZA 17-1327 of the Rechtbank Amsterdam

Case C-44/14 *Spain v European Parliament and Council*, EU:C:2015:554

Case C-327/18 *PPU-R O*, EU:C:2018:733

Case C-402/05 *Kadi and Al Barakaat International Foundation v Council and Commission* [2008] ECR I-06351

Case C-482/08 *United Kingdom v Council* [2010] ECR I-10413

Case C-673/20 *EP v Préfet du Gers and Institut national de la statistique et des études économiques*, EU:C:2022:449

Case 26/62 *Van Gend en Loos v Nederlandse Administratie der Belastingen* [1963] ECR 1

Case 238/81 *Srl CILFIT and Lanificio di Gavardo SpA v Ministry of Health* [1982] ECR-03415

Case 294/83 *Parti écologiste 'Les Verts' v European Parliament* [1986] ECR-01339

Case C-34/09 *Gerardo Ruiz Zambrano v Office national de l'emploi* [2011] ECR I-01177

Case C-77/05 *United Kingdom v Council* [2007] ECR I-11459

Case C-81/13 *UK v Council of the European Union*, EU:C:2014:2449

Case C-137/12 *European Commission and the European Parliament v the Council of the European Union*, EU:C:2013:675

Case C-159/90 *The Society for the Protection of Unborn Children Ireland Ltd v Stephen Grogan and others* [1991] ECR I-04685

Case C-184/99 *Rudy Grzelcyzk v Centre public d'aide sociale d'Ottignies-Louvain-la-Neuve* [2001] ECR I-06193

Case C-274/11 *Spain and Italy v Council*, EU:C:2013:240

Case C-377/12 *European Commission v the Council*, EU:C:2014:1903

Case C-431/11 *UK v Council of the European Union*, EU:C:2013:589

Case C-482/08 *United Kingdom v Council* [2010] ECR-I-10413

Case C-621/18 *Wightman v Secretary of State for Exiting the European Union*, EU:C:2018:999

Case C-656/11 *UK v Council of the European Union*, EU:C:2014:97

Case T-135/96 *UEAPME v Council* [1998] ECR II-2335

Case T-458/17 *Shindler and Others v Council*, EU:T:2018:838

Case T-496/11 *United Kingdom v ECB*, EU:T:2015:133

Danish Supreme Court Case 15/2014 *Dansk Industri, acting on behalf of Ajos A/S v Estate of A*

Lisbon, Judgment of the Second Senate of 30 June 2009, BVerfG, 2 be 2/08

Maastricht, German Constitutional Court Decision of 12 October 1993, BVerfGE 89
Brunner v European Union Treaty [1994] 1 CMLR 57
Matthews v United Kingdom (1999) 28 EHRR 361 (ECHR)
Opinion 2/13 on the accession of the EU to the ECHR, EU:C:2014:2454 (Full Court, 18 December 2014)
Opinion of Advocate General Campos Sánchez-Bordona in Case C-621/18 *Wightman v Secretary of State for Exiting the European Union*, EU:C:2018:978
Order of the Court of 11 July 1996 in Case C-445/93 *European Parliament v Commission* [1996] OJ No C 336/15
Order of the President of the Court of 19 October 2018 in Case C-621/18 *Wightman v Secretary of State for Exiting the European Union*, EU:C:2018:851
R (Factortame Ltd) v Secretary of State for Transport [1990] UKHL 13
R (Miller) v Secretary of State for Exiting the European Union [2016] EWHC 2768 (Admin)
R (Miller) v Secretary of State for Exiting the European Union [2017] UKSC 5
R (on the application of HS2 Action Alliance Limited) v Secretary of State for Transport and another [2014] UKSC 3
R (on the application of Miller) v The Prime Minister/Cherry and others v Advocate General for Scotland [2019] UKSC 41
R (Webster) v Secretary of State for Exiting the European Union [2018] EWHC 1542 (Admin)
Reference re Secession of Quebec [1998] 2 SCR 217 (Supreme Court of Canada)
Shindler v Chancellor of the Duchy of Lancaster [2016] EWCA Civ 649 (Court of Appeal)
Shindler v Chancellor of the Duchy of Lancaster [2016] EWHC 957 (Admin)
Texas v White 74 US 700 (1868)

III. Legislation and Treaties

The Constitutional Act of Denmark of 5 June 1953
Agreement on the European Economic Area [1994] OJ L 1/3
Agreement on the withdrawal of the United Kingdom of Great Britain and Northern Ireland from the European Union and the European Atomic Energy Community [2019] OJ C 384/1
An Act to give effect to the requirement for clarity as set out in the opinion of the Supreme Court of Canada in the Quebec Secession Reference SC 2000, c 26 Assented to 2000-06-29
Basic Law for the Federal Republic of Germany in the revised version published in the Federal Law Gazette Part III, classification number 100-1, as last amended by Article 1 of the Act of 28 March 2019 (Federal Law Gazette I p 404)
Belfast Agrement (1998)
Bill of Rights (1688)
Canadian Charter of Rights and Freedoms (1982)
Canadian Constitution Act (1982)
Charter of Fundamental Rights of the European Union [2007] OJ C 303/1
Civil Contingencies Act 2004
Commission Decision 2014/858/EU of 1 December 2014 on the notification by the United Kingdom of Great Britain and Northern Ireland of its wish to participate in acts of the Union in the field of police cooperation and judicial cooperation in criminal matters adopted before the entry into force of the Treaty of Lisbon and which are not part of the Schengen *acquis* [2014] OJ L 345/6
Commission opinion on the request by Ireland to take part in some of the provisions of the Schengen [2000] *acquis* SEC/2000/1439 final

Commission opinion on the request by the United Kingdom to take part in certain provisions of the Schengen *acquis* [1999] IP/99/550

Communication from the Commission to the European Parliament, the European Council, the Council, the European Central Bank, the European Economic and Social Committee, the Committee of the Regions and the European Investment Bank—Finalising preparations for the withdrawal of the United Kingdom from the European Union on 1 November 2019, Brussels, 4.9.2019, COM(2019) 394 final

Consolidated Version of the Treaty on European Union [2008] OJ C115/13

Consolidated Version of the Treaty on the Functioning of the European Union [2012] OJ C 326/47

Constitution of Ireland enacted by the People on 1st July 1937 in operation as from 29th December 1937

Council Decision 1999/435/EC of 20 May 1999 concerning the definition of the Schengen *acquis* for the purpose of determining, in conformity with the relevant provisions of the Treaty establishing the European Community and the Treaty on European Union, the legal basis for each of the provisions or decisions which constitute the *acquis* [1999] OJ L 176/1

Council Decision 1999/436/EC of 20 May 1999 determining, in conformity with the relevant provisions of the Treaty establishing the European Community and the Treaty on European Union, the legal basis for each of the provisions or decisions which constitute the Schengen *acquis* [1999] OJ L 176/17

Council Decision 2000/365/EC of 29 May 2000 concerning the request of the United Kingdom of Great Britain and Northern Ireland to take part in some of the provisions of the Schengen *acquis* [2000] OJ L 131/43

Council Decision 2014/836/EU of 27 November 2014 determining certain consequential and transitional arrangements concerning the cessation of the participation of the United Kingdom of Great Britain and Northern Ireland in certain acts of the Union in the field of police cooperation and judicial cooperation in criminal matters adopted before the entry into force of the Treaty of Lisbon [2014] OJ L 343/11

Council Decision 2014/857/EU of 1 December 2014 concerning the notification of the United Kingdom of Great Britain and Northern Ireland of its wish to take part in some of the provisions of the Schengen *acquis* which are contained in acts of the Union in the field of police cooperation and judicial cooperation in criminal matters and amending Decisions 2000/365/EC and 2004/926/EC [2014] L 345/1

Council Decision authorising the opening of negotiations with the United Kingdom of Great Britain and Northern Ireland for an agreement setting out the arrangements for its withdrawal from the European Union, Brussels, 15 May 2017 (21016/17 LIMITE BXT)

Council Directive 74/121/EEC of 18 February 1974 on stability, growth and full employment in the Community [1974] OJ L 63/19

Council Directive 94/80/EC of 19 December 1994 laying down detailed arrangements for the exercise of the right to vote and to stand as a candidate in municipal elections by citizens of the union residing in a member state of which they are not nationals [1994] OJ L 368/38

Declaration by the Government of the United Kingdom of Great Britain and Northern Ireland on the definition of the term 'nationals' [1983] OJ C 23/1

Denmark and the Treaty on European Union [1992] OJ C 348/1

Directive 2004/38/EC of the European Parliament and of the Council of 29 April 2004 on the right of citizens of the Union and their family members to move and reside freely within the territory of the Member States [2004] OJ L 158/77

Directive 2005/36/EC of the European Parliament and of the Council of 7 September 2005 on the recognition of professional qualifications [2005] OJ L 255/22
European Communities Act 1972
European Council Decision (EU) 2018/937 of 28 June 2018 establishing the composition of the European Parliament [2018] OJ L 165 I/1
European Council Decision taken in agreement with the United Kingdom extending the period under Article 50(3) TEU, Brussels, 11 April 2019 (EUCOXT 20013/19 BXT 38)
European Council meeting (18 and 19 February 2016)—Conclusions, Annex 1—Decision of the Heads of State or Government, meeting within the European Council, concerning a new settlement for the United Kingdom within the European Union—Brussels 19 February 2016 EUCO 1/16
European Parliament resolution of 16 February 2017 on possible evolutions of and adjustments to the current institutional set-up of the European Union [2018] OJ C 252/201
European Parliament resolution of 5 April 2017 on negotiations with the United Kingdom following its notification that it intends to withdraw from the European Union [2017] OJ C 298/24
European Parliament resolution of 18 September 2019 on the state of play of the UK's withdrawal from the European Union [2021] OJ C 171/2
European Parliamentary Elections (Franchise of Relevant Citizens of the Union) Regulations 2001
European Union Act 2011
European Union (Notification of Withdrawal) Act 2017
European Union Referendum Act 2015
European Union (Withdrawal) Act 2018
European Union (Withdrawal) Act 2019
European Union (Withdrawal Agreement) Act 2020
European Union (Withdrawal) (No 2) Act 2019
General Declaration on Articles 13 to 19 of the Single European Act [1987] OJ L 169/25
Montevideo Convention on the Rights and Duties of States, signed at Montevideo, 26 December 1933
Nineteenth Amendment to the Constitution Act 1998
Parliamentary Voting System and Constituencies Act 2011
Proposal for a Regulation of the European Parliament and of the Council on the establishment of an evaluation mechanism to verify application of the Schengen *acquis*, Brussels, 16.11.2010, COM(2010) 624 final
Protocol on Ireland/Northern Ireland, Agreement on the withdrawal of the United Kingdom of Great Britain and Northern Ireland from the European Union and the European Atomic Energy Community [2019] OJ C 384 I/92
Protocol on Ireland/Northern Ireland, Draft Agreement on the withdrawal of the United Kingdom of Great Britain and Northern Ireland from the European Union and the European Atomic Energy Community, as agreed at negotiators' level on 14 November 2018 TF50 (2018) 55
Regulation (EC) No 883/2004 of the European Parliament and of the Council of 29 April 2004 on the coordination of social security systems [2004] OJ L 166/1
Regulation (EU) 2016/399 of the European Parliament and of the Council of 9 March 2016 on a Union Code on the rules governing the movement of persons across borders (Schengen Borders Code) [2016] OJ L 77/11
Regulation (EU) No 492/2011 of the European Parliament and of the Council of 5 April 2011 on freedom of movement for workers within the Union [2011] OJ L 141/1

Representation of the People Act 1983
Representation of the People Act 1985
Single European Act [1987] OJ No L 169/1
TEU and TFEU, Protocol (No 4) on the Statute of the European System of Central Banks and of the European Central Bank
TEU and TFEU, Protocol (No 15) on certain provisions relating to the United Kingdom of Great Britain and Northern Ireland
TEU and TFEU, Protocol (No 16) on certain provisions relating to Denmark
TEU and TFEU, Protocol (No 17) on Denmark
TEU and TFEU, Protocol (No 19) on the Schengen *acquis* integrated into the framework of the European Union
TEU and TFEU, Protocol (No 20) on the application of certain aspects of Article 26 of the Treaty on the Functioning of the European Union to the United Kingdom and to Ireland
TEU and TFEU, Protocol (No 21) on the position of the United Kingdom and Ireland in respect of the area of freedom, security and justice
TEU and TFEU, Protocol (No 22) on the position of Denmark
TEU and TFEU, Protocol (No 30) on the application of the Charter of Fundamental Rights of the European Union to Poland and to the United Kingdom
TEU and TFEU, Protocol (No 36) on transitional provisions
The Schengen *acquis*—Agreement between the Governments of the States of the Benelux Economic Union, the Federal Republic of Germany and the French Republic on the gradual abolition of checks at their common borders [2000] OJ L 239/13
The Schengen *acquis*—Convention implementing the Schengen Agreement of 14 June 1985 between the Governments of the States of the Benelux Economic Union, the Federal Republic of Germany and the French Republic on the gradual abolition of checks at their common borders [2000] OJ L 239/19
Trade and Cooperation Agreement between the European Union and the European Atomic Energy Community, of the one part, and the United Kingdom of Great Britain and Northern Ireland, of the other part [2021] OJ L 149/10
Treaty amending, with regard to Greenland, the Treaties establishing the European Communities [1985] OJ No L 29/1
Treaty establishing a Constitution for Europe [2004] OJ C 310/1
Treaty establishing the European Economic Community [1957]
Treaty of Amsterdam amending the Treaty on European Union, the Treaties establishing the European Communities and certain related acts, signed at Amsterdam, 2 October 1997 [1997] OJ C 340/1
Treaty of Lisbon amending the Treaty on European Union and the Treaty establishing the European Community, signed at Lisbon, 13 December 2007 [2007] OJ C 306/1
Treaty of Lisbon, Declaration No 63 by the United Kingdom of Great Britain and Northern Ireland on the definition of the term 'nationals' [2007] OJ C 306/270
Treaty on European Union, signed at Maastricht on 7 February 1992 [1992] OJ C 191/1
Treaty on Stability, Coordination and Governance of 2 March 2012 T/SCG
Vienna Convention on the Law of Treaties. Done at Vienna on 23 May 1969. Entered into force on 27 January 1980. United Nations, Treaty Series, vol 1155, p 331

Index

For the benefit of digital users, indexed terms that span two pages (e.g., 52–53) may, on occasion, appear on only one of those pages.